French
Socialisms

ISBN: 978-1-960821-01-0

Cover Design by Mykell Gates Jamil and Priscilla MacClamrock.

Published by little big eye publishing, Charlotte, NC, 28205, USA, www.littlebigeyepublishing.com/.

French Socialisms

From 'Utopian Socialism' to 'Industrial Democracy'

Written by: Célestin Bouglé

Originally Published as:
Socialismes français.
Du «socialisme utopique» à la «démocratie industrielle»

Paris, Librairie Armand Colin, 1932
Collection Armand Colin (History & Economics Department) no. 149

Edited by: Cayce Jamil

Translated by: Shaun Murdock

little big eye publishing

Table of Contents

Appendices to the English Edition

Foreword to the English Edition

By Cayce Jamil

Célestin Bouglé (1870-1940), whose life symbolically paralleled the rise and fall of France's Third Republic (1870-1940), is occasionally viewed as the "alter-ego" of the prolific sociologist Émile Durkheim (1858-1917).[1] From 1897 until the outbreak of World War I (1914-1918), Durkheim led an unprecedented social movement geared around his journal, *L'Année sociologique,* which engaged in the collective production of scientific sociology.[2] Through the journal, which operated as a research hub and rallying point for the Durkheimians, the group offered scientific solutions to a number of long-standing philosophy problems, such as morality, religion, and the acquisition of socially-shared categories of thought. Additionally, with their cohesive division of labor, the Durkheimians spearheaded an unparalleled revaluation of the literature on ethnographies and shifted academic attention from industrial to archaic societies.[3] Prior to the *L'Année sociologique,* "sociology" was primarily undertaken by philosophers working in near isolation. The doctrinal heterogeneity and collaborative ethic among the contributors to the Durkheimian journal allowed for the unparalleled success of the group and the founding of sociology as a legitimate discipline. Although generally forgotten today, Bouglé was integral to the foundational journal and even appears to have been the key individual behind the creation of the journal, which Durkheim himself confirmed.[4]

---

[1] P. M. Sturges: *Social Theory and Political Ideology: Célestin Bouglé and the Durkheimian School.* Dissertation at City University of New York. 1978, p. 5.

[2] R. Collins: The Durkheimian Movement in France and in World Sociology. Pp. 101-135 in *The Cambridge Companion to Durkheim.* Cambridge University Press, 2005.

[3] V. Karady: The Durkheimians in Academe. A Reconsideration. Pp. 71-89 in P. Besnard (ed.): *The Sociological Domain: The Durkheimians and the Founding of French Sociology.* Cambridge University Press, 1983.

[4] P. Besnard: The 'Année Sociologique' Team. Pp. 11-39 in Besnard (ed.): *The Sociological Domain.* 1983.

Primarily through their contributions to the *L'Année sociologique*, the Durkheimians went from relative obscurity to becoming a symbol of the French university system. In contrast to other notable proponents of "social science" during their era, such as Frédéric Le Play (1806–1882), Gabriel Tarde (1843–1904), and René Worms (1869–1926), the Durkheimians crafted their methodology in alignment with the grandiose works of Saint-Simonism and Comtean positivism. Despite their overt professionalism, the Durkheimians were distinctly committed to socialism. Durkheim, Bouglé, Marcel Mauss (1872–1950), Henri Hubert (1872–1927), Robert Hertz (1881–1915), Lucien Lévy-Bruhl (1857–1939), Maurice Halbwachs (1877–1945), Paul Fauconnet (1874–1938), François Simiand (1873–1935), and Hubert Bourgin (1874–1955) were all tied to the French socialist movement.[5] The Durkheimians held significant roles within the Socialist School (1899–1902) and the Group for Socialist Unity (1899–?). They helped found the socialist paper *L'humanité* (1904–), with Mauss and Hubert being regular contributors, were active within the burgeoning socialist press, and maintained close friendships with the prominent socialist Jean Jaurès (1859–1914).[6] By the late 1890s, Durkheimian sociology had essentially become a stronghold for socialists within the French academic system.[7]

While the Durkheimians were dynamic participants in the socialist movement, they were careful to distinguish their political activities from their intellectual pursuits.[8] For instance, Durkheim made explicit connections between socialism with sociology in his lectures, but he largely refrained from political engagement in the public sphere. He notably broke his public silence during the Dreyfus affair (1894–1899), where the Durkheimians robustly defended a Jewish military officer wrongfully accused of treason, and again during World War I, writing

---

[5] Notably, Hubert Bourgin would later shift his allegiances to the far right during the interwar period.
[6] *Ibid.*, pp. 24–26.
[7] T. Clark: *Prophets and Patrons: The French University System and the Emergence of the Social Sciences.* Harvard University Press, 1973, pp. 188–194.
[8] Karady: The Durkheimians in Academe. A Reconsideration. 1983, p. 74.

2

against German aggression. Contrary to Durkheim's approach, Bouglé began regular political advocacy starting from the Dreyfus affair, emerging as the public spokesperson for the Durkheimians. His vocal involvement in the Dreyfus affair even led to his expulsion from his teaching institution in 1897, necessitating Durkheim's assistance in securing him another position in the middle of the academic year.[9] In response to the Dreyfus affair, Bouglé played a pivotal role in the establishment of the *Human Rights League* in 1898, where he also served as vice-president from 1911 to 1924.[10]

In the lead-up to World War I, Durkheim and Bouglé emerged as the most prominent sociologists in France.[11] However, Bouglé was more than a mere follower of Durkheim: he is often referred to as "the ambivalent Durkheimian." According to the Durkheimian scholar Salvador Juan, Célestin Bouglé was "without doubt, the most original and autonomous in relation to Durkheim. He gained significant fame in his era, thanks to his textbooks and his qualities as a speaker in his classes or in political debates."[12] Among the Durkheimians, Bouglé was the most consistent adversary of the then-popular inegalitarian theories and scientific racism.[13] In addition, Bouglé was the first of the Durkheimians to engage in-depth with the works of the German socialist Karl Marx (1818–1883).[14] Besides his numerous works on socialism and sociology, Bouglé was affiliated with the radical and radical-socialist party and ran

---

[9] Sturges: *Social Theory and Political Ideology.* 1978, p. 51.

[10] P. Vogt: Un durkheimien ambivalent: Célestin Bouglé, 1870–1940. Pp. 123–139 in *Revue Française de sociologie,* 20(1), 1979.

[11] Clark: *Prophets and Patrons.* 1973, p. 178.

[12] S. Juan: *Durkheim et la sociologie française: d'hier à aujourd'hui.* Éditions Sciences Humaines. 2019, p. 164.

[13] L. Mucchielli: Sociologie versus anthropologie raciale. L'engagement décisif des durkheimiens dans le contexte « fin de siècle » (1885–1914). Pp. 77–95 in *Gradhiva: Revue d'histoire et d'archives de l'anthropologie,* 21(1), 1997.

[14] J. Humphreys: Durkheimian Sociology and 20th-Century Politics: The Case of Célestin Bouglé. Pp. 117–138 in *History of the Human Sciences,* 12(3), 1999.

unsuccessfully for the Chamber of Deputies in 1901, 1906, 1914, and 1924.[15]

Bouglé's first book, *The Social Sciences in Germany*,[16] which initiated the dialogue between Durkheim and Bouglé, contained nearly all of his differences with Durkheim's approach. Notably, Bouglé held divergent views from Durkheim on several key topics, including the concept of "social facts," the relationship between psychology and sociology, the problem of causality, the significance of teleology, and the relationship between social structure and ideas. Compared to Durkheim, Bouglé applied a higher degree of theoretical complexity to his interpretation of history. He emphasized the possibility of social dynamics becoming static and didn't believe that the progression towards egalitarianism and "organic solidarity" naturally corresponded with the development of the division of labor. Moreover, in direct opposition to Durkheim, Bouglé rejected the notion that social science could dictate the goals that individuals should pursue. Bouglé displayed a more eclectic approach to sociology, showing sympathy towards the socialistic perspective of Durkheim's doctrine while also appreciating the individualistic stances of Durkheim's intellectual rivals, Gabriel Tarde and Georg Simmel (1858-1918). Nonetheless, despite their profound theoretical disagreements, Durkheim and Bouglé maintained a close friendship.[17]

Even though the majority of the Durkheimians had a background in philosophy, they became increasingly specialized in their studies over the course of the careers. In contrast, Bouglé continued to straddle the intersection of philosophy and sociology and grappled with the significance of sociology for society. Consequently, among the Durkheimians, Bouglé delved most deeply into the ideas of the classical French socialists, frequently writing and speaking about them, especially

---

[15] Vogt: Un durkheimien ambivalent. *Revue Française de sociologie*, 20(1), 1979.
[16] *Les sciences sociales en Allemagne* (1896).
[17] Sturges: *Social Theory and Political Ideology*. 1978, pp. 51-74.

4

during the inter-war period.[18] Bouglé aimed to unify various socialist concepts into a cohesive framework. This is evident when he wrote: "the synthesis of two traditions, which we have only the best reasons to celebrate... the two most beautiful rosettes in the crown of ideas fashioned by France in the first half of the nineteenth century: Saint-Simonism and Proudhonism."[19] Despite being the public face of the Durkheimians in his era and the most theoretically distinct among them, Bouglé's works, much like those of the early French socialists he studied, have since sunk into obscurity, rarely revisited by either academics or the general public. While Durkheim's nephew, Marcel Mauss, has gained considerable attention in recent decades, Bouglé's works have largely remained unexamined.

In the forthcoming sections, I intend to highlight the interconnection between the emergence of socialism and social science. First, I situate the rise of socialism in its historical context, emphasizing the emergence of the French Enlightenment and its roots in the Scientific Revolution. Next, I highlight the turmoil of the French Revolution (1789–1799) and the emphasis that was eventually placed on role of a social science in reorganizing society, which ultimately gave rise to socialist thought. I then explore Marx's positions on social science and his relationship with the ideas of the French socialists. Subsequently, I investigate the Durkheimians' stance on socialist theory as well as their disintegration leading up to World War II (1939–1945). Finally, I provide a brief overview of Bouglé's 1932 work, *French Socialisms,* situating it within the conflict-ridden backdrop in which it was written.

---

[18] P. Vogt: Durkheimian Sociology Versus Philosophical Rationalism: The Case of Célestin Bouglé. Pp. 231–247 in P. Besnard (ed.): *The Sociological Domain.* 1983.
[19] C. Bouglé: *De la sociologie à l'action sociale. Pacifisme, féminisme et coopération.* PUF, 1923, p. 114. Quoted in Humphreys: Durkheimian Sociology and 20th-Century Politics. 1999, p. 127.

The "Age of Enlightenment," or the "Age of Reason," was a philosophical movement that took place in Western Europe during the 17th and 18th centuries. This period, sometimes marked as starting after the 1637 publication of René Descartes' (1596-1650) *Discourse on the Method,* is widely accepted to have ended with the outbreak of the French Revolution in 1789. The Enlightenment tellingly followed the Scientific Revolution, which commenced following the deathbed publication of Nicolaus Copernicus' (1473-1543) *On the Revolutions of the Heavenly Spheres.* Copernicus proposed a heliocentric model, asserting that the Earth was in motion and orbited the Sun. This contradicted the widely held belief that the Earth was stationary at the center of the universe.

Interestingly, due to the technical nature of the book, only ten "Copernicans" have been identified in the 60 years following its publication.[20] One of these Copernicans, Galileo Galilei (1564-1642), significantly popularized Copernicus' theory in 1610 when he adapted the telescope, originally a tool designed for navigation and warfare, for astronomical purposes. By pioneering observational astronomy, Galileo discovered the moon's rough surface, the moons of Jupiter, the phases of Venus, hundreds of new stars, and sunspots.[21] Alarmed by the rising popularity of Copernicanism, the Catholic Church officially deemed heliocentrism as "foolish and absurd" and contradictory to the Bible, and in 1616, placed Copernicus' book in its Index of Forbidden Books. The philosophy of nature, previously integrated with theology, found itself

---

[20] R. Westman: The Copernicans and the Church. Pp. 76-113 in *God and Nature: Historical Essays on the Encounter between Christianity and Science.* University of California Press, 1986.
[21] T. Kuhn: *The Copernican Revolution: Planetary Astronomy in the Development of Western Thought.* Harvard University Press, 1957, pp. 220-225.

restricted and ostracized by religion. As a result, traditional wisdom increasingly faced skepticism.[22]

Influenced by Galileo, Descartes regarded mathematics as the key to the universe. By synthesizing various mathematical techniques of his time, Descartes became the most prominent French intellectual of his time. Starting in the 1620s, Descartes' originally sought to explain all physical reality using mathematical principles. In so doing, he attempted to demonstrate that reasoning could reveal all knowledge about the universe in a single sweep. However, by the 1630s, Descartes could only provide excuses for his inability to find the *a priori* mathematical principles that governed the universe. Learning of Galileo's conviction for heresy by the Church in 1633, Descartes quietly abandoned his grand ambition, fearing he might meet a similar fate.[23] To conceal his heliocentrism, Descartes shifted his analysis from the universe to less theologically-sensitive topics like the *cogito*–the thinking self. Famously, in his 1637 *Discourse on the Method,* Descartes penned the line *je pense, donc je suis,* later rendered in Latin in his 1641 *Meditations on First Philosophy* as *cogito, ergo sum*–"I think, therefore I am." He believed that by employing absolute doubt to grasp certainty, he had established a new foundation, based on skepticism, on which to build reliable knowledge. Like mathematics, Descartes argued that this reasoning was an unshakeable truth. Although he excessively favored 'rationalism' over 'empiricism,' Descartes' prioritization of reasoning became an important mainstay in modern philosophy, especially in France.[24]

Just as Copernicus is said to have ushered in the Scientific Revolution, so too has Cambridge professor Isaac Newton (1643-1727) often been seen as bringing its vibrant era to a close. This perception

---

[22] M. A. Finocchiaro: *The Galileo Affair: A Documentary History.* University of California Press, 1989.

[23] D. Clarke: *Descartes: A Biography.* Cambridge University Press, 2006, pp. 97-125.

[24] J. Seigel: *The Idea of the Self: Thought and Experience in Western Europe since the Seventeenth Century.* Cambridge University Press, 2005, pp. 64-74.

largely stems from his publication of the groundbreaking *Philosophiæ Naturalis Principia Mathematica* (often referred to as simply the *Principia)* in 1687. Until that point, the Aristotelian view of the universe, which portrayed Earth—the "terrestrial sphere"—as embedded within a distinct "celestial sphere" encased within a closed firmament, was believed to operate under fundamentally different laws. Newton, through an ingenious blend of observation and mathematics, dismantled Aristotle's two-sphere model. He proposed "universal gravitational attraction," a force that didn't discriminate between terrestrial and celestial, but pervaded the entire universe. The same gravity that causes an apple to descend to the ground also binds Earth in its orbit around the sun, Newton argued, thereby unifying the two spheres under a single set of laws. Armed with Newton's laws of motion, the trajectory of different objects anywhere in the universe could be predicted with astonishing precision. His mathematical derivations were nothing short of revolutionary, and Newtonian physics eventually displaced both Aristotelian and Cartesian models and became the new paradigm of reality.[25] More than just a physical model, Newton's vision of a cosmos dictated by immanent laws had far-reaching implications. It instilled a sense of confidence in later thinkers, empowering them to advocate for expanded individual freedoms and nurturing a steadfast belief in the possibility of applying scientific methods across other facets of nature.[26]

Following Newton's paradigm-shifting discovery, Enlightenment thinkers embraced his methods of induction and deduction to decode the mysteries of the universe. The Enlightenment's epicenter occurred during the 18th century, particularly in France, where the movement emphasized egalitarianism and freedom over arbitrary rule, thus sowing the seeds of socialist thought. A loosely organized group of prominent intellectuals collaborated on the *Encyclopédie*, whose subtitle translates to *A Systematic Dictionary of the Sciences, Arts, and Crafts* (1751–1772). This monumental work, spanning 28 volumes and over 70,000 articles penned by approximately 150 contributors, aimed to assemble all

---

[25] Kuhn: *The Copernican Revolution.* 1957, pp. 254–260.
[26] A. Koyré: *Newtonian Studies.* University of Chicago Press, 1965.

"useful" knowledge, with the intention of positively transforming human society. Implicitly anti-authoritarian and secular, the *Encyclopédie* featured contributors from luminaries such as Montesquieu (1689-1755), Jean-Jacques Rousseau (1712-1778), and Voltaire (1694-1778). These thinkers sought to uncover the laws of society while casting a skeptical eye on political institutions. The *Encyclopédie*'s progressive stance drew the ire of authorities. The Pope added it to the list of prohibited books, and starting in 1759, the *ancien régime*—France's political system, centered around an absolute monarchy—censored the project.[27] This suppression rallied the intellectual community against theology and clericalism, enhancing their sense of philosophical unity. The empiricism and materialism that flourished in France during this period was arguably a reaction against the dogmatism and metaphysical "idealism" fostered by the *ancien régime*'s ruling elite.[28]

Another significant contribution to French Enlightenment thought, particularly relevant to the development of social science, emerged from a group of economists connected to the *Encyclopédistes*. Known as the Physiocrats, a term derived from Greek meaning "government of nature," they were the first to bear the label *économistes*. At the age of sixty, the physician François Quesnay (1694-1774) shifted his focus toward the burgeoning economic issues plaguing France. He penned a series of articles for the *Encyclopédie*, though the *ancien régime* censored several of his contributions. Approaching society as a real, spontaneous whole, Quesnay endeavored to discover the immanent laws of economic relationships, seeking to establish a new science to guide economic policies. He posited that only the "productive" sector—labor in concert with nature—generates wealth and argued that it should be prioritized over the "sterile" sector, industry, which he saw as merely repurposing the wealth created by agriculture.

---

[27] W. Bristow: Enlightenment. *Stanford Encyclopedia of Philosophy,* 2017.
[28] A. Rustow: *Freedom and Domination: A Historical Critique of Civilization.* Translated by S. Attanasio. Princeton University Press, 1980, pp. 386-387.

As a reaction to mercantilism, Quesnay was the first to argue that surpluses were born from production rather than commerce. He also pioneered the definition of social classes and their empirical examination through income comparisons. Breaking with tradition, Quesnay considered the wealth of the poorest and most populous classes to be the best gauge of a country's overall wealth.[29] Quesnay's ideas quickly gained traction, earning him a group of fervent followers who disseminated his theories, influencing political leaders across Europe. Adam Smith (1723-1790), often dubbed "the father of economics," met and was notably influenced by Quesnay. Smith later replaced agricultural labor with labor in general as the producer of wealth in his landmark 1776 book *The Wealth of Nations*, leading to the notorious labor theory of value.[30]

Significantly, while the Physiocrats admired the values associated with British liberalism, particularly tolerance and liberty, they rejected their emphasis on intermediary political bodies, representation, and checks and balances. Under the *ancien régime*, intermediary institutions such as the church, guilds, universities, and communes were linked with medievalism, feudal tyranny, and clericalism. Consequently, these institutions faced hostility from the Physiocrats and French Enlightenment thinkers at large. For instance, Le Mercier de La Rivière (1719-1801), a key disciple of Quesnay, argued that without evidence, "the idea of establishing counterweights to prevent the arbitrary abuses of the sovereign power is obviously fanciful: the opposite of arbitrariness is evidence; and it is only the irresistible force of evidence that can counter the force of arbitrariness and of opinion."[31] Rejecting the idea of a pluralistic clash of arbitrary rationalizations, the Physiocrats asserted that liberty must be encouraged to align with the laws of nature.

---

[29] B. Milanovic: *Visions of Inequality: From the French Revolution to the End of the Cold War.* The Belknap Press, 2023, pp. 31-36.
[30] T. P. Neill: Quesnay and Physiocracy. Pp. 153-173 in *Journal of the History of Ideas,* 9(2), 1948.
[31] P.-P. Le Mercier de La Rivière: *L'ordre naturel et essentiel des sociétés politiques.* 1910: 345. Quoted in P. Rosanvallon: Political Rationalism and Democracy in France and in the 18th and 19th Centuries. Pp. 687-701 in *Philosophy and Social Criticism,* 28(6), 2002: 689.

For Quesnay and his disciples, human rights were the "essential laws of social order," and recognized three "fundamental" human rights: property, liberty, and security.[32] Indeed, the Physiocrats were pioneers in placing "natural human rights" at the heart of their political theory. In doing so, they connected law and economics, foreshadowing the relationship between human rights and economic liberalism that would become ubiquitous in the 19th century. Significantly, the Physiocrats perceived these "basic laws" as entirely independent of government and underscored the importance of reciprocal social duties. Le Mercier de La Rivière captured these ideas in the maxim: "No rights without duties, no duties without rights."[33] For these early human rights thinkers, the existence of rights and their implementation through reciprocal duties would create a balance that could shape the whole of society.

Although the term "social science" appears to have been coined during the early years of the French Revolution, the French Enlightenment ultimately paved the way for the concept. For instance, the Physiocrats popularized the dichotomy between science and art, endorsing the term "social art," which may have prompted the notion of a "social science." Relatedly, Marquis de Condorcet (1743-1794) was already discussing a "moral science" throughout the 1780s.[34] The works of Montesquieu and Jean-Jacques Rousseau were notably influential in spreading this conception of applying science to society. In his anonymously published *The Spirit of the Laws* (1748), Montesquieu drew a clear distinction between natural phenomena and social phenomena. He contended that while humans possess natural laws such as the right to preserve one's life and the right to eat, they also hold societal laws that vary according to time, place, and the specific conditions

---

[32] T. Carvalho: The Role of Physiocracy in the Birth of Human Rights. Pp. 61–71 in *Opera Historica,* 21(1), 2020: 62.

[33] P.-P. Le Mercier de La Rivière: *L'ordre naturel et essentiel des sociétés politiques. Œuvre doctrinale.* 2017: 115. Quoted in Carvalho: The Role of Physiocracy in the Birth of Human Rights. 2020: 65.

[34] K. Baker: The Early History of the Term 'Social Science.' Pp. 211–226 in *Annals of Science,* 20(3), 1964.

of the society under examination. Montesquieu categorized societies into different groups—particularly forms of government and their laws—which could then be compared and studied in a scientific manner. In contrast, Rousseau's key contribution was his concept of a "general will," which insisted that society contains an emergent, impersonal psychological force that was fundamentally distinct from the individuals that constitute society. This perspective—that society incorporates a *sui generis* moral entity—laid the foundation for a "science of society."[35] Collectively, the ideas of the French Enlightenment formed the bedrock for the French Revolution and the emergence of socialism.

The French Revolution

In the wake of the devastating Seven Years War (1756-1763), the expansion of the French state bureaucracy led to an escalating fiscal crisis, forcing France to declare bankruptcy in 1788. This, coupled with a particularly poor harvest season, led to a series of spontaneous riots in Paris. As a result, King Louis XVI (1754-1793) summoned the Estates General, a seldom-used advisory board composed of representatives from the clergy (the First Estate), the nobility (the Second Estate), and the commoners (the Third Estate). Dissatisfied with the proceedings, the Third Estate left the Estates General to form the "National Assembly" and invited the other Estates to join them. Amid rising bread prices and a breakdown of public order across France, the National Assembly decreed the cancellation and re-authorization of taxes and imposed limits on the role of the monarchy, effectively seizing political power. This marked the official beginning of the Revolution that would consume France for a decade. Unlike the revolutions in the Anglosphere, which aimed to preserve an existing tradition of liberty from attack, the French sought to establish liberty by completely destroying the existing order. As

---

[35] É. Durkheim: *Montesquieu and Rousseau: Forerunners of Sociology.* Translated by R. Manheim. The University of Michigan Press, 1960.

a result, the traditional bonds between the royalty, clergy, and nobility came under intense scrutiny and the *ancien régime* ultimately collapsed.[36]

Following the storming of the Bastille and the defeat of counter-revolutionary forces, the National Assembly adopted the collectively written *Declaration of the Rights of Man and of the Citizen* (1789). This significant document formally abolished serfdom and aristocratic privileges, emphasized equality, and proclaimed the universal right of each citizen (all citizens being men at the time) to "liberty, property, security, and resistance to oppression." The *Declaration* outlined the rights of man as a whole, not just those of Frenchmen. While the document drew inspiration from the 1776 *Declaration of Independence* in the newly formed United States of America, it was also influenced by the Physiocrats and the French Enlightenment.[37] This is particularly evident in the inclusion of "the right of resistance to oppression," the presence of which demonstrates the stark difference between the voluntarist "Anglo" approach to freedom and the anti-domination "Franco" approach. Furthermore, from the very onset of France's revolution, denunciations of all forms of obedience were regularly enacted. For instance, following the King's attempted escape from his virtual house arrest in 1791, upon his return to Paris, he was greeted by a silent crowd with their hats still on, a powerful symbol of non-compliance.[38]

However, the newly granted political rights did little to alleviate the economic turmoil that was engulfing Revolutionary France. In hopes of restoring public order, the revolutionaries attempted to put the Enlightenment philosophers' ideas into practice, but found little success. The first significant schism of the Revolution occurred in 1790 when the

---

[36] W. Doyle: *The French Revolution: A Very Short Introduction.* Oxford University Press, 2001.

[37] Carvalho: The Role of Physiocracy in the Birth of Human Rights. 2020, pp. 65-67.

[38] P. Ansart: La déférence ou le refus du pouvoir. Pp. 251-268 in *Communications,* 69, 2000.

Assembly decided to reorganize the Catholic Church and imposed an oath of obedience to the revolution on all clergy; approximately half complied. In 1791, the Pope publicly denounced the revolution, leading many clergy to retract their oaths.[39] In the same year, a massive slave uprising in the French colony of Saint-Domingue led to the first proclamation of the abolition of slavery in 1793, a decree that Napoleon overturned a decade later.[40]

Moreover, in an attempt to export the revolution's ideals, the French army attacked the Prussian and Austrian armies, resulting in disastrous defeats for the French. With military setbacks and an increasingly deteriorating economic situation, waves of unrest persisted, polarization among the French public intensified, and more radical voices began to emerge. Growing social divisions, widespread fear of a royalist revolt, and rumors of foreign enemies conspiring in Parisian prisons to overturn the revolution led members of the anti-royalist Jacobin Club to slaughter approximately 1,400 prisoners in what became known as the September Massacres. A few weeks later, after a series of skirmishes broke out between Revolutionary France and the neighboring monarchies, France officially abolished the French monarchy and declared itself a republic. In January 1793, the former king, now just referred to as a "citizen," was put on trial for high treason and publicly guillotined. The execution of Louis XVI further served to polarize the French public.[41]

By Autumn 1793, the more radical faction within the Jacobins, the Montagnards led by Maximilien Robespierre (1758-1794), had centralized power, called for a planned economy, and declared terror the order of the day. Fearing the Revolution to be losing its momentum, the Montagnards sought to create a new framework that would galvanize the masses. For instance, following their rise to power, the Montagnards

---

[39] Doyle: *The French Revolution.* 2001, pp. 45–47.
[40] *Ibid.,* pp. 72–73.
[41] *Ibid.,* pp. 50–54.

14

implemented several significant measures that attempted to discipline the popular movement:

- The abolition of political elections.
- A forced conscription of all males between the ages of 18 and 25 into the military.
- A law that made profiteering punishable by death.
- The "General Maximum," a law setting price limits on products.
- A decree weakening individual freedoms, such as denying the right for "enemies of the people" to defend themselves, known as the Law of Suspects.[42]
- A new 'revolutionary calendar' to replace the former 'Christian calendar.'
- A new deistic, state religion known as the Cult of the Supreme Being, intended to replace Catholicism, as well as the short-lived atheistic, state religion known as the Cult of Reason.[43]

The Montagnards even went so far as to suggest that children should be separated from their families for long periods of time and brought up collectively in boarding schools by the state.[44] However, after the French secured a significant victory against the Austrians at the Battle of Fleurus in June 1794, the public expected the government to roll back some of the wartime measures. When Robespierre objected to rollbacks to focus on enemies of the state, discord grew, and the Montagnards came under intense scrutiny. In July 1794, Robespierre and his supporters were publicly guillotined. Although the disorder and bloodshed didn't end, the apex of the chaos, known as the Reign of Terror, is considered to have to

---

[42] A. Soboul: Robespierre and the Popular Movement of 1793-4. Pp. 54-70 in *Past & Present, 5*, 1954.

[43] M. Schmid: Pentecost 1794: Robespierre's Religious Vision and the Fulfillment of Time. Pp. 259-276 in *Religion in the Age of Enlightenment, 5*(1), 2015.

[44] J. Israel: *Revolutionary Ideas: An Intellectual History of the French Revolution from the Rights of Man to Robespierre.* Princeton University Press, 2015, p. 389.

ended. In less than two years, roughly 16,000 people were guillotined, 20,000 died in prison, and 200,000 were killed in combat.[45]

By 1795, some civil rights, such as freedom of worship, were reinstated in France, and an elaborate set of checks and balances was implemented. Meanwhile, French armies became triumphant on almost all fronts. After leading successful military campaigns against the Austrian Empire and the Ottoman Empire, General Napoleon Bonaparte (1769-1821) gained significant prominence among the French public. This set the stage for him to stage a coup d'état in 1799, dissolve the First French Republic, and become the de facto leader of France.

A full decade after the onset of the Revolution, Napoleon's ascendancy effectively brought it to an end. In 1801, Napoleon negotiated with the new Pope to restore Catholicism in France. However, the property of the Church that had been confiscated and sold during the Revolution would not be returned. Napoleon's conquests abroad steadily dismembered the Holy Roman Empire of the German Nation, the oldest political entity in Europe.[46] According to historian François Furet (1927-1997), "Bonaparte had invaded the whole political theatre, and occupied it entirely on his own... infinitely more powerful and despotic than the old one, since there was no longer any intermediary body to oppose its domination over equal individuals."[47] At the end of 1804, Napoleon constituted the First French Empire and crowned himself emperor, a regime that lasted until 1815.

Although the French Revolution failed in nearly every realm and ultimately consolidated into a centralizing state, the peasantry across France gained significant control over property that formerly belonged to the feudal nobility. Unlike England, where control of agricultural land was increasingly concentrated into fewer and fewer hands, France effectively

---

[45] H. Gough: *The Terror in the French Revolution.* Bloomsbury Publishing, 2010, p. 2.
[46] Doyle: *The French Revolution.* 2001, pp. 70-73.
[47] F. Furet: *Revolutionary France, 1770-1880.* Translated by A. Nevill. Blackwell, 1992, p. 234.

decentralized control over the land. After the Revolution, most peasants were content with their new holdings and rarely participated in the tumult that frequently engulfed Paris. Beyond the desacralization of virtually every social institution, the substantial transfer of property from the Church and the nobility to the Third Estate was the most dramatic long-term outcome of the Revolution.[48]

In many respects, the Revolution embodied Enlightenment ideas by demolishing traditional intermediate groups associated with feudalism and consolidating power in the French state. This increase in state centralization, often at the expense of other groups, helped create a situation in which totalitarian leaders could thrive. In response to the obliteration of these intermediate groups, the concepts of a "social group" and "social science" began to proliferate. Early social thinkers critiqued the "administrative despotism" of the French Revolution, particularly the Rousseau-inspired Jacobins. They started to view social groups as entities that were more than the sum of their parts, rather than merely being representatives of the "general will" that encompassed the entire polity instead of these intermediate groups. Indeed, by relying on the state as the primary source of social integration, the Revolution accelerated societal disorder, leading to Napoleon's rise to power.[49]

The Emergence of Socialism

Following the tumultuous French Revolution, there was a significant shift in political philosophy. The focus moved away from political rulers and towards the people. A consensus of values emerged among the French regarding the inalienability of human rights and the unity of humanity through reason and liberty.[50] Instead of focusing on the relationship between atomized individuals and the state, these social

---

[48] G. H. Mead: *Movements of Thought in the 19th Century.* University of Chicago Press, 1936, pp. 418-421.
[49] R. A. Nisbet: The French Revolution and the Rise of Sociology in France. Pp. 156-164 in *American Journal of Sociology,* 49(2), 1943.
[50] I. Hamati-Ataya: The French Enlightenment. Pp. 1065-1070 in *The Encyclopedia of Political Thought.* Wiley Blackwell, 2014.

thinkers shifted their attention to intermediate social groups and economic rights. In essence, they reframed the problem of order altogether, which laid the basis for the development of socialism and sociology. As Émile Durkheim stated, "It was from this intellectual effervescence that Saint-Simonism, Fourierism, Comtism, and sociology simultaneously resulted."[51] Even more, Durkheim argued that Henri de Saint-Simon (1760–1825) was the founder of *both* sociology and socialism.[52] Marcel Mauss, in his key work on socialism, *The Nation* (which was not published in full until 2013), similarly contended that:

> "[Socialism was] born at the same time as social science, and Saint-Simon was... the founder of both.... This simultaneous birth of the social sciences, on one hand, and of socialism, on the other, along with its counterpart individualism at the core, and liberalism, is an important fact in the history of the sciences and human morality."[53]

Indeed, all French socialists of this era believed in the revolutionary potential of social science to remove arbitrary rule from the social order. As such, they saw it as fundamentally in opposition to the status quo. For instance, Auguste Comte (1798–1857), who coined the terms "sociology" and "positivism,"[54] originally served as Saint-Simon's

---

[51] É. Durkheim: Sociology in France in the Nineteenth Century. Pp. 3–24 in *Émile Durkheim: On Morality and Society*. Edited by R. N. Bellah. University of Chicago Press, 1973: 11.

[52] É. Durkheim: *Socialism*. Translated by C. Sattler. Collier Books, 1962, pp. 50, 134.

[53] M. Mauss: *La nation*. PUF, 2013, pp. 260–261.

[54] Tellingly, Comte considered positivism to be a form of socialism: "Socialism is spontaneous positivism, while positivism constitutes systematic socialism." (A. Comte to Laffitte: August 31, 1849. Quoted in M. Pickering: *Auguste Comte: An Intellectual Biography, Volume. II*. Cambridge University Press, 2009, p. 437.) Although "positivism" was a highly contentious topic during the 20th century, Comte's "positivism" is surprisingly modern, with contemporary commentators stating that Comtean positivism has more in common with "post-positivism" than the "logical-positivism" regularly associated with his name. For more on this distinction, see R. C. Sharff: *Comte After Positivism*. Cambridge University Press, 1995.

secretary and collaborator starting in 1817, until they had a bitter falling out in 1824. Comte, the "father of sociology," argued that this new science of society would emancipate mankind and was, therefore, antithetical to academia with its hyper-specialization and protection of the status quo.[55]

Above all, these early socialist thinkers critically examined the Church and the practice of religion more generally. Much like the later Durkheimians, the French socialists placed religion, particularly its relation to the state, at the heart of the social question. Comte, like the Saint-Simonians, aspired to replace Catholicism by creating a humanist religion informed by science. Charles Fourier (1772-1837) highlighted the role of religion in suppressing the passions, though his followers emphasized the compatibility of his thought with Christianity. Pierre-Joseph Proudhon (1809-1865) endeavored to overcome the practice of religion altogether, while simultaneously drawing attention to passages in the Bible.

Another commonality among the French socialists is that they sought to improve society as a whole. They believed that by approaching society scientifically, the ills that plagued society could be overcome in a mutually beneficial manner. Fascinated with Newton's "law of attraction," the French socialists held that this groundbreaking discovery held enormous implications for society. Contrary to the "passive expectation of a transcendent ideal state" that medieval Millenarianism embraced, by extending Newton's insight from physics to society (which Comte originally termed "social physics"), the French socialists emphasized an immanent social force that had the potential to emancipate humanity.[56]

Linked to this insight about an immanent social force, the French socialists were hostile toward government, which they generally perceived

[55] M. Pickering: *Auguste Comte: An Intellectual Biography, Volume I.* Cambridge University Press, 1993, pp. 666-672.
[56] J. Strube. Socialist Religion and the Emergence of Occultism: A Genealogical Approach to Socialism and Secularization in 19th-Century France. Pp. 359-388 in *Religion,* 46(3), 2016.

as a product of military rule. Indeed, the central theory of Saint-Simon's work was his prediction that the scientific society of the future would be 'administered' rather than 'governed.'[57] Similarly, Fourier rejected all external authority and positioned the individual's passions as the guiding force. For Proudhon, the "father of anarchism," government was systematic disorder while anarchy was inherently a state of order. Even Comte advocated for the dissolution of the state into decentralized regional units.[58] In his lectures on socialism, Durkheim stated that "[s]ince it is unnecessary to repress humanity to make it pursue its interests, [administrative] directors will have no need for an authority which raises them above those they direct. Governmental restraint will have no basis. That is the principle of socialist politics, that is the anarchistic creed."[59] For Durkheim, this insight about the "anarchistic" nature of socialism was something he attributed to not only the French socialists, but also Marx. For example, Durkheim wrote:

> "[S]ocialism, far from being authoritarian—as is so often said—far from demanding a stronger organization of governmental powers, was, on the contrary, in one sense, essentially anarchistic. We find the same attitude, even more pronounced, in Fourier as in Saint-Simon, in Proudhon as in Fourier, in Marx as in Proudhon."[60]

Moreover, the anarchistic approach of the French socialists didn't imply the negation of property. Contrary to the Marxist tradition, the French socialist tradition didn't aim to abolish property rights, but rather sought their modification. As Mauss described: "far from socialism being an adversary... of individual property, it presupposes it.... [T]his has been a consistent aspect of the doctrine since Saint-Simon and especially Proudhon; it aims to actualize individual property and to grant workers collective property... of the means of production and the fruits of labor."[61]

---

[57] G. Ionescu: *The Political Thought of Saint-Simon.* Oxford University Press, 1976, p. 3.
[58] R. Vernon: Auguste Comte and the Withering-Away of the State. Pp. 549–566 in *Journal of the History of Ideas,* 45(4), 1984.
[59] Durkheim: *Socialism.* 1962, p. 236.
[60] *Ibid.,* p. 194.
[61] Mauss: *La nation.* 2013, p. 287.

Skeptical of community, they viewed property as a safeguard for individual welfare.

Relatedly, the French socialists generally supported the populist demands of direct action, human rights, and social justice. By approaching society scientifically, they aimed to explain the populist movement that often found itself at odds with the establishment.[62]

Notably, all the French socialists also shared the use of the concept of "series." A series was used as a qualitative, historically-oriented tool to make sense of social processes. By tracing out a series, they argued that it illuminated the similarities and differences between social phenomena and also served to explain how particular processes emerged in history. In effect, ideas and actions were understood to have a reciprocal relationship with each other. Nonetheless, there were stark differences in how each thinker understood and utilized the conception of series.[63]

Saint-Simon, Fourier, and Proudhon

While it seems that Saint-Simon and Charles Fourier never met, they shared some striking similarities. Both were imprisoned and narrowly avoided execution during the Reign of Terror, lost their inherited fortunes during the Revolution, and began their writing careers under Napoleon. These early socialist theorists sought to understand how society functioned in hopes of preventing another destructive social upheaval. Despite both Saint-Simon's and Fourier's doctrines emerging during the first decade of the 19th century, Fourier would operate in the shadow of Saint-Simon until the latter's death.

Initially obscure, Saint-Simon began to attract some attention in the mid-1810s and his following gradually increased until his death in

---

[62] C. Calhoun: Classical Social Theory and the French Revolution of 1848. Pp. 210-225 in *Sociological Theory, 7*(2), 1989.
[63] J. Tresch: The Order of the Prophets: Series in Early French Social Science and Socialism. Pp. 315-342 in *History of Science*, 48(3-4), 2010.

1825. Saint-Simon emphasized the outdated elements of Catholicism but also acknowledged the positive role of religion in society. He believed that the most urgent need was to replace the spiritual power of the time, the Catholic Church, with social scientists. In his view, the Scientific Revolution had left Catholicism out of touch and, therefore, it had lost respect in the eyes of the masses. By applying science to society, it would allow humanity to replace outdated theology with empirically-supported theories that could then serve to harmoniously integrate humanity.[64]

> "[T]he crisis in which the European peoples are involved is due to the incoherence of general ideas: as soon as there is a theory corresponding to the present state of enlightenment, order will be restored, an institution common to the peoples of Europe will be re-established, and a priesthood adequately educated according to the present state of knowledge will bring peace to Europe..."[65]

By uncovering the laws of society, Saint-Simon believed they could be used to reorganize society in an orderly and mutually beneficial way. For Saint-Simon, the defining feature of science, especially when compared to religious dogma, is that it is based on demonstration and is, therefore, fundamentally testable and replicable. Saint-Simon notably laid the foundation for "positivism" by arguing that all scientific disciplines were interconnected and became "positive" sciences, capable of making accurate predictions, in a sequential order, with the least complex being first. Physiology was currently in the process of becoming a positive science. After physiology would come the "science of man," or "social physiology," in which morals, politics, philosophy, and religion would all be explained in a scientific manner. Once all the particular sciences became "positive," they would fit into one general science.[66]

---

[64] K. Taylor: Introduction. Pp. 13–61 in *Henri Saint-Simon: Selected Writings on Science, Industry, and Social Organization.* Croom Helm Ltd., 1975.

[65] F. M. H. Markham (ed.): *Henri Comte de Saint-Simon: Selected Writings.* Translated by F. M. H. Markham. Basil Blackwell, 1952, p. 27.

[66] *Ibid.*, pp. 21–23.

Repeatedly, Saint-Simon emphasized that all of these sciences were the products of the collective efforts of human activity and were ultimately grounded in economic production. For Saint-Simon, society was constantly being created, a process he referred to as "society in action." Rather than a transcendent order, society was an immanent, collective act. All social structures, including those based on science, were themselves products of this collective action, inherently interlinked with all other components within society.[67] "A conception of general science discovered in one period is always put into effect the following period," he argued.[68] Saint-Simon understood society to be engaged in a process of becoming conscious of itself through the different scientific disciplines. By organizing the sciences, he believed it would provide industrial society with a corresponding system of ideas on which to structure itself.[69]

Not long after meeting the economist Jean-Baptiste Say (1767–1832), Saint-Simon redirected his emphasis away from social science and toward economic issues and "industrialism," a term he coined. In his earlier works, Saint-Simon had made a distinction between governing and non-governing. Now, he distinguished between producers and non-producers and shifted his critique of government into the economic sphere.[70] Moreover, Saint-Simon aimed to provide a systematic explanation for why industrialism had failed to triumph during the Revolution. In his view, the French Revolution had essentially reconstituted feudalism by replacing the rule of nobles with that of the bourgeoisie. He attributed the failure to the lack of a shared, overarching

[67] G. Gurvitch: *Les fondateurs français de la sociologie contemporaine : Saint-Simon et P.-J. Proudhon.* Centre de Documentation Universitaire, 1955.
[68] Taylor: *Henri Saint-Simon.* 1975, p. 120.
[69] G. L. Gollin: The Sociology of Saint-Simon: Monument or Steppingstone? Pp. 188–196 in *Journal of the History of the Behavioral Sciences, 6*(2), 1970.
[70] P. Musso: Religion and Political Economy in Saint-Simon Pp. 809–827 in *The European Journal of the History of Economic Thought,* 24(4), 2017.

idea among industrials and their willingness to allow lawyers and jurists to commandeer their cause.[71]

Initially open to collaboration with anyone, Saint-Simon became increasingly embittered and disillusioned by the resistance of the upper classes to his proposals. Sensing a growing split between industrial leaders and the working masses, he began to differentiate between the owners of industry who profited without working, and the exploited workers. He identified property as the key to exploitation and sought to eradicate idler property owners.[72] Consequently, Saint-Simon began advocating for an alliance between the industrialists and the monarch, opposing the lawyers and jurists as well as the bourgeoisie.

However, Saint-Simon's revolutionary impulses were soon overshadowed by his concern for the development of a new system of morality. As his patience for science and economics began to wear thin, he devoted the last few years of his life to the construction of a moral framework suited to industrialism. Saint-Simon argued that without a superior force emphasizing mutual obligation, society would fall into egoism. Right up to his death, he continued to claim that the basis of morals could replace religious dogma with facts derived from observation but also posited that Christianity had laid down the principle of an industrial morality, particularly the concept of loving one's neighbor. He believed that a scientific approach to the topic would allow the moral 'oughts' to be removed and would lead to society being organized in a mutually beneficial manner.[73]

Days after Saint-Simon's passing, a small circle of his followers founded the popular journal *Le producteur*. Initially, this group didn't possess any systematic philosophy. The primary commonality among the contributors to the journal at this time was their shared view of history as

---

[71] H. Saint-Simon: On the Intermediate (Bourgeois) Class. Pp. 250–252 in Taylor: *Henri Saint-Simon*. 1975.

[72] Ionescu: *The Political Thought of Saint-Simon*. 1976, pp. 8, 31.

[73] G. Stedman-Jones: Saint-Simon and the Liberal Origins of the Socialist Critique of Political Economy. Pp. 21–47 in *La France et l'Angleterre au 19 siècle. Echanges, représentations, comparaison*. Créaphis, 2006.

an unfolding progression in science, industry, and art. Between 1825 and 1826, Comte collaborated with the Saint-Simonians and wrote several important articles in their journal. These articles elucidated Saint-Simon's often-confusing doctrine and outlined his "positive philosophy."

However, by the end of 1826, Comte suffered a mental breakdown and was institutionalized for two years. The journal soon fell apart in his absence. When Comte reemerged in 1828, the Saint-Simonians had evolved into a more religious and dogmatic group. Feeling threatened by Comte's return, they ridiculed Comte due to his continued focus on science as opposed to their newfound emphasis on spreading a religion. In response, Comte founded his own rival "positivist" school in Paris and began regularly delivering lectures from his apartment. From 1830 to 1842, Comte wrote his six-volume work *The Positive Philosophy,* laying the foundations for what would come to be known as "sociology."[74]

Starting in December of 1828, the Saint-Simonians held biweekly public lectures headed by Arman Bazard (1791–1832) and Barthélemy-Prosper Enfantin (1796–1864). These lectures were later collected together in a renowned book titled *The Doctrine of Saint-Simon: An Exposition,* which is sometimes referred to as "the Old Testament of Socialism." The theory the Saint-Simonians propounded, which departed from Saint-Simon's in several significant ways,[75] began with a philosophy of history that critiqued the entire structure of society, before offering proposals on how to reorganize it. In their view, philosophers had erred by failing to grasp the interplay between social action and collective ideas, and that societal progression is driven by morality. The Saint-Simonians aimed to regulate the market to enhance the capacities of workers by reconfiguring social institutions. They condemned high interest rates and rents, arguing that these served the idle instead of a society of producers. Consequently, they advocated for extending credit

---

[74] M. Pickering: Comte and the Saint-Simonians. Pp. 215–223 in *French Historical Studies* 18(1), 1993.
[75] G. G. Iggers: Elements of a Sociology of Ideas in the Saint-Simonist Philosophy of History. Pp. 217–225 in *The Sociological Quarterly,* 1(4), 1960.

to workers at minimal interest rates, and further emphasized the institution of property as the source of human exploitation.[76]

Starting in 1832, "networks" as a replacement for "power" became the central focus of the Saint-Simonians. They argued that networks consisted of both material components, which encompassed communication networks such as canals, railways, telegraphs, and roads, and immaterial components, comprising knowledge and financial credit. The two types of networks were fundamentally intertwined in such a way as to reduce distances between individuals and pave the way towards a universal association.[77] Enchanted by the idea of railroad networks, the Péreire brothers established the Crédit Mobilier in 1852, primarily to finance railways at low cost. Through their efforts, the French railroad network expanded five-fold by 1870. Encouraged by their success, they expanded operations into Austria in 1855, Spain in 1856, Russia in 1862, and Italy in 1863. Their successful model even influenced the historic banking Rothschild family, who began to follow their organizational pattern and moved towards large-scale investments in Europe.[78]

Although Saint-Simon emphasized the need to assist the poorest members of society, he never maintained a continued interest in their condition. Likewise, he expressed no tangible interest in the plight of women. This contrasted sharply with Charles Fourier, who placed the condition of the poor and women at the forefront of his concerns. For Fourier, the emancipation of women coincided with the emancipation of humanity. In May 1829, Fourier, who had a minuscule following compared to Saint-Simon, attended one of the Saint-Simonians' lectures and discussions. Despite reacting in a strongly negative manner, criticizing their moralism and "plutocratic tendency," he kept his thoughts to

---

[76] G. G. Iggers: Introduction. Pp. ix–xlvii in *The Doctrine of Saint-Simon: An Exposition. First Year, 1828–1829.* Translated by G. G. Iggers. Beacon Press, 1958.

[77] P. Musso: Network Ideology: From Saint-Simonianism to the Internet. Pp. 19–66 in J. L Garcia (ed.): *Pierre Musso and the Network Society: From Saint-Simonianism to the Internet.* Springer, 2016.

[78] J. C. Eckalbar: The Saint-Simonians in Industry and Economic Development. Pp. 83–96 in *American Journal of Economics and Sociology,* 38(1), 1979.

himself. At the same time, Fourier was astonished by the following and resources that the Saint-Simonians had amassed. Shortly afterwards, Fourier sent Enfantin a letter and initiated a correspondence with him. Fourier gifted Enfantin a copy of his 1829 book *Le nouveau monde industriel,* notably published in the publishing house where Pierre-Joseph Proudhon worked. Proudhon later wrote, "for six whole weeks, I was a captive of this bizarre genius."[79] Following Enfantin's encounter with Fourier, the Saint-Simonians incorporated the emancipation of women into their doctrine. They went on to claim that men and women were equal and that God was androgynous.[80]

Fourier's approach to social science was centered not on morality or economics, but squarely on "the passions." Fourier believed that radical social change could only occur by working with, rather than against, "the drive given [to] us by nature prior to any reflection; it is persistent despite the opposition of reason, duty, prejudice, etc."[81] Instead of philosophical speculation, Fourier claimed that his approach was based directly on concrete observations of social life. He viewed the Saint-Simonians as further repressing humanity in their attempts to create a new religion, arguing that they were "working *in denial of man,* and what is more, in denial of God since they want to change or stifle the passions which God has bestowed on us as our fundamental drives...."[82] For Fourier, the path to societal harmony was not through moralism, but by giving free rein to the forces present in society. By doing so, he argued, individuals would naturally form stable groups, which he termed a "phalanx." These phalanxes, as Fourier imagined them, would be akin to a planetary system held in harmony through the interplay of independent

---

[79] Quoted in G. Woodcock: *Pierre-Joseph Proudhon: A Biography.* Black Rose Books, 1987, p. 13.
[80] J. Beecher: *Charles Fourier: The Visionary and His World.* University of California Press, 1986, pp. 413–421.
[81] J. Beecher & R. Bienvenu (eds.): *The Utopian Vision of Charles Fourier: Selected Texts on Work, Love, and Passionate Attraction.* Translated by J. Beecher & R. Bienvenu. Beacon Press, 1971, p. 216.
[82] C. Fourier to V. Considerant: October 3, 1831. Quoted in F. E. Manuel. *The Prophets of Paris.* Harper & Row, Publishers, 1965, p. 207.

forces, collectively enabling the development of each individual's capacities.[83]

Like the Physiocrats, Fourier critiqued the role of merchants and highlighted the inability of commerce to generate wealth. He believed that the advancement of industry only served to increase the "wretchedness" of the people, and he linked the disorganization of industry with poverty. In contrast to the Jacobins, who advocated for strict equality, Fourier, like Saint-Simon, believed in the inequality of capacities and talents, and hence saw hierarchy as an inevitable feature of society. Instead of championing the equal distribution of rewards across society, Fourier argued for what he termed a "social minimum." He held that society must guarantee property to every individual, as well as the "right to work," which encompassed the rights of hunting, gathering, fishing, and grazing. In Fourier's view, these rights would allow the poor to escape degrading work by developing their talents and finding attractive work for themselves. Interestingly, the first proponent of what is now a popular idea, guaranteed basic income, was the obscure Belgian Fourierist, Joseph Charlier (1816–1896), who promoted the idea from 1848 until his death.[84]

Influenced by both Saint-Simon and Fourier, Pierre-Joseph Proudhon was also deeply interested in the emerging notion of social science. However, instead of pursuing a new religion (like Saint-Simon) or giving free rein to passions (like Fourier), Proudhon argued that the goal of this new science was to find a balance between reason and conscience. As he wrote, "if there is a contradiction between reason and conscience, between conscience and the law, that contradiction comes from us."[85] In Proudhon's view, an individual's will constantly finds itself pulled between two different impulses: the intellectual and the moral.

---

[83] N. V. Riasanovsky: *The Teaching of Charles Fourier.* University of California Press, 1969, pp. 179–214.

[84] J. Cunliffe & G. Erreygers: The Enigmatic Legacy of Charles Fourier: Joseph Charlier and Basic Income. Pp. 459–484 in *History of Political Economy,* 33(3), 2001.

[85] P.-J. Proudhon: *The Celebration of Sunday.* Translated by S. Wilbur. Corvus Editions, 2023, p. 46.

Reason arises from the individual's experience, while conscience originates from their social relations.

To Proudhon, only justice—the central pole of society—is capable of providing this balance between reason and conscience, and must therefore be the focal point of social science. He argued, "The practice of justice is a science which, when once discovered and diffused, will sooner or later put an end to social disorder, by teaching us our rights and duties."[86] Proudhon believed that the voluntary and rational recognition of the immanent principle of justice would facilitate the reorganization of social relations and ensure a pluralistic unity.[87]

Proudhon specifically positioned the philosophy of the Catholic Church in opposition to the philosophy of Revolution. Catholic philosophy is based around the belief in a transcendent force that structures social relations and serves to legitimize social hierarchy and inequality. In contrast, revolutionary philosophy paves the way for the immanence of justice and rights that uphold human dignity.[88] As Bouglé wrote, "Proudhon's paradoxical position in the history of sociology may be summed up thus: he forced collective reason to consecrate personal rights and assigned to the community the goal of protecting individual equality."[89]

In Proudhon's 1861 work *War and Peace,* he outlined a series of rights that derive from society, starting with "the right of war" and progressing to "political rights," "civil rights," and finally "economic rights." Economic rights pertain to work and the economy, and determine

---

[86] P.-J. Proudhon: *What is Property? or An Inquiry into the Principle of Right and of Government.* Translated by B. R. Tucker. Humboldt Publishing Co., 1876, p. 254.

[87] A. Prichard: *Justice, Order, and Anarchy: The International Political Theory of Pierre-Joseph Proudhon.* Routledge, 2013, pp. 104–106.

[88] G. Navet: Proudhon et la déclaration des droits de l'homme et du citoyen. Pp. 53-63 in *Revue d'études proudhoniennes,* 1, 2015.

[89] C. Bouglé: Proudhon, Pierre-Joseph. In *Encyclopedia of the Social Sciences, Volume XII.* Macmillan Publishers, 1935, p. 575.

what is considered to be a fair relationship between capital and labor.[90] Proudhon argued that only once economic rights are fulfilled through an "agricultural-industrial federation" can political rights actually be guaranteed. He wrote, "Who does not see that the mutualist organization of exchange... irresistibly push[es] the producers, each following his specialty, towards a centralization analogous with that of the State, but in which no one obeys, no one is dependent, and everyone is free and sovereign?"[91] In other words, Proudhon believed that only through the working classes becoming organized through mutual exchange and federations can rights fully take root.

By the time Durkheim and Mauss were writing around the turn of the 20th century, the classical French socialists were largely overlooked by both socialists and sociologists. It seems that outside of the Durkheimians, only the followers of Marx and Friedrich Engels (1820–1895) kept them alive in academia, albeit by labelling them as "utopian socialists." When the Marxists seized political power to form the Soviet Union in 1917, it effectively sidelined any other narrative of socialism, including British Fabianism, Russian anarchism, and other strains of German socialism.[92] The Soviet Union even went so far as to suppress sociology as a discipline in 1924, a prohibition that remained in effect until the mid-1950s.[93]

Still, while Marx and Engels relegated the French to the status of "utopian socialists," they nevertheless acknowledged their ideas as important steppingstones towards their own. As shown in *figure 1* below,

---

[90] P.-J. Proudhon: *War and Peace: On the Principle and Constitution of the Rights of People.* Translated by P. Sharkey. AK Press, 2022, pp. 213–225.

[91] Proudhon to Micaud, December 25, 1855. *Correspondence* Vol. 6, Lacroix, 1875, pp. 285–286. Quoted in S. Wilbur: Pierre-Joseph Proudhon: Self-Government and the Citizen-State. In *Contr'un*, 2, 2013, p. 26.

[92] B. D. Wolfe: French Socialism, German Theory, and the Flaw in the Foundation of the Socialist Internationals. Pp. 177–197 in J. S. Curtiss (ed.): *Essays in Russian and Soviet History: In Honor of Geroid Tanquary Robinson.* Columbia University Press, 1965.

[93] L. Greenfeld: Soviet Sociology and Sociology in the Soviet Union. Pp. 99–123 in *Annual Review of Sociology,* 14, 1988.

although still neglected today, the French socialists contributed to the genesis of several major intellectual movements of the 20th century: sociology, positivism, socialism, anarchism, and Marxism.

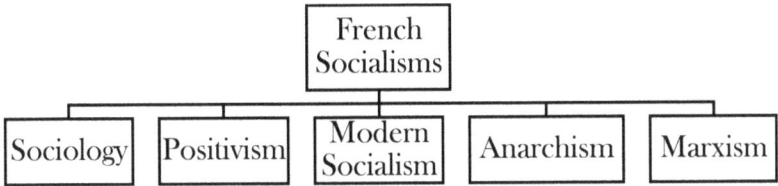

Figure 1: The major intellectual legacies of the key French socialisms.[94]

Marx and French Socialisms

Up until 1847, the writings of the French socialists had a profound impact on the young Karl Marx. For instance, in his *1844 Manuscripts*,[95] Marx advocated for a positivist conception of social science based on the natural sciences. He predicted that "Natural science will in time incorporate into itself the science of man, just as the science of man will incorporate into itself natural science: there will be *one* science."[96] Marx's early writings didn't yet adopt the stage theory that would later become central to his thought, which posited that a bourgeois revolution and the full development of capitalism were necessary prerequisites for a proletarian revolution. Instead, in the *1844 Manuscripts*, Marx argued that intellectual ideas would ultimately guide the proletariat to

---

[94] Adapted from: G. Ionescu: *The Political Thought of Saint-Simon*. Oxford University Press, 1976, p. 18.
[95] Published in 1932, along with Marx and Engels' *German Ideology*, by the Marx-Engels Institute of the Soviet Union, notably the same year as when this book by Bouglé was originally published.
[96] K. Marx: *Economic and Philosophic Manuscripts of 1844*. Translated by M. Milligan. Progress Publishers, 1959, p. 98.

31

communism.[97] Furthermore, during this period, Marx's views on communism and property were closely aligned with the French socialists:

> *"Fourier*, who, like the Physiocrats, also conceives *agricultural labor* to be at least the *exemplary* type, whilst *Saint-Simon* declares in contrast that *industrial labor* as such is the essence, and accordingly aspires to the *exclusive* rule of the industrialists and the improvement of the workers' condition. Finally, *communism* is the *positive* expression of annulled private property—at first as *universal* private property."[98]

The series of manuscripts written between 1845 and 1846 by Marx and Engels, known collectively as *The German Ideology,* can arguably be seen as a tribute to the French socialists. Not only do these writings contain sections defending the correct interpretation of the ideas of Saint-Simon, the Saint-Simonians, Fourier, and Proudhon, but the very philosophy that Marx and Engels expound, later labelled as "historical materialism" by Engels, appears to be a reiteration of French socialist thought. Like the French socialists, Marx and Engels argue that social reality originates from human activity. Consequently, they perceive the activity of production as the key to history, leading them to place significant emphasis on scientific and technological innovation as well as economic activity. Even the vocabulary Marx and Engels began to use in these manuscripts echoes the lexicon of the French socialists. For example, instead of German philosophical terms like 'species-being,' 'negation of the negation,' 'in-itself' and 'for-itself,' Marx and Engels shifted toward concepts common among the French socialists such as 'industry,' 'trade,' 'action,' 'social class,' and 'ideology.'[99] Relatedly, Marx and Engels' emphasis on the progress of industrialization creating the

[97] A. F. McGovern: The Young Marx on the State. Pp. 430–466 in *Science and Society,* 34(4), 1970.
[98] Marx: *Economic and Philosophic Manuscripts of 1844.* 1959, p. 87–88.
[99] P. Ansart: *Marx et l'anarchisme: essai sur les sociologies de Saint-Simon, Proudhon et Marx.* PUF, 1969.

viability for a more harmonious society in *The German Ideology* also appears to stem from the French socialists.[100]

However, by the time Marx published his first solo-authored book, and the only book he wrote in French, *The Poverty of Philosophy* in 1847, sometimes referred to as "Anti-Proudhon," there was a noticeable shift in his attitude towards the French socialists. This shift led Marcel Mauss to write in *The Nation* that "it is generally agreed that Marx was unfair to his predecessors as he was to Proudhon. In our opinion, he was most unfair to Saint-Simon.... [I]t is, on the part of Marx, supremely inaccurate not to have acknowledged the scientific depth of Saint-Simon's views on economic history, the connections it maintains with politics and law."[101] Rather than using science to uncover immanent forces within society, Marx began to assert that the social movement must become political above all else.

According to Marx, the entrenched antagonism between the two dominant classes must lead to a "complete revolution" in which the proletariat and bourgeoisie will engage in "a brutal conflict." Once the proletariat conquers political power, they "will exclude classes and their antagonism, and there will no longer be political power, properly speaking, since political power is simply the official form of the antagonism in civil society."[102] Only through a violent class struggle resulting in the seizure of political power will the oppressor class become absorbed into the oppressed class, ultimately leading to the disappearance of all alienation and antagonism. In other words, Marx's philosophy of history asserted that he had uncovered the teleology of society's movement, which in turn led Marx to reject the French socialist emphasis

---

[100] J. Sperber: *Karl Marx: A Nineteenth-Century Life*. WW Norton & Company, 2013, pp. 168–169.
[101] Mauss: *La nation*. 2013, p. 267.
[102] K. Marx: *The Poverty of Philosophy*. Translated by. H. Quelch. Prometheus Books, 1995, p. 190.

on social science and instead stress the need for the social movement to become a political movement.

Shortly after the publication of *The Poverty of Philosophy,* Marx collaborated with Engels to publish their now-classic 1848 work, *The Communist Manifesto.* Although it immediately fell into obscurity and was not republished until 1872,[103] the *Manifesto* eventually became a landmark critique of the French socialists. In this work, Marx and Engels provided a brief overview of the different socialists and communists of their day, and famously labeled Saint-Simon and Fourier (as well as Robert Owen) as "utopian socialists." They argued that, although these "utopians" recognized the class antagonisms deeply entrenched within society, their situation within "the early undeveloped period" of capitalism prevented them from seeing industry as spontaneously creating the conditions that would result in a proletarian revolution. "They therefore search after a new social science, after new social laws, that are to create these conditions,"[104] Marx and Engels argued, going on to ridicule "their fanatical and superstitious belief in the miraculous effects of their social science."[105]

Moreover, Marx and Engels labeled Proudhon a "conservative or bourgeois socialist" and suggested that instead of seeking to alter the relations between labor and capital, he merely sought to "lessen the cost, and simplify the administrative work of bourgeois government."[106] These comments on Proudhon stand in stark contrast to their remarks just three years prior, where they wrote in *The Holy Family* that Proudhon's "work is a scientific manifesto of the French proletariat..."[107]

---

[103] D. McLellan: *Karl Marx: His Life and Thought.* Harper Colophon, 1977, p. 188.

[104] K. Marx & F. Engels: *The Communist Manifesto.* Signet Classic, 1998, p. 87.

[105] *Ibid.,* p. 89.

[106] *Ibid.,* p. 85.

[107] K. Marx & F. Engels: *The Holy Family or Critique of Critical Criticism.* Translated by R. Dixon. Foreign Languages Publishing House, 1956, pp. 58–59.

Still, until the early 1870s, the French dominated the landscape of 19th century socialist and revolutionary movements. Within the International Workingmen's Association (1864-1876), the French section, particularly the group from Paris—a mix of former Saint-Simonians, Positivists, Fourierists, and Proudhonians—were by far the most influential within the organization throughout the 1860s.[108] At the last truly representative IWA congress, the 1869 Basel congress, the more radical Proudhonian theories began to dominate over other more reformist approaches. Reaching their apex in the IWA, the federalist, anti-authoritarian currents set the stage for the 1871 Paris Commune.[109]

When the Franco-Prussian War broke out in July 1870, Marx wrote the IWA's official statement on the war, condemning Napoleon III while also denouncing Otto von Bismarck (1815-1898) for using it as a premise for conquest. However, in private, both Marx and Engels sided with the German nationalist cause. Engels even established a German patriot committee in Manchester.[110] In a revealing, but prophetic letter written at the outbreak of the war, Marx wrote to Engels:

"The French need a thrashing... German predominance would also transfer the center of gravity of the workers' movement in Western Europe from France to Germany, and one has only to compare the movement in the two countries from 1866 till now to see that the German working class is superior to the French both theoretically and organizationally. Their predominance over the French on the world stage would also mean the predominance of our theory over Proudhon's, etc."[111]

---

[108] S. Hayat: The Construction of Proudhonism within the IWMA. Pp. 313-331 in *"Arise Ye Wretched of the Earth": The First International in a Global Perspective.* Translated by T. Labica. Brill, 2018.

[109] J. Bancal: Proudhon et la commune. Pp. 37-81 in *Autogestion,* 15, 1971.

[110] J. Sperber: Karl Marx the German. Pp. 383-402 in *German History,* 31(3), 2013.

[111] K. Marx to F. Engels. July 20, 1870. Translated by D. Torr. Marxists Internet Archive.

Over the next two years, a rapid power shift occurred: France suffered a humiliating defeat by the Prussians, Emperor Napoleon III capitulated, and the German Empire formally consolidated. Additionally, the brutal suppression of the short-lived Paris Commune of 1871 and the treatment of the Communards as pathological criminals resulted in what some have referred to as "the ultimate exorcism" of French socialism.[112] The recovery of socialism was slow in France and did not start to reemerge for well-over a decade. Relatedly, sociology waned and would not reemerge among the French until the 1890s.[113]

As Marx's writing career started to wind down, Engels' was ramping up. Indeed, it was through Engels' 1878 book *Anti-Dühring*, which appeared in installments in the official journal of the Social Democratic Party (SPD), that Marxist theory first began to find an audience. As the Soviet historian David Riazanov (1870-1938) described, *Anti-Dühring* was "epoch-making in the history of Marxism. It was from this book that the younger generation... learned what was scientific socialism, what were its philosophical premises, what was its method."[114] In this work, Engels notably dismissed coercion as the basis of social exploitation, which the French socialists had all maintained, and instead put exchange in its place.[115]

The first three chapters of *Anti-Dühring* were later used for the enormously popular pamphlet *Socialism: Utopian and Scientific,* translated and published in French in 1880 by Marx's son-in-law Paul Lafargue (1842-1911). This work cemented the legacy of French socialism as "utopian" and Marxism as "scientific." Just a few years after publication, Engels wrote in 1882 that "this little book circulates in ten languages. I am not aware that any other socialist work, not even our

---

[112] Furet: *Revolutionary France, 1770-1880.* Blackwell, 1992, p. 506.
[113] W. P. Vogt: The Confrontation of Socialists and Sociologists in Prewar France, 1890-1914. Pp. 313-320 in J. Falk (ed.): *Proceedings of the Fourth Annual Meeting of the Western Society for French History,* 1977.
[114] D. Riazanov: *Karl Marx and Friedrich Engels.* Translated by J. Kunitz. International Publishers, 1927, p. 210.
[115] C. Jamil: Resurrecting Proudhon's Idea of Justice. Pp. 141-167 in *Journal of Classical Sociology,* 22(2), 2022: 162-163.

Communist Manifesto of 1848 or Marx's *Capital,* has been so often translated. In Germany it has had four editions of about 20,000 copies in all."[116]

In his widely read pamphlet, Engels expounded his conception of "scientific socialism" (a term actually coined by Proudhon decades earlier[117]) for the first time. Echoing the conclusions from *The Manifesto* but now with "science" instead of just German philosophy, Engels stated that only after the capitalist revolutions on feudal society would there then be the historically-determined "*Proletarian Revolution,* solution of the contradictions: the proletariat seizes the public power and by virtue of this power transforms the social means of production, which are slipping from the hands of the bourgeoisie, into public property."[118]

Similarly, in *Socialism: Utopian and Scientific,* Engels presented a sketch of the "utopian" thought of Saint-Simon, Fourier, and Owen, and then proceeded to critically interrogate them. "Their immature theories corresponded to the immature state of capitalist production and the immature class situation... We can leave it to the literary small fry to quibble solemnly over these fantasies..." Engels quipped.[119] Above all, Engels stressed that the historical location of these thinkers didn't allow them to recognize that socialism would be "a necessary outcome" based upon the conflict between the two classes produced by the historical movement. Proudhon is mentioned only once in the text, and Engels inaccurately claims that Proudhon promoted labor notes, something he never actually advocated.[120] Engels goes onto argue that from these thinkers, "nothing could come but a kind of eclectic, average socialism...

---

[116] F. Engels: Introduction to the English Edition. Pp. 11-35 in F. Engels: *Socialism: Utopian and Scientific.* Foreign Language Press, 1975: 13.
[117] Proudhon: *What is Property?* 1876, p. 277.
[118] F. Engels: *Socialism: Utopian and Scientific.* Foreign Language Press, 1975, p. 85.
[119] *Ibid.,* p. 44.
[120] I. McKay: Proudhon's Constituted Value and the Myth of Labour Notes. Pp. 32-67 in *Anarchist Studies, 25*(1), 2017.

a mish-mash permitting of the most manifold shades of opinion..."[121] For Engels, "scientific socialism" could only be "an essentially German product..."[122]

Though France is often credited as the birthplace of the socialist movement, classical French socialist thought largely fell into disregard over the course of the late 19th century. In fact, in the twenty years following the Paris Commune, socialism as a whole waned. Contrary to the rest of the century, the late 19th century was a time of relative peace within Europe and was marked by growing social and political conservatism.[123] Socialism within the German Empire was notable in that it didn't elicit animosity towards the military and government. If anything, the German socialists generally applauded the newly formed empire as it afforded them much better opportunities to spread their propaganda, especially since they operated within the strongest country in Europe. As Bouglé argued just after WWI, German socialism was overtly militaristic, authoritarian, and nationalistic.[124]

Nevertheless, after a failed assassination attempt, Otto von Bismarck, the first Chancellor of the German Empire from 1871–1890, hobbled the emerging socialist movement when he implemented the Anti-Socialist Laws in 1878, which would stay in effect until his resignation. The persecution by the government during the 1880s pushed German socialists from the popular Lassallean theories of working through the state towards the then-relatively unknown Marxist theories that insisted on seizing control of the state. Largely due to the relentless efforts of Friedrich Engels, the SPD officially adopted Marxism in 1891.

This shift to Marxism by the SPD coincided with a period of rapid growth in the party, as well as a greater political leniency towards socialism

---

[121] Engels: *Socialism: Utopian and Scientific.* 1975, pp. 52–53.
[122] F. Engels: Preface to the First German Edition. Pp. 5–7 in *Socialism: Utopian and Scientific.* 1975: 6.
[123] J. H. Billington: *Fire in the Minds of Men: Origins of the Revolutionary Faith.* Basic Books, 1999, pp. 367–368.
[124] C. Bouglé: *Le memento du démocratie Française: dix vérités sur le socialisme Allemand.* Berger-Levrault, 1920.

within the Empire. For example, in 1871, the SPD held only two seats in the Reichstag, which increased to 12 seats in 1877 and then to 35 seats in 1890, with roughly one-fifth of the total votes.[125] By 1903, they received 81 seats and roughly a third of all votes, demonstrating the growing influence and acceptance of socialist thought within the German Empire.[126] Within the newly-formed Second International (1889–1916), the SPD dominated. The SPD served as a model for newly-formed social-democratic parties, including the Russian Social Democratic Labor Party (1898–1917) that would later split into the more well-known Bolshevik and Menshevik factions.[127] Consequently, primarily through the efforts of the SPD, socialism became widely associated with party politics.

Interestingly, in the premier journal on socialism in France, *La revue socialiste* (LRS) (1885–1914), Marx was the most frequently mentioned socialist theorist, with references peaking in 1901. According to Michel Bellet, "The mass of references to Marx in *LRS* is organized around a dominant orientation: the will to restore the sources and the contribution of French socialism to international socialism, to counter the weight of a German socialism strongly influential in the Second International..."[128] Initially, the journal sought a path of reconciliation with German socialism by attempting to synthesize French socialist ideas with Marxism. However, by 1894, the *La revue socialiste* became increasingly critical of Marx, with some contributors going as far to state that Marx and Marxism were "essentially anti-French."

For Eugène Fournière (1857–1917), the editor of LRS from 1898 until 1914, Marx's thought represented a divergence from socialist

---

[125] Billington: *Fire in the Minds of Men.* 1999, pp. 376–377.
[126] C. J. H. Hayes: The History of German Socialism Reconsidered. Pp. 62–101 in *The American Historical Review,* 23(1), 1917.
[127] L. T. Lih: The Impact of the SPD Model on Lenin and Bolshevism. Pp. 431–456 in T. Rockmore & N. Levine (eds.): *The Palgrave Handbook of Leninist Political Philosophy,* 2018.
[128] M. Bellet: The Reception of Marx in France: *La revue socialiste* (1885–1914). Pp. 1154–1199 in *The European Journal of the History of Economic Thought,* 25(5), 2018: 1160.

history, particularly on the questions of individualism and contracts. According to Fournière, "What Marx added to the concepts of Fourier and Proudhon" was simultaneously "a total erasure of the path imperfectly traced by them, and a deviation from the road up to that point followed by French socialism."[129] For several writers in the *La revue socialiste,* Marxism was perceived as the outcome of a German socialist tradition that veiled an imperialist nationalism that was not only alien but overtly hostile to the French socialist tradition.

The Durkheimians and French Socialism

Following their defeat in the Franco-Prussian War, the fall of the Second French Empire, the establishment of the Third Republic, and the ruthless overthrow of the Paris Commune, a bewildered yet inquisitive atmosphere reemerged among the French. As Célestin Bouglé wrote a couple of years before his death:

> "1871! I evoke that date, the date of our defeat, on purpose. For it was a defeat which caused much soul-searching, and gave birth to more than one resolution among intellectuals. One thing is curious: in order to prepare the necessary revival, it was not on the spirit of authority that most of them counted, but on the spirit of truth..."[130]

With the shock produced in 1871, France again found itself facing the same social questions, and as a result, sociology and socialism were eventually recovered among the French. Tellingly, Durkheim's 1893 dissertation, later titled *The Division of Labour in Society,* initially began as a study of the relationship between "individualism and socialism," which he modified to become a study of "individual personality and social solidarity." Although Durkheim strategically distanced himself from the socialist movement to focus on sociology, many of his ideas, particularly

---

[129] E. Fournière: Les systèmes socialistes (de Saint-Simon à Proudhon). Pp. 129–152 in *La revue socialiste,* 218, 1903: 146. Quoted in Bellet: The Reception of Marx in France. 2018, p. 1167.
[130] C. Bouglé: *Humanisme, sociologie, philosophie.* Hermann, 1938, pp. 23–24. Quoted in Sturges: 1978, p. 42.

on solidarity, resonated with the socialists of his day and were even incorporated to some degree within the syndicalist movement.[131]

In a series of lectures between 1895 to 1896, later compiled together as the book *Socialism,* Durkheim discussed the history of socialism, particularly Saint-Simonism, in-depth and its relation to sociology. Durkheim distinguished socialism from communism, with the former being much newer in comparison to the latter, and carefully defined socialism as "those theories which demand a more or less complete connection of all economic functions or of certain of them, though diffused, with the directing and knowing organs of society."[132] Insisting that communism predated socialism and was therefore not part of the socialist tradition, he defined communism as a theory that posits "that private property is the source of selfishness and that selfishness springs immortality" and, consequently, "holds to a common authority of abstract morality."[133] Although Durkheim's lecture series would come to an abrupt halt following the creation of *L'Année sociologique,* his stances on socialism do not appear to have changed. For example, in a letter just before his death in 1917, Durkheim wrote that "[o]ur salvation lies in socialism discarding its out-of-date slogans or in the formation of a new Socialism which goes back to the French tradition."[134]

However, WWI devastated the Durkheimians, and they worked throughout the interwar period to rebuild what was lost. Revealingly, Durkheim's last two publications before his death in 1917 were obituaries: one for his son, André, and the other for his student, Robert Hertz. When *L'Année sociologique* resumed publication in 1925, it opened with obituaries for seventeen people who had died since its last publication in 1912. In addition to the deaths, sociology in France

---

[131] M. Mauss: Introduction to the First Edition. Pp. 32–36 in Durkheim: *Socialism.* 1962.

[132] Durkheim: *Socialism.* 1962, p. 56.

[133] *Ibid.,* p. 73.

[134] É. Durkheim to L. Bourgin: March 30, 1915. Quoted in S. Lukes. *Émile Durkheim, His Life and Work: A Historical and Critical Study.* Allen Lane, 1973, p. 321.

attracted few students during the interwar period. Not only had many of their students died during the war, but young adults were now generally lacking among the French.

Consequently, the formerly tight-nit Durkheimians began to disintegrate into three subgroups. The first and most popular subgroup, led by Mauss and Hubert, specialized in prehistory, religion, and anthropology. The second, composed of Simiand, the Bourgin brothers, and Halbwachs, focused on economics and statistics. The last subgroup, centering around Bouglé, Paul Lapie (1869-1927), and Dominique Parodi (1870-1955), concentrated on "general sociology" and the relationship between philosophy and sociology.[135] As the rest of the Durkheimians increasingly became "micro-focused" in their empirical investigations, Bouglé's subgroup kept the philosophical torch lit by continuing to research and propagate the ideas of the French socialists.

Relatedly, Bouglé played a pivotal role in the revival of the thought and legacy of the French socialists. During the interwar period, Bouglé republished "the Old Testament of socialism," *The Doctrine of Saint-Simon*, with Élie Halévy (1870-1937) in 1924, and a selection of Saint-Simon's texts in 1925. He was a leading member of the group *Les amis de Saint-Simon,* and authored the 1918 work *Among the Socialist Prophets,*[136] the present 1932 book, and several journal articles and book reviews on the French socialists in general.[137] Additionally, Bouglé was the organizer of the first group to edit and republish Proudhon's completed works, the *Société des amis de Proudhon.*[138] He also published a second book on Proudhon's thought in 1930 titled *Proudhon* (the first, *The Sociology of Proudhon*[139] was published just before WWI in 1911), and

---

[135] J. Heilbron: *French Sociology.* Cornell University Press, 2015, pp. 92-100.
[136] *Chez les prophètes socialistes.*
[137] J.-C. Marcel: Célestin Bouglé, un demi-siècle de publications (1894-1940). Pp 77-109 in *Les études sociales,* 1(165), 2017.
[138] A.-S. Chambost: Une longue aventure éditoriale: L'édition des Œuvres (in)*complètes* de Proudhon chez Marcel Rivière. Pp. 59-80 in *Mil neuf cent. Revue d'histoire intellectuelle,* 1(40), 2022.
[139] *La sociologie de Proudhon* (1911), which has been translated and is forthcoming at *little big eye publishing.*

edited the 1920 book *Proudhon and Our Times.*[140] Bouglé was one of the few sociologists to routinely write and speak about the French socialists during the interwar period, and much of what he propagated fell into neglect following his 1940 death. For example, his *Société des amis de Proudhon* collapsed during WWII and their archives were never located.[141]

Bouglé's influence was not confined to his writings or the revival of French socialism. He also founded the first sociology research center in France called the *Centre de documentation sociale* (1920-1940). This center went on to significantly shape French sociology, influencing intellectuals such as Raymond Aron (1905-1983), Georges Friedmann (1902-1977), Jean Stoetzel (1910-1987), and Jean Cazeneuve (1915-2005).[142] As Durkheimism disintegrated during the interwar period, the Durkheimians collectively began to play important roles within newly formed intergovernmental organizations like the League of Nations (1920-1946). In particular, within the two wings of the League—the World Court and the International Labour Organization (ILO)—the Durkheimians essentially had a revolving door relationship in the latter. For example, the first director of the ILO, Albert Thomas (1878-1932), who served until his death, enlisted the help of many of Durkheim's former students. He also collaborated with the *Centre de documentation sociale*, coordinating theory with practice and providing internships for Bouglé's students. Like Bouglé, Thomas emphasized the importance of moral education and the practice of social justice.[143] Under Thomas's leadership, the ILO ratified the eight-hour workday among its member countries, and spearheaded what has been called "the silent revolution"—

---

[140] *Proudhon et notre temps.*
[141] C. Gaillard: 30 ans déjà!. Pp. 9-60 in *Bulletin annuel de la Société P.-J. Proudhon.* Archives Proudhoniennes, 2012.
[142] A. Savoye: Enquête sur les étudiants en sociologie de Célestin Bouglé et leur engagement en politique (1920-1940). Pp. 111-156 in *Les études sociales,* 1(165), 2017.
[143] M. Dhermy-Mairal: « Faire vibrer les cœurs à l'unisson » Célestin Bouglé et Albert Thomas, entre science et action (1920-1932). Pp. 31-49 in *Les études sociales,* 1(165), 2017.

a unification effort within the fragmented cooperative movement, particularly between agricultural cooperatives and consumer cooperatives, aiming to organize the social economy.[144]

French Socialisms (1932)

Published in 1932, Bouglé's *French Socialisms* was written against the backdrop of the Great Depression, a time when totalitarian and fascist leaders had either come to power or were in the process of doing so, setting the stage for World War II. At the time of the writing of this book, Mussolini was in control of Italy, Stalin ruled the Soviet Union, and the Nazis were gaining momentum in Germany. In contrast, France, where the sociologist Georges Gurvitch notes "the antistatist socialism of Saint-Simon, Fourier, and Proudhon were deeply rooted patterns of the French mental attitude..." managed to maintain an anti-authoritarian cultural tradition critical of war.[145] Despite this, the economic downturn reignited antisemitic sentiments in France, and the country was not immune to the rise of fascist and reactionary social movements.[146] And while Bouglé had great hopes for the League of Nations to mitigate "nationalist passions," he also recognized the organization's limitations, stating that it "is more of a mechanical than an organic work.... In short, the League of Nations needs the support of those psychic forces which the sociologist calls *collective conscience.*"[147] For Bouglé, lofty intellectual ambitions for world peace were ultimately powerless without moral individuals whose "hearts beat in unison."[148]

---

[144] M. Dhermy-Mairal: L'unification du mouvement coopératif au Bureau international du travail : la « révolution silencieuse » d'Albert Thomas. Pp. 15-29 in *Le mouvement social,* 2(263), 2018.

[145] G. Gurvitch: Social Structure of Pre-War France. Pp. 535-554 in *The American Journal of Sociology,* 48(5), 1943: 550.

[146] V. Caron: The Antisemitic Revival in France in the 1930s: The Socioeconomic Dimension Reconsidered. Pp. 24-73 in *The Journal of Modern History,* 70(1), 1998.

[147] C. Bouglé: *De la sociologie à l'action sociale. Pacifisme, féminisme et coopération.* PUF, 1923, pp. 8, 50.

[148] Dhermy-Mairal: « Faire vibrer les cœurs à l'unisson ». *Les études sociales,* 1(165), 2017.

These growing social divisions and authoritarian movements cast a shadow over Bouglé's pen in this succinct work. Yet, against this fragmented backdrop, Bouglé skillfully summarizes the key theoretical socialist traditions within France, and examines their impact on the world. *French Socialisms* is more than a study of the French socialists—it is an interrogation of how their eclectic ideas shaped the 19th and 20th centuries. In particular, Bouglé connects Saint-Simonism with large-scale industry and production, Fourierism with cooperatives and consumption, and Proudhonism with syndicalism and exchange. His work underscores that these movements, far from being marginal footnotes in history, have had a profound, almost unconscious impact on humanity. Indeed, the problems the classical French socialists grappled with—war, poverty, social fragmentation, hierarchy, and more—are still the very issues our societies confront today.

Bouglé launches his exploration with a discussion of the philosophers of the French Enlightenment and of the Physiocrats. He then delves into the legacy of the French Revolution, examining how it laid the groundwork for the socialist thinkers of the nineteenth century. The book then turns its focus to a thorough appraisal of the three key socialist traditions from France—Saint-Simonism, Fourierism, and Proudhonism—and their impacts on the world. Bouglé concludes with an overview of the consequences and perspectives of his analysis of French socialism.

As an additional resource, two articles written by Bouglé, one published in 1918, titled "Two Resurrections: Saint-Simonism and Proudhonism," and one published in 1938 titled "Variations of Marxisms," are included as appendices to the present volume. The first article discusses the revival of French socialism in the aftermath of World War I. The second article compares the Marxist movement of the 1930s with its more dogmatic antecedents. The book ends with an Afterword, where I return to delineate the developments on the world stage since the original publication of this book, and engage in a discussion of what French socialism implies for today. In an era marked by anti-establishment populism across the globe, the ideas of the French socialists arguably hold more relevance now than ever before.[149]

In terms of the presentation of the text itself, with the exception of one footnote that states "Note from Bouglé," all the footnotes are from the editor. I attempted to contextualize all the people and references for the unfamiliar reader, although there were a few exceptions that I was unable to locate. Unless mentioned, the nationalities of all the people in the footnotes are French. Additionally, all French titles in the text have been translated into English with a footnote of the original French title, along with the year of publication. All translated text, including the appendix articles, were translated by Shaun Murdock.

---

[149] E. Castleton: Untimely Meditations on the Revolution of 1848 in France. Pp. 244-269 in *Opera Historica,* 19(2), 2018.

Preface

History often serves as an escape from the present. This is particularly the case with the history of ideas. The intellectual constructs of the great thinkers provide a comfortable shelter for the mind, a *refugium ac solatium.*[150] We take solace in them, shedding the concerns of tomorrow at the threshold.

However, this tactic is not always easy to implement. When we are confronted with systems aimed at the reorganization of society—those under the purview of the social economy—and only a century or less separates us from when they were conceived, it becomes nearly impossible to silence the resonance, to detach ourselves from the ongoing issues they sought to address, and to disregard the concerns that remain relevant today. Particularly if we have engaged in social action in some capacity, we inevitably engage in a continuous comparison between these systems and life, striving to identify both what they have offered thus far and what they could offer in the future.

This sets forth the purpose and approach of this modest volume. Having been charged with teaching the history of social economy at the Sorbonne for nearly twenty-five years, my attention has been captivated by the doctrines that propose institutional transformation as a solution to social problems. It is well-known how numerous these efforts were in France during the first half of the 19th century. Our harvest of programmatic ideas from that era is unparalleled. Germany rightfully boasts of philosophers such as Fichte, Schelling, and Hegel, who followed Kant.[151] But France, too, has a trio of visionaries to honor: Saint-Simon and Fourier from 1800 to 1830, and a bit later, Proudhon, each of whom

---

[150] Latin for "refuge and solace," this phrase is derived from the Roman statesman Cicero's (106–43 BCE) oration *Pro Archia Poeta,* where the author defends a poet charged with illegally acquiring Roman citizenship.

[151] Johann Gottlieb Fichte (1762–1814), Friedrich Wilhelm Joseph Shelling (1775–1854), Georg Wilhelm Friedrich Hegel (1770–1831), and Immanuel Kant (1724–1804) were all German philosophers associated with the influential German idealist tradition.

constructed vast systems. These systems, arguably even more so than those of the Germans, were driven by a will to act and aimed more pointedly at a complete restructuring of social organization. But our "reformers"—a term Louis Reybaud[152] used derisively—also put forth principles, articulated laws of evolution, and beckoned the intellect on a kind of global intellectual journey. I have on several occasions, both at the Sorbonne and at the Centre de documentation sociale at the École Normale Supérieure,[153] endeavored to revive these thinkers, shining a light on the fecundity of their works for the new generation. Having also had the chance to closely observe the movements of parties and leagues, cooperatives and trade unions, I was able to directly discern numerous traces of the influence of these systems in the agendas of today's activists, or at the very least, tendencies in harmony with their spirit, whether acknowledged or not. Thus, in attempting to anticipate the shape of tomorrow, I found myself continuously shuttling between the realities of the present and the theories of the past.

And when universities abroad—in Belgium and Romania, Portugal and Argentina, Turkey and Germany—honored me by asking for my insights into the distinctive economic and social trends of contemporary France, I often drew upon the historical framework of the social economy: for instance, tracing a line from the Saint-Simonians to large-scale industry, from Fourierism to the cooperative movement, and from Proudhonism to syndicalism.[154]

---

[152] Marie Roch Louis Reybaud (1799-1879) was a journalist and economist, known for his critical examination of socialist theories in his influential 1840 work *Études sur les réformateurs ou socialistes modernes* ("Studies on Reformers or Modern Socialists"). Reybaud notably argued that the socialists were all religious reformers with an interest in a universal science.

[153] Bouglé founded and directed the Centre de documentation sociale (1920-1940), an institution for social research within the École Normale Supérieure (ENS). The ENS (1794-) is a *grande école* in Paris, in which Bouglé served as deputy director starting in 1927 and then director in 1935 until his death.

[154] Syndicalism is an anti-statist social movement that understands labor unions and their federations to be cells of a future socialist order and insists that labor unions must be completely independent from political parties. Syndicalism had great success in France between 1899 to 1937, particularly through the

I am not suggesting that all our captains of industry[155] are familiar with Saint-Simon, all our cooperative managers with Fourier, or all our union secretaries with Proudhon. Indeed, very few have likely read the works of these intellectual forebears. But isn't it often the case that a system, through various intermediaries, influences even those who are unaware of it? Activists who haven't read a single line from Hegel or Darwin[156] may still be imbued with Hegelian or Darwinian thought. There are ideas that are "in the air"; we inhale them without realizing it. Moreover, without drawing inspiration from a theory, whether indirectly or unconsciously, it happens that we fulfill predictions it had sanctioned or implement programs it had recommended. We then encounter it without acknowledgment. We don't apply it, yet we validate it. We prove its value through actions, aligned with its principles, that were not directly spawned by those principles. Call them coincidences, or perhaps spontaneous convergences, which are no less revealing to the historian than the so-called direct or indirect influences.

These observations are particularly applicable to what we refer to as the French socialist trinity: Saint-Simon, Fourier, and Proudhon. Needless to say, around them, and especially the first two, orbit many secondary figures whose influence also warrants acknowledgment. Buchez,[157] for instance, champions the cause of workers' associations and demonstrates what Catholic thinking can contribute to the social

---

Confédération Générale du Travail (French Confederation of Labor), which was founded in 1895 and still exists today.

[155] "Captain of industry," a term used to describe influential and innovative business leaders and entrepreneurs, was coined by the Scottish philosopher and historian Thomas Carlyle (1795–1881). Carlyle was notably associated with the Saint-Simonians.

[156] Charles Darwin (1809–1882) was a highly influential English biologist and naturalist known for propagating the theory of evolution, which argues that all species descend from a common ancestor, particularly through his 1859 book *On the Origin of Species by Means of Natural Selection.*

[157] Philippe Buchez (1796–1865) was a politician, historian, and former Saint-Simonian social theorist known for being a proponent of workers' associations and founder of Christian socialism.

problem. Louis Blanc[158] asserts the necessity of state intervention above workers' associations, envisioning the state as an organizer of labor in service to the people; he integrates socialist principles with a commitment to democracy. As we proceed, we will not overlook elements in today's institutions or agendas that echo these thinkers. However, we contend that by placing ourselves at the center of Saint-Simonian, Fourierist, and Proudhonian systems, we are well-positioned to trace the major paths French social thought has taken: they offer us the most informative vantage points. This alone suffices to explain the particular focus we place on these three schools of thought.

Nevertheless, to fully grasp their impact on the 19th century and their potential influence on the 20th century, it is essential to consider the trends they encountered along their path—those they opposed, those they advanced, and those they reconciled with. This rationale underpins the structure of this study: before assessing Saint-Simonism, Fourierism, and Proudhonism, I believe it necessary to briefly revisit the legacy of the 18th century and that of the French Revolution.

---

[158] Louis Blanc (1811–1882) was an influential socialist and politician who advocated for the creation of worker cooperatives as well as for guaranteeing work through government-funded jobs. His 1839 book *The Organization of Labour* was one of the most widely read socialist works in the mid-19th century. In 1848, accused of revolutionary activity, he went into exile in England for over 20 years and his popularity never recovered.

Chapter I

The Legacy of the 18ᵗʰ Century: Philosophers

What do we still owe to 18ᵗʰ-century philosophy today? Pinpointing this precisely is likely to be challenging for several reasons, not least because we are far from achieving consensus on the 18ᵗʰ century's contributions to French thought. Scholars disagree among themselves, no less than the philosophers in question might have disagreed. The century of Voltaire,[159] Montesquieu, Diderot,[160] and Rousseau has inspired diverse assessments and served as the birthplace of a wide array of intellectual trends.

It has often been said that the 19ᵗʰ century, the century of history, spent its time reacting against the 18ᵗʰ century, the century of *a priori* rationalism. There is undoubtedly some truth to this view. For example, Bonald,[161] who took *The Social Contract* with him in his luggage when he went into exile, regarded the French Revolution as the final volume of the *Encyclopédie*. He leveled one of the most severe indictments against "philosophism."[162] By contrasting the collective *we* with the individual *I*, the laws of nature—seen as manifestations of God's will—with contracts established by human will, and the spontaneous institution of the family

---

[159] François-Marie Arouet (1694–1778), known by his pen name Voltaire, was an Enlightenment writer, historian, and philosopher known for his wit, his criticism of Christianity (especially the Catholic Church), and his advocacy for freedom of speech, the separation of church and state, and civil liberties.

[160] Denis Diderot (1713-1784) was a philosopher, art critic, and writer. He was a prominent figure during the Enlightenment and is remembered for serving as co-founder, chief editor, and contributor to the *Encyclopédie* (1751-1772), which sought to encapsulate all useful knowledge.

[161] Louis de Bonald (1754-1840) was a counter-revolutionary philosopher and politician. A critic of the French Revolution, he is known for his traditionalist views and his influence on sociological theory, emphasizing the importance of religion and traditional social structures.

[162] *Philosophism* is a term used to describe a secular and critical approach to philosophy that seeks to apply reason and scientific thought to all areas of human activity and tends to be at odds with traditional religious beliefs.

with paper constitutions, he reminded us that the individual is shaped by and for society. A sociology grounded in theology is outlined here, parts of which many thinkers of the 19th century would retain, even as they turned their backs on theology and refused a return to the ancien régime.[163] Auguste Comte was no less harsh than Bonald on the "metaphysics" of human rights, and Taine[164] followed suit when he declared war on the intoxication of abstract ideas, which he believed to be the source of so many crimes. "The quintessential French error," declared Paul Bourget,[165] who endeavored to demonstrate that the mode of thinking of the precursors and enablers of the Revolution was diametrically opposed to the requirements of experimental science conducted in the manner of Claude Bernard.[166] Some thirty years ago, literary criticism seemed to unanimously share these aversions. I myself heard Ferdinand Brunetière[167] conclude a year-long course on Voltaire at the École Normale Supérieure by stating he didn't wish for his country to have many men of such stature. Around the same time, Jules Lemaître[168] took pleasure in airing Rousseau's dirty laundry, bombarded him with

---

[163] The *ancien régime* refers to the monarchic, aristocratic, social, and political system established in France from approximately the 15th century until the 18th century, under the late Valois and Bourbon dynasties. The term is typically used to emphasize the contrasts between the institutions of the old order and those of the more democratic post-revolutionary era.

[164] Hippolyte Taine (1828–1893) was a critic and historian who was skeptical of the abstract principles of the Enlightenment and the French Revolution. Taine advocated for a more empirical approach to understanding human behavior.

[165] Paul Bourget (1852–1935) was a novelist and critic, known for his conservative views and his critiques of the moral implications of modern society and the legacies of the Enlightenment.

[166] Claude Bernard (1813–1878) was a physiologist considered one of the founders of experimental medicine. His work established the principles of the scientific method in the field of biology.

[167] Ferdinand Brunetière (1849–1906) was a critic and professor who was known for his conservative, anti-revolutionary views and his opposition to the literary and philosophical legacy of Voltaire.

[168] Jules Lemaître (1853–1914) was a literary critic, dramatist, and nationalist known for his critical commentary on other authors.

sarcasm, and accused him of inconsistency. Less sarcastic, Émile Faguet[169] was hardly more sympathetic at heart, even towards Montesquieu.

Since then, the 18th century has undergone more meticulous scholarly examination. Microscopic critique has prevailed over telescopic critique. There has been a claim to greater objectivity, or at least an attempt to be more precise. It became apparent that the classic verdicts were somewhat simplistic and certainly inadequate for appreciating the complexity of the subject at hand. Gustave Lanson,[170] one of the first to call out these "excessive simplifications" and "hasty generalizations," took pains to illustrate the role of experience in shaping the rational moral philosophy to which the philosophers of that era aspired. Didn't many of these philosophers simply systematize the practices of the respectable people of their time and provide theoretical underpinnings for aspirations like widespread well-being, mutual goodwill, and tolerance, which aligned with the new currents of thought? Far from these principles being *a priori* constructs of reason lost in abstraction, they are often seen as emerging from situations that capture the public's reflective attention. Moreover, why assume that the concern for observation and inquiry was unfamiliar to the contemporaries of Voltaire or Rousseau? Daniel Mornet,[171] continuing Lanson's efforts, invites us to explore the "cabinets" of naturalists, which were fashionable at the time. In these spaces, collections were classified, microscopes were handled, and fights were

---

[169] Émile Faguet (1847–1916) was a literary critic and historian, noted for his conservative views and his critiques of Enlightenment thinkers like Montesquieu and Rousseau.

[170] Gustave Lanson (1857–1934) was a pivotal figure in literary criticism and historiography, noted for his rigorous methods of historical research and his emphasis on the social context of literature. His influential approach, referred to as Lansonism, sought to combine biographical studies of authors with the analysis of their works within the cultural and intellectual milieu of their times.

[171] Daniel Mornet (1878–1954) was literary scholar who furthered Lanson's scholarly methods. Mornet is particularly known for his research into the intellectual origins of the French Revolution. His work often focused on the analysis of previously neglected sources such as letters, diaries, and other personal documents to gain insight into the social and intellectual currents of the 18th century.

waged, with an arsenal of facts, against both the spirit of systematization and the traditions of theology. This process led to the accumulation of thousands of empirical insights that would facilitate the remarkable surge in scientific advancement witnessed in the late 18th century, on the eve of and during the French Revolution. One need only consult the authoritative depiction by Louis Liard[172] in his *Higher Education in France*[173] to recognize the extent to which free inquiry at the time exceeded the bounds of official pedagogy. It was not just in mathematics or astronomy but also in chemistry, physics, and biology that there was an extraordinary renewal. And when Henri de Saint-Simon, a nobleman with lofty intellectual aspirations, set out to synthesize the sciences he deemed essential, he may have claimed the honor of placing the dome atop the structure, but he was well aware that the pillars had been erected, stone by stone, by the fact-oriented minds that were so plentiful and active in the 18th century.

*

* *

Wouldn't it be astonishing if this curiosity halted at the threshold of the social world, where the philosophers, preoccupied with criticism, reform, and the declaration of rights, might be accused of systematically discounting facts? Is it plausible that they would deliberately choose to blindfold themselves? In truth, there is no reformer who is not, to some extent, an observer. And the thinkers and activists of the 18th century were more keenly observant of historical realities than any others. The "pack" of Encyclopedists, fervently attacking prejudices and privileges, likewise

---

[172] Louis Liard (1846–1917) was a philosopher and university administrator who played a key role in the reform of French higher education.
[173] *L'enseignement supérieur en France* (1888, 1894). This two-volume work is a comprehensive account of the development of French educational institutions that highlights the tension between traditional education and the new wave of scientific inquiry that characterized the lead up to the French Revolution.

engaged in the intellectual hunt so highly valued by Bacon.[174] Hubert,[175] in his recent work, has comprehensively assessed the contributions of the *Encyclopédie* to the social sciences. He demonstrated that many of its contributors continued, in their own ways, the efforts of the scholars whose findings they utilized: whether in ethnography or linguistics, on primitive societies or European society during the Middle Ages, on political institutions or religious beliefs, figures like Diderot, de Jaucourt,[176] and Boucher d'Argis[177] compiled and aimed to systematize empirical knowledge, paving the way for a philosophy of history that was meant to be something other than mere *a priori* normative speculation. From this perspective, it might be argued that robust researchers like Condorcet,[178] and following him, Saint-Simon and Auguste Comte, merely inherited and augmented this legacy.

Moreover, in order to gauge the narrowness of the critique so often directed at the spirit of the 18th century—accused of always being ready to reason about rights but incapable of bowing to facts—one name should suffice: Montesquieu. If we accept that the reformist philosophers who followed him allowed themselves to be intoxicated by commanding abstractions, didn't the author of *The Spirit of the Laws* offer in advance a kind of antidote? He sent dreamers back to the school of experience. He declared his intention to speak "based on history." He collected

---

[174] Francis Bacon (1561-1626) was an English philosopher whose advocacy for the empirical method laid the groundwork for modern scientific inquiry. His metaphor of "the hunt" represented the pursuit of knowledge in which nature's secrets were hidden beyond common sense and had to be sought out.

[175] René Hubert (1885-1954) was a historian of philosophy and pedagogy. He wrote several works on the Encyclopedists that demonstrated their contributions to early social science.

[176] Louis de Jaucourt (1704-1779) was a scholar and aristocrat. He wrote around a quarter of all articles in the *Encyclopédie,* and was its most prolific contributor.

[177] Antoine-Gaspard Boucher d'Argis (1708-1791) was a lawyer and major contributor to the *Encyclopédie.* He also wrote a number of legal treatises.

[178] Nicolas de Condorcet (1743-1794) was a philosopher who advocated for educational reform and the rights of women and African slaves. He is sometimes considered to have embodied the ideals of the Enlightenment. He died in prison during the Reign of Terror.

examples from all civilizations, focused on determining the factual conditions that make legal codes workable, and on reminding us that what is suitable for one society may not be suitable for another. A legislator who wants to create enduring work must take into account not only the variety of climates that he cannot defy, nor the nature of governments he should not "offend," but also the state of commerce, the character of religions, and what Montesquieu calls "the general spirit," the precursor to the *Volksgeist*[179] and collective consciousness.[180] For "laws have innumerable relations to innumerable things." Montesquieu thus opened up all sorts of paths for inquiry, but he warned us that in no field can we do without investigation. And while we wait to be able to gather and coordinate the results, he provides us with guidance grounded in cautious conservatism. Coming across the concept of prejudice, against which so many strong minds of the 18th century waged war, he solemnly proclaimed that the worst prejudice for a people is not to know itself, meaning: to be ignorant of the local and historical conditions to which it is in part captive. Are we not here squarely in the realm of relativism, diametrically opposed to that impatient, universalist rationalism, keen to legislate for all times and all countries, so often decried as the malevolent spirit that would lead France to the Revolution?

It goes without saying that Montesquieu was not completely immune to the prevailing currents of his century. The magistrate who wrote the *Persian Letters*[181] was not merely a deft satirist; he was also a philanthropic heart who was outraged by injustice and intolerance. Moreover, he recognized that above the laws regulating social norms or mutual dependencies—those social facts uncovered through observation among various societal phenomena—there exist eternal moral laws, expressions of divine will. And when he encountered slavery, he declared

---

[179] *Volksgeist* is a German term that refers to the "spirit" (*geist*) of a people (*Volk*).

[180] *Collective consciousness* (sometimes translated as *collective conscience*) appears to derive from the work of Proudhon and was popularized by Émile Durkheim. The term denotes a set of shared values and attitudes.

[181] *Lettres persanes* (1721). This satirical work by Montesquieu presents a critique of French society through the fictional letters of Persian travelers.

it against nature, though in some countries it was founded on what was considered a 'natural' rationale. Here, two currents meet head-on: as Lanson has wisely noted, idealism and realism, reformist rationalism, and conservative determinism are interwoven, each tempering the other, in Montesquieu's thought. But his greatest originality, in his time, was to remind us that political and social realities themselves are subject to natural laws, decipherable through patient observation. In this light, it is not surprising that Auguste Comte hailed him as one of his most immediate forerunners, nor that Durkheim dedicated a thesis to the classification of social types according to Montesquieu.

Ultimately, this trend truly found its full development with Auguste Comte and his followers. In Montesquieu's time, from the publication of *The Spirit of the Laws* to the *Declaration of the Rights of Man*, the balance ultimately didn't tip in favor of his cherished realism. Despite my necessary caveats against this dichotomy, which has been used and abused, it remains true that the majority of 18th-century philosophers—militant thinkers, almost swashbuckling intellectuals, always battling oppressive traditions—drew chiefly on the emancipatory power of rationalism. As active disciples of Descartes, who in matters of physics and psychology mostly favored Newton and Locke[182] over Descartes, promoting sensualism over innatism,[183] they appropriated methodical doubt for widespread use, and upheld a belief in the power of clear and distinct ideas, along with the idea that since common sense is the most widely shared thing in the world, society itself can and must be remade by reason. And thus, they wielded reason like an axe, hacking away at the sacred groves that Descartes—the "masked philosopher," as

---

[182] John Locke (1632-1704) was an influential English philosopher and physician who is widely regarded as "the father of liberalism." Locke was an important developer of empiricism, which considers empirical observations to be the chief source of knowledge.

[183] Sensualism is a philosophy that emphasizes the role of the senses in acquiring knowledge, asserting that all knowledge is based on sensory experience. Conversely, innatism is the philosophical doctrine that posits certain ideas or principles are inherent in the human mind, not acquired through experience.

Maxime Leroy[184] likes to say—had prudently chosen not to enter. D'Alembert,[185] in the *Preliminary Discourse to the Encyclopedia of Diderot*, likened him to a conspirator who remains in the shadows and does not witness the outcome of the plot he has nonetheless devised. Faithful to what they believed was his underlying inspiration, they generalized his skepticism and spread the "restless and troubled dispositions" he personally found repugnant, and no reverence for tradition held them back: religious beliefs, political customs, social conventions, all were subjected to the scales of criticism. Nature, Reason, Humanity—these were the only deities before which they bowed. And when the men of the Revolution echoed Rabaut Saint-Étienne's[186] words, "Our history is not our code," it was the same philosophical stance that motivated them, a philosophism at odds with historicism. The natural right they held in highest regard was the individual's capacity to judge society and the authority to rebuild it from the ground up, if necessary, in accordance with the demands of reason.

In this regard, *The Social Contract* was deemed more influential by the architects of the Revolution than *The Spirit of the Laws*. Historical relativism was overshadowed by the legal rationalism championed by

---

[184] Maxime Leroy (1875-1957) was a historian, sociologist, and political theorist known for his work on the history of ideas, particularly in relation to the development of socialism and social economy. His writings often explored the impact of philosophical thought on social movements and political institutions. Leroy is remembered for his detailed studies of key figures in the Enlightenment and the French Revolution.

[185] Jean le Rond d'Alembert (1717-1783) was a prominent mathematician, physicist, philosopher, and music theorist. As one of the leading intellectuals of the Enlightenment, d'Alembert was a co-editor and a major contributor to the *Encyclopédie*. His contributions to the *Encyclopédie* include a preliminary discourse, published in 1751, that outlines the project's goals and is considered to be a key text of the Enlightenment.

[186] Jean-Paul Rabaut Saint-Étienne (1743-1793) was a Protestant pastor and political figure during the French Revolution. He was a member of the National Assembly and an advocate for religious freedom and constitutional government. Rabaut Saint-Étienne's quote, "Our history is not our code," reflects the revolutionary desire to break from the past and establish a new legal and social order based on Enlightenment principles rather than on historical precedent. He was guillotined during the Reign of Terror.

Jean-Jacques Rousseau—the Rousseau of *The Social Contract*—who stands out as its most genuine proponent. A society formed by and for individuals, where conventions give rise to laws, and the citizens' consent to governance is contingent upon the stipulations of a general will that is legitimate only when it strives for equality—these principles are succinctly encapsulated by the concepts of popular sovereignty and equality of citizens, as Lakanal[187] highlighted in his report to the Convention regarding the transfer of Rousseau's remains to the Panthéon.[188] These indeed are the theses that seem to distill, as if into a series of intellectual detonations, the daring ideas of the 18th century. In them, Bonald correctly perceived the repudiation of all forms of traditionalism.

*

* *

Should we then say that the rallying cry that emerges from this is individualism at any cost, without reserve or measure, and that the philosophy of the 18th century thus unleashed upon France, at the risk of making any organization impossible, a proud, defiant spirit of freedom, always ready to make demands but never concessions? This perspective would blame the same philosophy for the severe discontents that Western civilization endured when nascent industrialism allied with liberalism, and the prevailing wisdom was to solve all problems, social and economic alike, by adhering to the principle of "laissez faire, laissez passer."[189] If this absolute form of economic liberalism is indeed the direct result of the demands made by Diderot's associates or Rousseau's followers, it becomes clear that there is no common ground between this philosophy and socialist doctrine, rendering communication between

---

[187] Joseph Lakanal (1762-1845) was a rhetorician and politician who helped reform France's educational system during the French Revolution.
[188] The Panthéon (1790-) is a monument in Paris that was originally intended to be a church but was repurposed during the French Revolution. It now serves as a secular mausoleum and is considered to be a symbol of French identity. It houses the remains of several notable philosophers and revolutionaries.
[189] "Let do, let pass," a motto advocating for minimal government intervention in the economy. Usually shortened in English to "laissez faire."

them impossible. Consequently, one could use the philosophy of the 18th century to argue against socialism, or conversely, use socialism to argue against the philosophy of the 18th century.

Efforts have long been made to clarify this misconception. In *The Idea of the State*,[190] professor Henry Michel[191] argued that in the 18th century, individualism didn't possess the absolute, clear-cut, and negative characteristics it was sometimes ascribed in the 19th century. Back then, it was capable of bending to the demands of human solidarity.

Didn't Montesquieu himself want public granaries to ensure the subsistence of all? Didn't Condorcet, who considered public services a sacred obligation of society, propose the creation of accumulation funds to support a system of mutual credit and social insurance? Furthermore, is it surprising that these philosophers, who place individual rights above all, would call for welfare or social security measures, or even accept restrictions on property rights for the common good? Provided that these rights are secured for all, isn't it logical for them to endorse or call for changes to institutions that are found to be harmful to the majority upon application? From this angle, it seems that the supposed dichotomy between individualism and socialism may itself be based on a misunderstanding—a topic to which we will return.

Moreover, who doesn't know that genuinely socialist constructs were not lacking in the 18th century? They were, in fact, quite prevalent. André Lichtenberger[192] recently showcased a variety of theoretical systems in which property was either proposed to be abolished or at least

---

[190] *L'idée de l'état* (1896).
[191] Henry Michel (1859-1904) was a philosopher and disciple of Charles Renouvier. He was notably Bouglé's teacher at the Lycée Henri IV.
[192] André Lichtenberger (1870–1940) was a sociologist and novelist of the late 19th and early 20th centuries, known for his studies on the social and psychological aspects of economic life.

60

regulated to preserve equality. Morelly[193] and Mably[194] meticulously crafted plans for communist cities, drawing inspiration from both religious communes and ancient republics. They cast aside private property as the root of all evil. Other reformers, not as extreme, at least proposed establishing income tax, limiting or abolishing inheritance, capping wealth, expanding sumptuary laws,[195] creating public workshops, and supporting workers' associations. What does this signify if not that, from the 18th century onwards, the concept of a socialist regime was already captivating many minds appalled by the vices of the wealthy and the poverty of the poor? These plans, however, as Lichtenberger points out, retained the nature of literary utopias—dream cities floating in the air like those in Aristophanes' *The Clouds*.[196] They lacked a foundation in historical reality. There wasn't yet a class of proletarian workers to champion socialism. At that time, it was largely the speculative fancy of isolated intellectuals.

However, it should be noted that such constructs presuppose a series of critical reflections on the existing economic order, which may later be integrated into a coherent system. And it's not the utopian dreamers, whether communists or socialists, who lend these ideas credence. The many sow while the few reap, profit is all too often inversely related to labor, wages are kept low due to competition among workers themselves, those who control of the means of subsistence wield insurmountable power over those who don't, and the people always constitute the most destitute yet essential segment of the nation—observations like these, pregnant with implications, are not only echoed

---

[193] Étienne-Gabriel Morelly (1717-1778) was a philosopher who proposed communist systems in his work, most notably in his 1755 *Code de la Nature*.

[194] Gabriel Bonnot de Mably (1709-1785) was a philosopher who criticized private property and advocated for communal living.

[195] Sumptuary laws are regulations designed to restrict excessive spending on personal goods, often enacted to maintain hierarchies or moral standards.

[196] Aristophanes (446-386 BCE) was a comic playwright in Ancient Greece, sometimes considered "the father of comedy," whose play *The Clouds* famously satirized the intellectual fashions of classical Athens.

in the works of Morelly, Linguet,[197] and Rousseau; similar sentiments are found in the *Encyclopedia*, and in the writings of Holbach[198] and Turgot.[199] Reflecting on this tradition led Léon Cahen[200] to assert, regarding the concept of class struggle in the 18th century, "that a foundational thesis of contemporary socialism is not a result of the development of large-scale industry and the emergence of a working-class proletariat, but rather the logical and rational outcome of 18th-century French philosophy."

In this area too, Rousseau garnered a vast following. He performed his typical role of synthesizing and igniting passion. He may not have delved deepest into the analysis of economic mechanisms, nor defined concepts like profit, wages, and competition with utmost precision. But everything he touched, he imbued with fervor—a fervor arising not just from his own fiery nature but also from the experiences he endured. According to Louis Blanc, with Rousseau, a new class of citizens emerged, demanding its rightful place in the world. As early as his *Discourses*, the indignation of a Protestant appalled by the vices of the civilized mixes with the bitter lament of a plebeian outraged by inequality. Does this make him, as Louis Blanc insisted, a complete precursor of modern socialism? If by modern socialism we mean a theory that includes the condemnation of private property and the glorification of the

---

[197] Simon-Nicholas Linguet (1736-1794) was a writer, journalist, and advocate who gained notoriety for his radical political views and criticism of the ancien régime. He was also a critic of Enlightenment philosophers like Voltaire and advocated for a form of welfare state. Linguet was guillotined during the Reign of Terror.

[198] Baron d'Holbach (1723-1789) was a prominent Franco-German philosopher and Encyclopedist. Holbach is best known for his materialist and atheistic philosophy, which argued that everything in the universe could be explained by the laws of nature and that religious explanations were deceptive and misleading.

[199] Anne Robert Jacques Turgot (1727-1781) was an economist, philosopher, and statesman who served as a Controller-General of Finances under Louis XVI. He is remembered for his economic reforms, advocacy for free trade, and attempts to rationalize the French economy.

[200] Léon Cahen (1874-1944) was a historian known for his comprehensive studies on the history of socialism and his detailed examination of political movements in Europe. His work traced the lineage of socialist ideas back to the Enlightenment, demonstrating the long-standing nature of the critique of social inequalities.

working-class proletarian, it's clear that Rousseau didn't formally develop either stance. Might one not find as many texts where he justifies property as those where he denounces it? As for the factory workers in cities he loathed, Rousseau didn't foresee their rise. He didn't contemplate this new class that would emerge with the advent of large-scale industry. The peasant in his thatched cottage, the craftsman in his workshop—these were the usual companions of his dreams. At the very least, he presents an unwavering contrast, not just between individuals and the state, but between the common people and the elite. "It is the people who constitute the human race." The people are noble in two respects: they are closer to nature through their customs, and they are the most beneficial to the nation's life through their labor. For far too long, the power of the law has been wielded against them by owners primarily focused on protecting their property, by the privileged who cling tightly to their advantages, and by the idle who are scarcely distinguishable from thieves. Let the upheaval, the moment of vengeance, come: it would only be justice. The calls for a new law that will restore and preserve equality are distinctly heard in the *Discourses, The Social Contract,* and *Émile.*[201] Therefore, it is no wonder that the revolutionaries wished to honor their author, not just for having "revived the useful arts,"[202] but for teaching them to rediscover, "beneath the veneer of false social conventions," the notion of the inherent equality of all humans.

---

[201] These are all works written by Rousseau.

[202] The term *useful arts* historically referred to crafts, trades, and practices that resulted in the production of goods and services that served practical needs of society. In contrast to the "fine arts," which encompass creative endeavors like painting, sculpture, and music for aesthetic and cultural expression, the "useful arts" were oriented towards functionality and utility. During the Enlightenment and subsequently during the French Revolution, there was an emphasis on valuing the useful arts that reflected a shift in social values, especially concerning the dignity of labor. In Rousseau's writings, the celebration of the useful arts is tied to his advocacy for a society structured around natural rights and equality, challenging the prevailing social hierarchies that favored the leisure class and the ornamental over the productive and the practical.

*
* *

To what extent do these dominant ideologies— rationalism, individualism, socialism—which have alternately merged and diverged since the 18th century, continue to exert influence on the political and social life of France today? They were fiercely opposed immediately following the Revolution, as we have noted. And in the counterarguments presented, science seemed to succeed theology. It was believed that the positivist approach, when applied to the study of human societies, could provide an unexpected rebuttal for the supporters of the monarchy and the church, who faced the severe criticism of the "metaphysicians" of natural rights. It would prove that democracy, born of philosophy, is "antiphysical"; aren't its desires at odds with the laws of nature, which demand, among other things, respect for differentiation and heredity for the advancement of humanity as well as animal species? Thus, the way would be made clear: the ideas of the 18th century should be finally seen as outdated and inadmissible in the governance of a major nation.

To make such a claim is to jump to conclusions. In fact, the argument that pits science against democracy is—as I have often attempted to demonstrate—highly debatable. Neither the laws of differentiation nor those of heredity apply straightforwardly to the human domain: there are unexpected possibilities and necessities that are unknown in the animal kingdom that come into consideration. Furthermore, even if the soundness of the principles held dear in the 18th century could not be scientifically proven, these principles would still maintain a practical role: at the very least as value judgments, expressing the desires of the masses and acting as focal points for their collective efforts.

There's an assertion that contemporary sociology would logically dismiss these tendencies if it were truly following in the footsteps of thinkers such as Bonald and Comte. But who says it is beholden to their influence? One can benefit from their insights without pledging allegiance to their systems, whether sociocratic[203] or theocratic in nature. Today's sociologists, inherently less ambitious and more dedicated to observing specific social phenomena, consider as premature any broad syntheses that label the aspirations of democracy as contrary to the natural laws of social organization. If provisional trends can be discerned from methodically limited sociological studies, they appear to be quite compatible with liberal and egalitarian ideas. Upon recently reviewing the work of the *L'Année sociologique*, I noted that several contributors appeared to validate, through 19th-century methodologies, many of the practical conclusions of the 18th century. Doesn't Durkheim himself, in his own way, support the claims of modern individualism? His thesis on *The Division of Labour* argues for a new kind of solidarity that enables individuals to differ, to seek their paths, to take their chances, to think independently: the reverence for the human person, according to his perspective, should be at the forefront of the collective consciousness. Indeed, anticipating a reform of the current organization to ensure human rights for all, he envisions a balance between the bloated state and isolated individuals by re-establishing intermediate centers that would create not only moral discipline but also a new economic order. This opens the door to syndicalism, and through syndicalism, to socialism. Yet, it is in pursuit of fulfilling the equal rights of individuals that the leader of my sociological school advocates for these protections. In this regard, he remains loyal to the *Declarations of Rights*, which partly represent the intellectual culmination of the 18th century: he would no doubt have deemed these principles still applicable for the current transformations of law.

Indeed, today there is no lack of thinkers eager to establish contrasts within this very field. By shedding light on what he terms the "revolt of facts against rights," Morin,[204] for instance, takes pleasure in

---

[203] Coined by Auguste Comte, "sociocracy" was a proposed system of administration led by sociologists.

[204] Gaston Morin (1877–1959) was a legal theorist and philosopher who studied civil law. He gained notoriety for his 1920 work *La révolte des faits contre le*

highlighting the deficiencies of the Civil Code,[205] which reflects the individualistic ethos of the 18th century. He points out that the Civil Code fails to offer solutions to the challenges posed by the contemporary organization of labor; the collective bargaining it mandates is fundamentally different from contracts between individuals. Furthermore, Duguit,[206] following in the footsteps of Comte, has long since deemed legal notions that endow all rights to the individual and all power to the State as outdated. He advocates for a rule of law based solely on objective grounds: public order should be structured so that each person can perform their social role in line with the demands of solidarity. However, there are diverse forms of solidarity: some undervalue individual rights, while others afford them ample room. If we choose the latter, is it not by virtue of value judgments that still resonate with echoes of *The Social Contract*? From this perspective, Charmont[207] has spoken of a "revival of natural law," noting that the main goal of "social law" is precisely to offer more protections to individuals.

Furthermore, when dedicated sociologists like Davy,[208] with his book on *Law, Idealism, and Experience*,[209] join the debates among legal scholars, don't they, in their own way, seek to justify idealist assertions—

Code ("The Revolt of Facts Against the Code"). Morin was notably also known for his campaigning for women's suffrage.

[205] The Civil Code (*Code civil des Français*), also known as the Napoleonic Code, was promulgated in 1804 and is regarded as one of the most influential civil law codes in history. It was the first legal code to be adopted with a pan-national scope, and it influenced the law of many countries formed during and after the Napoleonic Wars. While it has undergone numerous amendments, it remains the backbone of French civil law.

[206] Léon Duguit (1859-1928) was one of the leading scholars on public law in France. He was a prominent socialist thinker who rejected the idea of state sovereignty and argued that the state's role was social and not political. Duguit argued that laws must respect the objective principles of solidarity and justice.

[207] Joseph Charmont (1859-1922) was a jurist, legal theorist, and collaborator with Gaston Morin.

[208] Georges Davy (1883-1976) was a Durkheimian sociologist and philosopher known for his work on the sociology of law.

[209] *Le droit, l'idéalisme, et l'expérience* (1922). Davy's book explores the interplay between legal theory and the broader societal ideals and experiences that shape it.

what G. Séaille[210] termed "affirmations of the modern conscience"—that drive the evolution of law? Yet these assertions are no longer presented as timeless truths. They are not proclaimed from Mount Sinai[211] but laid at our feet by the tides of history. They embody aspirations tied to specific circumstances that reflect the changes occurring within the structures of our societies. We have attempted to demonstrate recently that the rise of *Egalitarian Ideas*[212] is greatly aided by the ebb and flow that diminishes barriers between specialized and hierarchical domains, by the social complexity that interweaves the various groups an individual may belong to, and by the myriad currents—sometimes contradictory—that simultaneously homogenize and individualize us. In this way, as we have said, egalitarian ideas are not a gift from the heavens. They are not meteorites but rather vines, drawing sustenance from the very soil we tread upon.

Therefore, it is possible to sociologically justify the principles initiated by 18th-century philosophical rationalism and to explain the enduring prestige they hold among us, particularly within groups that stand to gain from a "democratization" of political and social institutions.

---

[210] Gabriel Séailles (1852–1922) was a philosopher who specialized in aesthetics. He was a prominent neo-Kantian and sought to reconcile Kant and German idealism with evolutionary theories.

[211] In Judeo-Christian tradition, Mount Sinai is the mountain where Moses received the Ten Commandments from God. It is often invoked as a symbol of divine law and eternal truths.

[212] *Les idées égalitaires: étude sociologique* (1899). Bouglé's dissertation explores the interplay between social structures and ideology to elucidate the emergence of socialist ideologies in Europe. Bouglé posited that the increasing interconnectivity among social groups paralleled structural changes such as the expansion of state functions and the establishment of formal legal equality, which, in turn, fostered the spread of egalitarian thought. To provide a contrasting examination, his 1908 *Essays on the Caste System,* delves into the Indian caste system's reinforcement of distinct social divisions and its promotion of inegalitarianism.

It is quite clear that both theocratic reasoning and, later on, positivist arguments have not achieved significant practical success. They failed to stop the "men of progress" from advancing, rallying an ever-growing body of supporters under the banner of the 18th century's gods: Nature, Reason, and Humanity.

Perhaps it would even be fair to generalize and agree that, setting aside partisan interests and passions, the French intellect often still bears an imprint of the 18th century. The modes of reasoning that prevailed then are still recognizable among us, even in those who feel no particular affinity for the philosophy of the *Encyclopedia* or *The Social Contract*, much less for the political and social implications derived from them. *Nolentes trahunt*—the fates drag the unwilling.[213] This is the impression many foreign observers have, who note this distinctive mark on French people of various persuasions. An English statesman in Geneva, during a discussion on the best way to organize security, humorously remarked: "We, the English, believe that human types are differently shaped, and clothing must be tailored accordingly. You French seem to always believe that the same suit should fit everyone." This echoed the famous reflection: "I do not know man; I know men"—a common thread in the criticisms of Burke,[214] Savigny,[215] de Maistre,[216] and Taine against the 18th-century conception of natural law. Couldn't it be said that the same

---

[213] Seneca (4 BCE–65 CE) wrote *Ducunt volentes fata, nolentes trahunt* which translates to "The fates lead the willing and drag the unwilling."

[214] Edmund Burke (1729–1797) was an Irish philosopher and statesman who is considered to be a founder of the philosophy of conservatism. He opposed the French Revolution and supported British colonialism of India.

[215] Friedrich Carl von Savigny (1779–1861) was a German historian and jurist. He opposed rationalism and *a priori* principles and argued that the law emerges from the people (*Volk*) according to their historical context.

[216] Joseph de Maistre (1753–1821) was a Savoyard philosopher, lawyer, and diplomat who is also considered to be a founder of the philosophy of conservatism. He opposed the Enlightenment and the French Revolution.

68

tradition informs the characteristic that Salvador de Madariaga,[217] a psychologist who has observed a wide array of ethnic peculiarities in Geneva, attributes to the French: primarily legal reasoners, ever ready to establish universal principles from which they inexorably draw conclusions? Furthermore, when we contrast German political psychology with that of France, and seek to explain, for instance, why democracy has not taken the same form in Germany as it has in France despite the Weimar Constitution,[218] aren't we returning to the same benchmarks? Vermeil[219] laments that the Germans do not grant the same authority to the state, which is tasked with upholding democratic will, nor do they place the same emphasis on the individual, who should remain capable of independent thought. Isn't this a lament that Germany has not been directly touched by the radiance of a Voltaire, a Diderot, or a Rousseau?

But it goes without saying that their spirit would be found significantly more vibrant among men of action, those with popular demands to champion, facing the same foes the 18th century so vigorously exposed. It is hardly surprising that proponents of secularism, intent on protecting the state from ecclesiastical dominance and the individual from the clutches of traditional doctrines, would strive to counter Bonald's rebuttals by invoking Voltaire. Proudhon himself, contrasting *justice* in the Revolution with *justice* in the Church, explicitly claimed the legacy of

---

[217] Salvador de Madariaga (1886-1978) was a Spanish diplomat and historian who promoted international cooperation through organizations like the League of Nations. An outspoken critic of fascism, he notably went on to be awarded the Charlemagne Prize, given for service related to European unification, in 1973. His major works include *Englishmen, Frenchmen, Spaniards* (1928) and *The League of Nations* (1930).

[218] The Weimar Constitution governed Germany from 1919 to 1933 and is known for its attempt to establish a democratic framework after WWI.

[219] Edmond Vermeil (1878-1964) was a Germanist and historian. Vermeil was a professor at the Sorbonne and an influential figure in the study of German civilization. He was particularly known for his analysis of German thought and its evolution leading up to the rise of National Socialism.

d'Alembert and his colleagues. Likewise, Jules Ferry,[220] a reader of Proudhon, repeatedly traced his intellectual lineage to the same wellsprings from which Proudhon professed to draw. As a fledgling lawyer, didn't he choose for his inaugural lecture, requested by Pierre-Antoine Berryer,[221] the topic: "The Influence of Philosophical Ideas on the Legal Profession in the 18th Century"? And in 1870, when he pledged to devote himself to the education of the people, it was Condorcet who inspired him, the very Condorcet whose *Memoirs on Public Education*[222] would later be reissued by Ferdinand Buisson.[223] Thus, the 18th-century library offers secularists the richest arsenal of arguments they could ask for.

Certainly, this library would address many other concerns. However, the predominant theme of the majority of its collected works is the emancipation of the human individual and the development of strategies to guarantee, even against the states themselves, the protection of its fundamental rights.

---

[220] Jules Ferry (1832–1893) was a prominent statesman and republican. He was twice Prime Minister of France's Third Republic (1880–1881, 1883–1885). His administration is remembered for his laws expanding and modernizing France's public education, known as the Ferry Laws, which established free education (1881) and mandatory and secular education (1882). Ferry is also known for his anti-clericalism as well as his for advocacy of colonialism and for his role in expanding the French colonial empire.

[221] Pierre-Antoine Berryer (1790–1868) was a celebrated lawyer and politician, known for his defense of the liberties of the press and of individuals. Although Berryer was a staunch monarchist, he often defended republicans and was respected across the political spectrum for his commitment to legal principles. His request for a lecture on the influence of philosophical ideas on the legal profession in the 18th century showcased his recognition of the importance of Enlightenment thought on the evolution of French law and society.

[222] *Mémoires sur l'instruction publique* (1792).

[223] Ferdinand Buisson (1841–1932) was an academic and politician who played a key role in the establishment of secular education in France. As a supporter of the republican values of the Third Republic, Buisson reissued the works of Condorcet, an Enlightenment thinker who advocated for a system of public education. He was notably a Nobel Peace Prize laureate in 1927 for his work as the president of the League for Human Rights.

70

However, one might say that it's not merely or even primarily about democracy today; it's about socialism. And for those interested in traversing between the present and the past, the most compelling inquiry would be to determine whether, by succumbing to the trend toward socialism, we are still following the distant impetus of the Revolution's forerunners. We shall undertake this investigation. Yet here, it seems impossible to dissociate the recollections of 18th-century philosophy from those of the Revolution itself. The general public is inclined to assume that through the Revolution, the social ideas of philosophers experienced a baptism of fire: at that juncture, they drew nearer to reality in order to govern it. It is hardly surprising that these ideas remain haloed by this trial in the view of the parties now struggling for the transformation of today's world, and that what is most remembered is the moment when they seemed inclined toward action. Therefore, we will wait until we have more precisely defined the legacy of the Revolution to decide if today's socialism retains any elements of the philosophy that seemed to be the Revolution's offspring.

Chapter II

Legacy of the 18ᵗʰ Century (Continued): Physiocrats and Rural Folk

Before delving into the crucible of the Revolution to identify the combinations and separations that occurred, and the compounds that resulted, we must turn our attention to a school of thought that carved out a significant place under the sun in the latter half of the 18ᵗʰ century: the economists known as the Physiocrats, disciples of Dr. Quesnay. They constituted a 'sect' that became increasingly distinct from the 'pack' of philosophers. Regarding not only economic but also political and social issues, their stance was markedly different from that of Montesquieu, and even more so from Rousseau and his followers. In particular, while the latter were seen as bringing us closer to socialism, the Physiocrats, on the contrary, seemed to steer us away from it: at least, their central theory takes us to the polar opposite of the one contemporary socialism, influenced by Marxism, has made familiar to us, which derives all value from industrial labor and elevates the working class above all else. Quesnay's school is decidedly neither "laborist" nor "workerist," and if it elevates one class above all, it is that of rural landowners.

Starting in 1750, Voltaire remarked, all of France began to obsess over grain. The philosopher was thus paying tribute, perhaps not without a hint of irritation, to the success of a certain doctor who boldly claimed to have a cure for the kingdom's financial distress. Quesnay—the physician to Madame de Pompadour,[224] an avid reader of Malebranche,[225]

---

[224] Madame de Pompadour (1721-1764) was the influential mistress of King Louis XV of France and a patron of the arts and Enlightenment figures, including Voltaire and Quesnay.
[225] Nicolas Malebranche (1638-1715) was a philosopher best known for his doctrines of Vision in God—the idea that we see all things in God and that God is the immediate cause of all our perceptions—and Occasionalism—the theological doctrine that posits God as the only true cause, with what we perceive as causes in the world being merely occasions for divine action.

and owner of a modest estate in Nivernais—published an *Economic Table*[226] in 1758 that made a significant impact. Expounding on the renowned saying, 'Poor peasant, poor kingdom; poor kingdom, poor king,' he used intricate logical 'zigzags' to compare various sources of income, concluding that the key to replenishing the state's treasury was to bolster agriculture, the true generator of wealth. Quesnay's theory attracted several distinguished figures, among them the Marquis de Mirabeau.[227] The Marquis, known as "the friend of man" after his work bearing this title, would later write *Rural Philosophy* in 1763, a work Grimm[228] dubbed the Pentateuch[229] of the nascent sect. Dupont de Nemours[230] extolled *The Origins and Progress of a New Science*. Le Trosne,[231] the king's attorney in Orléans, proved *The Freedom of Trade in Grain, Always Useful and Never Harmful*. Le Mercier de la Rivière, former administrator in Martinique, delineated *The Natural and*

---

[226] *Tableau économique*. This is a pivotal work that represents the first input-output model in economic theory, illustrating the flow of goods and money in an economy.

[227] Marquis de Mirabeau (1715-1789) was an influential Physiocrat economist often known by the title of his 1756 book, *L'ami des hommes*, or "Friend of Man." He later wrote the 1763 *Philosophie rurale*.

[228] Friedrich Melchior, Baron von Grimm (1723-1807), was a German-born French author, diplomat, and Enlightenment philosopher. Grimm is known for his 1753-1790 newsletter *Correspondance littéraire, philosophique et critique* ("Literary, Philosophical, and Critical Correspondence"), which provided a comprehensive survey of the cultural life of his time and was circulated widely among the elites of Europe.

[229] The Pentateuch consists of the first five books of the Old Testament.

[230] Dupont de Nemours (1771-1834) was a chemist, economist, and government official who later emigrated to the United States. His son founded DuPont de Nemours, Inc., commonly known as DuPont. He wrote the 1768 *De l'origine et des progrès d'une science nouvelle.*

[231] Guillaume-François Le Trosne (1728-1780) was a lawyer and economist and a member of the Physiocratic school. He contributed to the development of economic theory, particularly in the area of law and governance. He wrote the 1765 *La liberté du commerce des grains, toujours utile et jamais nuisible.*

Essential Order of Political Societies.[232] The abbot Nicolas Baudeau,[233] who wrote a *First Introduction to Economic Philosophy; or, Analysis of Civilized States*, directed the *Ephemerides of the Citizen.*[234] In short, a School was established and equipped, whose influence on public opinion has been meticulously chronicled by Georges Weulersse[235] in his book *The Physiocratic Movement in France*, with a methodical patience that seems to exhaust the topic.

What, then, was the doctrine that the Physiocrats were advocating? The very titles of the books we've just mentioned serve as a reminder. They sought to persuade the king, his advisors, and his subjects that all prosperity stems from agriculture, and that agriculture itself thrives on freedom. The first misconception to be dismantled, in order to prevail with this argument, was the mercantilist[236] fallacy: the notion that a nation enriches itself by maximizing its foreign exports and minimizing its imports of manufactured goods. Wouldn't this lead to the accumulation of the world's gold in its vaults? This is why the state found it beneficial to provide incentives to the export industry. Such illusions were dangerous, the Physiocrats contended. The true wealth of nations isn't the concentration of gold, but the abundance of the earth's produce.

---

[232] *L'ordre naturel et essentiel des sociétés politiques* (1767). La Rivière's best known work in which he argued that governments should allow the laws of nature to govern society without interference.

[233] Nicolas Baudeau (1730-1792) was a Catholic monk, economist, and a prominent advocate of Physiocracy. Baudeau worked to apply Physiocratic principles to the reform of French fiscal policy. He wrote the 1771 *Première introduction à la philosophie économique; ou, Analyse des états policés.*

[234] *Éphémérides du citoyen* (1765-1772, 1775-1779) was a journal in which many Physiocratic ideas were published. An ephemeris is a book of tables concerning the trajectory of astronomical objects.

[235] Georges Weulersse (1874-1950) was a historian who specialized in the history of economic thought. He wrote the two-volume *Le mouvement physiocratique en France* (1910), which remains a seminal text in understanding the development and impact of Physiocratic ideas in pre-revolutionary France.

[236] Mercantilism is an economic policy that dominated Europe from the 16th to the 18th centuries. It held that the wealth of a nation was based on its stockpile of precious metals, typically gold and silver, which could be increased through a positive balance of trade with other nations.

Consequently, what is important is not to lavish support on industry, but to remove the obstacles to agriculture.

There seemed to be a deliberate effort to complicate the movement of grain. Mandated and increasingly scarce markets, prescribed days and locations for sales, zones where transport was prohibited, and compulsory stockpiling—all appeared to conspire to obstruct farmers from earning a fair price for their crops. It was against these obstructions, which seemed to cloud their future, that the Physiocrats tirelessly campaigned. Hence, they embraced the politics suggested by the renowned maxim: "Laissez faire, laissez passer." The maxim was coined by Gournay,[237] who, as Turgot points out, began at the merchant's counter, in contrast to Quesnay who began with the plow. Quesnay's sole concern was the fair pricing of grain; it is important to emphasize this point to clearly define his brand of economic liberalism, which has been described as a liberalism of convenience rather than one of principle. Had Quesnay perceived a threat to the country's agricultural output from foreign competition, mightn't he have shifted to its antithesis, protectionism? Nonetheless, he boldly advocated for a policy of high prices in his "maxims": "Only a high price can procure and maintain the wealth and population of a kingdom through the success of agriculture. That is the alpha and omega of economic science." He also asserted: "Abundance without value is not wealth. Scarcity and high prices mean misery. Abundance and high prices signify opulence."[238]

*

* *

Does the economic liberalism necessary to cultivate this opulence inherently lead to political liberalism? Did the Physiocrats advocate for systematic safeguards against the abusive interventions of authority? It was

---

[237] Jacques Claude Marie Vincent de Gournay (1712–1759) was a Physiocrat economist who actually only popularized the term. It appears to have been coined around 1680 by a merchant named Le Gendre during his conversation with a politician on what the government could do to help him.

[238] F. Quesnay: *Quesnay's Tableau économique.* Translated by M. Kuczynski & R. L. Meek. Augustus M. Kelley Publishers, 1972, p. 9.

here, as has been correctly observed, that the Physiocrats most distinctly parted ways with the philosopher-jurists, who were keen on devising laws for the protection of rights. The checks and balances championed by Montesquieu were no more appealing to them than Rousseau's concept of the general will. They willingly acknowledged a sort of co-ownership of lands by the royal authority, as long as it preserved the necessary freedom for rural property ownership. They were not convinced that despotism was inherently harmful; rather, it must become enlightened by agricultural science. The regime they particularly admired was that of China: didn't the Emperor himself plow the soil? This is why, after being subjected to Mably's scorn, the economists were later praised by one of the royal censors, believed to be Moreau,[239] according to Weulersse. He commended them for having the insight to support "a government by one," at a time when "a certain philosophy had quite openly declared itself in favor of republican systems."

However, let's not be deceived by this seeming surrender. If the economists welcomed even the idea of despotism without concern, it is because they placed absolute trust in the natural laws they uncovered, which are so evident that they apply even to princes. In this regard, it's important to recognize that they didn't forsake the concept of natural law, which was highly esteemed in the 18th century, but instead planted it in the soil, so to speak. They founded the moral order on the physical order, which, according to Quesnay, is obviously most advantageous to humanity. Mirabeau also declared, "It is by things that men are governed," a statement that redirects focus to the concrete, to the laws governing the production and distribution of wealth. The fundamental rights of individuals cannot be secured if these laws are not observed. The foremost among these laws is the freedom of trade, which calls for the safeguarding of property rights. Hence, the economist's primary petition to the despot is to refrain from making any kind of intervention by means

---

[239] Jean Victor Marie Moreau (1763–1813) was a general under Napoleon. However, Moreau didn't support Napoleon's rise to power and was banished from France in 1805 and emigrated to the United States. He later returned to Europe, fought against Napoleon, and died in battle.

of the theoretical co-ownership they are presumed to hold over all the possessions of their subjects. Quesnay's saying was often echoed: "If I were king, I would do nothing." In other words, he advocated for strict limits on governmental action: while the sovereign authority can and should establish laws to curb clear disorder, it must not encroach on the natural order of society. "The gardener must remove the moss that damages the tree, but should be careful not to cut into the bark that channels the sap that nourishes its growth."

Dupont de Nemours was blunter, asserting: "If sovereigns' decrees were contradictory to the laws of social order, they would be nonsensical acts that would bind no one."

This implies that the Physiocrats' seeming acceptance of 'despotism' didn't equate to an endorsement of state control—quite the opposite. Their faith in the natural order was so strong that they were convinced that the highest levels of prosperity would naturally occur if only people were free and guided by Physiocratic principles. In this sense, Gurvitch,[240] building upon the observations of Hector Denis,[241] correctly noted that they laid the groundwork for the significant distinction between the realm of the state, a world of constraints and regulations, and civil society, where contracts and exchanges reign supreme. Hegel's utilization of this distinction in his *Elements of the Philosophy of Right* is well-documented. Variations of this concept appear in the works of Saint-Simon, Fourier, and Proudhon. Indeed, the embryonic form of this idea is present in the comprehensive worldview of Quesnay's followers, which could be described as a form of liberalism grafted onto naturalism.

---

[240] Georges Gurvitch (1894–1965) was a Russian-born French sociologist primarily interested in the study of law and the sociology of knowledge. After WWII, he was one of the leading sociologists in France. Gurvitch promoted a pluralist, multidimensional sociology and he notably wrote several books on the ideas of the classical French socialists.

[241] Hector Denis (1842–1913) was a Belgian economist, sociologist, and socialist politician. Like his collaborator Guillaume de Greef (1842–1924), he was interested in synthesizing the ideas of Comte with Proudhon. Denis wrote the 1897 *Histoire des systèmes économiques et socialistes.*

Furthermore, this liberalism was not absolute; it was driven by agricultural interests. Should these be threatened, it would be amenable to compromise. In the realm of international relations, it has been contended that Physiocratic economics would likely endorse a measure of protectionism if the price of grain were to drop due to foreign competition. By the same token, this rationale applies even more to the case for interventionism within the nation. The Physiocrats expected the state not only to shield farmers from 'usurpations,' property infringements, and various forms of violence but also, with the help of "public instructors," to promote the universal education they valued so highly: "A so-called civilized state that believes it can establish authority on anything other than universal education is like trying to build a pyramid with the apex at the bottom." They also entrusted the government with a third role: administration in the strict sense, which they understood as encompassing all activities aimed at enabling and facilitating land cultivation, not just maintaining roads and clearing ditches, but also reclaiming and preparing wild, uncultivated land. Such endeavors would necessitate "sovereign advances." The Physiocrats were willing to let the state handle these tasks. Moreover, considering that Quesnay himself suggested that the state might need to cap interest rates in certain scenarios, their liberalism was far from categorically excluding government action.

*

*   *

Does this suffice to conclude, as Lichtenberger and later Gurvitch suggest, that they too made room for socialism? Such a claim would have to be interpreted very broadly. It must be remembered that no institutions, measures, or reforms interested the Physiocrats unless they favored agriculture. Two key elements characteristic of contemporary socialism were conspicuously absent from their system: the glorification of industry and that of the laborer. Indeed, they provided strong arguments against both. Weulersse aptly described them as anti-industrialists. And considering their veneration for property coupled with their skepticism of industry, they might too be labeled as anti-socialists.

We need to uncover the underlying reasons for these sympathies and antipathies. They are rooted in Quesnay's purely economic theories concerning the net product.[242] It's possible they even reach into the core of his philosophical beliefs. Recall that he was a devoted reader of Malebranche, who rejected the idea of human beings having any causal power. Wasn't Quesnay, the "agronomist" and disciple of the oratorian Malebranche, predisposed to value the gifts of nature above human labor?

Nevertheless, when Quesnay compared the various types of expenditures in the renowned zigzag table that made him famous, he believed he had demonstrated that only investments in agriculture yield productive returns. In this instance alone does the income generate a surplus. In every other case, it is expended without any net yield, effectively dissipating. The wealth that arises from the earth is privileged to perpetually regenerate itself like the phoenix. Agriculture is, as Mirabeau put it, a "divine manufacture where the maker partners with the creator of nature." As Weulersse also astutely points out, we find here a form of agrarian deism or pantheism. The farmer, as a direct collaborator with the divine force, is the sustainer of the entire nation. Such was the Physiocrats' belief in the fecundity of this annually renewed creation that they boldly proposed a tax system that would be borne entirely by landowners, custodians of the sole genuine source of revenue.

On the contrary, they argued for the rehabilitation and exaltation of farmers, to honor them as nurturing patriarchs. Quesnay's foremost wish was that "farmers no longer be relegated to the class of citizens whose professions are deemed contemptible and degrading." The correspondent from the Société d'Agriculture de Paris, writing from Bussy Saint-Georges, attributes this desire to the peasants themselves. He portrays them speaking with a threatening assertiveness: "Begin by giving us status and treating us as useful individuals, a recognition denied to us until now... Impress upon the elite this harsh but vital truth: that by our

---

[242] Net product refers to the total output or yield of a production process after deducting the costs associated with creating that output.

industry, we can do without you." The Marquis de Mirabeau, in *The Friend of Man*, had previously conveyed the social implications of this observation, with a kind of solemnity and as though he were himself startled and concerned: "If all stems from the land, then the man who most effectively cultivates its yields is the foremost man in society. It is alarming to declare, but the king, the army general, and the minister could not survive without agriculture, yet agriculture would continue without them."

The culmination of these reflections is the advocated preeminence of the classes that till the soil. In truth, they alone merit the designation "productive." The other citizen groups, which figures like Sieyès[243] and Saint-Simon would have acknowledged, were either overlooked or undervalued by Quesnay's school, systematically pushed into the "sterile" classes.

It's not just those who subsist on income without labor that are called into question. Socialist writings from both the 18th and the 19th centuries label them as parasites. In principle, Physiocracy does not disagree. It takes a hard stance against rentiers who coast through life without lifting a finger, contributing nothing to the cultivation of the land. Saint-Simon would liken them to hornets. Mirabeau likened them to wolves.

But what of the active professions? Commerce? Industry? Are they to be deemed sterile? The Physiocrats boldly pronounced such a judgment. The transporters of goods and products are undoubtedly necessary, but one should not be mistaken into thinking they generate any new wealth. If that were the case, wouldn't simply circulating goods around the globe multiply their value a hundredfold? The Physiocrats approached the view that merchants levy an excessive toll for the costs of

---

[243] Emmanuel Joseph Sieyès (1748–1836) was a clergyman and political theorist known for writing the defining manifesto of the French Revolution, *What is the Third Estate?* (1789). After the Revolution, he served in the Directory government but lost influence during Napoleon's rise to power.

circulation. Their strictness here presages Fourier's critique. Baudeau proclaimed, "The expenses and profits from all transport, from all traffic, are clearly an additional burden on both producers and consumers." Mirabeau, on his part, noted, "The merchants complain about the Economists and the audacity they showed in shaking the exalted throne that these times of prestige and illusion had raised for the mercantile profession and its labor suppliers." And Quesnay himself, recalling that a state would run to ruin if it abandoned the plow to become a "carrier," was the very first to check the pride of intermediaries: "Just as rope that pulls the bucket to fetch water from the bottom of the well does not produce the water, so too does trade not produce value."

But industry itself, which shapes raw materials and transforms them into usable products, didn't earn the approval of the Physiocrats. Ultimately, they would not be displeased to reduce it to the bare minimum. Isn't its principal function to expand the production of luxury goods that could, if necessary, be foregone? It is a mistake to think that promoting such production—such as the manufacturing of silk stockings, which Quesnay addresses in a treatise—enhances the nation's renewable wealth. Industry transforms and trade transports, but neither creates. Therefore, their contributors cannot be welcomed into the esteemed ranks of the productive classes.

This holds true not just for business owners, but also workers, and especially factory workers. In reality, they do not create any new value. They consume the value of what they produce just to maintain themselves. "The artisan destroys as much through his living expenses as he creates with his labor." "The value of the artisan's work does not cover its costs." And to deliver the final blow: "The industrious class aids production through its expenditure, yet this expenditure benefits only as would that of an idler living off a portion of income: in this respect, the idler and the worker are one and the same."

*
* *

The closing of the 18th century thus set us on a course diametrically opposed to the one fervently pursued in the 19th century. The glorification of factory workers' labor as the creators of all wealth became the central theme of socialism, which aligned itself with large-scale industry and championed its achievements: socialism sought to correct industrial chaos only to reap the benefits of its endeavors. And it is well-known that this celebration of the worker was underpinned by an economic theory, a 'theory of value' that Marx adapted from David Ricardo.[244] Ricardo claimed that all value is measured by labor. For Marx, all value originates from the labor power[245] that the worker sells to the employer. We find ourselves in the realm of "ponocracy," in stark contrast to Physiocracy. The reverence for labor, *ponos*, has supplanted the worship of *phusis*, the productive nature.[246]

To fully appreciate the distance the Physiocrats lead us away from socialism, we should note a particular distinction: they were more interested in landowners, especially large landowners, than in day laborers. They favored those who could extract the highest yields from the land by investing the necessary capital for its cultivation. The common complaint was that agriculture lacked workers. Yet, Quesnay had noted: "It is not so much men, but wealth that we must draw to the

---

[244] David Ricardo (1772-1823) was an English political economist. His "labor theory of value" posits that the value of a good is fundamentally determined by the amount of labor necessary for its production.

[245] In Marxist theory, labor power is the capacity for work, in contrast to the physical activity of labor, which is the source of all surplus value—the difference between the actual wage paid to the laborer and the value produced by the laborer. Marx's adaptation was that while labor created value, the capitalist system allowed capitalists to extract this surplus value from their labor power, which ultimately engendered class struggle.

[246] *Pónos* (πόνος) is a noun from Ancient Greek that translates to 'work' or 'toil,' while *Phúsis* (φῠ́σῐς) is a noun that translates to 'nature' or 'property.'

countryside."[247]   And Baudeau more pointedly countered: "Hands? Hands? That is exactly what our current operations do not need. Advances, advances—that is what the land needs, that is what is missing from yours. Sovereign advances, real estate advances, movable advances from productive farms that conserve labor instead of multiplying it." He also stated that his ideal was "a large and robust agricultural workshop on rich estates." These remarks are telling and lend credence to Marx's characterization of the Physiocrats' system as part feudal, part capitalist. Indeed, their ideal was the gentleman landowner who managed a large enough estate to profit from advancements in agricultural technique, made possible by the capital he invested. In this regard, what they established was in fact agrarian capitalism, which is arguably opposed to the socialism of the working class in two respects.

*

*   *

The Physiocrats have been characterized as anti-mercantilist and anti-interventionist, champions of rural property rights, with a penchant for large-scale farming operations. They prioritized the societal role of the classes involved in land cultivation, which they saw as the sole source of wealth. Defined in this manner, what influence does their philosophy hold in contemporary France? Is it still a source of inspiration? Or, perhaps without mentioning it by name, do we remain loyal to their principles?

The overview of ideas we've just compiled offers at least one benefit: it brings back into focus a significant segment of French social reality that socialist literature seemed to have neglected or made us overlook for years. Marxism is fundamentally an analysis of the advances of mechanization in factories. It is deeply intertwined with industrialism. It draws its support from the masses of proletarians that big industry gathers in its 'factory nests.' It advocates for the workers, tailors its agenda to their circumstances, and explores the strategies they could employ and

---

[247] F. Quesnay: *Quesnay's Tableau économique.* Translated by M. Kuczynski & R. L. Meek. Augustus M. Kelley Publishers, 1972, p. 8.

the policies that might benefit them. In contrast, the peasants, dispersed across the land they till and often own, do not fit as neatly into the framework of *The Communist Manifesto* or *Capital*. Hence, there was a tendency to overlook them, or at the very least, an instinctive effort to downplay their importance, to undervalue their contribution. The unique lifestyle and labor of the peasantry were viewed as peripheral, or at least as a fleeting phase: mere dust particles that wouldn't stop the wheel of big industry from turning, and after grinding down numerous victims, would eventually grind down the economic system itself.

In recent years, there seems to have been an awakening to the paradox in this earlier tendency to overlook the peasantry. Indeed, France's economic evolution has not entirely followed Marxist projections. The consolidation of industries and, even more so, of property ownership has not advanced as rapidly as anticipated. Nonetheless, the peasantry has maintained its dominance. In this context, it was the Physiocrats who proved to be the accurate forecasters. Their aspiration has been partially realized: agriculture is now a primary focus of public interest. An increasing number of speakers and writers are eager to remind France that it is fundamentally a rural nation. It's not just that Ministers in the Chamber of Deputies or at agricultural assemblies are prone to declare, quite naturally, that agriculture is "the sturdy, enduring framework of the nation"; but to convey the distinctive mindset of France, emphasis is placed on the peasant influence. Lucien Romier[248] in his *Explanation of Our Time* would find common ground with André Siegfried[249] in his *Portrait of Political Parties in France*. Foreign

---

[248] Lucien Romier (1885-1944) was a conservative politician and journalist. He later joined the Vichy government and served as minister of State from 1942 to 1943. He died while being arrested by the Gestapo. He wrote the 1925 *Explication de notre temps*.

[249] André Siegfried (1875-1959) was a geographer and centrist political commentator. He served as a Senator from 1933 to 1940 and then as an ambassador to the US from 1940 to 1944. He wrote the 1930 *Tableau des partis politiques en France*.

commentators like Sieburg[250] are even more inclined to concur. "Peasants first"—could this be the unofficial motto ascribed to the contemporary French? It would surely gladden the heart of the "agronomist" doctor and his followers.

It's clear, however, that this kind of dominance is waning. Rural folk no longer hold the position in our society that they used to. With each passing decade, their numbers shrink in comparison to those of other social groups. The industrial revolution, which Mantoux[251] has expertly analyzed in terms of its development and impact, began as a British phenomenon. But it is well known that the so-called British system took root and thrived in France as well. Here too, machinery has been applied to the processing of cotton, wool, flax, knitwear, and metallurgy; factory nests have proliferated. Major regions—Lorraine and Dauphiné among them—have established industrial infrastructures that rival those of Germany or England. France's output of manufactured and semi-manufactured goods is on the rise.

It's no wonder that this drive, which draws people toward sprawling cities, has resulted in a relative decrease in the countryside population. Two statistics illustrate this trend: in 1845, the urban population made up only 24% of France's total population; by 1926, it accounted for 49.1%.[252]

The scales are almost balanced. Whereas eighty years ago the rural population was three times as numerous as the urban population, they are now on the verge of parity.

---

[250] Friedrich Sieburg (1893–1964) was a German journalist and literary critic. He was also a German nationalist who later supported the Nazis and worked in the German embassy in occupied France.

[251] Paul Mantoux (1877–1956) was a historian best remembered for writing the 1906 book *La revolution industrielle au XVIIIe siècle* ("The Industrial Revolution in the Eighteenth Century").

[252] France's post-WWII policies greatly accelerated this trend towards urbanization. Consequently, the urban population in France in 1960 was roughly 62% and in 2023 was around 81%.

The 1926 census of the active population, whose preliminary results have only recently been released, enables us to assess the rapidity of these shifts in proportion since the war. Agriculture, including forestry, has lost 821,275 workers in five years, while industry, including mining, has gained 615,725, and commerce has seen an increase of 195,563. Altogether, the agricultural sector has experienced a loss of nearly 10% since 1921.

As Pierre de Monicault[253] noted at the 12th Congress of French Agriculture, more than half of French workers (farmers and other agricultural workers) rely on farming; the entirety of French agricultural production accounts for 44% of France's overall income; the total output of the steel industry, for instance, doesn't reach the value of the total wheat production, nor does the total production of automobiles surpass that of oats. This leads to the conclusion that even today, agriculture holds at least as much economic significance in France as industry does. It is precisely this balance that constitutes one of the unique characteristics of our nation.

*

*　*

From this economic structure, what social consequences arise? To discern this, we must first establish the ratio of salaried workers to owners within agriculture. Marx's predictions of concentration and proletarianization do not seem to be confirmed here. He claimed that "[i]n the sphere of agriculture, modern industry has a more revolutionary effect than elsewhere, for this reason: it annihilates the peasant, that bulwark of the old society, and replaces him with the wage-laborer."[254] Yet over extensive periods, the bulwark remains strong. Rather, the type of person favored by the Physiocrats, the rural proprietor, continues to dominate. Within the category of forestry and agriculture, there are

---

[253] Pierre de Monicault (1869–1953) was a politician associated with the conservative *Fédération républicaine* ("Republican Federation") party.
[254] K. Marx: *Capital: Volume I.* Translated by S. Moore & E. Aveling. Charles Kerr & Co., 1906, p. 554.

(excluding women) 2,452,777 heads of farms, 4,262 managers, 1,684,785 workers, and 585,912 solitary laborers. This indicates that there are still four times as many small-scale farm operators as there are true agricultural laborers.

Do these landowners cultivate their land according to the methods the Physiocrats advocated? Are they expanding their estates and engaging in the necessary reconsolidation of land so that the yield of the soil can be increased through technological enhancements, which typically require a sizeable area of operation? Or on the contrary, do small plots remain the norm? It is difficult to give an exact answer to this question. The response would differ depending on the region and the type of crop. What applies to vineyards and sugar beets might not hold for wheat or flax. What is true in Brittany may not be the case in Picardy.

One thing is certain: after the war, amid widespread anticipation for a more rational reorganization of production and heightened awareness of the drawbacks of land fragmentation, there were concerted efforts to consolidate land systematically. Efforts were made in the reclaimed territories to form larger plots than before. However, on the whole, fragmentation continues to be the norm. The numerous peasants who purchased land upon their return from the front lines rarely had the opportunity to create extensive estates.

But in the countryside, a new force has emerged—or rather has grown remarkably—offering benefits to small farmers that could compensate for the lack of land redistribution: the power of association. Did the Physiocrats anticipate the extent to which it could expand and the variety of services it could provide? Their advocacy was, without a doubt, an encouragement to band together. They urged farmers to recognize and defend their shared interests. This suggests that they would have viewed the growth of agricultural societies favorably. Some were established before the success of Quesnay's *Tableaux*; many more followed. The Physiocrats found in their ranks natural correspondents, invaluable informants, and designated advocates for their theory. They outlived revolutions, and their legacy continues to underpin the foundation of the

Palace erected by the Société des Agriculteurs de France. However, it's clear that the remembrance of the Physiocrats, in whatever form it has endured, was not the unique or primary catalyst for the significant movement we are observing. In an era when the concern for various shared interests led to the formation of numerous advocacy groups, it was only natural that farmers would be prompted to wield the same tool. They benefited from a law not originally intended for them: the law allowing the creation of syndicates was, in its creators' minds, primarily a worker's law. It was aimed at the proletariat in factories and their wage struggles. Farmers took advantage of the opportunity. They established hybrid associations with mixed attributes, part trade union and part cooperative, whose proliferation, as de Rocquigny[255] accurately observed, was one of the pivotal events of the late 19th century. Michel Augé-Laribé,[256] in *Agricultural Unions and Cooperatives*, has compiled compelling evidence of this. The Bulletin of the Ministry of Labor now lists more than 9,000 agricultural unions, encompassing over 150,000 farmers, 9,000 of which function as purchasing cooperatives, and close to 4,000 as production cooperatives.

Since the war, there has been not just a proliferation but also a coordination of these types of associations. They have managed to establish a National Confederation of Agricultural Associations which has a permanent secretariat, has convened its 13th Congress, and serves as a sort of professional parliament.

In addition to the large and influential group of deputies from various parties that has formed to defend rural interests, we have recently witnessed the creation of an agrarian party. This party aims to send deputies to Parliament who will represent agriculture exclusively, without

---

[255] Henri-Marie-Robert, comte de Rocquigny du Fayel (1845-1929) was a statesman and journalist. He carried out field missions for a variety of institutions on topics related to agriculture.

[256] Michel Augé-Laribé (1876-1954) was a politician and economist who specialized in rural political economy. He was a Senator from 1924 to 1941 and advocated for gold-backed currency and free trade. Augé-Laribé wrote the 1926 *Syndicats et coopératives agricoles*.

any political affiliation, and whose sole purpose is to amplify the "Voice of the Earth."

Karl Marx appeared to think that rural folk, missing the shoulder-to-shoulder solidarity of the factory, would forever be incapable of developing a class consciousness; hence why he scornfully likened them to a sack of potatoes.[257] Furthermore, numerous other observers have noted what seems to be an unshakable individualism among, in particular, French peasants. Even André Siegfried seems to succumb to this conventional wisdom. However, the establishment of the various bodies we've just discussed amply demonstrates that both the worker-focused socialists and the individualists have overstated the peasants' inability to come together.

Despite their multitude, these groups maintain a number of common tendencies. Are these tendencies in alignment with the Physiocratic tradition?

On one key point, there is no question. The type of rehabilitation that Quesnay and his followers called for is being demanded by our farmers with unmatched vigor. Jules Méline,[258] in *The Return to the Land*, already noted that agriculture, being our foremost industry, "still suffers from its former humility." Daniel Halévy,[259] in his *Visits to the Peasants of the Center*, encountered among them a kind of bruised pride, a bitter feeling of being treated as second-class citizens. Since the war, Romier notes, this peasant pride has been restored. Aware of their sacrifices and stung by comments about their profits, the farmers have pointed out in

---

[257] See Chapter 7 of Marx's (1852) *The Eighteenth Brumaire of Louis Napoleon*. Similarly, in Volume III of *Capital* (Chapter 47), Marx referred to the peasantry as "a class of barbarians standing half outside society."

[258] Jules Méline (1838–1925) was a conservative politician and the prime minister of France from 1896 to 1898. He advocated for protectionist policies and advocated for peasants' interests. Méline wrote the 1905 *Le retour à la terre*.

[259] Daniel Halévy (1872–1962) was a historian and journalist. Although he originally was a Dreyfusard, he later moved to the far right and supported the Vichy regime. He wrote *Visites aux paysans du centre* (1921).

their Congresses that for too long, industry has been treated like a favored child: they now insist on speaking not as subordinates, but as equals.

Another point of convergence is the issue of education. We've seen the importance the Physiocrats placed on it and how they relied on the work of public educators not just to popularize their doctrine but also to disseminate the technical knowledge necessary to enhance agricultural productivity. Organized farmers are revisiting this issue. They are looking for ways (see, for example, their Congress in Rouen) to have their associations work together with teachers and to tailor the curriculum of rural schools to better meet agricultural needs.

But from this angle, we can hardly expect anything but stopgaps, or at least slow corrections that will have long-term effects. To maintain agricultural prosperity, which is vital to France's health, there are urgent measures that must be taken. And the rural world has known what these are for years. Protectionism is its hope. The primary goal is to prevent foreign wheat, produced more cheaply, from competing with French wheat. A price collapse could occur, which might lead to farmers abandoning their fields in despair. And so, France would lose not only the privilege of living off its land but also its reserve of rural folk who are the backbone of its strength. This argument, familiar as it is, stands in clear opposition to the Physiocrats' principle, epitomized by Gournay's maxim 'Laissez faire, laissez passer,' which advocates for the removal of all barriers to the free movement of grain. Yet what the rural world seems to call for here are barriers that can be adjusted depending on France's state of production, so that our farmers are always appropriately compensated for their work. Here, its desires are diametrically opposed to those of the agronomist doctor.

However, let's not overplay this overly simplistic contrast: it may be softened in several ways. Firstly, we've noted that the Physiocrats' liberalism—as historians from Oncken to Truchy[260] have long observed—

---

[260] August Oncken (1844–1911) and Henri Truchy (1864–1950) were both economists and historians.

may not be a principled liberalism, an uncompromising one. Just as Méline would not have surrendered to the complaint of *pain cher* ("expensive bread"),[261] their primary concern was to ensure good living and working conditions for the farmers who sustain the entire nation. Had they been shown that these conditions were threatened by foreign competition, they probably would have shifted their stance and, to save wheat, sacrificed liberty.

Conversely, it's important to note that an increasing number of today's agricultural opinion leaders are eager to show farmers that it's a big mistake to put all their trust in protectionism. At the 1930 French Agriculture Congress, Queuille[262] presented a report specifically dedicated to this topic: "Methods of Assisting and Protecting Agriculture Beyond Tariffs."

Pushing back against what he termed the mystique of customs, and putting his own spin on the well-known phrase "the kingdom of God is within you,"[263] he pointed out that in many cases, while it might be unavoidable to use tariff protection or even administrative protection against the overwhelming competition of low-priced goods, other, potentially more effective long-term remedies should be considered: "General education, technical training, scientific research, collective defense against diseases and fraud, cooperation, credit, insurance, mutual aid, transportation rates—all of these areas are just getting started and need improvement. They could provide as much, if not more, efficacy in safeguarding farmers than customs tariffs."

---

[261] Jules Méline earned this nickname in the (left-wing) radical press after the Méline tariff, a protectionist measure, was introduced in 1892. In 1897, the politician Albert Bedouce (1869–1947) published a pamphlet, *Le pain cher*, in which he vigorously attacked Méline's protectionist policy.

[262] Henri Queuille (1884–1970) was a politician associated with the Radical political party and was notably minister of agriculture eleven times. He later went on to be the prime minister of France from 1948 to 1954.

[263] A Bible quote attributed to Jesus when he spoke to the Pharisees, from Luke 17:21.

Clearly, implementing this agrarian policy, deliberately distinct from politics, hinges on three elements: agreements with foreign countries, state aid, and coordinated efforts from rural associations. To gauge the advancements our agriculture has made and the strides it still needs to take in these three aspects, one can refer to the report submitted at the end of 1930 to the National Economic Council by Augé-Laribé, Secretary-General of the National Confederation of Agricultural Associations. To address the instability of the costs and sales prices of farm products, prevent the depletion of certain markets and the overflow of others, determine quotas, and channel surplus, whether incidental or regular, in order to benefit regions in need, each country must establish regulatory bodies for production, domestic consumption, and international exchange. How can we achieve this sort of rationalization? By utilizing producer cooperatives, connecting them with consumer cooperatives, and placing their collective efforts under the oversight of the state, serving as both support and mediator.

Could this path not lead to an excessive expansion of the State's role in economic matters? This concern was raised right when the project we're summarizing was introduced. And we must concede that the actions taken or suggested since then—to address the poor sales of wine, for example—do not seem to comfort the advocates of traditional liberalism. Isn't it even being proposed that the government should determine the quota of vines that each winegrower may plant or maintain? This new agrarian policy necessitates ongoing collaboration, in a wide array of forms, between the government as the overseer and the associations as the managers.

Some argue it could be labeled 'socialism,' which departs significantly from the principles championed by the Physiocrats. Indeed, the program being attempted now is the antithesis of laissez-faire and doesn't appear to align with the classic ideal of individualism. Yet this doesn't necessarily mean it would have been strictly rebuked by Quesnay and his followers. We've recognized their primary concern is the improvement of agriculture; perhaps they would have conceded: "If

liberal principles must be sacrificed to save French agriculture, so be it."
It's also worth noting that this "socialist" agenda, which seems to be driven
by the desire to protect the peasant, shares little with the socialism
promoted by Marxism: there's no talk of a working-class dictatorship, nor
of centralizing all property under state control. A "socialism for the
peasants," if it were ever to materialize, would need to make numerous
concessions to the freedoms that peasants hold dear, especially the right
to property. From this perspective, the rural classes, for whom the
Physiocrats were staunch advocates, remain a significant force in French
politics and economics. When considering the future of socialism in
France, we often overlook this important point—a significant oversight,
which remembering the Physiocrats might help us avoid.

Chapter III

Legacy of the French Revolution: The Third Estate and the Fourth Estate

What did the men of action of the French Revolution retain from the theories developed by 18th-century thinkers? Did they derive socialist implications from them, and to what degree? As a result, can those pushing contemporary France towards socialism legitimately seek refuge in the memory of the Revolution? Or conversely, does the Revolution give their adversaries a stronger foundation for a counter-offensive?

Anyone looking to delve into this research today might run into an initial hurdle that's particularly popular among those most interested in socialism. Is it perhaps giving too much credit to theories, philosophy, and ideology to question their past roles or potential current influence? There was a time when the power of ideas was credited with explaining everything. They were either celebrated or condemned for birthing the Revolution, depending on one's perspective. But historical materialism has since arrived, as we've seen, and it's changed all that. The clash of economic forces is what drives deep changes in society's structure. The back-and-forth of ideas is just a shadow play on the wall. Ideas are more often than not the products rather than the causes, or at the very least, they serve more as excuses than actual driving forces. Marxist philosophy, by flipping Hegelianism on its head and planting it firmly on the ground, has gotten us used to this shift in viewpoint.

Whether one buys into this framework or not, one thing is for sure: the very advancement of historical research on the Revolution seems to have led to ideas being knocked down a peg or two in the ranking of causes. We no longer attribute the stages of the Revolution to the dominance of one thinker after another, like Montesquieu followed by Rousseau, as was the case in Louis Blanc's era. Now, there's a stronger focus on economic variables, the force of necessity, and the trials they forced upon lawmakers. Realism has also gained ground in this area.

No one would think to question these findings anymore. It's indisputable that the work of the Committee for Economic Studies of the Revolution, along with that of Sagnac and Mathiez,[264] has uncovered a variety of economic circumstances impacting the everyday lives of urban and rural populations—factors that the Revolution's earliest historians hadn't fully appreciated. As Lefebvre's[265] insightfully pointed out, the severe trials Europe has endured during and after the war have undoubtedly made us more capable than ever of grasping, for instance, how significantly the issue of food supply can influence the direction of a nation in turmoil.

Additionally, it's noteworthy that even the protagonists of the drama often referred to the underlying forces they felt compelled by. Mirabeau himself declared, "The Revolution is owed more to the sense of our sufferings than to the progress of the Enlightenment." Throughout the Revolution, several assembly members noted that experience had opened their eyes and helped them appreciate the value of principles they had previously deemed impractical. Lakanal, extolling Rousseau, even stated, "In a way, it was the Revolution that explained *The Social Contract* to us." Carnot[266] claimed, "A person does not start out as a revolutionary; they become one." And Saint-Just[267] observed, "Perhaps the force of circumstances is leading us to outcomes we had not anticipated." According to these accounts, many men of action during the revolutionary crisis moved from experience to theory rather than from theory to experience.

---

[264] Philippe Sagnac (1864–1954) and Albert Mathiez (1874–1932) were historians remembered for their interpretations of the French Revolution.
[265] Georges Lefebvre (1874–1959) was a historian known for his work on the peasantry and the French Revolution. He emphasized "history from below," namely a focus on the experiences of common people.
[266] Lazare Carnot (1753–1823) was a mathematician and member of the Committee of Public Safety during the notorious Reign of Terror. He later served as Minister of War under Napoleon.
[267] Louis Antoine de Saint-Just (1767–1794) was a political philosopher, prominent Jacobin, and member of the Committee of Public Safety, nicknamed the "archangel of terror" during the Reign of Terror. He was executed alongside Robespierre during the Thermidorian Reaction.

Yet they deemed theories to be useful, and they commended those who had crafted them, carrying the ashes of great thinkers, the liberators of the nation, to the Pantheon with great ceremony. They clearly recognized that theories not only provided guidance for the actions of legislators but also served as focal points for strong collective emotions. Even amid the fervor of the revolution, these theories were like an intellectual scaffold that people were glad to rely on. Karl Marx, with a hint of irony, noted the ancient trappings beloved by the revolutionaries of the era—lictors' fasces,[268] senators' robes, curule chairs[269]— and remarked that shadows of Rome cast themselves over the cradle of the Revolution. They were not merely there for show. In invoking them, wasn't there a belief that they could bestow a distant, ancient strength upon the nascent giant? The same could be said, and even more so, of the concepts recently formulated in France. Faced with all sorts of challenges, the Revolution's architects were naturally drawn to the well of "advances in ideas" laid out by the philosophers.

In a petition launched on the eve of the summoning of the Estates-General[270] by the students of Nantes, the signatories stated that they were drawing on the "sense of their own strength," while also expressing a desire to "reap the benefits of 18th-century philosophy." Thus, they embraced both approaches, striking the chords of both realism and idealism. It's likely that most of the figures involved in the Revolution shared this same synthetic frame of mind. Doctrines, even if they weren't seen as creative forces, were still regarded as essential intermediaries. Language, or more specifically, the language of principles, was valued

---

[268] A fasces is a bundle of wooden rods attached to a blade. In Ancient Rome, it symbolized the magistrate's power to punish and represented unity and authority, later becoming emblematic of the fascist movement.

[269] A curule seat is a transportable chair that symbolized political power in Ancient Rome and was reserved for high-ranking officials such as magistrates and senators, denoting their status and authority.

[270] The Estates General of 1789 was the general assembly summoned by the King of France to represent the three estates that marked the beginning of the French Revolution. The assembly ended when the Third Estate, as well as some members within the other estates, formed the National Assembly.

because it seemed useful. And history cannot afford to overlook the impact that they derived from it.

*

* *

However, from the "advances of ideas" established by the 18th century, more than one interpretation can be drawn. In this sense, while the ideology of the Revolution may not have been entirely ineffective, it may well have lacked complete unity. In the multitude of speeches, pamphlets, and articles, often contradictory ideas have been voiced. Amid this confusion, isn't there a risk of finding support for a wide range of views, some for, others against property; some for, others against socialism?

Nevertheless, given the topic at hand, we can identify major trends, some more prevalent in the early stages of the Revolution, others later on. We can look for the expression of the earlier trends among the advocates of the Third Estate, such as Sieyès, Rabaut Saint-Étienne,[271] and Barnave,[272] and of the later trends among the advocates of the Fourth Estate[273] (a term used from the start of the Revolution), like Dolivier,[274] Lange,[275] and Roux,[276] who continued the actions and expanded the

---

[271] Jean-Paul Rabaut Saint-Étienne (1743-1793) was a Calvinist pastor and politician who advocated for religious toleration. He was guillotined during the Reign of Terror for his association with the Girondins.

[272] Antoine Barnave (1761-1793) was a moderate Jacobin politician and orator. He advocated for a constitutional monarchy and was executed during the Reign of Terror for counter-revolutionary activities.

[273] While the "Third Estate" referred to everyone besides the nobility and clergy, the "Fourth Estate", in this context, referred to the poor and downtrodden.

[274] Pierre Dolivier (1746-1830) was a priest who defended the poor and questioned the heredity of the ownership of land during the French Revolution. He is considered an important precursor of socialism.

[275] François-Joseph Lange (1743-1793) was a proto-socialist pamphleteer during the French Revolution who sought to develop a coherent social democracy. He was executed during the Reign of Terror.

[276] Jacques Roux (1752-1794) was a radical Catholic priest and leader of the popular far-left. After learning he was to be tried by the Revolutionary Tribunal for withholding funds, he committed suicide.

98

thoughts of Robespierre and Marat.[277] Are the doctrines they developed thus antithetical? And must we concede that the earlier trends aimed to articulate the agenda of an individualist bourgeoisie, while the later trends aimed at that of a socialist proletariat? This would be too simplistic, as we shall see: concepts like individualist bourgeoisie or socialist proletariat, perhaps suitable for the contemporary era, don't quite fit the economic and social realities of the Revolution. But it is clear that the theorists who spoke more prominently in the later phase, those we refer to as advocates of the Fourth Estate, will bring us much closer to the conceptions that can indeed be called socialist.

*

*　*

As we have seen, the author of *What is the Third Estate?* certainly didn't shy away from invoking natural law. He made a case for the need to establish the state's fundamental laws through a constituent power. Undoubtedly, he would have readily echoed Rabaut Saint-Étienne's sentiment, "our history is not our Code," and dismissively relegated to the past those who cry heresy at the mention of innovation. The advocates of the Third Estate recognized that the moment had arrived to innovate, to act on principles, since no appeal to precedent could solve the nation's problems. And they made no secret of their annoyance with the historical justifications that had been used and abused in these matters right up until the eve of the Revolution.

This should not be taken to mean that the advocates of the Third Estate despised all of history. They were quite adept at identifying a number of historical events—specifically economic ones—that could support the claims of their order. They went beyond simply observing

---

[277] Jean-Paul Marat (1743–1793) was an anti-monarchist politician who called for violence against the enemies of the revolution. He was notoriously assassinated in his bath by Charlotte Corday (1768–1793), a murder that became one of the most iconic events of the French Revolution.

that Philip the Fair[278] had established prosperous towns whose citizens possessed rights that were to be honored. In a broader sense, they emphasized the comprehensive material power of the men of the Communes, which was intertwined with a rising intellectual power, thereby attesting to the superior value of one class: its economic force engendered its rights. This is where we see the emergence of the theory that connects the revolutionary movement with the movement of the historical Communes, a theory with a significant future, later to be developed by Augustin Thierry,[279] Auguste Comte, and most notably by Saint-Simon himself, who recognized in the industrialists not just the descendants of the Gauls oppressed by the Franks, but also the heirs of the artisans and merchants of the Communes. Thus, the stage was set with the belfries of the Communes, just as it had been set with the forests of Franconia for the apologists of the nobility. Most notably, the key to the Revolution was no longer sought in abstract ideology, but in economic history.

The thinker who most lucidly expressed this interpretation was perhaps Barnave. And Jaurès[280] was not exaggerating when he observed that an initial outline of historical materialism was drawn by the author of the *Introduction to the French Revolution*,[281] who represented one of the most industrial regions of that era, Dauphiné, in the Constituent

---

[278] Philip IV (1268–1314), known as Philip the Fair, was the King of France from 1285 until his death, noted for his conflict with the papacy and the Knights Templar, which shaped his reign as well as French history.

[279] Augustin Thierry (1795–1856) was a historian, early follower of Saint-Simon, and was Saint-Simon's secretary from 1814 to 1817. Thierry would later develop his own picturesque approach to history and was a pioneer in archival research. Marx would later call him the "father of class struggle."

[280] Jean Jaurès (1859–1914) was a popular socialist leader who helped found the *Parti socialiste français* (1902–1905) and the *Section française de l'Internationale ouvrière* (1905–1969) political parties. He was notably associated with the Durkheimians and was tragically assassinated around the outbreak of WWI.

[281] *Introduction à la rèvolution française.* The book, published after Barnave's death and written while he was imprisoned, has been argued to prefigure the ideas of Auguste Comte as well as Karl Marx.

100

Assembly.[282] In the book, Barnave explicitly stated that a new distribution of wealth leads to a new distribution of power. He noted that the Revolution in France became possible because, alongside the ownership of land, the ownership of movable property had surged: "Just as land ownership elevated the aristocracy, industrial property uplifts the power of the people."[283]

The people, whose circumstances, according to Barnave, legitimize their aspirations, consist of all "active" individuals, those who produce the necessities for the nation's sustenance. He certainly differentiates among categories, but not classes. Jaurès points out that when Barnave spoke of workers, he immediately grouped them with merchants. Indeed, Barnave also suggested that non-property owners could well form a dangerous, "restless and corrupt" class. However, this was merely a fleeting moralistic judgment. The author was far from considering non-property owners capable of inciting a revolution. Moreover, although he acknowledged a growing antagonism between industrial owners and landowners, he didn't extend the same analysis to the dynamics between property holders and wage earners.

Sieyès encompassed within the Third Estate not only peasants and workers but also merchants, members of the liberal professions, and civil servants. He perceived and desired them to be in solidarity, forming a united front. Within this united front, there were no layers, no division between the privileged and the underprivileged. It is true that Sieyès acknowledged that the interests among the categories he identified may vary. But it was permitted, even encouraged, to set aside these differences in the struggle for rights that the Third Estate must engage in as a single, undivided force.

---

[282] The National Constituent Assembly (1789–1791) was the formal name given to the National Assembly.

[283] A. Barnave: *Introduction to the French Revolution.* Ch. 3. Translated by E. Chill. In *Power, Property, and History.* Harper & Row, Publishers, 1971, p. 82.

What was the primary objective of this conflict? It aimed not so much to alter the system of property ownership but to transform the mechanisms of authority. Regarding property, the approach aligns with the doctrine of the Physiocrats; it is codified in the *Declaration of the Rights of Man*, affirming the individual's inviolable and sacred right to ownership. As for authority, the lessons drawn from the philosophers' advocacy are clear. Remember that the state is not an end unto itself; its obligation is to uphold and ensure the equal rights of all. How to ensure control by the majority and provide safeguards for the individual? It was this twofold problem that the leaders of the Third Estate primarily sought to address. In this respect, they truly merit the label of *legalists* that Saint-Simon, the industrialist, scornfully hurled at them. It can indeed be said that the period of the Revolution, marked by their predominant influence, was first and foremost a revolution of jurists.

This Revolution, as we mentioned, proclaimed the principle of private property. From this standpoint, it was conservative. Yet it brought about significant changes in the economic order, perhaps the most serious that our history has ever documented. It freed the fields from the burdens imposed by the feudal system, it partitioned the estates of the nobility and the clergy, and in their stead, it elevated a host of small landowners. Numerous petitions from the Third Estate had respectfully called for this liberation, and since the summoning of the Estates-General, the peasants—pitchforks at the ready, poised to burn down châteaux and terriers[284]—had imperatively demanded it.

The primary preoccupation of the Revolutionary Assemblies was to fulfill these demands. The Legislative Assembly, followed by the National Convention, finished the task initiated on the night of August 4th. Following the decrees they issued, peasants could henceforth, as Sagnac notes, become free and absolute owners of the land at no cost.

---

[284] *Terriers* refers to the records of land holdings, sometimes including a list of tenants, their holdings, and the rents paid. In this context, the peasants' intent to burn the terriers signifies their rejection of the legal and systemic structures of land ownership.

Certainly, it wasn't always the peasant who ended up as the final owner. Many members of the bourgeoisie stepped in to purchase national properties. And in some areas, large landowners managed to hold on to extensive estates. But overall, an economic revolution was achieved in favor of those who cultivated the land. It can be asserted that France, by the end of the 18th century, had successfully carried out the endeavor that various countries in Central and Eastern Europe attempted following the last war: it freed and parceled out the land, thereby establishing the necessary conditions for the emergence of a rural democracy, a democracy comprised of landowning citizens.

That doesn't mean, however, that socialism didn't benefit from the process. It gained the memory of a precedent that could be invoked later, with the necessary adaptations; a "colossal transfer of property has occurred." One class was essentially expropriated for the benefit of another. The principle of property, which was intended to be preserved, was simultaneously undermined. Titles were burned, and properties were auctioned off without the consent of their owners. The partitioning of estates and the individuation of rural properties, one of the most definitive outcomes of the Revolution, was preceded by a principle of socialization: there was a moment when the Nation, exercising a sort of supreme authority, redrew the map of property ownership in favor of a group of citizens who, after long oppression, sought to take control of their destiny.

*
* *

Yet the French Revolution was to forge other, more direct avenues for socialism. It heard demands that might already be termed proletarian. Driven by the urban masses, who raised their voices ever higher and lamented with increasing fervor as their suffering intensified, the Revolution faced challenges to the very right to property, which it believed resonated with the deepest desires of the peasant populace.

Of course, these were not strictly workers' demands. At that time, workers didn't have a significant enough impact on the overall economy of the nation to spawn and steer an ideological movement. It has already been observed (by Roger Picard[285] in his study *The Cahiers of '89 and the Working Class*) that issues of wages and unemployment occupied a small place in the people's lists of grievances on the eve of the Revolution. During the Revolution itself, Jaffé,[286] while researching *The Workers' Movement in Paris*, found little more than a few petitions from carpenters and masons demanding the right to associate or pointing out that the Rights of Man should encompass the right to life.

Yet in the absence of a distinct working class, there was an urban populace in turmoil, exerting pressure that the Assemblies could not ignore. To the "poor day laborers, the sacred order of the unfortunate" that Dufourny de Villiers[287] identified as constituting a Fourth Estate, was added a diverse throng of common folk—artisans, shopkeepers—who sought to wield their slice of political power to alleviate the economic hardship that constricted them. Even at the time of calling the Estates General, when the method of election and the census tax rate were debated, isolated protests emerged: the propertyless had opinions to express—shouldn't they too have a say? With each passing month, as the suburbs instigated riots against the Assemblies and recognized their own strength, and as they concurrently faced food scarcities and rising prices, these protests grew more forceful, more defiant.

The masses felt increasingly formidable just as they felt increasingly deprived. It was only natural that they would find advocates whose voices carried with growing authority. It was during this time that the concept of "the people" became more defined. The term was no longer universally applicable; it began to be reserved for those who toiled.

---

[285] Roger Picard (1884–1950) was a historian who wrote the 1910 *Les cahiers de 89 et la classe ouvrière*.

[286] Grace M. Jaffé (1897–1996) was a historian who wrote the 1924 *Le mouvement ouvrier à Paris*.

[287] Louis Pierre Dufourny de Villiers (1739–1796) was an architect and politician in the French Revolution who defended the poor. He was arrested during the Reign of Terror but avoided execution.

104

For Robespierre, the people were the vast, hardworking class untouched by the corrupting influences that had degraded what were referred to as the upper classes. Marat preferred the term "the little people" and proclaimed, "It was the little people who made the Revolution." The pamphlets of Dolivier, Lange, and Roux repeatedly hammered home these ideas. They became the standard rhetoric in the Clubs and Committees. They were used to justify the rationing and requisition measures that the Committee of Public Safety had to enforce when France turned into a fortified camp.

Certainly, these were measures of circumstance. However, they came with an undercurrent of theoretical reassessment that reached back to the very principle of property rights. It is known that Robespierre no longer regarded property as a natural right, but rather as a right granted by society and that could be limited, if necessary: if the interests of the masses seemed to require it, why shouldn't this right be subjected to increasingly stringent restrictions? While the Physiocrats, who mainly considered the rural population, had consecrated property rights, these rights were now under threat at their very core by the revolutionaries, who were primarily concerned with the toiling and destitute urban masses.

Once this period of introspection commenced, Pétion[288] was indeed justified in his lament over the division of the Third Estate. A fresh ideology was emerging, tailored for the Fourth Estate, and this ideology indeed paved the way for distinctly socialist ideas.

*
* *

The red flower that bloomed at the end of this stem was Babouvism. The doctrine crafted by François-Noël Babeuf,[289] the former

---

[288] Jérôme Pétion de Villeneuve (1756–1794) was the mayor of Paris from 1791 to 1792 and was associated with the Girondins. After the Jacobins came to power, he went into exile and ultimately committed suicide.
[289] François-Noël Babeuf (1760–1797) was a journalist and political agitator who advocated for radical egalitarian and communist ideas. He helped form the

land registry commissioner,[290] to animate and direct the conspirators he encountered at the Society of the Pantheon, indeed bears the hallmarks of a synthetic summary as well as a draft proposal: it intertwines recollections of 18th-century theories with those of the Revolution's experiences, and alongside a blueprint for insurrection, it lays out a plan for communist organization.

For a significant portion of the progressive public, the Babouvists arrested on 21 Floréal, year IV[291] were quintessential conspirators. The documents brought forth during the major trial of the 64 at Vendôme reveal the methodical precision with which they had orchestrated their attempted coup. Proclamations, banners, songs, and the allocation of tasks among patriots deemed "suitable for governing and stirring revolution within a secret Directory,"[292] as well as the recruitment of women who could "rally" the soldiers by presenting them with wreaths—all was in place for a "plebeian Vendée."[293]

The conspiracy failed. Yet the determined will to succeed that had driven its formation made a lasting impression on the imaginations of rebellious men of action. Thanks to Buonarroti's[294] *History of Babeuf's Conspiracy for Equality* (published in 1828), Babouvism became and remained a symbol of unity for insurgents throughout the century.

---

secret society "Conspiracy of the Equals," and was executed shortly after the conspiracy was uncovered.

[290] The *commissaire à terrier* was responsible for maintaining land registry records, reflecting the feudal rights and obligations, a role that Babeuf held before becoming a revolutionary leader.

[291] The date on the French Republic's calendar refers to May 10th, 1796, on the Gregorian calendar.

[292] *Le directoire* (1795–1799) was the five-member governing committee during the French Revolution.

[293] The War in the Vendée (1793–1796) was a counter-revolution in the Vendée region of France, which was brutally suppressed with an estimated 200,000 victims. The Vendée region continued to experience uprisings in 1799, 1815, and 1832 but were much smaller in scale.

[294] Philippe Buonarroti (1761–1837) was an influential Italian-French socialist writer and follower of Babeuf. He was involved in the "Conspiracy of Equals" and went into exile in Switzerland and later in Britain.

106

Nonetheless, for Babeuf the insurrection was merely a prologue. He aspired to compose the entire drama. His goal was to equip his contemporaries with all the tools needed to rectify a Revolution that, despite its myriad promises, had led to numerous disillusionments. To engage in positive, constructive labor was the ambition that had fueled him throughout a life replete with toil and conflict.

To achieve this, it was first necessary to restore the honor of the principles that too many men of the Revolution, inclined toward easy compromises, seemed to have forgotten. This was the role of 18th-century philosophy. It set the tune for the Babouvists—quite literally, as they had composed awakening songs that called upon nature and declared equality. Hence, it was not without reason that Babeuf, naming his son Émile,[295] transcribed passages from Rousseau, especially the one stating: "You are lost if you forget that the fruits are for everyone and the earth belongs to no one." The Babouvists also shared the skepticism of nature's advocates towards civilization, suggesting that refining and complicating our means of action risked exacerbating inequality. Like Rousseau, the Babouvists fundamentally detested large cities. They favored an agricultural life. Preferring the Spartan over the Athenian—to use the contrast familiar to the men of the Revolution, highlighted by Buonarroti—they would choose the equality of black broth[296] over opulence monopolized by a few. It was undoubtedly this aspect that Marx and Engels had in mind when, in the *Communist Manifesto*, they criticized as inherently reactionary the revolutionary literature that promoted, alongside a rudimentary egalitarianism, a universal asceticism.

This Rousseau-inspired emphasis on virtue didn't prevent the Babouvists, particularly Buonarroti, from acknowledging the beneficial role of commerce and industry: in a way, they too have been the lictors of liberty. The wealth accumulated by the members of the Communes, the artisans, and merchants of the Third Estate, became a tool for

---

[295] *Émile, or On Education* (1762) was a book written by Jean-Jacques Rousseau on the nature of education.
[296] In antiquity, black broth was a regional cuisine from Ancient Sparta.

emancipation that was meant to benefit the entire nation. Moreover, while large cities are breeding grounds for corruption, they are also centers of unrest. The Babouvists were prepared to defend Paris, anticipating the leading role to be taken by the urban proletariat. They even recognized the value in the hardships endured by the masses. Isn't the people's distress the most palpable evidence of the harms caused by inequality? Thus, the very setbacks of the past Revolution and the hardships it exacerbated could advance the cause of the coming Revolution, which aspires to achieve genuine equality through a systematic restructuring of the economic system.

Moreover, didn't the recent Revolution also show us, alongside its ills, a potential remedy? As France turned into a fortified camp, a war factory, didn't we manage, in the face of common danger, to demand sacrifices from the privileged, to ensure provisions for the dispossessed? Weren't there rations, requisitions, price caps, and the establishment of granaries of plenty? The widespread application of these measures is precisely what Babouvism advocated: that in peacetime, we should do for the nation what was done out of necessity in wartime. This historical experience serves as the strongest foundation for the system they intended to implement, which could already be termed collectivist. To defend not just the urban workers but also the countless ranks of the oppressed, they proclaimed with somber lyricism, "Let's work to make gold as valueless as sand and stones." As a result, the blueprint for all collectivist plans was boldly outlined here: the confiscation of the assets of émigrés,[297] enriched officials, and neglectful landowners; the abolition of inheritance; communal exploitation by all able-bodied members of society; the allocation of labor; and the centralization of goods and produce in public stores, from which they would be distributed across regions.

And now there can be no doubt: at its extreme, the French Revolution paved the way to socialism.

---

[297] Émigrés refer to the people who fled France, mostly aristocrats, during the French Revolution.

The advocates of the Third Estate were primarily focused on establishing a regime of legal equality that, while facilitating the transfer of properties into the hands of peasants, left the fundamental principle of property untouched.

Babouvism discounted this principle because it sought nothing less than complete economic equality—equality or death.[298]

---

[298] This phrase echoes the revolutionary cry of "liberty, equality, fraternity or death," which became a rallying call for revolutionaries seeking not just political freedom but also social and economic equality. "Death" was later dropped for being too closely linked to the Reign of Terror.

Chapter IV

Legacy of the French Revolution (Continued): Liberals, Radicals, Socialists

We've attempted to identify the various tendencies that emerged from the tumult of the French Revolution. Specifically, to determine whether it leads to socialism, we've noted the importance of distinguishing between different factions and periods. We must now consider how much these recollections continue to live and influence us, and whether they can be found in the platforms of today's political parties.

It is undeniable that memories of the Revolution have long retained significant prestige in France: they are an integral part, or for many seem to be the entirety, of our national tradition. This backdrop, against which countless dramatic, inspiring, or horrifying scenes unfolded, prevents them from looking back to the ancien régime, to a past which they, like Sieyès, would eagerly refer to as the era of Gothic nonsense. At the very least, they regard the *Declaration of the Rights of Man* as the quintessential product of the French mind, the crowning achievement of our history.

In truth, this attitude itself took a while to become commonplace. For many years following the Revolution, even those who wished to preserve as much of its principles as they could scarcely dared to speak of it openly: it seemed to inspire a kind of revered dread. We recall Lamartine's[299] description: "Holy wishes, vain utopias, atrocious methods." The most that its proponents could do was to cast a veil over

---

[299] Alphonse de Lamartine (1790–1869) was a writer and politician who helped found the Second Republic (1848–1852). He served as the Second Republic's first Head of Government from January to February 1848.

its excesses and chaos, to allow the guillotine[300] and the assignat[301] to fade into oblivion.

However, the opposition that stood against the Restoration couldn't afford to remain silent about the Revolution. It couldn't ignore the powerful impact that such dramatic images had on those it brought together in clubs or secret societies. Between 1820 and 1840, histories of the Revolution proliferated. The connection was rekindled. After the events of 1830,[302] the Republic may have been sidelined, but the revolutionary spirit was reawakened. It inspired societies such as the Society of the Rights of Man[303] and the Friends of the People.[304] Having attended one of their meetings, Heinrich Heine[305] remarked with sly insight: "The gathering smelled like an old, dirty, greasy, and worn copy of the 1793 *Monitor.*"[306]

A meticulous review of the themes in Republican propaganda at the onset of the July Monarchy[307]—like the one conducted by Gabriel Perreux[308]—in club gatherings and in newspaper columns, in Paris and

---

[300] The guillotine was a device first invented around the onset of the French Revolution that attempted to execute convicts in a more humane manner.

[301] Assignats were a form of paper money that came into use during the French Revolution.

[302] Known as the July Revolution of 1830, citizens set up barricades in Paris and fought against the royal army, which led to the overthrow of King Charles X (1757-1836), who had been reinstated as king following the fall of Napoleon Bonaparte. Charles' cousin Louis-Philippe I (1773–1850) was then crowned the first "King of the French" and ruled until the Revolution of 1848. The July Revolution was an important event in that it substituted popular sovereignty for the principle of hereditary right.

[303] *Société des droits de l'homme* (1830–1840).

[304] *Amis du people* (1830–1832).

[305] Christian Johann Heinrich Heine (1797–1856) was a German literary critic and poet whose revolutionary political views forced him to live in exile in France starting in 1831 for roughly 25 years.

[306] *Le Moniteur Universel* (1789–1868) was the main newspaper during the French Revolution.

[307] The July Monarchy (1830–1848) was a liberal constitutional monarchy under Louis-Philippe I, which started following the July Revolution of 1830 and ended with the Revolution of 1848.

[308] Gabriel Perreux (1893–1967) was a journalist and historian.

across the provinces, reveals the extensive revolutionary references made by the opposition, who would soon become conspirators. "Fantasy Jacobinism," as François de Corcelle[309] put it, played a pivotal role at the Pellier riding school,[310] dubbed the "Jeu de Paume[311] of the new Revolution." The Robespierrist definition of property, in particular, received a lot of attention because it seemed to offer a way to connect the memories of '93 with socialist ambitions. This is precisely the bridge that the Revolution of 1848, in its initial phase, set out fervently to build. And again, as can be clearly seen not only in manifestos like those of Louis Blanc and Victor Considerant[312]—*The New Cordelier, Father Duchêne, The Friend of the People*[313]—and in the titles of political groups such as the "Montagnards,"[314] the first, great Revolution was invoked; it was declared that the mission was to continue it, to complete it, to fulfill its logical promise by moving from political reform to social reform.

Following the Second Empire, which scrubbed the motto *Liberty, Equality, Fraternity* from the walls and outlawed the singing of *La Marseillaise*,[315] when the time for the Republic came around again, it was

---

[309] François de Corcelle (1802-1892) was a writer and politician who opposed the Second French Empire. He was the grandson of Lafayette. He is also known for his correspondence with Alexis de Tocqueville.

[310] The Pellier riding school was turned into a meeting place for parliamentary assemblies during the French Revolution. The Pelliers taught at the riding school after the Revolution until it was destroyed in 1830.

[311] Jeu de Paume ("palm game"), often called "real tennis," is a ball-and-court game that originated in 17th century France and gave rise to the modern game of tennis.

[312] Victor Considerant (1808-1893) was a social theorist and the most influential disciple of Charles Fourier. He led an experimental Fourierist phalanstery in Texas, which ultimately failed.

[313] *Le nouveau cordelier, Le père Duchêne,* and *L'ami du peuple.* The titles evoke those of Camille Desmoulins' journal *Le vieux cordelier* (1793-1794), Jacques-René Hébert's journal *Le père Duchesne* (1790-1794), and Jean-Paul Marat's newspaper *L'ami du peuple* (1789-1792).

[314] The Montagnards were members of *La montagne* ("The mountain"), the more radical group within the Jacobin Club (1789-1794).

[315] La Marseillaise is the national anthem of France. Written in 1792 and adopted as the national anthem from 1795-1799, it was outright banned during the

once more under the influence of the Revolution that the men who were poised to seize control collaborated and strategized their efforts.

Jules Simon,[316] defining *Radical Politics*,[317] repeatedly stated in his public lectures that he was a man of '89. The Belleville Program of 1869[318] was drafted in the form of a Cahier[319] intended to evoke the Cahiers of the Third Estate, and Gambetta, upon accepting it from his constituents, declared: "This method seems to me consistent with the rights and traditions from the first days of the Revolution." On September 4th, when he sought to calm the people storming the Palais-Bourbon, sensing that the age-old idea was haunting the crowd and fueling their drive, he proclaimed: "A representative of the Revolution speaks to you." Later, in 1881, when Clemenceau[320] felt the need to rally a more fervent radical-socialist group to champion the people's claims, he aligned himself with the tradition of the Montagnards. He urged his supporters to "prepare for the great social transformation that will be the culmination of the French Revolution." And soon he would emphatically call on Republicans to embrace the Revolution in its entirety. More recently, Ferdinand Buisson, in defining the radical and radical-socialist Republican Party, tasked it with the goal of continuing the work of the First Republic and adapting the principles of the *Rights of Man* to the present day. It's likely that such historical references have awakened

---

Bourbon Restoration (1814–1830). It has officially been readopted as France's national anthem since 1870.

[316] Jules Simon (1814–1896) was a philosopher and Prime Minister of France from 1876 to 1877. He advocated for modernizing France's educational system, which brought him into conflict with the Church.

[317] *La politique radicale* (1868).

[318] Léon-Michel Gambetta (1838–1882) was a politician and one of the founders of France's Third Republic. His election program, the "Belleville Manifesto," defined the agenda for the new republic. Gambetta was known for advocating freedom of the press and educational reforms.

[319] Cahiers were lists of grievances written by the three estates during the French Revolution.

[320] Georges Clemenceau (1841–1929) was the Prime Minister of France in 1906–1909 and 1917–1920, and a leading member within the Radical Party. He is remembered for glorifying the achievements of the French Revolution as well as consolidating power and curtailing civil liberties during WWI.

114

political callings even in our times. Herriot,[321] reflecting on his journey to becoming a radical-socialist, mentions that in his youth, he encountered the spirit of the Revolution on several occasions: he was shown the grave of a member of the National Convention[322] in his village, learned of the struggles between the Chouans and Republicans[323] that he was told about in the Bocage Vendéen,[324] and finally, at the École Normale, during an age when one devours the works of philosophers, he came upon Hegel's own assessment: "The bath of the Revolution has cleansed the French nation of many institutions that the human spirit had outgrown, just as a child outgrows their shoes."[325] Undoubtedly, many others on the left could attest to being influenced in similar ways.

But as we've said, it would be unfair to let those who strive to bridge the gap between the Republic and socialism hold a monopoly on this: many of those who aim to deepen the divide or erect a barrier between the two also claim the right to draw from the same well of memories. Indeed, the majority of today's conservatives, at least in intellectual circles, seem to have resolved to condemn the spirit of the Revolution as the root of all our troubles. We recall Renan's[326] stern reflections after the defeat of 1870 on *Intellectual and Moral Reform*: "France today is paying the price for the Revolution"; and again: "The failed experiment of the Revolution has cured us of our faith in reason."[327]

---

[321] Édouard Herriot (1872–1957) was the Prime Minister of France in 1924–1925, 1926, and 1932 as well as a historian. He notoriously denied the Holodomor famine at its height in 1933 during a visit to Ukraine

[322] The revolutionary assembly that governed France from 1792 to 1795 during the French Revolution.

[323] The Chouan brothers led a counter-revolutionary royalist uprising from 1794 to 1800.

[324] The Bocage Vendéen is a well-wooded natural region in Western France.

[325] G. W. F. Hegel to C. G. Zellman. January 23, 1807.

[326] Ernest Renan (1823–1892) was an influential philosopher and Semitic scholar. He critically examined religious texts and promoted an anticlerical, scholarly approach to religious scholarship. Renan wrote the 1871 *La réforme intellectuelle et morale*.

[327] E. Renan. *What is a Nation? And Other Political Writings.* Translated by M. F. N. Giglioli. Columbia University Press, 2018, p. 206.

Taine echoed this sentiment with his well-known fervor in his volume on the Revolution, seeing in it little more than a frenzy of animalistic instincts unleashed by an excess of ideology. Taine and Renan have had many successors. It's said to be rare these days to find a notable man of letters in the salons who dares to uphold the principles of '89. Most literary figures are "right-thinking," which first and foremost means they would concur with Paul Bourget in labeling the Revolution "the quintessential French mistake": they agree that to reorganize France, the pack of "liberties" that have ravaged its traditions must first be reined in.

Yet closer to the political fray, there are conservatives of a different stripe: those who wish to preserve the economic status quo while not politically supporting for a rollback or surrender of the freedoms that have been won.

These individuals proclaim themselves advocates for both political and economic liberalism, searching for ways within the individualism championed by the French Revolution to stifle any socialist tendencies. Didn't the Revolution claim to liberate individuals from all hindrances to their professional and intellectual pursuits? Didn't the Physiocrats, whose ideas are reflected in the *Declaration of the Rights of Man*, call for laissez-faire and the protection of private property? There is nothing better than letting citizens voice their opinions, assemble for their defense, and express their desires through decisions of assemblies: this aligns with the noble traditions of the French Revolution. However, if these assemblies begin to disrupt the "natural laws" of the economy, or if this democracy turns towards socialism, it must be checked. Tocqueville[328] rightly noted in 1848 that these two concepts are at odds when combined: he believed that by favoring *equality*, we risked losing all the achievements of *liberty*. Are the tragic circumstances of certain classes invoked in vain? The Revolution abolished class distinctions; our current laws don't acknowledge them; resurrecting them would only hinder the

---

[328] Alexis de Tocqueville (1805-1859) was a diplomat, liberal political philosopher, and historian. He is considered a pioneer in comparative political science for his detailed observations, not only of politics in the US compared to Europe, but also on the ancien régime compared with the French Revolution.

116

normal operation of politics, which is both liberal and democratic. Wouldn't we soon be tempted, not just to limit the individual's right to move freely, choose their profession, and trade at will, but also to trample over the system of public liberties? Thus, law, the safeguard of freedom, would soon be put out to pasture. When the centenary of the 1830 Revolution was celebrated, one paper summarizing this argument boldly claimed that the socialists would be akin to petty Polignacs[329]: their decrees would pose a far greater threat than those of the original Polignac to the Revolution's ideological legacy.

*

* *

One can imagine what the parties known as the left—radicals or socialists—would have to say in response to this conservative liberalism. Radicals would claim to be the most devoted of all to the cause of freedom, consecrated in their view by the Revolution itself. They recognize that an atmosphere of freedom is essential, not just for the government to be held accountable by the masses, but also for the flourishing of individuality. That's why they are committed to preserving not only the unhindered operation of parliamentary institutions, the principal means of legal leverage for a modern democracy, but also secular public education. By liberating the state from the control of the Church, this education allows individuals to pursue their own opportunities, measure their own worth, and ultimately choose their own ideas while shaping their own circumstances.

"No one shall be disturbed for his opinions, including his religious beliefs," that is, even regarding religion: Article 10 of the *Declaration of the Rights of Man*, as Herriot wrote in 1920, logically leads to the secularization of public services, education included. It insists that the dogmas that divide us must be left at the door of the nation's schools. It does not permit asking future citizens for a confession of faith, nor, for

---

[329] The Polignacs were a powerful noble family who were close with the royal family leading up to the Revolution. They went into exile following the storming of the Bastille in 1789.

that matter, a certificate of atheism. And this is how secularism[330] complements the intellectual politics of the Revolution.

But it also marks the beginning of a social politics desired by the Revolution. It wished to recognize no other social distinction than that of virtues and talents. And the public utility it called upon also required enabling the most capable, the most deserving, to take on leadership roles. Wasn't this a call for equality of opportunity for all children from the start? Wasn't this an early justification for the so-called *école unique*[331] comprehensive school project? Making elementary education accessible to everyone and higher education available to the most capable is, according to radicals and Condorcet, and reiterated by Ferdinand Buisson, the best means of combating both privilege and prejudice. In this regard, the social issue is primarily one of education.

Is that all there is to it? And won't it be necessary to use more direct methods to address the economic pressures that render freedom an illusion for the majority? Might this not lead us away from the perspective of the advocates of the Third Estate, who asserted the inviolability of private property? Radical-socialists are not willing to concede to other socialists that the abolition of private property would definitively cure all our social ills. However, they acknowledge that it could be subjected to increasing restrictions and limitations. It is no longer what it once was. Why, then, should it remain what it is now? The Radical Party is "first and foremost a party of evolution." And if the men of the Third Estate truly lacked an evolutionary perspective, if they genuinely believed that property rights would remain static, then on this point, enlightened by experience, we must revise their doctrine; or at

---

[330] "Secularization" in this context refers to *laïcité*, a French concept of secularism that goes beyond the separation of church and state. It embodies the absence of religious involvement in government affairs, and the absence of government involvement in religious affairs, ensuring freedom of thought and religious practice. In France, *laïcité* is a principle that applies to public services and education, promoting a neutral public space where people can express their personal beliefs without the interference of the state.

[331] After WWI, some teachers lobbied for the creation a unique school system entitled *école unique,* which sought equality of opportunity for all.

least, while preserving their ultimate goal—the free development of human personalities—we must accept that new circumstances require new methods.

Including state intervention? Why not? One of the "elements" of the "radical doctrine," as Alain[332] puts it, is certainly a mistrust of all public authorities, even those elected, and all the more so of government administrations. Every government is fundamentally reactionary; every administration needs to be constantly challenged. For the citizen, resisting any and all power is the beginning of wisdom—a Cartesian tradition, some say, or at the very least a revolutionary one. And there is no doubt that radicalism retains a bit of this quasi-anarchist streak. But another revolutionary tradition may provide a different impetus when necessary: Jacobinism. Jacobins are prepared to strike hard when they believe they represent and defend the will of the masses; they are ready to smash any barrier to take action. Isn't this Jacobin tradition, which Kautsky[333] notes "casts a youthful glow upon the bourgeois radicalism of France," what many recognized in the vigor of Combes,[334] "that Robespierre in slippers," and which partly accounted for his popularity with the plebeian masses? Louis Blanc had already stated that we must use the state as a tool, lest it become an obstacle. Once the people exert their influence on the state, it ceases to be the master and becomes the servant. And it is no longer off-limits to harness its power for the task of economic organization that our current situation demands. For instance, it seems natural that certain industries that enjoy de facto monopolies should be returned to the state. It would at least be logical for the state to levy the greatest tax burden on

---

[332] Émile-Auguste Chartier (1868-1951), also known as Alain, was a philosopher and essayist. He was influential in promoting republican and humanist ideals of citizenship and opposing totalitarianism.

[333] Karl Kautsky (1854-1938) was an Austrian-German Marxist theoretician and one of the key leaders of orthodox Marxism. He advocated for a slower, democratic transition to socialism and came into conflict with the Bolshevik party for their advocacy of vanguard party-led insurrections.

[334] Émile Combes (1835-1921) was a radical politician and the Prime Minister of France from 1902-1905. He pursued an aggressive policy of laïcisation that aimed for a strict separation between church and state.

accumulated wealth, ensure a minimum of leisure time for workers, and establish a social security system. The solidarist doctrine, developed by Léon Bourgeois,[335] was designed precisely to enable the Radical Party to curtail classic individualism.

But the most significant innovation he was compelled to accept wasn't state intervention; it was the formation of trade unions. The law of 1884 allowed workers to organize for the defense and study of their professional interests. We're well aware of what has sprung from this seed and the proliferation of unions that now cover the landscape of big industry. Would the men of the Revolution have desired this as well? Anyone who recalls the Le Chapelier Law[336] would find it paradoxical to assert that they would have supported such a thing. It explicitly prohibited workers from uniting "for their so-called common interests." And this veto wasn't the result of a worried assembly making a decision in a fleeting fit of bad temper; it reflected a mindset common among many revolutionary activists, who were themselves influenced by 18th-century philosophers, including Rousseau, who would not tolerate any intermediary bodies between the state and the individual. The abuses of the guilds and, more broadly, the kind of fragmentation that plagued the kingdom—nearly every group having privileges harmful to the whole as well as to industry—explain this near consensus. Proponents of trade unionism today are quick to point out that unions—organizations defending wages, and therefore with a limited goal, open to all workers within the same trade—should bear no resemblance to the calcified guilds of the ancien régime.

Regardless, trade unionism represents a crack in the individualist system cherished by the French Revolution. And at first glance, it appears challenging to simultaneously serve these two masters. This may explain

---

[335] Léon Bourgeois (1851–1925) was a political philosopher and Prime Minister of France from 1895 to 1896, as well as President of the Senate from 1920 to 1923. He pioneered "solidarism," which emphasized social interdependence and collective responsibility and advocated for the expansion of the welfare state.
[336] Le Chapelier Law was enacted at the start of the French Revolution that banned guilds and made the association of employers or workers illegal.

120

some uncertainty among the ranks of the Radicals. There are notable figures, like Joseph Caillaux,[337] who suggest that trade unionism could threaten not just individual freedom but also the authority of the state, and could ultimately "give rise to a new feudalism": thus, Jacobinism might be quite incompatible with trade unionism. However, the majority have come to accept these new approaches. They are convinced that without the backing of the unions, the state alone would be incapable of fulfilling its economic duties, and that workers would lack the most effective means to advocate for their interests. Wage labor is not forever: "As much as any other party," states the Declaration of the 1927 Congress, "the Radical-Socialist Party, which places the moral value of the individual and human rights at the core of its doctrine, declares that workers are not merchandise, and that wage labor should not be seen as the ultimate form of human labor." But if the wage labor system is indeed to be replaced by a true associative system, can one imagine that such a transformation could occur without the organized action of the trade unions? Thus, unions serve as both a shield for the individual and a lever for the state. Consequently, radicalism is eager to adopt, as a minimum program, the one formulated by the General Confederation of Labor[338]: it believes that by allying itself with trade unionism, it remains true to the spirit of the *Rights of Man*.

*
* *

It's clear that there wouldn't be as many subtleties or hesitations in communist thinking. It regards the *Declarations of Rights* as little more than hypocritical pretexts. In this context, it embraces Karl Marx's perspective, noting that in the French Revolution, the peak of idealism coincided with the peak of realism. Didn't emerging large-scale industry

---

[337] Joseph Caillaux (1863–1944) was a politician and the Prime Minister of France from 1911 to 1912. He was a fierce opponent of WWI and was an early advocate of a national income tax.
[338] The General Confederation of Labor (CGT) was founded in 1895 as a confederation of trade unions. It still operates today as the first of the five major French trade union confederations, with around 700,000 members.

need, to freely hire workers and impose its conditions, for French society to be reduced to a mere dust of atoms?

But wasn't this precisely the goal of the Revolution's axe as it chopped down the trade guilds? In this case, the idea was merely the servant of self-interest. In that case, what's the point of fretting over whether we remain true to "principles" that primarily express a bourgeois will to power?

Additionally, if we examine the mechanisms of democracy closely, we quickly realize that it operates through and for money; its entire apparatus is yet another sham. Therefore, those who seek genuine liberation for the working and peasant proletariat would be wise not to hold these principles or mechanisms in high regard. Workers should only heed their present economic circumstances and the unstoppable power they create by coming together.

Yet there is a chapter in the history of ideas during the French Revolution that communists must enjoy revisiting: the final chapter, the Babouvist chapter, cast to the winds in what Jaurès describes as the sublime convulsion, the final throes of the Revolution. We've already noted the prestige that Babouvism quickly reclaimed when Buonarroti, the former conspirator, fed the story of the Conspiracy for Equality to the youth hungry for revolution. The book became the bible for insurgents. Blanqui,[339] in particular, seems to be imbued with it, constantly preparing for decisive strikes and appearing to count on a successful skirmish to impose a new law. It is undeniable that Blanqui's tactics, and through him those of Babeuf, have helped shape one of the traditions that the Communist Party leans on: the tradition of decisive, swift action, foreshadowing and paving the way for the dictatorship of the proletariat.

However, Babouvist ideas could have reached contemporary communism through another conduit: the *Communist Manifesto* itself.

---

[339] Louis Auguste Blanqui (1805–1881) was a socialist philosopher. He advocated for the violent overthrow of the government and "revolutionary opportunism." As a result, Blanqui spent much of his life in prison.

Following Charles Andler's[340] authoritative commentary, it is no longer up for debate that the *Manifesto* primarily serves as a synthetic summary of earlier doctrines. And it has been established that its constructive portion draws direct inspiration from the French Revolution's experiments, shaped into decrees by Babouvism. Isn't it Babouvism that tasks the state—a state transformed by the conquest of workers, a proletarian state—with centralizing products and organizing production? Marx and Engels infuse Babouvism with industrialism while stripping away its asceticism. However, they preserve its collectivism. Therefore, when communists today praise the potential benefits of their ideology, we shouldn't merely dismiss it as the importation of some kind of Asian socialism tested in Russia: they too can legitimately lay claim to one of the traditions of the French Revolution.

*
* *

What, then, differentiates the Communist Party from the Socialist Party on this matter? It might be conceded that the Socialist Party isn't confined to the final chapter of the French Revolution; it can embrace a more extensive inheritance. Specifically, it wouldn't entirely renounce the sort of democratic idealism shaped by 18th-century philosophy, which the communists tend to discount.

Truthfully, when it comes to doctrinal structure, it is quite challenging to discern between socialism and communism in our times. Experience doesn't seem to have filled the frameworks outlined by Durkheim in his lectures on socialism. He posited that communism would chiefly focus on regulating consumption, while socialism would concentrate on reorganizing production. Yet in practice, 19th-century communism also criticized the anarchy of production, seeking to remedy it through the proletarian state's control over nationalized industries.

---

[340] Charles Andler (1866–1933) was a philosopher and Germanist. He established France's first German studies program in 1898 and wrote studies on Nietzsche, Fichte, and Marx. In 1901, Andler translated and incorporated commentary on Marx and Engels' *Le Manifeste Communiste*.

Meanwhile, the Socialist Party in France[341] seems to have sidelined its reformist tendencies, which also contained a critical stance towards Marxism, especially since it agreed to the unity pact. On the day this pact was signed, Guesde[342] triumphed over Jaurès. The merger was carried out under the auspices of the *Communist Manifesto*. And despite the significant revisionist efforts of recent times, it is the Marxist theories—capitalist concentration, the increase in the number of proletarians and the worsening of their conditions, the dictatorship of the proletariat, the transformation of private property into collective ownership—that still remain, at least in principle, the ABCs of both socialism and communism. These are the theories that supply the propaganda themes for both parties. Having undoubtedly experienced their persuasive power among the working masses, socialism is not willing to cede these advantages to communism.

However, there are undeniable differences in tone between the literature of the two parties. They may share the same underlying doctrine, but their practical stances are worlds apart. Communists cut and slash with the uncompromising attitude of a group far from the threshold of power in France. They express utter contempt, not just for all the reforms attempted thus far, but also for the peaceful and legal methods of action that a democratic system, in theory, offers to the masses. Didn't Lenin[343] declare, "Democracy is a state form that sanctions the

---

[341] The French Section of the Workers' International (SFIO) (1905-1969), which later became the Socialist Party (1969–), formed as a merger between the Marxist and Blanquist Socialist Party of France (1902-1905) and the Jaurèsist French Socialist Party (1902-1905).

[342] Jules Guesde (1845-1922) was one of the early popularizers of Marxism. He helped found the French Workers' Party (1880-1902) that merged with the Blanquist Central Revolution Committee (1881-1898) to become the Socialist Party of France. He served in the Chamber of Deputies for roughly 20 years.

[343] Vladimir Lenin (1870-1924) was a Russian Marxist political theorist, leader of the Bolshevik party, and the founding head of government of the Soviet Union from 1917 until his death. His "Marxist-Leninist" ideology was a prominent influence within the international communist movement.

124

subordination of the majority to the minority"?[344] And Trotsky,[345] in turn: "The proletarian doctrine views democracy as an instrument of bourgeois society"?[346] In light of this, their followers are prepared to choose social war—the only legitimate war, that of the proletarians of all nations against the privileged of all nations—over such hypocritical conventions. They embrace the prospect of systematic violence with open arms. And when questioned about what violence can build, they have an answer at the ready: "Look at what's happening in Russia."

What's happening in Russia doesn't spark the same fervor among socialists. They remain skeptical that the nationalizations they dream of could be implemented in a country that, according to Marxist theory, should have been the least prepared for them, given its lack of industrial development. In any case, they observe the trampling of both individual rights and the system of public liberties there, not just with respect to the bourgeoisie but also regarding the "majority" socialists. Nevertheless, they cling to these freedoms as a legitimate means for the disenfranchised to voice their concerns and demand a restructuring of the social order itself. They consider it natural for a nation fortunate enough to have such freedoms to defend this legacy. This implies that they are not willing to forsake the legacy of the Jacobins, the sans-culottes,[347] and the patriots of '93; they readily identify as heirs of the French Revolution. Certainly, they seek to extend its victories and to tackle issues that the Revolution only managed to raise, but they intend to do so by employing the principles it proclaimed and the weapons it forged. This means that they hold in equal

---

[344] V. I. Lenin: *The State and Revolution.* International Publishers, 1932, p. 68.
[345] Leon Trotsky (1879–1940) was a prominent Russian Marxist political theorist alongside Lenin. Following Lenin's death, Trotsky was outmaneuvered by Joseph Stalin (1878–1953) and fell from power. He wrote polemics on Stalin in exile, but was assassinated in his home in Mexico City by a Soviet agent.
[346] L. Trotsky: *Terrorism and Communism: A Reply to Karl Kautsky.* Translated by M. Schachtman. University of Michigan Press, 1961, p. 40.
[347] The sans-culottes were common people within the lower classes during the French Revolution. They were a key driving force during the Revolution and were generally seen as "radicals" pushing for direct democracy.

esteem the idea of equal rights for all humans and that of the sovereignty of the people.

The tradition shines most clearly and brilliantly in the ideas of the man who for so long led the Socialist Party in France, whose memory is revered not only by socialists but also by a broad swath of democrats: Jean Jaurès. His thinking was especially complex, weaving together very diverse elements. In it, the traditions of German socialism converge with those of French socialism. Hegel maintains his presence in this multi-denominational temple, alongside Fourier and Saint-Simon. And Marx's contributions are highly celebrated for combining the teachings of German dialectics with those of English political economy, positioning the entire history of the world around the struggles of one class, the working class, whose crucifixion destines them as the instrument of universal salvation. Jaurès recognized the truth in this philosophy. He was also aware of its proven propagandistic power. Since the unity pact, the disciplined Jaurès appeared to have muted his critique of Marxism. However, he couldn't resist enhancing it, even correcting it in his own way. Many of his corrections seem to draw from his deep reverence for the French Revolution. Let's revisit the preface of his monumental history of the Constituent Assembly. He was loath to accept, after recounting so many significant intellectual battles and acts of heroism, that the mind is strictly bound by material forces, that principles merely reflect self-interest, or that heroes are merely agents, and "acted upon" at that, in economic history. This is why he unexpectedly brought together three names, placing his history under their combined patronage: Marx, Michelet,[348] and Plutarch.[349]

Moreover, he believed there is much worth preserving from the principles the Revolution proclaimed, and that they could still serve a

---

[348] Jules Michelet (1798–1874) was a historian considered to be the founder of historiography. He attempted to explain history through the perspective of commoners and was a pioneer in archival research.
[349] Plutarch (46–119) was a Greek Platonist, Apollonian priest, and historian. He is primarily remembered for his biographies of well-known Greek and Roman emperors and philosophers.

useful purpose. By comparing the ideal they represent with today's social reality, as shaped by large-scale industry, couldn't the people logically demand a number of substantial reforms? In this regard, Jaurès certainly didn't scorn the values enshrined in the *Declaration of the Rights of Man*. Without the sentiments it inspired and popularized, would we react to economic injustice in the same way? Furthermore, it's clear that the principles it espouses would remain ineffectual for the majority, if a new organization of industrial life didn't safeguard genuine freedom for all: "Only socialism can fully realize the *Declaration of the Rights of Man* and actualize true human rights." Elsewhere, Jaurès endeavored to systematically bridge the terms that others have systematically set in opposition, those who wish to widen the chasm between the traditions of the 18th century as embodied in the Revolution and the goals of socialism: "Socialism is individualism, but logical and complete." The ultimate goal is always the liberation of human beings. But if we want this liberation to be more than a mere platitude for the majority of workers, who are essentially serfs of the industrial machine, we must be willing to employ methods beyond the "laissez-faire" approach so cherished by economic liberalism.

Jaurès thus strove in every way to closely weld democratic idealism with socialist realism. As for the extent to which his thinking still dominates in the socialist party today, that is hard to pinpoint. It's well known that very different currents are clashing within the unified socialist party at this very moment. Yet it's noteworthy that representatives from these various currents turn to the bust of Jaurès, set up at the lectern of their congresses, and call upon his authority. His prestige has not diminished. And it's probable that if his work continues not only to enlighten minds but also to stir souls, it is partly due to the role he assigned to the memories of the French Revolution within socialist philosophy.

Chapter V

Assessment of Saint-Simonism: Past

The centenary of Henri de Saint-Simon's death, commemorated in the grand amphitheater of the Sorbonne in 1925, appears to have sparked a resurgence of interest in Saint-Simonian studies.

Maxime Leroy, who had already published *Socialism of the Producers*,[350] has authored *Life of the Count of Saint-Simon*.[351] Alfred Péreire[352] has reprinted *Letters of an Inhabitant of Geneva to His Contemporaries* according to the original edition, accompanied by two previously unpublished works, *Letters to the Europeans* and *Essay on Social Organization*. Following the *Doctrine of Saint-Simon*,[353] a series of lectures from 1829 that I reissued with the help of Elie Halévy,[354] I have made *The Work of Henri de Saint-Simon*[355] available to the public with a selection of organized excerpts ("Philosophy of Sciences," "Organization of Peace," "Socialist Industrialism," "Religion of the Future"). Henry-René d'Allemagne[356] has published a comprehensive volume recounting *The History of the Saint-Simonians from 1827 to 1837*. Richly illustrated, it brings to life their personalities and the

---

[350] *Socialisme des producteurs* (1924).

[351] *Vie du Comte de Saint-Simon* (1925).

[352] Alfred Péreire (1879–1957) was a historian and the grandson of Isaac Péreire. He reprinted the *Lettres d'un habitant de Genève à ses contemporains* (1803), *Lettres aux Européens,* and *Essai sur l'organisation sociale* in 1924.

[353] *Doctrine de Saint-Simon* (1829–1830). Republished by Bouglé and Halévy in 1924.

[354] Élie Halévy (1870–1937) was a historian, philosopher, and close friend of Bouglé's. He wrote several works on British utilitarianism and 19th-century England. He was the brother of Daniel Halévy.

[355] *L'œuvre de Henri de Saint-Simon* (1925).

[356] Henry-René d'Allemagne (1863–1950) was a librarian and historian who published on many different topics. He wrote the 1930 *Les Saint-Simoniens, 1827–1837*.

caricatures they inspired. Jehan d'Ivray[357] has penned *The Saint-Simonian Adventure and Women*. Lastly, Charléty[358] after presenting *Extracts from Enfantin* in the Social Reformers collection, has reissued his own thesis from 1895, *History of Saint-Simonism*, shortly after G. Weill's[359] work on *A Precursor of Socialism: Saint-Simon and His Work*, which has significantly aided the sort of resurgence we are observing, supplements the bibliography from the first edition with a list that includes over 130 titles.

Now is therefore an opportune moment to conduct an assessment of Saint-Simonism, catalog the ideas its followers have introduced to the world, and identify which have gained acceptance. Benedetto Croce[360] has written a renowned book titled *What is Living and What is Dead of the Philosophy of Hegel*. All other things being equal, we would like to undertake a similar examination of Saint-Simonian thought.

"The world will divide our remains," Enfantin, the pope turned businessman, proudly declared, all the while maintaining his deep faith. And Karl Grün,[361] one of the Germans who came to Paris between 1830 and 1848 to gauge the new France, remarked, "Saint-Simonism is like a box full of seeds: the box has been opened, its contents have scattered to

---

[357] Jehan d'Ivray (1861–1940) was a writer who primarily wrote on the topics of Egypt, the Orient, and feminism. She lived in Egypt for over 40 years but returned to France after the death of her husband in 1919. She wrote the 1930 book *L'aventure Saint-Simonienne et les femmes*.

[358] Sébastien Charléty (1867–1945) was a historian specializing in classical antiquity and 19th century history. He was a Dreyfusard and had deep interest in Saint-Simonism. Charléty wrote the 1930 *Extraits d'Enfantin* as well as the reissued his thesis as *Histoire du Saint-Simonisme* in 1931.

[359] Georges Weill (1865–1944) was a historian specializing in socialism and republicanism. He wrote the 1894 book *Un précurseur du socialisme: Saint-Simon et son œuvre*.

[360] Benedetto Croce (1866–1952) was an Italian historian, philosopher, and politician. He is generally considered one of the last great idealist philosophers and argued that Hegel's ideas offered a third way between positivism and Marxism. He notably opposed Mussolini's fascist regime.

[361] Karl Grün (1817–1887) was a German socialist and former Young Hegelian. Like Marx, Grün spent some time in Paris where he associated with socialists like Victor Considerant, Pierre Leroux, and Proudhon.

parts unknown, but each seed has found a furrow and we have watched them emerge from the earth one by one."

Have these prophecies been fulfilled?

*
* *

It may come as a surprise that the modern world owes much to Saint-Simon and the Saint-Simonians. Despite their tumultuous lives, adventures, and eccentricities, many of their ideas have proven fruitful, practical, and well-suited to societal needs. Reading through the history that Charléty narrates with a particularly delightful blend of sympathy and irony, we encounter a procession of hotheads, agitators, zealots, and dabblers. Are we then to believe, as Sir James Frazer[362] is fond of saying of primitive peoples, that here too, "madness mysteriously gives way to reason"?

Saint-Simon is immediately captivating. His biography reads like a beautiful novel, or better yet, a beautiful film! The opening scene: a young nobleman, who dreams of his ancestors Count de Vermandois and even Charlemagne, is awakened at five in the morning by his valet reminding him, "Remember, my lord, you are destined for great deeds." From an early age, he believes that aristocrats must distinguish themselves by the brilliance of their service to humanity. As the young count reaches adulthood, America stirs, the world is in upheaval, and the flag of rebellion is raised against England. Saint-Simon sets sail with Lafayette[363]

---

[362] James Frazer (1854–1941) was a Scottish anthropologist largely focused on comparative religion. His work also explored the interplay between rationality and irrationality in order to make sense of how different cultures interpret the world, often in ways that seemed "mad" from the Western perspective.

[363] Gilbert du Motier (1757–1834), better known as Lafayette, was an aristocrat who volunteered in the Continental Army during the American Revolutionary War (1775–1783). He later severed in the National Assembly during the early years of the French Revolution. Additionally, he commanded the French National Guard but fell out of favor and fled to Austria where he was imprisoned from 1792 to 1797. Lafayette is sometimes argued to have embodied the ideals of democracy, cosmopolitanism, and Franco-American cooperation.

later stating that his goal was to defend the cause of "industrial liberty" on American soil. He bravely performs his duty, suffering a wound to the thigh in a naval battle. Yet beneath the soldier's exterior, the engineer and businessman are already piercing through. Saint-Simon suggests to the Viceroy of Mexico the creation of a canal connecting the Atlantic and Pacific Oceans through Panama. His primary interest is already the exploitation of the globe, and he recognizes the necessity of science. Upon his return to service in Belgium, he is found eagerly pursuing knowledge, attending Monge's[364] lectures with great enthusiasm. But to gain knowledge, one also needs the means provided by wealth. Saint-Simon takes advantage of the Revolution, which complicates life for the nobility, to become a kind of *nouveau riche*. In partnership with a German, de Redern,[365] he dives into business, establishes bazaars, bids for the lead roofing of Notre-Dame, and speculates on national properties. It's a period of opulence, of grand receptions. Saint-Simon gathers scholars of all sorts at his table, seeking to learn from them between courses. He even marries, claiming it to be in the name of science, asking Mlle de Champgrand[366] to maintain his household with the appropriate splendor. After his marriage quickly dissolves, he considers marrying Mme de Staël,[367] imagining their union could produce genius. She declines. Saint-Simon finds solace in writing the *Letters from an Inhabitant of Geneva to His Contemporaries* in 1803, urging the peoples of Europe to properly honor science and its practitioners by providing the best among them with the means to free themselves, unite, and

---

[364] Gaspard Monge (1746–1818) was a mathematician and politician during the French Revolution. He made important contributions in descriptive geometry and helped to establish the École Polytechnique. Monge also held prominent positions in the French Republic and the First French Empire.

[365] Sigismund Ehrenreich Johann von Redern (1761–1841) was a German-French aristocrat and diplomat.

[366] Alexandrine-Sophie Goury de Champgrand (1773–1860), who went by the penname Baroness Sophie de Bawr, was a highly successful writer, playwright and composer who married Saint-Simon in 1801.

[367] Germaine de Staël (1766–1817) was a political theorist and influential salon hostess who was persecuted by Napoleon I and forced into exile multiple times. She was a prominent advocate of representative democracy as well as greater freedoms for women.

132

enlighten the world. However, the scene soon darkens. His partner de Redern is bankrupted. To make ends meet, Saint-Simon takes a job as a copyist at the pawnshop, with assistance from his valet. Nonetheless, the gentleman-copyist pens *Introduction to the Scientific Works of the Nineteenth Century*,[368] followed by *Memoir on the Science of Man*[369] and *Work on Gravitation*.[370] He also vehemently criticizes the members of the Bureau of Longitudes,[371] branding them anarchists for not recognizing the importance of his efforts towards higher coordination: he aimed to advance science by a "Napoleonic leap." Soon, more urgent issues demand his attention: on the eve of the Congress of Vienna,[372] he and his secretary Augustin Thierry draft an ambitious plan for the reorganization of European society. But can peace truly be established without the orderly advancement of industry? From 1817, Saint-Simon becomes the champion of industry, the advocate for industrialists. For their sake, to elevate their role in the world, he composes "Catechisms" in collaboration with Auguste Comte. Yet many grow weary of supporting him, and Saint-Simon himself becomes exhausted from constantly seeking assistance. In a moment of despair, he shoots himself in the head. After a miraculous recovery, he regains his fervor and is thrilled to see

---

[368] *Introduction aux travaux scientifiques du XIXème siècle* (1808).

[369] *Mémoire sur la science de l'homme* (1813).

[370] *Travail sur la gravitation* (1813).

[371] The Bureau des Longitudes (1795-) is a scientific institution focused on technological improvements that was created during the French Revolution.

[372] The Congress of Vienna (1814-1815) was a set of international diplomatic meetings among the European powers to decide on the political arrangement of Europe following the downfall of Napoleon Bonaparte.

distinguished men like Olinde Rodrigues,[373] Léon Halévy,[374] Duveyrier,[375] and Carnot[376] rally around him. And when he passes away in 1825, entrusting them to publish his *New Christianity*,[377] he exclaims with great passion: "The future is ours."

This elite group, which was destined to grow, became excited about his teachings. Graduates of the École Polytechnique,[378] like Enfantin, and financiers such as the Péreire brothers[379] joined the original disciples. They published a magazine, *The Producer*,[380] which in itself was a statement of intent, and it was followed by *The Organizer*,[381] another rallying cry. They held numerous conferences and developed an entire philosophy of history to justify their trust in revitalized industry, which soon took on the characteristics of a religion. Here, the lecturers turned apostles retreated to Ménilmontant,[382] where they practiced solidarity and

---

[373] Olinde Rodrigues (1795-1851) was a banker, economist, and philosopher. He was an early advocate for worker cooperatives and argued that capitalism tended to monopolies. He expressed early suppositions about marginal utility theory and concepts related to equilibrium that anticipated marginalism.

[374] Léon Halévy (1802-1883) was a historian and dramatist. He was the last secretary of Saint-Simon from 1824 to 1825, as well as the grandfather of Élie Halévy and Daniel Halévy.

[375] Charles Duveyrier (1803-1866) was a playwright and propagator of Saint-Simonism. He was also the father of the famous explorer and geographer Henri Duveyrier (1840-1892).

[376] Nicolas Léonard Sadi Carnot (1796-1832) was a mechanical engineer and military scientist, commonly referred to as the "father of thermodynamics." He was a major influence on later physicists, including Clausius, Kelvin, and Maxwell. He died at only 36 years old, most likely from cholera.

[377] *Le nouveau christianisme* (1825).

[378] The École polytechnique (1794-) is a grande école in France that specializes in science and engineering.

[379] Émile Péreire (1800-1875) and Isaac Péreire (1806-1880), were brothers known for developing France's finance system during the Second French Empire and challenging the powerful Rothschild banking family.

[380] *Le producteur* (1825-1826).

[381] *L'organisateur* (1830-1831). It was named in homage to Saint-Simon's political magazine of the same name that ran from 1819 to 1820.

[382] Ménilmontant is a neighborhood in Paris that was once a hub for Saint-Simonism. Following the 1831 schism in the Church, Enfantin and his followers formed a short-lived community in the neighborhood.

labor, tilled the land while singing hymns written by Félicien David,[383] and during days of riots, they carried their pacifying banner through the suburbs. But Enfantin and Bazard,[384] in the process of becoming Popes, soon clashed. Enfantin voiced some peculiar claims about women and the rights of the high priest in matters of love. Discord intensified, leading to a split. The group, adopting the moniker *Compagnons de la femme* ("Companions of Woman"), dusted the ingratitude of the big city off their shoes and set sail for the East. After a series of adventures, they found themselves in Egypt, where the entrepreneurial and organizational skills of the Saint-Simonians resurfaced. Among other initiatives, they developed a plan for the piercing of the Suez Isthmus.[385] Forced out of Cairo by the plague and returning to France, most of them resumed using their business acumen. Enfantin himself, with the help of the Péreires, took the helm of enterprises like the Crédit Mobilier and the P.-L.-M. Company.[386] The disciples of Saint-Simon became intermediaries between industry and finance, not only drilling through isthmuses but also laying down railways. "We must march forward on the railways," Enfantin often said. But he was convinced that through the railways, through the expansion of industry, the Saint-Simonian idea would succeed in conquering the world.

---

[383] Félicien David (1810–1876) was a popular composer known for integrating eastern musical influences into western classic styles. He travelled with the Saint-Simonians to the Egypt and wrote music for them. David later received widespread acclaim for his symphonic poems, ballets, and operas.

[384] Saint-Amand Bazard (1791–1832) was one of the key founders of the religion of Saint-Simonism. His heated arguments with Enfantin on the issue of the emancipation of women led to them getting into a violent altercation, in which Bazard died from his injuries.

[385] The Isthmus of Suez is a 78 mile-wide (125 kilometer) land bridge that divides Africa and Asia.

[386] Crédit Mobilier and Compagnie P.-L.-M were immensely successful banking and railway companies, respectively, created by the Péreire brothers, that heavily influenced the development of Europe.

*
* *

What is this idea, or rather, what are these ideas that to which the Saint-Simonians clung above all else, even after they had rejoined the ranks of the mainstream?

I deliberately say *ideas* because, although the system was meant to be tightly integrated, some parts of it could remain vibrant, while others might wither. Religion, pacifism, industrialism, socialism—these tendencies are distinguishable, and they would not necessarily share the same fate.

Religion serves as the pinnacle, the culmination of all Saint-Simonian thought. Saint-Simonism didn't start out as a Church. But very soon, as acknowledged by most of the contributors to *The Producer*, the School felt the need to transform into a Church. "Saint-Simonian Religion" was, to the great surprise of the associate Jules Vinçard,[387] the headline on the posters that Saint-Simon's followers soon plastered on the walls of the Latin Quarter[388] to invite the people to their gatherings. By 1829, when they interpreted the Saint-Simon's teachings in *Doctrine of Saint-Simon,* Bazard's notable series of lectures, they hinted that although they used the language of science and employed reason and evidence, it was merely a concession to the times. They were keen to invoke emotion to guide souls back to faith—not just any vague humanitarian longing, but a true faith, anchored in a doctrine and upheld by a hierarchy. Saint-Simonism, too, aimed to erect a cathedral. If we wish to grasp its true nature, we cannot ignore this endeavor.

Did Saint-Simon himself dream of or want this? Commentators argue about it. Georges Dumas[389] has long portrayed the great man as an exalted messiah. In contrast, Maxime Leroy leads us to admire him as a

---

[387] Jules Vinçard (1796–1878) was an artisan, writer, and Saint-Simonian.
[388] In Paris, the Latin Quarter is around the Sorbonne and is known for its student life.
[389] Georges Dumas (1866–1946) was a leading psychologist and medical doctor who wrote several works on Saint-Simon and Auguste Comte.

clear-headed individual, a true secularist, a child of the 18th century. And indeed, he shares much with the Encyclopedists: he, too, relied on scientific progress to foster human progress of humanity. Yet he aimed to surpass the perspective of the "critical periods,"[390] which his disciples would later scrutinize. He commended theocrats "for having understood the utility of systematic unity." Ultimately, he authored *New Christianity*, which, while criticizing Protestantism and Catholicism for their lack of zeal in transforming the earth for the betterment of the masses, intimates that a faith that unites and inspires is a valuable asset for improving their physical and moral fate. On his deathbed, he was to declare: "People thought that all religious systems were bound to vanish because the obsolescence of the Catholic system had been proven. They were mistaken: religion cannot disappear from the world; it merely changes. Rodrigues, do not forget this, and also remember that to accomplish great things, one must be passionate."

Is it any wonder that, with such memories, the disciples found, as Charléty notes, the makings of a redeemer and the substance of a religion?

Once united, and fired up by their very union, they leaned heavily in this direction, steering their vessel toward the mystical. In response to the excess of the positive mindset that they felt was threatening to engulf them, they energetically rejected the prevailing notion that religion was a thing of the past, obsolete and outdated. Proudhon would eagerly emphasize this point. And Auguste Comte—who, having left Saint-Simon, withdrew into his own domain; Erdan[391] calls him the Achilles of Saint-Simonism—seemed, even in 1830, to maintain the same stance.

---

[390] To Saint-Simon, society moved from "organic periods," where social and political forces harmoniously reinforced each other, to "critical periods," where they fell into conflict and war with each other.
[391] Alexandre André Jacob (1826–1878), whose pen name was Alexandre Erdan, was a writer and journalist known for being a fierce critic of clerics.

But Bazard and Enfantin, in the 17th Session of the *Exposition of the Doctrine of Saint-Simon*, closely contested the conclusions that might be drawn against religion from a misinterpreted law of the three stages. On closer examination, we find that each stage of humanity's development is marked by a growth in the intensity and breadth of religious ideas. Beliefs are purified and expanded. Yet humanity never ceases to have beliefs. To prepare humanity to embrace ours, tailored to its current needs, we should strive to convince it that a great religious future lies ahead. The time has come to unfurl the banners once more.

It's no surprise, therefore, that Sainte-Beuve[392] commended Saint-Simonism primarily for having "provided the concept of a religion and respect for this social form, the highest of all, to many who were previously without"—or that Carlyle[393] lamented not having learned earlier that near the Palais-Royal,[394] "amid the cafés and billiard rooms of your youthful city," as he wrote to d'Eichthal,[395] "a group of apostles was nurturing a new religion within its midst."

The religion that was being nurtured would itself spawn "dogmas" quite scandalous to the Christian faith. Christianity, accustomed to dualism, often contrasts the spirit with the flesh, nature with God. It is this very dualism that the Saint-Simonians aimed to abolish at any cost. A core part of their mission of reconciliation was to vindicate the flesh, which for them signified not so much a license for passions—as has been too frequently claimed—but rather an advocacy for labor, a call for well-being, and a celebration of industry. A sort of pantheism among the graduates

---

[392] Charles Augustin Sainte-Beuve (1804–1869) was a novelist and literary critic, particularly of biographies and history.

[393] Thomas Carlyle (1795–1881) was an important Scottish historian and philosopher who was influenced by the Saint-Simonians. He wrote the renowned 1837 work *The French Revolution*. Carlyle was a prominent conservative public intellectual and coined the term the "dismal science" in reference to economics.

[394] The Palais-Royal is a former royal palace and shopping arcade in Paris that, during the French Revolution, became known as the Palais de l'Égalité.

[395] Gustave d'Eichthal (1804–1886) was a Saint-Simonian philosopher and economist interested in Hellenism and the Greek language.

of the École Polytechnique, envisioning God as a colossal worker, is apparent in their effusive expressions.

*

* *

If humanity were to rally behind this banner, we wouldn't just see advancements in industry, but also the establishment of peace—a deeply held belief among all Saint-Simonians. And this belief, at least, they can confidently claim to have adopted directly from their master. We've noted that Saint-Simon wrote *Letters from an Inhabitant of Geneva* in 1803, and in 1814, with the help of Augustin Thierry, he produced the *Plan of Works Necessary for the Organization of Humanity.*[396] In the former, he called on nations to send a number of scholars to Geneva, to gather around Newton's tomb and agree on the course for humanity. In the latter, urging nations to emulate England and France, which have established parliamentary systems, he envisioned the "supremacy of a general Parliament"—what we would now call a super-Parliament. Positioned above all national governments and endowed with the authority to settle their disputes, this body would not only serve as an arbiter but also coordinate and oversee projects of international public benefit, ultimately making Europe "livable" and fostering in the hearts of the new generations the development of a "European patriotism."

The disciples were determined to prove, through a genuine philosophy of history, that such an undertaking was both possible and necessary, and that this edifice stood as a culmination. They did not deny the scale and significance of war, acknowledging that the past has largely been an expansive, systematized state of warfare. However, they observed a gradual shift where cooperation was increasingly triumphing over conflict. Battles between groups or within them, which once perpetuated each other, were progressively diminishing. The realms of security were expanding. The City was uniting families. The Nation was enforcing a shared order among the cities it united. Churches were extending beyond

---

[396] *Plan des travaux nécessaires pour l'organisation de l'humanité.*

the boundaries of Nations. And the Saint-Simonians simultaneously proclaimed and summoned the rise of an even broader and novel grouping, one that should probably embody aspects of both the state and the Church. The concept remained slightly vague. The river forged ahead through the fog. Yet regarding the course and force of the stream, these philosopher-apostles harbored no doubts.

The force that drives everything else, it is well known, should be sought in industry. This militia of apostles was a corps of engineers. A better exploitation of the globe was their central ideal. And their hymns strongly reacted against the ascetic tendency, hostile to the progress of material civilization, justified by various memories: the anathemas of Christianity against the flesh, Rousseau's indictments against the sciences and arts, or even Spartan declamations against luxury. Buonarroti, as we have seen, in recalling the work of Babeuf, reminded us of the duel that took place during the Revolution itself, between the "Athenians," apologists for commercial expansion, and the "Spartiates," ready to reduce everyone's consumption to ensure equality. But equality in deprivation was the most opposite directive to the wishes of the Saint-Simonians. They were convinced that their highest hopes—the religious future of humanity, the organization of peace—would remain dead letters if the wheel of industry were to stop. They were grateful to their initiator for having pushed this wheel. "Everything through industry, everything for it," Saint-Simon had cried out, transposing a sentiment that would later be echoed by Lincoln.[397] And from 1817 onward, his primary focus was to elevate a new class to prominence: the industrialists. It was he who transformed this adjective into a noun, edited the *Papers of the Industrialists*[398] to spotlight their specific claims, and most clearly implied that through the improved methods of exploiting the earth, a new economic power has emerged, demanding an increasing share of political power. Shouldn't the eminent services of a class secure it a higher right?

---

[397] Abraham Lincoln (1809–1865) was the president of the US from 1861 until his assassination during the American Civil War. In the Gettysburg Address, he stated, "Government by the people, for the people..." and emphasized a system of governance accountable to its people.
[398] *Cahiers des industriels* (1823–1824).

"We set out," Saint-Simon declared, "to raise industrialists to the highest level of esteem and power." In his eyes, human labor, the transformation of matter, holds the utmost value; fundamentally, in his view, industrial labor creates all values, both social and economic, the value of people as well as things. And this is why the engineer was Saint-Simon's preferred figure. He certainly didn't demote the farmers, revered by Quesnay, to unproductive status: he assigned them their place next to the merchant and the manufacturer. But in the end, the latter, servants of progress, production, and consumption, constantly went up in his estimation. He would undoubtedly support the petition presented by the banker Laffitte,[399] with whom he maintained regular relations, when Laffitte lamented that by wanting to base national representation on land tax, one might indirectly strip commerce and industry of their undeniable rights, to sacrifice the active element vitalizing the entire society to the inert substance, to the land that bears it: "this land still bearing the marks of superstition and anarchy."

By championing these demands, Saint-Simon not only directly contradicted Quesnay on certain matters, he also went beyond and eclipsed Sieyès. He too undoubtedly spoke as an advocate of the Third Estate, successor to the Communes, and even a distant representative of the "Gauls" so long oppressed by the "Franks." Yet he was an advocate with little patience for lawyers;[400] or the military, for that matter. "Sword-wielders" and "talkers" were both seen as equally perilous in his view. That's why he wouldn't envision the hierarchy of social classes in the same manner as Sieyès, the legalist. He explicitly blamed the legalists for the Revolution's failure. It was time to make way for the men of action, those who work on tangible things, who handle matter, who prepare for a better arrangement of the world not just through speeches, decrees, or

---

[399] Jacques Laffitte (1767–1844) was a prominent banker and the first Prime Minister of France during the July Monarchy from 1830 to 1831. During the Revolution of 1830, Laffitte funded and helped organize the liberal groups that overthrew Charles X in order to put Louis-Philippe I on the throne.

[400] The original French, *c'est un avocat qui n'aime pas les avocats*, is a play on words, the word *avocat* meaning both "advocate" and "lawyer."

141

memos, but through actual production: placing producers not just above aristocrats, but also above the bourgeoisie themselves, like bees over hornets.

It's crucial not to conflate producers with workers in the sense of laborers or proletarian servants to machinery. The Saint-Simonians would later declare that the time had come to establish the "workers' party," and some, spreading the gospel in the suburbs and setting up a "workers'" rank, would draw ever closer to the proletariat. However, when Saint-Simon issued his rallying cry, he didn't draw this distinction within the collective he represented. The workers were not seen as distinct from their natural leaders. Indeed, for Saint-Simon, it was evident that they could accomplish nothing without their leaders. Most Saint-Simonians would stay true to the master's vision, which was hierarchical in nature. They were as opposed to inheritance as they were confident in individual abilities: let these abilities have the freedom they need, even if it means offering incentives. Saint-Simonism is, above all, an endorsement of business leaders, technicians, and organizers of production. And at the pinnacle, above the business leader himself, sits the banker: a general who coordinates the efforts of those whom Carlyle would famously dub the "captains of industry." Hadn't Saint-Simon himself already asserted that the banking industry's role was to connect the disparate groups of farmers, manufacturers, and merchants?

It's worth mentioning that in this system, intellectuals (yet another term Saint-Simon sought to elevate) maintain their significance. His followers would certainly emphasize this point. Industry, more than anything, requires the expertise of scientists. It also requires the creativity of artists if the public is to become excited about its achievements. This is why Enfantin, with the help of Arlès-Dufour,[401] would later advocate for the concept of *Intellectual Credit*. He would call for an increase in scholarships to nurture talent. He recognized, and often reiterated, that intelligence is the primary wealth of nations. Yet within this framework,

---

[401] François Barthélemy Arlès-Dufour (1797–1872) was a Saint-Simonian inventor, watchmaker, and railway pioneer. He is considered one of the founders of Swiss watchmaking due to his innovations in horology.

intelligence remains dedicated to serving industry, and its advancement is seen as the introduction to all other progress.

Yet there's a crucial condition that the Saint-Simonians would emphasize more and more: the improved exploitation of the earth must also lead to reduced exploitation of human beings by one another; industrialism must be enhanced, and if needed, restrained by socialism.

*

* *

The term "socialism" wasn't used by the Saint-Simonians, but the concept certainly was. The term had been attributed to Grotius[402] as far back as the 18th century. By the early 19th century, it was employed to describe the theories and experiments of Robert Owen.[403] Pierre Leroux[404] introduced it in France between 1830 and 1835, opposing it to individualism. The Saint-Simonians were fond of this same dichotomy, but they didn't use the same language. Sometimes they referred to it as "collectivism." More often, they were content with the term "association." And when they repeatedly professed that the era of association would succeed the era of antagonism, it should be understood that they were heralding the advent of a socialist regime. Its time had arrived; it stood on our threshold.

---

[402] Hugo Grotius (1583-1645) was a Dutch politician, philosopher, and jurist. He is considered to be a pioneer in the promotion of international law and held that it should be based on international cooperation, natural reason, and morality. Grotius was notably imprisoned and exiled for his views.

[403] Robert Owen (1771-1858) was a Welsh manufacturer who sought to reform industrial working conditions. He advocated for cooperative communities and secular education. He set up several experimental communities in the US, the most notable being in New Harmony, Indiana, that all failed within a few years.

[404] Pierre Leroux (1797-1871) was a political economist, philosopher, and a former Saint-Simonian. He coined the term "socialisme" in a disparaging reference to the Saint-Simonians. For example, see Leroux's 1834 essay "Individualism and Socialism" (translated by Shawn Wilbur and available on *The Libertarian Labyrinth*).

Should we then say that in this respect as well, Saint-Simon himself blazed a trail for his followers, and accept, in line with the notable assertion, that the last of the gentlemen was also the first of the socialists? It has been pointed out that he maintained ongoing relationships with financiers, employers, and the upper-middle class. He adopted many of their claims as his own. Didn't he serve them as much as, or even more than, he used them? Maybe. But what if, amid these dealings, he was pursuing his vision? And what if that vision was indeed to end economic chaos for the benefit of the laboring masses? He had long stated that the top priority of the budget should be to ensure employment for the able-bodied and provide for the disabled. His disdain for the "drones," for anyone who could live idly without lifting a finger, became increasingly evident; he identified the ultimate goal of humanity's progress as the improvement of the material and moral condition of the most numerous and poorest class. And when he finally penned his intellectual will, *New Christianity*, it was to solemnly remind the world's elite, in a reproach that echoed like a warning, that one concern should trump all others: the social welfare of the poor.

But in the end, these were merely aspirations and beginnings. From these foundational stones, the disciples would erect an entire structure. And it is truly to them that the credit is due for creating the reservoir of arguments that would sustain socialism for many years to come.

Very deliberately and systematically, they set their perspective against that of liberal political economy, the support for the social order or, more accurately, disorder of their time. Political economy lacks a sense of history as well as a social awareness. It has no clear understanding of wholes or phases. It fails to recognize the measures essential to the very existence of groups, to the harmony of their components. It also doesn't grasp that these measures can change over time, based on the structure of these groups and the level of development they have reached. In itself, it represents a phase of economic life that is in the process of being surpassed.

What this means is that the Saint-Simonians were prepared to challenge the sacred tenet of economic liberalism, the institution touted as eternal, universal, and immutable: private property. They vehemently exposed the abuses it led to. Ultimately, they disputed the very principle of private property itself.

Inheritance was undoubtedly seen by them as the ultimate scandal. Having clashed with their families when they were wealthy, or, if they were from poorer backgrounds, having faced various hurdles to their success, they understood personally what it means to be an unrecognized talent. They recognized the perilous and unjust advantage that notoriously lesser men possess, bolstered by the fortunes their parents left them, rendering them incapable of fulfilling the social duties demanded by their economic status. That's why the Saint-Simonians began by calling for the abolition of collateral inheritance, followed by a tax on direct inheritance. They ultimately contemplated, without any trepidation, the elimination of an institution that, by rewarding the luck of birth, stood as the primary barrier to their ideal of allowing each individual to contribute according to their abilities and be compensated according to their deeds.

But would simply eliminating heirs be enough? More broadly, can the existence of rentiers be justified? Should the ability to live without working be preserved in a society where everything relies on labor? "Idlers versus workers," Chateaubriand[405] noted, is an antithesis of great importance. The Saint-Simonians emphasized this with relish. They cheered the famous definition of aristocracy proposed by General Foy[406]: "a class that wants to consume without producing"; they noted that this mark of shame applies to anyone who lives off their investments. Thus, they celebrated the reduction of rental income. They would heartily

---

[405] François-René, vicomte de Chateaubriand (1768–1848) was a writer, historian, and politician. He played a major role in the development of Romanticism in France. Chateaubriand promoted anti-Enlightenment and sentimental Catholic perspectives.
[406] Maximilien Sébastien Foy (1775–1825) was a prominent military officer, politician, and writer. He was an ardent defender of civil liberties and outspoken critic of ultra-royalist policies.

145

endorse its complete elimination. Here, the Saint-Simonians fervently undertook what would become a major theme in socialist literature: the struggle against unearned income.

The core of all this reasoning is the notion that property is a historical category. Here again the word *socialism* is absent. It wouldn't be spoken until Rodbertus,[407] yet a Rodbertus who seems to have been profoundly influenced by the teachings of the Saint-Simonians. No one did more than they to immerse the absoluteness of property in the Heraclitean[408] stream. There was a time when people owned other people; now, we only own things. The right to bequeath was once completely unrestricted; now, it's constrained by numerous limitations. It's no longer what it once was; why should it remain what it is now? Everything changes. Even the most revered institutions must adjust to meet the evolving needs of humanity.

However, it's easy to demonstrate that humanity has not achieved complete fulfillment within the current legal framework. The clearest evidence lies in the existence of a proletariat, whose freedom is merely in name. Proletarians are depicted by the authors of the *Exposition of the Doctrine of Saint-Simon* as the direct descendants of slaves, commoners, serfs. Though less oppressed than their forebears, they are still oppressed, lacking the material means to leverage their abilities or to be compensated according to their deeds. For them, too many proclaimed rights remain theoretical, which they are unable to realize in practice. Therefore, it cannot be claimed that humanity's progress in harnessing

---

[407] Johann Karl Rodbertus (1805–1875) was a German economist, socialist, and a politician within the Prussian government, often remembered as an advocate for the labor theory of value. Rodbertus promoted state intervention and the collective ownership of land.

[408] Heraclitus (around 500 BCE) was a pre-Socratic Greek philosopher who taught that everything is in permanently in flux and in a constant state of "becoming." He stated that: "No man ever steps in the same river twice." Heraclitus also argued that fire was the most fundamental element and the source of all change.

the world's resources has eradicated the exploitation of one human being by another in all its forms.

What, then, is required? What measures must be taken? In short, what is the positive aspect of this socialism, the negative aspects of which we have just outlined?

Everything that the "laissez-faire, laissez-passer" philosophy relinquishes in this system is acquired by the state. However, it is a state of a new kind, bolstered by the influence of banks and revitalized by industrial methods.

As the universal heir, the state is set to become the primary lender, the allocator of labor, and the planner of production. The Saint-Simonians didn't shy away from this form of collectivism. They relied on it to reshape institutions and customs that are remnants of the military regime. Consider how Michel Chevalier,[409] especially during his period of Saint-Simonian zeal, describes the role of prefects[410]:

> "The time will come when it will seem just as ludicrous for someone to claim to be the chief magistrate of Seine-Inférieure,[411] for instance, without any involvement in the production and trade of cotton fabrics, as it would be to appoint a bishop to lead a regiment of riflemen or hussars.[412]"

Here he is again, envisioning the industrial armies of the future:

---

[409] Michel Chevalier (1806–1879) was a political economist, engineer, and a leading figure in Saint-Simonism. Chevalier was a senator from 1848 to 1876, best known for negotiating the Franco-British Free Trade Agreement of 1860.
[410] In France, a prefect is the state's representative within particular regions or departments.
[411] Since 1955, Seine-Inférieure has been known as Seine-Maritime. It's located on France's northern coast.
[412] A hussar was a form of light calvary that originated in Central Europe around the 15th century.

"Men will no longer be recruited to learn the art of destruction and killing, but rather to learn the arts of production and creation. Regiments will become trade schools where all may enter from the age of sixteen. Artillerymen will become mechanics, metal casters will produce steam engines, the corps of laborers will handle transportation, sappers will be miners, pontoon units will build bridges over rivers, and the line infantry will span a wide range of professions. Industry will be organized as something appealing and honorable. The state is envisioned as becoming the primary allocator of employment, compensation, and a universally accessible pension."

But then on which power must we depend to reach this grand outcome? The power of the bank. Nothing can be accomplished without credit. The difficulty lies in opening and closing the credit tap wisely, considering both individual capabilities and the common good. According to the Saint-Simonians, this is the task that private banks perform, albeit very imperfectly, as they are too committed to preserving old privileges. State banks, they believed, would be less prone to panic over decreased annuities or a drop in interest rates. They would be capable of funding public utility ventures. In addition, a central bank would play the role of coordinating their efforts. And this bank would be nothing less—in the words of the Péreires—than the government in the secular realm, a government that would nonetheless remain at the service of the state, which in turn is formed by the association of workers.

This is enough to shed light on the distinctive characteristics of Saint-Simonian socialism: a socialism of producers—as Maxime Leroy and Élie Halévy have rightly emphasized—more focused on increasing the wealth available to a humanity that would increasingly learn to harness the earth's resources than on regulating consumption or adjusting production to suit it. To succeed in this endeavor, let's make room for talent! The Saint-Simonians, in their own way, were "hierarchs," as they put it. They had no intention of reinstating castes. However, they absolutely required a guiding elite. And if it becomes necessary to better compensate these elites, "to pay them according to their deeds," the Saint-Simonians were not daunted by the prospect. They were prepared to acknowledge the reign of the engineer. And it was understood that above the engineer himself, they would place the banker, the supreme commander of the peaceful armies of the laboring masses: a commander-in-chief who would also, in truth, need to be an apostle...

In any event, to avoid being intimidated by this excess of state control, let's firmly remember that the state, in line with the Saint-Simonian vision of industrialism, would be a state transformed, rejuvenated, and, if one may be so bold, cleansed—cleansed of the vestiges of inept authoritarianism, the harmful legacy of militaristic politics. The methods of industry, which has no fondness for coercion, would take precedence over those of politics. "The government of persons will be replaced by the administration of things"[413]: a maxim not originally from Saint-Simon, but one that precisely reflects the deepest inclinations of the school, its founder, and its followers. And it is undoubtedly through this aspect of their thought that they were destined to leave the most enduring mark on the modern world.[414]

---

[413] Marx and Engels would also later reiterate the claim that government needs to be replaced by administration.

[414] **Note from Bouglé:** Let's revisit the kind of summary that I. Péreire provided regarding the contributions of Saint-Simonism. "There exists a school more pragmatic than others, a school that, grounded in the philosophical analysis of the past, has sought the governing principles of all observed phenomena to chart their course and predict the future: the work of this school is simply the study of civilization itself. It has revitalized the underpinnings of philosophy, history, and political economy. It has influenced every facet of human endeavor, including fine arts, science, and industry. It has outlined the agenda for the 19th century. It is the pioneer of railways in France. It revisited the concept of piercing the Isthmus of Suez and laid the groundwork for its realization. It has proposed innovative ideas on the restructuring of credit. Ultimately, it has produced individuals of utility in numerous domains, individuals who have managed to implement parts of its agenda and who have disseminated its principles across all strata of the social order; they have been present in the corridors of power as well as among the ranks of the republicans."

Chapter VI

Assessment of Saint-Simonism: Present

After their Egyptian venture, the Saint-Simonians scattered; their own era of diaspora had arrived. They returned to France and each settled down, more or less peacefully, to earn a living.

Their Saint-Simonian theories—the great doctrine, the fervent belief that had once inspired them—were no longer a topic of conversation. It wasn't that everyone had forsaken it—some held it close in the depths of their hearts—but in the end, its hymns were no longer sung, its banners no longer raised in public squares; one might assume that the Saint-Simonian idea was dead and buried. Yet perhaps it lived on beneath the surface; perhaps it was destined for a revival. It would then become apparent that, in meeting the desires of the times, it still possessed a potential for productivity that had been thought lost.

To confirm this, let's recall the various missions Saint-Simonism appeared to take on: to rejuvenate religion, to pave the way for peace, to champion intelligence, to structure industry, and to forge socialism.

*
* *

We won't linger on the first point: the Saint-Simonian religion is the most neglected part of the old Ménilmontant garden. Saint-Simonism as a religion wasn't even as lucky as Positivism in maintaining a few sects, a few chapels that were still standing. Although Father Enfantin, stubborn and wanting to reassure himself that he remained true to his youthful dreams, was able to write a meditation on *The Science of Man and Eternal Life*[415] in 1850, it would find no echo. The religion that he held dear seemed to have completely dissipated, as if it had vanished into thin air.

---

[415] *La science de l'homme et la vie éternelle.*

Does this imply that the needs it aimed to address—needs for enthusiasm, faith, unity, and guidance—are felt less acutely in 1930 than they were in 1830?

It's hard to say. It's often said that, after the war, there was a renewed and more urgent sense of religious longing. Assuming this is true, there hasn't been a noticeable drift of souls back to Saint-Simonism. Why? Because other options were available to them, most notably Christianity. Christianity asserts its capacity to adapt to the demands of our era, particularly its social demands. Didn't we witness, in the middle of the 19th century, figures like Buchez, Pecqueur,[416] and Louis Blanc intertwining the cause of Christianity with that of socialism? The Saint-Simonians objected to this conflation, criticizing the Christian tradition for its dualism, for pitting spirit against matter. In contrast, they aimed to vindicate the flesh, to justify not only the progress of industry but also the call for the welfare of the downtrodden classes.

Yet the Saint-Simonian dichotomy seems to be contradicted by how events have unfolded. In reality, many people in our era can stay devoted to or even revert to Christianity without forgoing their concern for well-being and the valorization of productive labor. On this issue, as on many others, the traditional religion in France has shown remarkable adaptability. It has managed to reconcile itself with war; why wouldn't it do the same with industry? At the end of his life, Michel Chevalier was impressed that a bishop had come to bless a locomotive. Such blessings would hardly raise an eyebrow today. The Church, despite its ascetic roots, has unmistakably come to terms with mechanization. This indicates that, contrary to the Saint-Simonian position, there's no contradiction in being both an industrialist and a Catholic.

Moreover, other moral forces might play the role that the *Exposition of the Doctrine of Saint-Simon* ascribed to religions, even without adopting Saint-Simonian forms. Socialism is one such force. This

---

[416] Constantin Pecqueur (1801–1887) was an economist and socialist. He was critical of capitalism and private property and advocated for a planned, cooperativist socialism with community ownership.

statement might surprise those who consider Marxism the predominant form and culmination of socialism and, on the other hand, view it as a science, the ultimate science. Yet even in its Marxist guise, socialism is a belief system. It drives action by inspiring enthusiasm. Will it allow traditional forms of faith to coexist, or will it aim to supplant them entirely? Young socialists are engaging in this very debate, and in a most interesting manner, as they try to define the relationship between their treasured doctrine and Christianity or secularism. It's evident that many of them look to socialism to be "integral,"[417] to offer them a worldview that strives for a total transformation of civilization. It may have been this unifying power that Durkheim—himself influenced by Saint-Simonism— had in mind when, at the conclusion of his work on the *Elementary Forms of Religious Life*,[418] he hinted that our era might witness new, fervent movements capable of creating binding moral values.

However, this isn't all that the Saint-Simonians themselves sought. If one revisits the final lessons of the *Exposition*, from the first year, it becomes clear that a vaguely defined religiosity would not have sufficed for them, no matter how great the cause it is connected to. They made a heroic effort to establish an actual religion complete with its own dogmas, hierarchy, and ceremonies. On this front and in this sense, their failure was absolute.

*
* *

On the contrary, we cannot say the same about the second tendency we've recognized in Saint-Simonism: the goal of organizing peace through the expansion of association. Today, few ideas are more

---

[417] Benoît Malon (1841–1893) was a writer, socialist, communard, and member of the First International, who sought to synthesize Marxist and other socialist tendencies with his emphasis on "integralism." He founded the influential journal *La revue socialiste* (1885–1914) and heavily influenced Jean Jaurès.
[418] *Formes élémentaires de la vie religieuse* (1912).

vibrant and influential. The League of Nations,[419] which personifies these ideas, stands as evidence that they have triumphed, capitalizing on the reactions to the recent war to generate a formidable wave of public sentiment.

Certainly, the Saint-Simonians were not the only ones to have desired such an organization. A history of its forerunners should not overlook, for instance, Abbé de Saint-Pierre[420] in France, nor Kant in Germany. However, the concepts developed by the Saint-Simonians, initially by Saint-Simon himself during his collaboration with Augustin Thierry, might be the ones most aligned with today's realities. They envisioned more than just a tribunal to adjudicate the law or calls for arbitration to move Europe out of the "violent state" they perceived it to be in. Saint-Simon held that for the law to prevail among nations, it was essential for them to grow increasingly accustomed to collective action, to form associations, to bind themselves to one another in large-scale projects of common utility. Isn't this the notion that has taken hold in Geneva? Whether directly or indirectly, through its own agencies or via the institutions it operates, the League of Nations tackles issues of health, transportation, and finance. Aware that all aspects are interrelated, and that political issues are invariably intertwined with economic ones, the League endeavors to make the management of the world's resources more rational, just as the Saint-Simonians intended.

Some might say these ideas were rediscovered rather than directly inspired by Saint-Simonism, suggesting analogies rather than lineages. Perhaps. Saint-Simon has not been honored with a statue in Geneva, and the delegates of the Nations who convene there have not felt compelled to pay him the solemn tribute they have paid, for instance, to Rousseau. However, we should not hastily dismiss the possible avenues of influence.

---

[419] The League of Nations (1920-1946) was the first worldwide intergovernmental organization that sought to maintain world peace. The organization was succeeded by the United Nations (1945-).

[420] Abbé de Saint-Pierre (1658-1743) was a Catholic abbot, political theorist, and philosopher. He is seen as one of the earliest promoters of international peace organizations and disarmament. Abbé de Saint-Pierre was notably an important influence on Enlightenment thought.

For example, no one would argue against the fact that the Leagues of Peace established in Europe before 1870, and again before 1914, smoothed the path for the League of Nations. Notably, one of the most influential of these leagues, the League of Peace and Freedom,[421] which convened a Congress in Geneva as early as 1867, is the beloved progeny of Lemonnier,[422] who founded *The United States of Europe* newspaper, and Lemonnier was in his time graced with Saint-Simonian allure. Here we have threads of influence that, though perhaps still unseen in some respects, are nonetheless tangible.

Among all the ideas that the League of Nations strives to embed within its institutions, there is one that merits particular attention for its special place in Saint-Simon's heart and for epitomizing a facet of Saint-Simonian politics: the concept of international intellectual cooperation. A bust of Henri de Saint-Simon has been rightfully installed at the International Institute of Intellectual Cooperation[423] on Rue Montpensier. It's a fitting tribute. Saint-Simon is at home there, near the Palais-Royal where he once passionately discussed his grand designs. And one of his early visions from 1803, conceived in Geneva itself, is beginning to be realized here (we've already mentioned the *Letters from an Inhabitant of Geneva* that Saint-Simon is said to have written to console himself after being spurned by Madame de Staël). An international subscription to build a mausoleum for Newton; around the mausoleum, a consecrated territory for the construction of a library, a school, and model laboratories; and to guide the enterprise, a council of scholars free to work and to issue directives to national councils—the plan is grandiose. And while no one can seriously consider implementing it exactly as it was

---

[421] League of Peace and Freedom (1867-1870) was created in response to the growing tensions between the Second French Empire and the Kingdom of Prussia. It was a precursor for the League of Nations and UN.

[422] Charles Lemonnier (1806-1891) was a Saint-Simonian journalist and advocate of international peace. His newspaper *Les États-Unis d'Europe* (1868-1870) was the organ of the League of Peace and Freedom.

[423] The International Institute of Intellectual Cooperation (1924-1946) was an organization founded in Paris associated with the League of Nations that promoted intellectual cooperation.

proposed, within this mythological framework, one can discern the outlines of feasible ideas. The focus is rightly placed on the necessity of both freeing and organizing the power of the mind to assist the world in finding its equilibrium.

The disciples would hold on to this concept of the primacy of intelligence and derive numerous implications from it.

Thus, they were led to forge new paths that others have begun to travel since the war. It has been recognized that intelligence too deserves defense. In the post-war upheaval, it was observed that intellectual values faced a concerning decline. This was not only due to the disorganization among those in intellectual professions, who risked diminished status and influence, but also because pure culture, a source of great richness, risked losing its rightful place and the support it requires. To address such concerns, organizations like the International Confederation of Intellectual Workers[424] and the Companions of Intellectual Professions[425] were established. On this front as well, the Saint-Simonians were pioneers and could serve as guides, not least because they emphasized that the conditions for productive intellectual labor deserved as much attention as those in the material realm—an idea that men like Otlet and La Fontaine[426] in Brussels had independently revived or rediscovered before the war. The Saint-Simonians went so far as to say, "The scientific community must be managed just as we have said the industrial community should be managed, catering to the needs of intellectual production and

---

[424] The *Confederation internationale des travailleurs intellectuels* (CITI) formed in 1923, in connection with the French trade union *Confederation des travailleurs intellectuels* (1920-), was one of the first international unions dedicated to an intellectual occupation. At its peak in the 1920s, it had members from over 30 countries. However, the rise of fascism and competition from other labor groups led to its decline.

[425] *Compagnons des professions intellectuelles.*

[426] Paul Otlet (1868-1944) and Henri La Fontaine (1854-1943) were Belgian peace activists known for creating the Universal Decimal Classification scheme. Additionally, they co-founded the International Association of Legal Science and helped establish standards for international documentation exchange and information science. La Fontaine won the Nobel Peace Prize in 1913 for his advocacy for international peace.

156

consumption through the adept distribution of workers, labor, and products." It must be added that they were always keen to identify talent wherever it may be. In this sense, despite their wariness of uncompromising egalitarianism, they championed what the French call equality in education, and the English call equality of opportunity. Vandervelde[427] was not wrong in presenting Ernest Solvay,[428] the soda ash magnate and founder of numerous initiatives to promote scientific research, as "a new Saint-Simon." He particularly lauded him for challenging the randomness of inheritance, where some are thrown naked into the arena while others enter fully armored, and for predicting, "No man would wish for another's start in life what he would not wish for his own. In this arduous journey of existence, the most serious of all, there shall therefore be fair equality at the starting point." Today, no advocate of universal education is more critical of educational inequality at the starting point than the authors of the fifth lesson of the *Doctrine of Saint-Simon* were in 1829: "Undoubtedly, the necessary education, without which access leaves even the most distinct vocations barren, is not available to everyone indiscriminately, but it remains a privilege granted by wealth, and wealth itself is a privilege almost always disproportionate to the merit of its holders."

The means to remedy this injustice, so perilous for social progress, would undoubtedly be a new structuring of the various levels of education—and on this point, the Saint-Simonians certainly have a plan that would make significant room not only for a unifying general education but also for professional training of a technical nature. A stopgap measure, in the meantime, would be a new organization of intellectual credit, which would provide advances to those with talent. *The*

[427] Emile Vandervelde (1866–1938) was a Belgian socialist, political theorist, and president of the Second International from 1900 to 1918. He adopted an internationalist viewpoint that called for cooperation between socialists. Vandervelde was also the Prime Minister of Belgium from 1926 to 1927.
[428] Ernest Solvay (1938–1922) was a Belgian chemist who earned considerable wealth from his patents and founded the company Solvay in 1863, the largest multinational company up until WWI. Solvay was known for his large donations and for promoting education and social welfare.

Producer, the recent journal that has revived the title of the 1825 publication, rightfully declares in an issue dedicated to this topic that it hopes, with the new strength provided by unionism, to resurrect and advance this grand Saint-Simonian idea. Scholarships, honor loans, and more recently the National Science Fund—all these institutions embody this very concept. And it is evidence that knowingly or not, our intellectual policy, as it is sometimes referred to today, is steeped in Saint-Simonism.

*
* *

But it's obvious that the core, the heart of Saint-Simonism, lies in industrial policy. To say it better, and to echo the words of Saint-Simon himself, in the eyes of his followers as well as his own, politics without industry is a hollow concept. If they had the opportunity to glimpse our era, it would undoubtedly be the attempts of industry to multiply its power through more rational organization that would have captured their keenest interest.

And here, it's easy to demonstrate that the Saint-Simonians not only foresaw and called for, but also directly laid the groundwork for, the major efforts of coordination that we have witnessed and that continue to unfold before us.

Canal builders and railroad constructors—as mentioned, the Saint-Simonians were predominantly driven by engineering pursuits. They were, above all, daring captains of industry. We've pointed out their involvement in developing the Suez Canal project in Egypt. The idea was formulated by Fournel,[429] embraced by Enfantin, and later revisited by Michel Chevalier. Yet none of them had the honor of turning the idea into reality. That had to wait for Lesseps.[430] But Enfantin could justifiably

---

[429] Henri Fournel (1799–1876) was a mining engineer and Saint-Simonian. He travelled with Enfantin to Egypt and was later a pioneer of mineral prospecting in Algeria.

[430] Ferdinand de Lesseps (1805–1894) was a diplomat who helped develop the Suez Canal in 1869. He later tried but failed to develop the Panama Canal in the 1880s.

158

express, with a blend of pride and wistfulness: "Certainly, it will be both good and fair for future generations to acknowledge that the initiative for this colossal undertaking was taken by those whom the old world dismissed as mere utopians, dreamers, and lunatics. But trust in History for that..."

Their role in the creation of railway networks is even better recognized today. As early as 1826, in *The Producer*, Dubochet[431] confidently predicted that "iron-grooved roads" would be "abundant sources of wealth and social improvements," that they would trigger a major revolution in societal conditions, perhaps on par with the impact of navigation itself. Between 1830 and 1850, the Saint-Simonians revisited these prospects repeatedly. In *Mediterranean System*[432] in 1832, Michel Chevalier was thrilled at the thought of the iron network that would shrink the globe by encircling it. That same year, the Flachat brothers,[433] assisted by Lamé and Clapeyron,[434] detailed their visions in *Political and Practical Views on Public Works in France*.[435] The Péreire brothers, with fervent intellectual vigor, worked to realize these visions, as evidenced by the extensive volumes that have been devotedly compiled of their writings. Supported by contributors, among whom were about twenty Polytechnique graduates influenced by Saint-Simonism, they established the Lyon–Saint-Etienne line in 1832, the Alais–Beaucaire line in 1835, and the Paris–Saint-Germain line in 1842, securing the passage of the crucial bill despite Thiers'[436] lack of imagination in opposing it.

---

[431] Jacques-Julien Dubochet (1798–1868) was a lawyer and journal editor.
[432] *Système de la Méditerranée.*
[433] Stéphane Mony-Flachat (1800–1884) and Eugène Flachat (1802–1873) were brothers, engineers, and Saint-Simonians who helped build the railways between Paris–Saint Germain and Paris–Versailles.
[434] Gabriel Lamé (1795–1870) and Émile Clapeyron (1799–1864) were close friends and engineers. They lived in Russia from 1820 to 1830. Upon their return to France, they helped the Flachat brothers build railways.
[435] *Vues politiques et pratiques sur les travaux publics en France.*
[436] Adolphe Thiers (1797–1877) was a politician and historian. He opposed Napoleon III and was exiled from France from 1851 to 1870. Thiers was the first President of the Third Republic from 1871 to 1873. Despite his left-wing

Furthermore, they didn't overlook the need to prepare for the consolidation of the various companies that had been established to manage the railways. And Enfantin himself, having become an administrator of the Paris–Lyon–Mediterranean Railway (PLM), eagerly engaged in this task of coordination, a hallmark of Saint-Simonian ingenuity.

Coordination and even concentration are indeed the watchwords of the former collaborators of *The Producer* and their followers. Wouldn't allowing companies to proliferate and expand haphazardly, with no connections among them, surely be the best way to perpetuate industrial anarchy? But how can these agreements be established if there are no entities—industry sponsors, as Rouen[437] called them in *The Producer* in 1826—to provide credit to businesses? This underscores the critical role of banks in Saint-Simonian thought: to them, the banker is to industry what the general is to the military. The Péreires, the most pragmatic of visionaries, took it upon themselves to act. They founded the Crédit Foncier in 1852, followed by the Crédit Mobilier.[438] Would you like to see how they defended the latter enterprise?

"The concept of Crédit Mobilier emerged from the inadequacy of credit facilities available for organizing the country's major business endeavors and the isolation of financial forces due to the lack of a hub powerful enough to unite them. It arose from numerous factors: the market need for a steady influx of new capital to meet the growth of public and industrial credit; the excessive conditions imposed on public fund lending and the subsequent challenges in the secure placement of top-tier securities; the need to centralize the financial and administrative operations of large companies, particularly regarding the capital

---

sympathies, he was generally regarded as an enemy of social reform by his contemporaries.

[437] Pierre-Isidore Rouen was a lawyer, jurist, Saint-Simonian, and frequent contributor to *Le producteur.*

[438] Crédit Foncier ("land credit") (1852–2019) and Crédit Mobilier ("movable credit") (1852–1867) were major banking companies in France that financed various infrastructure projects.

each one successively controls, to conserve shared resources for the companies and their numerous shareholders; and finally, the imperative to introduce into circulation a new intermediary, a new form of fiduciary currency."

Seldom have we witnessed more deliberate thinking from financial architects. In this, we can discern the mindset of those who would later describe the bank as the "economic soul" and assert that, within the secular realm, it would amount to nothing short of a government.

How much are these ideas still alive today? Have these examples been emulated? Have these master planners found successors who, whether aware of their legacy or not, carry on their mission of coordination?

The French have long been labeled as individualistic in industry, incapable of adhering to discipline or forging agreements, thus suggesting that cartels and trusts would struggle to establish themselves in our country. However, this notion must now be abandoned. Even before the war, major industries had managed to establish types of syndicates—with the Committee of Steelmakers[439] as the most notable example—and had formed agreements for setting prices and distributing orders. Robert Pinot,[440] recognized as an expert in this field, has observed that in France, the preference has traditionally been for the more flexible, adaptable small business model over trusts or cartels, better suiting our customs. Nonetheless, under various guises and names, agreements were made that limited laissez-faire. Clearly, these restrictions became more stringent during the war. By placing themselves "at the service of the nation," as Pinot notes, the major industrialists were inevitably compelled to

---

[439] The Comité des forges (1864-1940) was an influential organization made up of members from the French iron and steel industry that took protectionist attitudes toward trade and was dissolved by the Vichy regime.

[440] Robert Pinot (1862-1926) was a sociologist and long-term secretary-general of the Committee of Steelmakers known for his lobbying.

negotiate among themselves, under state oversight and control. Many believed that memories of this wartime system would fade once the conflict ended. However, didn't the post-war disorder make it necessary to redouble organizational efforts? Charles Rist,[441] writing in the updated *Political Economy Review*,[442] asserted that we were in greater need than ever for a dose of Saint-Simonism. In fact, significant constructive work has been carried out. For instance, Villey's 1922 book *Organization of Employers in French Industry*,[443] describes the emergence of a variety of groups, not only professional but also inter-professional and regional. These groups are both federating and specializing, coordinating to influence the customs regime, labor laws, equipment and techniques, and professional training. They have unmistakably shifted from a "defensive character" to an "active character," and their shared scope of action expands daily. This trend has prompted many business leaders to establish a General Confederation of French Production,[444] which, utilizing the laws of 1884 and 1901, creates various "Unions," classifying them, federating them, and driving them to tackle problems collectively— not only social and labor issues but also economic and commercial challenges that concern all "producers." Thus, we are witnessing the rise of new structures all around us. They may not have reached their definitive form yet, but since they are designed to defend industry, through association, against the anarchic effects of laissez-faire, they would have delighted the collaborators of *The Producer* and *The Organizer*: all this architecture is indeed in the Saint-Simonian style.

*
* *

But can such an organization thrive without state support or oversight? When it comes to setting prices, determining wage levels, or

---

[441] Charles Rist (1874–1955) was an economist and banker who advocated a return to the gold standard. He was an economic advisor to several prime ministers of France during the interwar period. Rist later was the editor of *Revue d'économie politique* from 1932 to 1955.

[442] *Revue d'économie politique* (1887–).

[443] *Organisation des employeurs dans l'industrie française.*

[444] Confédération générale de la production française (1919–1936).

162

distributing credits, doesn't the entity that represents the whole nation inevitably have a role to play? The Saint-Simonians would certainly have thought so, as they aimed to make the state the universal regulator. But we've noted that this is under the strict condition that the state must change its approach, that it must not interfere with the oppressive coercive power inherited from political practice, and that it must learn to manage by governing less. In other words, as Saint-Simon himself suggested in his parable of the two caravans,[445] it must treat people less as subjects and more as associates, which means welcoming, in this new style of administration, the involvement of stakeholders and experts. Saint-Simonian statism can only be a tempered form of statism, seeking to exert control while imposing limits on itself, eager to find leadership beyond political rulers, and to prioritize technical expertise over political maneuvering.

But aren't these mixed formulas, these hybrid systems, exactly what our era is fervently searching for from every angle? Syndicalists and cooperativists, jurists and economists, and advocates of "directed

---

[445] "Let us imagine a large caravan telling its leaders: *Take us to where we will be best off.* From that moment on, the leaders are everything, the caravan is nothing; it proceeds blindly because for such a journey to continue, even for just twenty-four hours, the caravan must grant its leaders unlimited trust, complete passive obedience. It is thus entirely at the mercy of their dishonesty and ignorance. The caravan can reserve no other right for itself than to declare that the desert to which it has been led is unsuitable and that it must be taken elsewhere; but this right can hardly serve it except to make, at its own expense, a series of experiments that will always be useless as long as it allows its guides to determine the journey's destination.

On the contrary, suppose the caravan says to its leaders: *You know the way to Mecca, lead us there.* In this new situation, the leaders are no longer chiefs, they are only guides; their roles, though very important, are merely subordinate; the main action comes from the caravan. Each traveler retains the right to critically evaluate the chosen path whenever they deem appropriate and to propose, according to their understanding, the changes they believe to be beneficial. Since the discussion can only ever concern a very precise and easily judged issue (*are we moving away from or closer to Mecca?*), the caravan, assuming it is somewhat enlightened, no longer obeys the will of the guides, but *its own conviction*, based on the evidence presented to it."

economy" or "mixed economy" all underscore the need for these new creations. Take Maxime Leroy, who was among the first to herald the rise of the fourth power, the professional power, and relies on it, along with the action of not just unions, but also various types of official bodies, to prompt the state to finally alter its sovereign administrative methods. Take Bernard Lavergne,[446] who rejoices in the formation of cooperatively structured businesses where the state, as a shareholder, retains its controlling interest. Take Jouhaux,[447] who, with the concept of industrialized nationalism, insists that while protecting companies from the chaos of competition, they must also be shielded from being smothered by state bureaucracy: the new type of national enterprise must counter both individual and capitalist exploitation methods and the traditional bureaucratic management of monopolies. Léon Blum,[448] regarding the railways, suggests finding an entity capable of defending itself and us against the aggressive resurgence of industrial feudalism, but that also harnesses for the public good the fruitful elements of private sector practices. Finally, François-Poncet,[449] inaugurating a session of the National Economic Council—a framework quite in line with Saint-Simonian ideals, as noted by Maxime Leroy—where representatives of labor, capital, the general public, and consumers are invited to collaborate with representatives of the state, highlights a series of new developments in the economic realm that signal a shift from the individual to the

---

[446] Bernard Lavergne (1884-1975) was an economist. He was an influential member within France's cooperative movement and worked alongside the economist Charles Gide (1847-1932).

[447] Léon Jouhaux (1879-1954) was the secretary general of the CGT from 1909 to 1947. He used a pragmatic approach that focused on negotiation rather than revolution. Jouhaux was a co-founder of the International Federation of Trade Unions (1919-1945) and he received the Nobel Peace Prize in 1951 for promoting justice.

[448] Léon Blum (1872-1950) was a socialist politician who co-founded the French Section of the Workers' International Party. Blum was later the Prime Minister of France three times in 1936-1937, 1938, and 1946-1947. During Nazi occupation, he was sent to Buchenwald concentration camp from 1943 to 1945.

[449] André François-Poncet (1887-1978) was a politician that served as the ambassador to Germany from 1928 to 1932 and then the ambassador to Italy until 1938. François-Poncet provided expertise on fascism to the French and was imprisoned for three years by the Gestapo during WWII.

collective, from the national to the international stage, and from a paradigm of economic liberty to one of economic structure: "In light of the sweeping and unceasing transformations with unforeseeable impacts that define the contemporary economic world, the state must serve as arbitrator, regulator, mediator, and guide. It's crucial that we do not fall back into the pitfalls of classical statism. What we need is an economic system that neither gravitates toward socialist economics nor remains anchored in the outdated liberal economy."

In the search for this hybrid, intermediary system, it's evident that the Under-Secretary of State for National Economy is likewise haunted by Saint-Simonian echoes. He made this clear in his address to the Chamber, outlining his vision for the spirit of modern capitalism, a neo-capitalism imbued with an understanding of its social responsibility and a recognition of the interdependence of all elements of production: "This capitalism is not about regressing; we are firmly convinced, rather, that it represents progress, the future. It is this future that must refresh and enrich the concept of politics and teach us that, just as Saint-Simon predicted, politics will soon become nothing more than the science of production."

Many of the organizers we're discussing likely channel Saint-Simon's ideas as Monsieur Jourdain spoke in prose, unknowingly.[450] Yet as recent examples have shown, some are fully conscious of the tradition they aim to resurrect. Indeed, to embody this aspiration, a group formed that intentionally revives the old banner of Saint-Simon's earliest followers: between 1920 and 1923, a new *The Producer* emerged. Backed by engineers, financiers (among them alumni of the École Polytechnique, as before), and intellectuals, *The Producer* solemnly

---

[450] Monsieur Jourdain is a character whose house is the setting for Molière's five-act comedy *The Bourgeois Gentleman,* which premiered in 1670. In it, Jourdain, a middle-aged "bourgeois," seeks to be accepted as an aristocrat and spends lavishly in order to do so. His name is sometimes still used to refer to someone who make pompous claims to dignity that they don't actually possess.

enlists under the patronage[451] of Saint-Simon. It doesn't simply adopt the traditional heritage of Saint-Simonism in its entirety, but both distills and enriches it. For instance, it integrates an advocacy for the individual—seemingly influenced by Stendhal's[452] attitudes and Bédier's[453] battles against the excesses of Romanticism in epic literature—a stance that is somewhat challenging to reconcile with what might already be termed the 'sociologism' of the Saint-Simonians, equally pronounced among the disciples as it was in the founder. But regarding our current issue—the interplay of economics and politics—the contributors to the new *Producer* align with the essence of the original. "Do not ask us for our views on domestic or foreign policy. For now, we can only respond indirectly with terms like: coal, nitrogen, fertilizer, hydroelectric power, credit, organizational bureaus, technical education, general culture." Francis Delaisi,[454] who eagerly echoes this statement in his preface to his book on oil, indeed seems to regard it as a sort of declaration of war on politics: it's time to block the path to the outdated notions that politics brings into the realm of commerce. The Chamber of Deputies,[455] Marquet[456] declares, is a Museum of Doctrines. A deputy is a man of doctrine. Therefore, drawing on the Saint-Simonian tradition, the goal is to suppress "doctrines," to quiet the noise and clashes of opinion, and to convene the individuals or entities who represent interests and hold expertise in a "straightforward and open" manner. According to this framework, a

---

[451] This is a play on words related to saints as patrons.

[452] Marie-Henri Beyle (1783–1842), known as Stendhal, was a novelist and practitioner of realism. His novels offered nuanced psychological portraits of its characters and insights into contemporary social issues.

[453] Joseph Bédier (1864–1938) was a writer, medieval historian, and philologist. He held the chair of Romance literature at the prestigious Collège de France from 1909 to 1936.

[454] Francis Delaisi (1873–1947) was an economist and trade unionist. During the interwar period, he advised socialist and labor organizations and advocated for the democratic organization of the global economy to prevent future wars. Delaisi wrote the 1920 *Le Pétrole,* which was published by *Le producteur.*

[455] The Chamber of Deputies (1814–1848, 1875–1940) was a parliamentary body in France.

[456] Adrien Marquet (1884–1955) was a socialist politician who later moved to the far right. Along with Marcel Déat, he formed the neo-socialist party in 1933 and supported the Vichy regime during WWII.

federation of technical bureaus and professional associations may well be the shape the state of the future will assume.

Truth be told, one aspect seems to be overlooked, or at least often downplayed, in this neo-Saint-Simonian publication: the social issue itself, the problem of the conditions faced by workers, particularly the working masses employed by industry. Do the authors believe that improving the production system will sufficiently enhance the living conditions for all producers, including the most modest laborer? Some of them seem to rely on their organizational agenda to wrest the labor movement from the clutches of socialism. Technical offices, Darquet proclaims, will no longer recognize class distinctions. A worker with a proposal will find as much credit there as anyone else. Moreover, he will have his designated spot in the "savers' union." Is there thus nothing left for him to demand as a worker? Are we being presented with a diluted form of Saint-Simonism, stripped of the reformist power of the central teachings of *Exposition of the Doctrine*?

But we are well aware that to harvest these seeds, other inheritors have emerged, notably the French Section of the Workers' International. Fundamentally a Marxist party, you might say, borrowing its themes from the *Communist Manifesto*, *Capital*, and *Anti-Dühring*. It clings firmly to these works, largely due to the success in propaganda that the interpretation of these "dogmas" has brought. Wouldn't it be open to drawing from new sources today? Perhaps. But the wellspring from which it drinks is itself fed by higher mountain lakes. Marxism is in part a new version of Saint-Simonism. Marx was particularly harsh toward the Saint-Simonians: "half prophets, half swindlers." Could it be precisely because he sensed a significant debt to them? At any rate, Charles Andler has long since demonstrated in his commentary on the *Communist Manifesto* that the influence of the authors of *The Doctrine of Saint-Simon* is apparent. Examining passages where Marx and Engels portray workers as the heirs of serfs, plebeians, and slaves, and where they expose the evils of industrial anarchy, he was able to state: "Bazard is the constant source of the *Manifesto*."

Needless to say, the stock of socialist traditions is formed from a multitude of diverse contributions, in addition to that of Saint-Simonism. The disciples of the aristocratic messiah, proud of their own abilities, and convinced that production can only be properly organized through a hierarchy that places talent at the top, are by no means "workerists," as we would say today. Nor are they democrats. And they are certainly not revolutionaries. The organization they envision, which they deem absolutely essential, is a top-down organization, rather than a bottom-up one. They do not immediately recognize workers' solidarity as a prerequisite for transforming property relations. Similarly, they do not seem to place much importance on the role of popular pressure on governments for the implementation of the reforms they envisage. Finally, the notion of a forceful takeover by resolute proletarians declaring a Revolution would appall them, if it could even be seriously entertained in their minds. It is under different influences that these three elements—workerist, democratic, and revolutionary—would be integrated into socialist doctrine.

Nevertheless, when socialism seeks not just to critique classical liberalism but to sketch a constructive plan of action, it naturally turns back to Saint-Simonism. Isn't it concerns inherited from Saint-Simon that differentiate socialists from parties that are neither democratic nor seem to believe that enacting the reforms demanded by the proletariat requires the strong-arm tactics favored by Jacobin politics? Drawing a distinction between socialists and Jacobins, one of the most influential young speakers at the Socialist Congresses,[457] Marcel Déat,[458] pointed out that socialists should primarily draw inspiration from the Saint-Simonian tradition. This tradition advocates for preparing the "administration of things" through various organizations that, being outside the realm of

---

[457] Within the SFIO, and later the Socialist Party in France, the Socialist Congresses are the highest body which establish the political line as well as elect the leadership of the party.

[458] Marcel Déat (1894–1955) was a socialist politician and writer. In 1933, Déat led the split of the French section of the Workers' International to form a neo-socialist party that moved to the far right. He collaborated with and held office under the Vichy regime and was later condemned *in absentia* and died in hiding.

politics, do not resort to its methods and can only utilize the state by transforming it. By adopting this position, the new leader is not only challenging the radical-socialists. His shots also indirectly hit certain members of his own party who, satisfied with parroting slogans designed to rouse the proletarian masses, appear to believe that as soon as these masses have seized power—be it through the ballot box or through forceful struggle—all would be achieved, the ovens preheated, and the bread ready-baked for socialism. According to the author of *Socialist Perspectives*,[459] such a transition requires a completely different kind of preparation: it necessitates the involvement not only of trade unions, but also cooperatives, and not only workers, but also farmers. In devising the necessary plans for this positive action, Déat is led to construct a kind of neo-socialism tinged with Saint-Simonism, just as François-Poncet seemed to be constructing a neo-capitalism under the same banner. And perhaps, upon a foundation of Saint-Simonian sediment, the battles and agreements between these two forces—neo-capitalism and neo-socialism— constitute the crucial part, the very essence, of the complex drama unfolding before our eyes.

---

[459] *Perspectives socialistes* (1930).

Chapter VII

Assessment of Fourierism: Past

The notion that Saint-Simonism has handed down fertile ideas to posterity, suitable for integration into modern economic and social practices, may appear paradoxical to those who consider the adventurous nature and the tumultuous lives of both the founder and most of his followers. The success of Fourierist concepts is equally surprising. Not that the head of this particular school was a restless dabbler: few careers were as tranquil or as monotonous as that of Charles Fourier, the "shop sergeant." Yet this mild-mannered clerk possessed a boundless imagination that seemed unstoppable by any reality. He belongs to the lineage of Campanella, Morris, and Wells.[460] At times, he even reminds one of Alphonse Allais.[461] He was the king of the utopians, if not to say the Pope of madmen. In his world, dreams of an architect, florist, ballet master, and chef abound and intertwine. Palaces and grand hotels spring up, connected by gallery-lined streets, amid fields of flowers tended by cheerful groups singing and dancing. Children flit back and forth, from the kitchen to the Opera, finding joy in performing even the foulest of street works. Fourier vividly imagined these characters and meticulously planned for the fulfillment of their every need. He seriously contemplated the most peculiar problems: for instance, how to make use of tough poultry? Or how to get a young girl who loves garlic to enjoy

---

[460] Tommaso Campanella (1568–1639), William Morris (1834–1896), and H. G. Wells (1866–1946) were eccentric thinkers and utopian writers. Campanella was an Italian theologian best known for his 1602 *The City of the Sun,* which imagined an ideal society based on common ownership. Morris was an English novelist and socialist who wrote several novels that depicted ideal versions of medieval societies. Wells was an English writer who is sometimes called "the Father of Science Fiction." His novels envisioned cooperative societies built around rational planning and science.

[461] Alphonse Allais (1854–1905) was a journalist and humorist. He was a founding member of the Dada movement and pioneered techniques like anti-art and irrational logic. Allais was a significant influence on surrealism and absurdist humor.

mathematics? It must be acknowledged that these speculations, couched in an unusual lexicon—pivots and postfaces, ascending and descending vibrations—can bewilder, if not outright deter, the uninitiated reader.

But let's muster the courage to move forward. Here, too, let's seek the 'substantial marrow'[462]: let's search for the deity within the clay doll, as Charles Gide,[463] our own prophet of Charles Fourier, suggests. When we tally up the truths uncovered, the possibilities recognized, and the necessities demonstrated by this great "romantic" visionary, we'll see that Fourier's foresight is significant not just in the particulars, but also in the grand scheme. He wasn't just the sharpest, most bitter critic of his era—for this dreamer could at times be a veritable Jeremiah[464]—but by combining critique with construction, he sketched out segments of the future with unmatched clarity and precision.

*
* *

What was the foundation of his philosophy? A systematic rejection of asceticism. He was repulsed by all the restrictions that moralists place on human nature. He was particularly critical of Christianity for its devaluation of luxury and its condemnation of instincts. We know that even at the start of the 19th century—with Buonarroti's reflections, among others, as evidence—the Christian and Spartan tendencies, with their holy oils and black broth, were united against the Athenian tendency, which was in favor of increasing products and refining needs. Fourier wholeheartedly adopted this latter view. He was

---

[462] The phrase "substantial marrow" originates from François Rabelais, who used it in his book series *Gargantua and Pantagruel* (1532-1564) to describe the essence or the most substantial part of something.

[463] Charles Gide (1847-1932) was a historian and economist who wrote on cooperatives. He played a leading role in founding the International Cooperative Alliance in 1895. Gide was also the founding editor of *Revue d'économie politique* (1887-) and served in this role until his death.

[464] Jeremiah (650-570 BCE), known as the "weeping prophet," was a figure in the Old Testament known for denouncing false prophets and their greed as well as condemning idolatry. He promoted the idea of a new covenant between God and Israel centered on forgiveness and inward devotion instead of empty rituals.

172

undoubtedly the most pagan of modern moralists. Even more fervently than the Saint-Simonians, he was prepared to vindicate the flesh. And he was determined not just to spare children any pain, but to refuse nothing to the passions. Wouldn't denying these passions ultimately be an affront to God Himself? If God has placed such irresistible impulses within us, wouldn't it be foolish for Him to forbid us from acting on them? This is the essence of the enigmatic phrase that Fourier's followers inscribed on his tombstone: "Attractions are proportional to destinies." This is also why the most basic wisdom tells us to "surrender to the siren" that is nature,[465] heed its warnings, interpret its symbols, and finally obey the law of attraction in the moral world that Fourier, a new Newton, has unveiled. Instead of the iron chains of coercion, let us boldly embrace the "chain of flowers" that binds the universe.

Fourier, in his quest to fulfill passions, identified more than 800 nuances. He labored with extraordinary precision to define them clearly so they could be fully satisfied. Let's focus on the overall outcome of this psychology: it serves as a timely counterpoint to the oversimplified psychology used by the creators of the homo economicus, whom Fourier scorned just as much as the moralists. They thought human activity could be boiled down to a single motive: profit. But in reality, even in economic life, people enjoy collaborating, comparing results, competing in groups, and most importantly, diversifying their pleasures. This "butterfly" passion, more so than the "composite" or the "cabalist,"[466] has been widely

---

[465] "We must in the end give in to its siren voice and study its laws." C. Fourier: *The Theory of the Four Movements*. Edited by G. S. Jones & I. Patterson. Cambridge University Press, 1996, p. 78.

[466] In Fourier's typology of the passions, there are twelve "radical" passions and one harmonious passion known as "unityism." Of the "radical" passions, five were sensuous, or "luxurious," with one corresponding to each of the five senses. Next, there were four affective, or "group," passions concerning family, friendship, ambition, and love. Lastly, there were three "distributive or serial" passions that ensured a coordination between sensual and affective passions: butterfly, composite, and cabalist. The *papillonne* or butterfly referred to periodic variety, the composite encompassed "blind" and uncalculating enthusiasm; and the cabalist passion was associated with competition and

discussed. There was a belief that Fourier advocated for, above all, a licentious approach to love. And this notion has contributed to the long-standing portrayal of socialists in France—from Louis Reybaud's "reformers" to those who are seen as destroyers not just of property, but first and foremost of the family. Fourier was certainly not opposed to greater sexual freedom. However, it is labor that he was most concerned with, labor whose monotony he wanted to break and transform into pleasure, a pleasure constantly renewed in pursuit of his ultimate goal: an unheard-of, unprecedented, and immeasurable increase in production.

We know what form this earthly paradise would take: the Phalanstery, Fourier's crowning achievement, where his dreams as an architect, gardener, and chef come together. A grand palace stands at the center of an experimental canton measuring a substantial square league, accommodating 1,600 members; it is equipped with a library, study rooms, and lounges. The wings are home to work and play areas for children. The buildings are linked to one another by enclosed, heated walkways. On the tables of the communal dining hall, 30 to 40 different dishes await the diners. As workers, they have already experienced the joy of variety, since they are divided into teams that flit from one task to another, from woodworking to gardening, from tending cherries to roses. These "passional series" lead to an unparalleled level of productive splendor. Fourier was convinced that this system could quadruple the actual yield and increase the relative yield twentyfold, multiplying the sum of pleasures to an extraordinary extent.

Confronted with this vision, Fourier was beside himself with excitement. He worried that if this "societal fairyland" were to be unveiled to people too abruptly, they might die of astonishment. Regardless, he felt sorry for them, having waited centuries for a formula that could deliver their salvation.

After such flights of fancy, it's hardly surprising that Marx categorized Fourier among the inventors who disregard the phases of

---

intrigue. For more detail, see D. Bell: Prophet of Eupsychia. Pp. 41–58 in *The American Scholar*, 38(1), 1968–69.

evolution. Proudhon, for his part, labeled him a mesmerized ideomaniac, likening him to a ballet master who whimsically arranges the movements of his groups. He thus stands accused of failing to recognize that there are laws of history, and that certain gradual transformations are necessary before other changes emerge as possibilities. A hasty verdict: like nearly all utopians critiqued by Karl Marx, Fourier too constructed his own philosophy of history. He was well aware of the stages that societies must go through to transition from "barbarism" to "civilization," and from there to "guaranteeism." He specifically acknowledged that "at least twenty centuries were necessary to elevate industry, science, and the arts to the level of refinement required for the establishment of the combined order."[467]

*
* *

Yet more than his theory of the past, it's Fourier's visions of the future that captivate us: these are the directives that the present can seek from his system.

A primary theme clearly stands out, setting Fourierism apart from Saint-Simonism: the primacy of consumers. What to do to dress and feed them well, enhance their wellbeing, and increase their pleasures tenfold—these are the challenges to which Fourier applied his meticulous ingenuity. With every technique or method introduced to him, his foremost question seemed to be, "will it result in better-provisioned tables?" He took particular joy in bringing to humanity recipes as a hotelier–philanthropist. The skill he aimed to impart to the many families living meagerly due to isolation was none other than the skill of collective housekeeping, only feasible within a broadened domestic association.

---

[467] C. Fourier: *The Theory of the Four Movements.* Cambridge University Press, 1996, pp. 96-97.

It's these kinds of concerns that explain why today, those who aim to remind political economy that the era of the consumer must finally come are eager to invoke Fourier's name.

Another aspect that sets Fourier apart from the Saint-Simonians, and aligns him with the Physiocrats, is his preference for agriculture, which he cherished particularly in the form of horticulture. The primary ambition of the Phalanstery was to make the land yield an exuberant profusion of vegetables, fruits, and assorted flowers. Manufacturing was always just an accessory, a supplement. Fourier seemed to accept industrial operations with reluctance, particularly if they led to risky speculation. Didn't he express his readiness to shatter the illusions of industrialism? While he envisioned industrial armies (complete with *bayadères* and *bacchantes*),[468] it was mainly to reclaim land for cultivation, to clear land, and to build levees, not to erect factories. The industrial backdrop of large-scale industry, so familiar to Enfantin and the Péreires, stirred no fondness in Fourier: it was amid orchards, among fields of carnations or roses, that he preferred to roam in his mind.

Moreover, with a lucidity unsurpassed by the editors of *The Producer*, he was keenly aware of the drawbacks and the numerous dangers posed by the current form of large-scale industry, as England had introduced it to the world. His thoughts here align with those of Sismondi,[469] the author of *New Principles of Political Economy*, the father of social economy, the man who most distinctly set the demands of

---

[468] *Bayadères* were Hindu dancing-girls and *bacchantes* were female revelers and followers of Dionysus, the god of wine-making, fertility, and ritual ecstasy in the religion of Ancient Greece.

[469] Jean Charles Léonard de Sismondi (1773–1842) was a Swiss political economist and historian who is remembered for his critiques of laissez-faire and coining the term *proletariat*. He was one of the first economists to analyze economic crises and advocated for cooperative alternatives to pure competition. Sismondi wrote the 1819 *Nouveaux principes d'économie politique*.

"philanthropy" against the ambitions of "chrematistics,"[470] and who exposed the harms of overproduction coupled with underconsumption.

Following in Sismondi's footsteps, yet infusing the economist's arguments with his own earthy eloquence, Fourier criticized "false, fragmented, repulsive, deceitful industry." He illustrated how the "frenzy to produce indiscriminately" triggers "plethoric crises" where poverty emerges from abundance itself. When competition among industrialists leads to concentration, does it benefit the masses? Not yet. The worker is given no assurance of sharing in the growing wealth. Fourier even asserted: "Factories prosper at the expense of the workers' impoverishment." With his methodical meticulousness, he identified and cataloged the "misfortunes of the industrious," the severe afflictions they endure, directly or indirectly: not just the poverty impacting their health and their families', but also the "mental miseries" they suffer from comparing themselves to others, the opportunities denied to them, and the uncertainty of their situation. Who has more vehemently exposed the repercussions of industrial anarchy?

However, there is one aspect of our civilization that particularly repulsed Fourier. It could be said that merchants were, to him, a personal enemy. As a commercial employee himself, he witnessed firsthand, from his father's drapery business, the petty cheats or "licenses for deceit" at the sales counter. He was astounded to see the price of an apple increase tenfold from Besançon to Paris. He held the class of middlemen responsible for the high cost of living, labeling them "an unproductive, deceitful, malevolent, economy-killing class." He asserted that nine-tenths of merchants and two-thirds of transportation agents are superfluous and therefore detrimental. He was outraged that agriculture, a principal function, is enslaved to commerce, a secondary function. Fourier was

---

[470] Deriving from Ancient Greece, *chrematistics* was the accumulation of wealth for its own sake, especially by usury. In contrast, *economics* was understood as the sale of goods at a right price.

relentless on this subject, saving his most scathing insults for the defenders of commercial parasitism.

This shows that the thought of the quintessential utopian was also critical in nature. The scourges he condemned are the same that socialism would vigorously fight against; the arguments at the heart of his denunciation are the same that socialism would elaborate on extensively.

*
* *

Yet if we consider the constructive rather than the critical aspect of his work, toward what type of socialism does he guide minds? Toward a socialism that would be neither democratic nor collectivist, that places little emphasis on political freedom or complete equality, and that endorses neither class struggle nor the transfer of the means of production to the state.

Fourier felt just as much disgust as Saint-Simon for a leveling egalitarianism. He was also not inclined to declare that everything is owed to the workers, that all value originates with them and should be returned to them. He asserted that capital and talent are as essential as labor for the successful operation of enterprises. He allotted each a share when the time came to distribute profits. In truth, he didn't wish for the eradication of classes, but rather for the softening of the conflicts that divide them in the current order, or rather disorder. He lamented and criticized the nature of their interactions in a striking summary: "an upward scale of hatred and a downward scale of contempt." He believed that his systems, which encouraged people of various backgrounds to collaborate in intersecting groups, could lead to a "fusion of classes through affectionate agreement." Meanwhile, he cautioned that his aim was to "enrich all classes of citizens without robbing any."

At any rate, there is one door Fourier was determined to keep shut: that of politics. The strategy he deemed necessary toward the parties vying for constitutional reform or the seizure of power was that of "absolute avoidance." Fourier, who had suffered in Lyon because of the

Revolution, was almost as critical as Comte would be of the philosophy that, in preparing for the Revolution, could only destroy and promise a freedom it was unable to guarantee. It offers diatribes where innovations are required. The distinction between formal freedoms—the powers of choice—and actual freedoms—mastery over nature—which Charles Andler has shown to be influential at the roots of German socialism, is starkly evident here. "How amusing a sovereign is," Fourier exclaimed, "when that sovereign is dying of hunger." And he challenged constitutionalism and liberalism to grant the people in our cities as many tangible rights as savages once had, when they could freely forage for their sustenance. In a "civilized" society, a proclamation of the Rights of Man is nothing more than an empty vessel.

Needless to say, Fourier's deep skepticism toward the system of political freedoms did not stem from a desire to reinstate the principle of authority. If he resisted following the lead of Sieyès or Barnave, it wasn't to rush into the embrace of Bonald. In the economic system he envisioned, the potential for arbitrary decisions would be minimized. He also believed that "authorities" should perform administrative roles rather than governmental ones. All leadership roles, or rather management positions, would be elective and, in theory, open to everyone. It's also worth noting that in these Phalansteries, where it's obvious to all that every regulation aims to maximize the satisfaction of passions, no regulation is seen as an oppressive burden: "Double and quadruple charms instead of double and quadruple discord." Collective discipline is "passionately agreed upon," all the more so because those who are dissatisfied always have the option to leave. This means that, through his belief in the power of passionate attraction and the harmonies it orchestrates, Fourier addressed the problem of authority in the most effective manner: by rendering it obsolete, or at least by rendering it inconspicuous. The human beehives he conceived naturally achieve the utmost in freedom and well-being.

Furthermore, the best safeguard Fourier offered against the misuse of authority and the excesses of regulation is precisely that he established no centralizing power within the nation at large. He didn't envision a state as a universal heir and universal regulator of labor, as the Saint-Simonians did. Instead, he saw the reorganization of the whole starting from the bottom up, not from the top down. If such a reorganization is to take place, it would be through the influence of a number of rejuvenated economic units, attracting one another and agreeing to set up mutually beneficial exchanges. This confirms that Fourier's aspirations were not toward a collectivist socialism, but rather toward a federalist socialism.

This federalism would involve new, broadly applicable methods of production and distribution. It would necessitate an effort to harmonize not just interpersonal relationships within groups, but also relationships between different groups. Consequently, an external, interphalansterian economy would need to be structured. And it is expected that this would, at the very least, require the involvement of councils that might resemble state bodies. Consider, for example, how these "communal bazaars" that Fourier envisioned for the era of guaranteeism are supposed to operate.

To assist the farmers of the Commune in selling their produce and purchasing fertilizers and equipment, there would be federal warehouses and rural banks. It would become necessary to integrate the labor of the factories with that of agriculture. Wouldn't the state, as the natural intermediary between associations, eventually establish a Ministry of Manufacturing? Didn't Fourier himself mention the need to create a league between the government and agriculture to counteract the industrial privateers?

But despite these foundational elements, Fourier's preferences lay with the structures built by small groups, each starting on their own land. And though in this system, centralized commands should be issued as infrequently as possible, it can be inferred that to address industrial anarchy, the creator of the Phalanstery, an adversary of all coercion, appeared to rely chiefly on an anarchistic form of socialism.

180

*

* *

Fourier, like Saint-Simon, had disciples. Influenced by figures such as Muiron,[471] Madame Vigoureux,[472] and Victor Considerant, a sort of school took shape. However, unlike the other, it never aspired to become a Church wracked with religious fervor. It also didn't contribute many new theories beyond those sketched by the master. The focus was on refining these ideas, discarding the eccentricities that dotted them, elaborating on the philosophy of history they entailed, and striving to adapt them to contemporary issues. In essence, the goal was to make Fourierism practical and, first and foremost, understandable, by removing its fantastical elements and increasingly presenting it as an experimental approach.

Considerant didn't just rehash Fourier's "novel of well-being"; he proved both the necessity and the feasibility of Fourier's proposed reforms. They are feasible because we are in a period of "ascending evolution"—the essential "apex resources" have been accumulated through scientific progress— and they are necessary because it is glaringly apparent that the masses are not reaping the benefits of these resources as they should. The masses are burdened with a new kind of feudalism, an industrial feudalism, "an aristocracy as oppressive as it is despicable," that capitalizes on the downfall of small merchants to dictate terms and swell its own share. Meanwhile, the workers' share diminishes. Like modern Sisyphuses, Tantaluses, and Danaïdes,[473] they exist in a true

---

[471] Just Muiron (1787–1881) was a journalist known for being Fourier's first disciple. He notably attempted to synthesize Fourier's theory of passionate attraction with Christianity.

[472] Clarisse Vigoureux (1789–1865) was a journalist who was first introduced to Fourierism by Muiron. She later moved to the short-lived Fourierist colony near Dallas, Texas known as La Réunion (1855–1857).

[473] In Greek mythology, Sisyphus, Tantalus, and the Danaids are residents of Tartarus, a deep abyss used as a dungeon for the wicked, as the prison for the Titans, and as the place where souls were judged after death.

"social hell." Would you like a glimpse of the phrases where Considerant summarizes his observations?

> "Our free-market industrialism is a colossal mechanism of immense power that ceaselessly siphons national wealth into the vast tanks of a new aristocracy while churning out famished legions of the poor and the proletariat."

Capitalist concentration, proletarianization, pauperism—the core tenets of "scientific" socialism are all present here in their nascent forms, and it's evident that Georges Sorel[474] wasn't mistaken in regarding Considerant's *Principles of Socialism* from 1843 as one of the manifestos that most directly paved the way to the *Communist Manifesto*.

However, let's clarify this. To move toward socialism, proponents of Fourierism would be willing to make increasingly greater concessions to democracy, but never to communism. Democracy was gaining dominance in the 19th century and was on its way to becoming the "modern dogma." This was a reality that Considerant acknowledged in 1843, pleased if he could persuade the advocates of this dogma that the political innovations they prized so highly were merely introductory: their own principles should alert them to the fact that the social problem was significantly more critical than the political one. But events progressed, the unforeseen happened, and the Republic was declared. The Fourierists, some of whom had slipped many of their master's ideas into the groups that laid the groundwork for the Revolution, aligned with the Republic: perhaps with more enthusiasm than their master would have preferred, they were swept up by the tide. Their newspaper, *Peaceful*

---

[474] Georges Sorel (1847–1922) was a political theorist known for advocating for the general strike and revolutionary syndicalism. Sorel's best-known work, the 1908 *Reflections on Violence,* argued that violence was necessary in order to create social change. His ideas were a major influence on the rise of fascism.

Democracy,[475] also embraced this motto: social reform is the goal, the Republic is the means.

Considerant readily agreed with the synthesis that the unfolding events seemed to demand. "All socialists are republicans. All republicans are socialists." There is a logic to the century. And 1848[476] is the logical heir to 1789, provided, however, that we indeed remember that an heir doesn't mean a repeat; the Republic, after the growth of industry and its various consequences, requires a new order, which can only be a socialist order.

Considerant passionately argued this point in the book he published in 1848, after the June Days,[477] *Socialism before the Old World, or the Living before the Dead.*[478] "The Revolution is not finished... In 1830, socialism was nothing, now it is everything." And the problem it must solve to prevent society's demise is indeed "the transformation of wages, the last form of dependency." Yet to address this issue, several solutions are suggested. Considerant, in his review, didn't conceal his dread of the authoritarian, coercive, and negative forms of socialism. Specifically, he spoke out against a "simple and gnarled" socialism that would halt at the mere emancipation of the serfs of capital. This indicates that Fourier's follower was positioning himself against any socialism advocating class conflict, the dictatorship of the proletariat, or the

---

[475] *La démocratie pacifique* (1843–1851) was a Fourierist newspaper that was suppressed by Louis-Napoléon Bonaparte (1808–1873) following the coup d'etat of December 2, 1851.

[476] The Revolution of 1848 forced the abdication of King Louis-Philippe I and brought about France's short-lived Second Republic (1848–1852), which was rife with tribalistic tendencies. The revolution was crushed when conservative and capitalistic forces took control with a coup d'etat by Napoleon Bonaparte's nephew Louis Napoleon and proclaimed himself the "Emperor of the French."

[477] The June Days uprising occurred in June 22–26, 1848 when civilians rebelled after the announcement that the government had closed the National Workshops that guaranteed work, as well as two socialist-leaning newspapers. The uprising was crushed and lead to over a thousand insurgents being killed and 10,000 arrested.

[478] *Le socialisme devant le vieux monde, ou les vivants devant les morts.*

nationalization of all wealth: Considerant was confident that Phalansterian socialism, optional and voluntary, would act as a counter to communist socialism.

Chapter VIII

Assessment of Fourierism: Present

Of the multitude of ideas stirred up by Fourier or his followers, how many have taken root or are in the process of taking root in today's reality? Did these peculiar "clouds" drift across the sky merely to entertain our gaze, or have they, in turn, enriched the earth?

A series of books can aid us in responding to this question: Gaumont's[479] on *The History of Cooperation*, Friedberg's on *Fourierism and the Contemporary Social Movement*,[480] Poisson's[481] on *Cooperation and Socialism*, Bernard Lavergne's on *Cooperative Order*,[482] and most importantly, those by Charles Gide, whose name is indelibly linked with that of Fourier.

Charles Gide, renowned for his appreciation of bold and imaginative ideas, has often taken pleasure in illustrating that Fourier, more than any other utopian thinker, deserves credit for a number of predictions that have come to fruition. It is not necessarily the case that contemporary innovators consciously drew from his theories when devising new techniques or practices. Yet their successes are proof that this visionary was endowed with a kind of second sight, possessing an almost prophetic intuition of future forms. At the dawn of the 19th century, Fourier foresaw a time when one could depart Paris in the morning, have lunch in Lyon, and dine in Marseille. He envisioned astronomers capable of alerting England, via the airwaves, of a ship's arrival in China. He predicted that through reforestation, humans would gain the ability to influence the climate. Thus, from among Fourier's thousand and one

---

[479] Jean Gaumont (1876–1972) was a historian of cooperatives who wrote the 1923 *Histoire de la coopération*.
[480] *Le Fouriérisme et le mouvement social contemporain* (1926).
[481] Ernest Poisson (1882–1942) was a lawyer, political economist, and cooperativist who wrote the 1922 book *La coopération et le socialisme*.
[482] *L'ordre coopératif* (1926).

inventions, a significant number have, in one form or another, become a reality.

Perhaps more intriguing than this colorful array of toy-tools are the overarching methods he championed, stemming from his concerns as a moralist, many of which are beginning to be implemented today. Leading the way are his thoughts on education, which are being embraced or rediscovered by proponents of "New Education." He significantly bolstered the liberal traditions of Montaigne[483] and Rabelais,[484] which were overshadowed in France by the favored methods of the Jesuits[485] and Napoleon. He advocated for a "unitary" education that brings people together and accustoms them to collaboration, but above all, he desired it to be "libertarian," respecting the diversity of children's tastes and their need for variety; he also envisioned it as "laborist," encouraging children to contemplate the impact of their actions and tightly integrating schools with workshops and fields. It's also worth noting that he advised educators to employ the technique of "absorbing substitution" to align children's emotions with the demands of community life, thus prefiguring what would later be termed "sublimation."[486] These examples alone are telling.

---

[483] Michel de Montaigne (1533–1592) was an influential Renaissance philosopher who pioneered the genre of personal introspection and self-examination. He expressed doubts about religious dogma and was an advocate of free thinking and open-mindedness.

[484] François Rabelais (1494–1553) was a Franciscan monk and writer during the Renaissance. His works were enormously popular and known for their humor and anti-establishment messages. Rabelais satirized ignorance, intolerance, and the abuses of religion.

[485] The Jesuits (1540–) are a religious order who are directed by the Pope and make an oath of "perpetual poverty, chastity, and obedience." The Jesuits established many schools, universities, and ministries around the world and have been advisors to powerful rulers due to their diplomacy.

[486] Sublimation is a psychological defense mechanism where socially unacceptable impulses and behaviors are transformed into socially acceptable impulses and behaviors.

From Fröbel,[487] who was familiar with Fourier, to Montessori[488] and her followers, one can appreciate how extensively ideas dear to the proponent of passionate attraction have been trialed in kindergartens and school-workshops.

Another group that owes him special tribute is the feminists. Fourier was clearer in his assertions than Saint-Simon—who only made a couple of references to the rights women might claim (notably, he suggested they vote for a subscription to Newton's tomb[489])—and had a broader perspective than Enfantin, who was primarily focused on the sexual relationship between the Priest and the Woman-Messiah. Fourier comprehensively addressed the issues central to feminist demands[490]—not that he had much interest in extending voting rights to women, which would be surprising given his political stance, but at least in the social realm, he protested against all institutions that have prevented women from realizing their full potential. Far from confining women to the Proudhonian dilemma of housewife or courtesan, he advocated for opening up all sorts of careers to them, careers that are in fact better suited to their nature than to men's. Although not particularly egalitarian in

---

[487] Friedrich Fröbel (1782–1852) was a German pedagogue known for opening the first kindergarten. He argued that play was essential for children's learning and development and sought to instill a sense of wonder, creativity, and social skills through self-directed play and interaction.

[488] Maria Montessori (1870–1952) was an Italian pedagogue and physician known for developing the Montessori method of education that involves incorporating student's interests, hands-on learning practices, and self-directed activities into the teaching method.

[489] In Saint-Simon's 1803 *Letters of an Inhabitant of Geneva to His Contemporaries,* he suggested to open a subscription at Newton's tomb to nominate artists and scientists to command the *Council of Newton,* which would oversee the progress of humanity.

[490] Fourier's key work on feminism and sexual liberation, *Nouveau monde amoureux* ("New Amorous World"), shocked his disciples so much that it was not published until 1967. Consequently, today, there is even more literature on the relationship between Fourierism and women's liberation in comparison to when Bouglé was writing. For more detail, see L. F. Goldstein: Early Feminist Themes in French Utopian Socialism: The St.-Simonians and Fourier. Pp. 91–108 in *Journal of the History of Ideas,* 43(1), 1982.

many other areas, Fourier, as Gide notes, claimed equality for men and women not only under the law but also in terms of morality. And it was he who asserted clearly that the progress of societies can be measured by the degree of emancipation granted to women. It's thus understandable why a reformer like Flora Tristan,[491] who in *The Workers' Union* of 1843 defended the equally sacred causes of workers and women, turned to Fourier and chose a quote from the great initiator as the epigraph for her book.[492] Do today's feminists remember this? No one has worked more than Fourier toward this revolution in customs, laden with diverse consequences, which Lucien Romier suggests calling "the Promotion of Women."

*
* *

But of course, what is most important to us is to assess the extent to which Fourier's visionary ideas, established to address the social question whose tragic importance Victor Considerant so tenaciously emphasized, have been integrated into the economic institutions of today.

Fourier placed his utmost trust in the establishment of Phalansteries. Has the experiment been attempted? Did it produce the expected outcomes? The inventor would undoubtedly argue that the experiment has not been conducted, because nowhere have his plans been applied in their entirety—and he clearly wouldn't have compromised even in the slightest. However, a number of communities were established under his influence. In founding them, there was an intention to at least follow the broad strokes of his philosophy. It was believed that

---

[491] Flora Tristan (1803-1844) was a French-Peruvian socialist known for her contributions to feminism. She was one of the first thinkers to emphasize women workers and promoted the emancipation of women. Tristan wrote the 1843 *L'union ouvrière*.

[492] In the epigraph of Tristan's posthumous *L'emancipation de la femme* ("Emancipation of the Women") (1846), she quotes Fourier: "Social progress and changes of periods occur due to the progress of women towards freedom, and decadence of social order occurs due to the decrease in women's freedom... In summary, the extension of women's *privileges is the general principle of all social progress.*"

188

his grand plan was being put to the test. Whether in Condé-sur-Vesgre or Cîteaux in France, or Brook Farms or Texas in America, attempts were made to organize both serial labor and communal living, in line with the principles of the Agricultural Domestic Association. In Texas, it was the master's foremost disciple, Considerant, who personally organized the venture. But there were failures upon failures: Gide, the latest historian of these *Communist and Cooperative Colonies*,[493] acknowledges that those claiming inspiration from Fourier were among the least fortunate. Sometimes a fire consumed the house, other times the enterprise lacked funds. But most often, it was harmony that was sorely lacking. The members proved incapable of maintaining the complete association that Fourier envisioned, one that combined both production and consumption.

But perhaps, even without full implementation, Fourierist ideas might find partial applications. Perhaps production cooperatives embody one aspect of his vision, while consumer cooperatives embody another? The pieces are valuable, so why shouldn't they be useful even when separated?

No one would suggest that cooperative production associations owe their existence entirely to Fourier's theories. Before him, Lange, concurrently Buchez, and subsequently Louis Blanc, all championed this same solution. By pooling their resources, organizing their labor among themselves, and distributing the profits it yields, couldn't workers eliminate the need for capital, or at least limit the control of the employers?

This was one of the great hopes ignited by the events of 1848. What Louis Blanc primarily sought from the state was its support for workers' associations through model regulations, financial aid, and a guaranteed customer base. These associations were intended to act as the driving force behind the new type of state he envisioned, aiming to establish an order that was both democratic and socialist. Following the

---

[493] *Colonies communistes ou cooperatives* (1927–1928).

collapse of 1848, the rise of the Empire spelled disaster for most of the associations of tailors, hatters, and carpenters that had been established. It wasn't until 1865, as the Empire increasingly recognized the need to appease the working class, that similar associations began to re-emerge. There was another surge under the Republic. A consultative chamber was set up, providing workers' associations with model statutes, striving to standardize their structure and synchronize their activities. Yet diversity remained the norm. An exhibition of workers' associations? As Charles Gide would say, it's primarily a Museum of Samples. Some were independent, while others were affiliated with a union or a political party. Some were established without any capital, while others utilized capital to different extents.

Where might we find those that have succeeded in implementing a portion of the Fourierist agenda?

Some have drawn direct inspiration from it, such as the *Familistère*[494] at Guise, founded and sustained by Godin,[495] an admirer of Fourier. He wasn't satisfied with simply establishing a "Social Palace" for communal living among the workers next to the workshops where stoves were manufactured. He aimed for the workers to share in the enterprise's profits and, through their share of the profits, become its shareholders. Different categories of workers were recognized, based on the shares they received: auxiliaries, participants, members, and associates. Directors and members of the Supervisory Board received 18%, talent's share as prescribed by Fourier. In the end, a number of cherished Fourierist ideas

---

[494] The Familistère—a portmanteau of *famille* ("family") and *monastère* ("monastery")—was a type of social housing experiment inspired by Fourier that was designed to provide workers and their families with comfortable living conditions. It included not only housing but also communal facilities like schools, shops, and laundry facilities. Its design was intended to foster a sense of community among its inhabitants.

[495] Jean-Baptiste André Godin (1817–1888) was a political theorist, social innovator, and industrialist who started a self-contained community in Guise, France in 1856 known as the Familistère de Guise. He sought to emancipate workers from capitalist exploitation through cooperatives.

were realized in this model association, which regrettably remained the only one in existence.

Certainly, there are a few others that hold on to elements of the Fourierist ideal. For instance, a painters' association, Le Travail, allocates its profits in line with Fourier's principles: 37% to capital, 13% to management, and 32% to the workers, plus 17% for their pensions.

Overall, workers' production associations have not retained much of Fourierism. Nor can it be said that they have inadvertently stumbled upon the methods Fourier believed should govern labor organization or profit distribution, even if they have forgotten his teachings. Above all, it cannot be claimed that they have significantly contributed to the overall transformation of the economic and social regime whose faults he criticized. Certainly, their future should not be dismissed. They can serve a useful purpose in various forms, as Dubreuil[496] suggests in *The Industrial Republic*, outlining the necessary conditions. However, to date, despite the recent solemn acknowledgment of their efforts, workers' production associations have had only a limited impact. Even with state subsidies or orders, they are not equipped to compete with large capitalist companies.

*

* *

Consumer cooperatives might, in all respects, achieve more substantial results and more directly fulfill a grand Fourierist vision: the fight against intermediaries by unifying consumers. By joining forces to purchase goods and commodities, reselling them to themselves at the fairest prices, and then distributing the profits based on their purchases, aren't cooperatives also enacting a revolution? It's a quiet revolution, but

---

[496] Hyacinthe Dubreuil (1883–1971) was a writer and syndicalist. He advocated for autonomous workshops with the aim to educate workers and provide economic, intellectual, and moral fulfillment. Dubreuil wrote the 1923 *La république industrielle*.

191

one perhaps more productive than others, gradually transforming the workings of the modern economy, penny by penny.

Here we are confronted with a movement of a different magnitude than that of the production cooperatives. "No noise, lots of hard work"—isn't this the motto in action here? By 1925, it was estimated that, assuming four members per cooperative family, the buying and selling activities of "distributive" cooperatives involved nearly 10 million French people. Bernard Lavergne, who eagerly calls our attention to this development, encapsulates it in a few key numbers:

> "Two and a half million cooperative members enrolled in our societies, annual sales of 1.8 billion, a National Federation that includes more than half of all cooperators and two-thirds of the nation's cooperative strength if we measure by turnover, a central cooperative for purchasing and production, also known as the Wholesale Store, with sales surpassing 350 million a year, and a Bank of Cooperatives that since October 1925 has held over 120 million in public deposits and operates more than 1,000 auxiliary cash desks or branches—these are the main achievements of French cooperatives, captured in a few overall figures."

It's noteworthy that this type of cooperative takes pride not only in the number of people it feeds but also in the level of organization it has achieved. Cooperative stores, once isolated and individualistic, have collectively recognized the importance of federation, of mutual support through coordinating their orders and setting terms with producers. This is what has enabled them to provide invaluable services during and after the war. It also accounts for the influence they can wield over production, as they become shareholders, owners, and managers of large factories where they are the main customers, thereby striving to facilitate a more rational alignment of production with consumption. This is why Albert Thomas[497] was not mistaken a few years back in commending the

---

[497] Albert Thomas (1878–1932) was a socialist, the first director of the International Labour Organization (ILO), and a collaborator with Bouglé. He

192

Cooperative Federation for being on track to become a public institution destined to spawn various social transformations.

Furthermore, as Bernard Lavergne suggests, we might be on the verge of uncovering and implementing a formula that could, through the expansion of cooperatives, address one of the most compelling issues of our time: to socialize without nationalizing. The author refers to what he calls cooperative utilities: public interest ventures authorized by the state but maintaining their independence. For instance, a company for operating a railway, a potash mine, water distribution, or river development, consisting of various legal entities (the state, municipalities, a consortium of users), would only recognize its consumers as shareholders, wouldn't be focused on generating profits per se, and would allocate surpluses to a reserve fund. Their primary aim would always be to enhance consumption conditions without disrupting the technical needs of production. The author believes this is the only path toward achieving "industrialized nationalizations" that are as technically proficient as private enterprises. It is the cooperative spirit that opens not only this path but also endless other possibilities.

But whether we're talking about first or second-degree cooperatives, those that combine individuals or legal entities, how much do we recall Fourierist principles? Or at least, how much do we adhere to them unwittingly? This is what I aim to determine. Yet experts disagree—*grammatici certant*.[498] For Gide, the lineage is clear: in his talks on consumer cooperatives, he consistently cites Fourier as the quintessential forerunner, whose shadow he is glad to stand in. Isn't it just a matter of properly interpreting Fourier's utopias, adapting his concepts of the collective household known as the phalanstery, in order to glean numerous useful tips for the families of consumers? Poisson and

---

played an important role in the formation of the ILO and helped to solidify labor regulations, workers' welfare, and support for unions.

[498] Translates from Latin as "Grammarians dispute." The phrase comes from "Grammatici certant, et adhuc sub iudice lis est" (Horace, Ars Poetica, 78): "Grammarians argue, and the dispute is not over yet."

Lavergne are less convinced. In the practices of today's consumer cooperatives, they struggle to see the imprint of the master. The cooperative's golden rule, which dictates that the year's profits be distributed back to the buyers in proportion to their purchases—wasn't it a humble flannel-wearing worker, Charles Howarth,[499] a member of the Rochdale Society of Equitable Pioneers,[500] who first enshrined it in the charter of his association? Therefore, this particular innovation seems to have emerged from the workers' instincts, shaped by everyday experience, rather than from the grand scheme of a philosopher.

Indeed, we may not find any evidence of this vital technique for consumer cooperatives in Fourier's writings. But does that mean they owe him nothing? Gide's own example could be used as evidence. In the social economics he taught to so many students, which significantly contributed to the 'great thaw' of orthodox political economy, two distinct sources of inspiration converge. It's as if two spirits dwell within this structure: the Protestant tradition, emphasizing social duty, and the Fourierist vision, aiming for the complete fulfillment of all human passions, for both rich and poor alike. It is along this path, the fragrant road of passional attraction, that the author reached the belief that the consumer cooperative is a redemptive principle for humanity, which has been marred by the laissez-faire attitude of big industry. And considering the unparalleled contributions this professor made to the cooperative movement, stunning audiences with his eloquence and knowledge, and compelling the often-disparate elements of the movement to coordinate their efforts and elevate their ideals, there can be no doubt that, at least through Gide, the French cooperative movement owes a great deal to Fourier. Technicalities aside, the battle against parasitism and the defense

---

[499] Charles Howarth (1814–1868) was an English co-operator and Owenite who helped establish what is now known as the Co-operative Wholesale Society (1863–), a British co-operative federation.
[500] Formed in 1844, the Rochdale Society of Equitable Pioneers was a consumer cooperative known for forming the basis of the modern cooperative movement, primarily through their Rochdale Principles. The group was formed by 28 workers who had been laid off during a depression.

of consumers, those two rallying cries that would resonate for a long time, were without a doubt initiated by the creator of the Phalanstery.

Regarding second-degree cooperatives, which unite legal entities to form direct management enterprises, it can still be said that the inspiration is Fourierist, since they involve replacing private enterprise with businesses that don't seek capitalist-style profits, all for the benefit of consumers. However, Fourier doesn't seem to have anticipated anything in his plans similar to the structures we see today. We've noted that he recommended the establishment of communal counters to offer a variety of services to community members, and he wasn't opposed to the idea of enlisting the state's help against industrial pirates. But how the state could participate in public-interest enterprises without hindering them is something the creator of the Phalanstery didn't specify. These efforts at a mixed economy are more reminiscent of Saint-Simonian blueprints. And as Bernard Lavergne, a proponent of cooperative management, first points out, this approach, allowing for Fourier's favored tactic of complete detachment from politics, would likely be one of the best ways to realize "Saint-Simon's magnificent concept of the administration of things separate from the government of people." Here, the two streams would come together to power the wheels of the new mills...

*

* *

After these analyses, it might be easier now to assess what Fourierism has contributed to today's socialism. We've observed that between 1830 and 1848, several followers of the Fourierist school, inclined towards action, had essentially prepared a pool of ideas that the Revolution would later attempt to implement. Fourierism thrived not only in the works of Considerant but also in those of Louis Blanc, Pecqueur, and Vidal,[501] who proposed frameworks for organizing workers' associations. These were fleeting endeavors. Following the

---

[501] François Vidal (1812–1872) was a lawyer and socialist politician known for being critical of liberal economics. He was first associated with Saint-Simonism but later became associated with Fourierism.

backlash after the unsuccessful revolution, one could say that even the memory of these efforts was nearly lost.

But didn't Fourierism have another means of resurgence later on? Aren't fragments of it found within the ranks of Marxism? Weitling,[502] who wrote *Guarantees of Harmony and Freedom*, also read Fourier. And as Charles Andler has demonstrated, Weitling's thought was familiar to the authors of the *Communist Manifesto*. Marx and Engels owe a debt to him, and through him to Fourier, not just for a compelling critique of industrial anarchy, but also for the concept of what could be expected from the "armies" of workers. One could argue that Marxism, a formidable synthesis, incorporates Fourierism just as much as Saint-Simonism. Marx, in overshadowing his forerunners, utilized them. It could be said that he kept their ideas alive by causing us to forget their origins.

Of course, he added much more to it, in particular everything that was suggested to him by his recollections of German philosophy, along with the influence of his experiences in England: the idea of necessary catastrophes, closely tied to Hegelian dialectics, which demands the negation of the negation before the final synthesis; the concept of class struggle as the essential engine of history; and the notion of the dictatorship of the proletariat seizing state power, a necessary step toward establishing a socialist regime. If any of these ideas prove to be mistaken or simply inadequate when confronted with reality, shouldn't we seek foundations in the earlier, more complex and adaptable systems that Marxism only partially employed? Won't this prompt us to look to Fourierism, for instance, for means to temper the authority of Marxism?

Indeed, despite the dominance of Marxism and its established doctrine within the unified socialist party of France, it wouldn't be

---

[502] Wilhelm Weitling (1808–1871) was a German inventor, political activist, and communist. He helped to establish an underground communist movement in Germany known as the League of the Just (1836–1847), later to be the Communist League (1847–1852). He wrote the 1842 *Garantien der Harmonie und Freiheit*.

196

challenging to demonstrate that in the thinking of various French socialist leaders—such as Rouanet,[503] Millerand,[504] G. Renard,[505] and Jaurès—one can detect echoes of Fourierism, along with a certain regret for having allowed its vital essence to dissipate. Specifically, couldn't it be the influence of Fourierism that led Jaurès to connect his aversion to asceticism with his skepticism toward state control, and his favoring of the reconciliatory nature of federalism that counts on the collective endeavors of both trade unions and cooperatives?

Perhaps, as facts increasingly convince socialists that it's futile to await an economic revolution from a political power play, and that it's irresponsible to not construct anything positive in anticipation, we might witness a return to the practical lessons drawn from Fourier's utopias. Take, for example, the optimism we find in Marcel Déat's *Socialist Perspectives* regarding the progress of cooperatives, driven by a socialist vision eager to act within the economic sphere. When we hear him proclaim that cooperatives might one day become the Church of a new era, it becomes clear that the Fourierist forest is not entirely barren.

Need we say that both radical-socialists and traditional socialists alike might harvest resources from its trees? Fourierist socialism was among the first ideologies to advocate for the abolition of wage labor without necessarily abolishing property ownership. And we have observed similar proposals at recent congresses of the Radical Party. A pragmatic socialism and a socialism-infused radicalism could continue to work together for a while longer under the banner of Fourierism.

---

[503] Gustave Rouanet (1855–1927) was a journalist, socialist politician, and a disciple of Benoît Malon.

[504] Alexandre Millerand (1859–1943) was a politician who helped found the French section of the Workers' International socialist party. He was France's first socialist president and served from 1920 to 1924.

[505] Georges Renard (1876–1943) was a philosopher of law and socialist intellectual. He was a follower of Maurice Hauriou (1856–1929) and promoted a Christian philosophy of law based in the Renaissance and the Revolution.

Meanwhile, cooperatives eager to stay independent and above partisan politics find in the legacy of phalansterian ideology the means to unite those who, without resorting to class conflict, aim to lay the groundwork for the social reconstruction that appeared necessary after the war.

Let's revisit the "Manifesto" that was signed in 1921 by two hundred intellectuals and academics for the inaugural issue of the *Journal of Cooperative Studies*.[506] It echoes Jaurès' description of cooperatives as "laboratories of social experiments." They demonstrate that a business can thrive "without the enticement of profit or the push of competition." They employ capital, but deny it the power to dictate or hoard the enterprise's earnings. Far from aiming to swap the tyranny of capital for that of labor, they reject the notion that producers alone are qualified to represent the public interest. They place their bets on organized consumers, who "can have no other interests than those of the general populace."

The primacy of consumers, the fight against intermediary profit, and the roles assigned to both capital and labor—we may acknowledge these as the core tenets of Fourierism, now highlighted by its most esteemed expounder, Charles Gide, and showcased as a doctrine that is both redemptive and reconciliatory.

---

[506] *Revue des études cooperatives* (1921–). The journal was renamed in 1984 and is now known as the *Revue internationale de l'économie sociale*.

Chapter IX

Assessment of Proudhonism: Past

Proudhon doesn't belong to the lineage of the great inventors. He's not to be placed in the second tier, but rather in the second phase of French social economy of the 19th century. Born in 1809 and dying in 1865, he witnessed a succession of philosophical systems and political regimes. The trials of the Revolutions prompted his deep contemplation. He stood ready to push back not only against blind traditionalism, but also against reckless utopianism. Completely devoid of any romanticism, the term 'utopian socialism' hardly fits his stance: a more accurate term, as Stein[507] pointed out as early as 1842 in his authoritative work on socialism in France, is the ultimate 'critical socialism.'

But what, after all, does this socialism want, where does it aim, if it indeed qualifies as socialism? How should we categorize the author whose early writings deny property, while one of his later works affirms it? Every time we think we've pinned down this enigmatic genius with a formula, we realize he has slipped away: he is fond of opposition in all its forms, fundamentally a conciliator, yet playing with antitheses and antinomies; at once affable and fierce, arguing against and then for property or associations; a sociologist and an individualist, critical of democracy, yet even more critical of authoritarian regimes. Between the two poles of *What is Property?*[508] from 1840 and *Theory of Property*[509] from 1865, through the *System of Economic Contradictions*,[510] *Justice in*

---

[507] Lorenz von Stein (1815–1890) was a German economist. He wrote several influential works on socialism, including the 1842 *Der Sozialismus und Kommunismus des heutigen Frankreich* ("The Socialism and Communism of Today's France"), and helped to introduce socialist ideas into Germany.

[508] *Qu'est-ce que la propriété ? ou Recherches sur le principe du droit et du gouvernement.*

[509] *Théorie de la propriété.*

[510] *Système des contradictions économiques: Philosophie de la misère* (1846).

the Revolution and in the Church,[511] and *War and Peace,*[512] how many shifting nuances there are in his multifaceted thought! Ultimately, Proudhon is Proteus[513]: unclassifiable.

Let's attempt to first understand the diversity of his tendencies, the experiences that inform them, and the solutions they lead to. Let's take a closer look at this compelling and vexing figure—perhaps compelling *because* he is vexing? Consider him as an egalitarian commoner, individualist sociologist, anticlerical moralist, mutualist accountant, federalist, and syndicalist; only then might we be able to discern to what extent he remains both a democrat and a socialist, and decide, among the numerous successors who claim his legacy today, who truly resonates with the depth of his thought.

*
 * *

A distinct trait sharply distinguishes Proudhon from Saint-Simon and Fourier. Fourier, the merchant's son, himself became a small-time commercial clerk. Saint-Simon, regardless of his circumstances, always remained a nobleman. Proudhon was born and fundamentally remained a commoner. The son of a cooper and a cook, he assisted his father in the cellar, tended animals in the fields, became a typographer, then co-director of a small printing shop, and finally an accountant in a transport company—always in close contact with those who eked out a meager living from their labor, faced the constant dread of unemployment, and always fiercely defending them with both pen and passion. When the Academicians of Besançon awarded him a scholarship, the Suard pension, to pursue his studies, he warned them, with both charity and irony, that he would never abandon the cause of his "brothers in labor and poverty." It was with them in mind that he devoured the books of the Besançon Library and the Institute, attended lectures at the Sorbonne,

---

[511] *De la justice dans la Révolution et dans l'Église* (1858).
[512] *La guerre et la paix: recherches sur le principe et la constitution du droit des gens* (1861).
[513] In Ancient Greek mythology, Proteus was the elusive god of sea change and symbolized fluidity.

200

the Collège de France, and the Conservatory of Arts and Crafts,[514] studied Adam Smith, and sought to understand Hegel. His capacity for absorption was formidable. He was the autodidact who aspired to become an encyclopedist. Yet he was never a detached intellectual, proud to isolate himself in thought. When addressing the plight of workers, he remained a man who had personally "suffered from an accounting error"; he could not refrain from—using his own term—uttering genuine roars of rage. No matter how learned he became, he remained *filius fabri.*[515]

This likely explains one of Proudhon's deeply rooted tendencies: the will to establish equality among people. This will is not found to the same degree in Saint-Simon or Fourier. Far from it: as we have seen, Saint-Simonism, critical of nobles and heirs, calls for a bonus for "capabilities." Fourierism, for its part, reserves a share for "talents." Proudhon did not share this view. He advocated for the equivalence of roles and even faculties. From the collective perspective, since all roles are necessary, aren't they all fundamentally equal? As for the faculties bestowed by nature, what are they worth compared to what society contributes? A well-conceived polytechnic education, which would expose a child to a range of human arts, could enable every worker to attain the necessary philosophy. Genius itself, rather than a deity, is a "sublime child." This ultimately means that Proudhon staunchly denies anything that could justify inequality. He confidently asserts: "The tendency of society is toward the equality of intelligences and the leveling of conditions."

However, from the outset we must recognize a limit where his egalitarianism falters: the question of women's rights. We have seen how Saint-Simonism and Fourierism are prepared to expand them. Proudhon, on the other hand, insisted on keeping women within the domestic sphere. In his eyes, the family is sacrosanct. It is the pillar of

---

[514] The *Conservatoire national des arts et métiers* (1794–) is a grande école promoting education and research.
[515] This is a reference to Matthew 13:55 in the Bible, where Jesus is referred to as *filius fabri*, which translates from Latin as "the son of a carpenter."

justice, even within the social order. And for a just society to emerge, it is imperative that the man remains the master within the familial group. Grounded in rural tradition and recalling the Roman *pater familias*,[516] Proudhon systematically aligns more closely with Bonald and theocrats than with his forerunners in socialism, those reformers, denounced by Louis Reybaud, who sought to dismantle the family.[517]

Yet should one try to classify him among the traditionalists who advocate for authority, one would face stern rebuffs from our man, "the man of individuality above all," as he himself declared! His preference is for the "unsubmissive" and "reasoning" personality. This personality is the salt of the earth, and it alone, upon closer inspection, prevents societies from disintegrating. Hence Proudhon's famous hymn to vengeful irony. Hence his incessant appeals to liberty: "Charm of my existence, without which work is torture and life a prolonged death." Thus, in Proudhon, we see the constant resurgence of the most ungovernable character: a temperament that could be described not only as liberal but as libertarian.

What's remarkable, or perhaps surprising, is that this libertarian also happens to be the most decisive of sociologists. This was demonstrated long ago in my *The Sociology of Proudhon*[518]: one of the theories he was most proud to have developed is a "metaphysics of the group," which accounts for the specific effects of collective force, the reality of the social being, the revelation of reason manifesting in and

---

[516] In Roman law, *pater familias* referred to the oldest male in a household, who legally held authority.

[517] For a detailed analysis of Proudhon's antiquated views of women and his anti-feminism, see: A. Copley: Pierre-Joseph Proudhon: A Reassessment of His Role as a Moralist. Pp. 194–221 in *French History*, 3(2), 1989. Proudhon, like Charles Fourier and Karl Marx, was also notoriously antisemitic. A substantial amount of Fourier and Proudhon's antisemitism appears to derive from their negative reactions to Saint-Simonism, whose leaders were predominately Jewish. For more information, see Z. Szajkowski: The Jewish Saint-Simonians and Socialist Antisemites in France. Pp. 33–60 in *Jewish Social Studies*, 9(1), 1947.

[518] *La sociologie de Proudhon* (1911), which has been translated and is forthcoming at *little big eye publishing*.

through society. "For society is a person, do you understand?"[519] Overall, Proudhon's sociological sense was as developed as Comte's himself. And when writing to Cournot[520] about morality—here anticipating Durkheim and Lévy-Bruhl[521]—he contended that morality primarily reflects a "collective essence."

Nevertheless, the practical conclusions Proudhon reached are diametrically opposed to those of Comte, and when establishing the foundation of justice in moral terms, he spoke a "personalist" language that more readily evokes Renouvier.[522] "Respect yourself," for him, is ultimately the fundamental precept of morality. And he never wavered in prescribing that modern society should respect the individual. He accomplished the remarkable feat, as we've said, of compelling collective reason to sanctify personal rights.

To achieve such foundations, it is clear that Proudhon employed not only sociology proper but also a philosophy of history, and especially a dialectic that illustrates how reason reveals itself through a succession of oppositions. It is known that Proudhon prided himself on applying a Hegelian method. It is also known that Marx claimed Proudhon had misunderstood it. According to Marx, Proudhon, fundamentally eclectic as dictated by his education and his position as a "petty bourgeois," was

---

[519] P.-J. Proudhon: Resistance to the Revolution: Louis Blanc and Pierre Leroux. *La Voix de Peuple,* 1849. Translated by B. Tucker. In *Property is Theft! A Pierre-Joseph Proudhon Anthology.* AK Press, 2011, p. 483.

[520] Antoine Augustin Cournot (1801–1877) was an economist known for the economic concept of 'Cournot competition.' He was one of the first to introduce mathematics into economics and he developed novel concepts of equilibrium points and supply and demand graphs.

[521] Lucien Lévy-Bruhl (1857–1939) was a philosopher and sociologist associated with the Durkheimians. He helped to establish sociology in academia and made several important contributions to early anthropology and theories of relativity through the study of non-Western societies.

[522] Charles Renouvier (1815–1903) was a philosopher who was a major influence on Durkheim. He was a neo-Kantian who attempted to reconcile science with faith and developed the concepts of pluralism and free will. Renouvier was also an important precursor of existentialism and phenomenology.

concerned with preserving the good in everything and eliminating the bad. He did not realize that "it is the bad side of history that makes history,"[523] that evil must be denied through relentless struggle, a prerequisite for the anticipated syntheses. This verdict may be disputed. Isn't it Proudhon who wrote, "Come, Satan, let me embrace you,"[524] and also, "God is evil"?[525] Life is a battle, he tells his brother, both for societies and for individuals. Proudhon would be the last to deny that in order to advance, humanity needs to be spurred by suffering. The real difference between the Hegelian dialectic, as interpreted by Marx, and the Proudhonian dialectic lies elsewhere. Proudhon's characteristic trait is his renunciation of synthesis. From a certain moment, he became aware that this hope was unrealistic. Therefore, he no longer expected reconciliatory formulas, or at least, he did not believe in "universal reconciliation" except through "universal opposition." Oppositions are eternal. They cannot be resolved; one can only balance the social forces at play and maintain them in equilibrium under the law of justice. Services for services, products for products—with such principles guiding exchanges, a just peace may be achieved. But even this peace preserves the diversity of the forces involved, like rams that only come to a halt when they face each other. What emerges here in Proudhon is not eclecticism but rather pluralism, or to use a term he himself employed—a term restored to honor by Louis Ménard[526] after '48—a form of philosophical "polytheism," implying that at the heart of all social and natural reality lies a multitude of "irreducible and antagonistic elements."

Proudhon drew significant implications from this fundamental antagonism. It's crucial not to extinguish it if we want reason to be illuminated. Progress in reason requires "mutual contradictions," the

---

[523] K. Marx: *The Poverty of Philosophy.* Translated by H. Quelch. Charles H. Kerr & Co. 1913, p. 132.
[524] P.-J. Proudhon: *Justice in the Church and the Revolution. Eighth Study.* Translated by S. Wilbur. *Libertarian Labyrinth,* 2024.
[525] P.-J. Proudhon: *System of Economic Contradictions: Volume 1.* Translated by B. Tucker, 1888, p. 323.
[526] Louis Ménard (1822-1901) was a poet, philosopher, and socialist known for the concept of "mystical paganism." Ménard was associated with Comtean positivism but differed in the spiritualism that he advocated.

"balance of the self by the self," the "war of ideas." And so, Proudhon concluded that without free, universal, fervent controversy, even extending to provocation, there can be no public reason, no public spirit.

*
* *

If such is the bedrock of Proudhonian philosophy, one can imagine his antipathy toward any system seeking to impose unity through authority, especially any religion. For Proudhon, the quintessential function of religions is to unify, and he was adamantly opposed to any unification that inevitably entails the sacrifice of freedom. Thus explains his severity toward the series of messiahs and pontiffs who proliferated in France between 1800 and 1840, and whom Erdan would later study in *Mystical France.*[527] To Proudhon, these appeals to sentiment, faith, and discipline represented a particularly loathsome form of romanticism. Because he revolted against these then-numerous processions in our country, young revolutionaries from all nations, particularly Germans gathered in Paris and disconcerted by the pervasive scent of incense, greeted and thanked him as a liberator. Having been emancipated from Hegelian idealism by Feuerbach, they named him the French Feuerbach.

But it is not only new religions that the great emancipator assailed with his invective. Established religion too bears the brunt of his critique. And Catholicism, in particular, was his preferred target because it is the staunchest shield of authority: "The greatest school of respect that humanity has known," as Guizot[528] asserted. This is precisely why Proudhon resented it.

He was firmly convinced that the ideal of the Revolution can only be realized once the Earth is first liberated from the transcendence so cherished by the Church. Point by point—whether concerning labor,

---

[527] *La France mystique* (1858).
[528] François Guizot (1787–1874) was a politician, historian, and Prime Minister from 1847 to 1848. He was a proponent of constitutional monarchy and a leader of the conservatives.

property, or marriage—he contrasted the doctrine of the Church with that of the Revolution. He delighted in deepening the chasm between them. Religion may have provided some services at the dawn of society, which Proudhon did not fail to recognize. But, countering the Saint-Simonian and Comtean theses, he declared that religion is condemned by history. "It tends to die rather than to live."[529] Consequently, for anyone who prioritizes equality on Earth, religion can only be an obstacle, not a support. It muzzles not only freedom but also postpones justice; it depreciates labor, which alone should be the religion. On all these aspects, Proudhon was relentless, vehemently proclaiming the necessity to continue the task of liberation begun by the philosophers of the 18th century. He seems to bring more zeal to this task than they themselves did, for he spoke as a rural man who had seen his brethren suffer the abuses of the clerical party, and as a virtuous countryman, by no means libertine, whose only concern when demanding greater freedom was to establish greater justice: anti-clerical and even anti-religious because he was libertarian and egalitarian.

It's understandable, then, that the author of *Justice* was concerned with making as few concessions as possible to statism. Although a sociologist, his sociology did not lead him to place the state above all, to see it as a divine incarnation—a romantic notion fit for Hegel. On the contrary, it is civil society—society that organizes itself through exchange contracts between workers—that he wished to invigorate in opposition to, and eventually above, the state as a governing power.

"We deny the government of the state," he declared, "because we affirm the personality and autonomy of the masses."[530] If he envisioned society as a singular Prometheus, it is precisely to render nothing unto Caesar.[531] Hence his abhorrence of communism, which in his eyes is a

---

[529] P.-J. Proudhon: *The Creation of Order in Humanity.* Translated by S. Wilbur. *Libertarian Labyrinth,* 2024.

[530] Proudhon: Resistance to the Revolution. 1849. In *Property is Theft!.* AK Press, 2011, p. 483.

[531] "Render unto Caesar" is a phrase in the Bible attributed to Jesus concerning the payment of taxes to Caesar, which essentially summarizes the relationship between the Church and government.

form of Catholicism that could not establish itself without crushing the individual. Hence also his mistrust in democracy itself, if it relies on the force of the public power to enact its social program. Wasn't this Louis Blanc's error? That's why Proudhon heaped with criticism on him, going after the progeny of those who believe in the effectiveness of political means in social matters. The main purpose of The *General Idea of the Revolution in the Nineteenth Century,*[532] as with the *Confessions of a Revolutionary,*[533] is indeed to uproot this illusion, a beloved sin of democrats. It's essential to remind them, and especially them, that the economic must absorb the political: "the workshop will replace the government."

*
* *

Where, then, are the answers to the issues faced by the working world to be found? The direction seems to point towards banking solutions, namely, a reform of financial circulation that would enable free credit and equitable exchange. Proudhon, an accountant by trade, had a keen understanding of the balance of accounts and held in low regard anyone who lacked the art of bookkeeping. In the corridors of the 1848 Assembly, he surprised Victor Hugo[534] by stating, "I am a financier." He imagined establishing an exchange bank, which he referred to as the People's Bank, where workers could indeed exchange products for products and services for services, obtain necessary advances based on promises of labor, and avoid the extortionate conditions of usurious banks. This would lead, step by step, to a genuine revolution, the most profound and effective of all, since by becoming their own bankers, the people would become their own masters.

---

[532] *Idée générale de la révolution au XIXᵉ siècle* (1851).

[533] *Confessions d'un révolutionnaire* (1849).

[534] Victor Hugo (1802–1885) was a writer and politician, best remembered for writing *The Hunchback of Notre-Dame* (1831) and *Les Misérables* (1861). He was an important leader within France's romantic era and engaged in passionate debates promoting democratic and progressive views.

Revolution through mutualism, then, is Proudhon's cherished recipe. This alone would enable the organization not only of mutual insurance, mutual credit, and mutual aid, but also "mutual guarantees of market access, the good quality and fair price of goods."[535] Faced with these liberating prospects, Proudhon's enthusiasm knew no bounds, accompanied by an immense disdain for other reformers.

They persisted in wondering how to seize control of the state, how to use the force of public power; but he didn't need any of that apparatus. He unhesitatingly envisaged the "dissolution of government into the economic organization."[536] To establish justice, he needed only "modest" groups extending credit to each other and exchanging the products of their labor at their true value. They would be able to permanently replace hierarchical relationships with relationships based on reciprocity. And so his mutualism was supported by a federalism, an indispensable article of faith for Proudhon: "The twentieth century will inaugurate the age of federations."[537]

It goes without saying that Proudhon would not go as far as the extreme anti-statism he hinted at here. He eventually acknowledged the need for the strength of the community, in some form or another. Gurvitch, in his thesis on *The Idea of Social Law*,[538] rightly noted that as Proudhon's thought became more constructive and aimed to envision how economic life might be organized, he seemed to concede that the state would have to play a role as a balancing force. But the dominant tendency remains the same. Proudhon consistently sought safeguards against the resurgence of an authoritarian state. And this explains the evolution of his attitude toward two institutions that he initially criticized

---

[535] P.-J. Proudhon: *The Political Capacity of the Working Classes.* Translated by J. Duda. In *Property is Theft!.* AK Press, 2011, p. 730.

[536] P.-J. Proudhon: *General Idea of the Revolution in the Nineteenth Century.* Translated by J. B. Robinson. Freedom Press, 1923, p. 12.

[537] P.-J. Proudhon: *The Principle of Federation.* Translated by R. Vernon. University of Toronto Press, 1979, p. 12.

[538] *L'idée du droit social* (1931). Extracts from Georges Gurvitch's dissertation on the "Proudhonian Synthesis" have been translated into English by Shaun Murdock and are available in *The Anarchist Library.*

vehemently but later recognized as essential, at least in certain forms, in providing significant services: association and property.

For as surprising as it may seem, Proudhon long presented himself as an enemy of association. In *The General Idea of the Revolution in the Nineteenth Century*, he emphasizes its dangers more than its advantages. This is because for many of his contemporaries—starting with Buchez, the Saint-Simonian who returned to Christianity and exerted so much influence on the workers of *Atelier* newspaper[539]—association was seen as a panacea. And nothing annoyed Proudhon more than these panaceas proposed by his contemporaries. He reproached them for believing they have resolved all problems when they have only introduced a concept. And indeed, behind this concept were hidden things that Proudhon always feared. An integral, all-absorbing association worried him; this monolithic entity meant nothing good to him. But what about limited-purpose groupings that leave the individual with more freedom than they take and offer a number of guarantees—wouldn't these find favor in Proudhon's eyes? They had to: without them, he could not effect the economic renovation he dreamt of. That's why he eventually counted on the action of "worker companies" capable of managing large enterprises and, by practicing fair exchange among themselves, fostering a new economic system. Here we encounter Proudhon's adoption of contractualism, albeit in a critical stance against Rousseau. He found absurd the idea of a single social contract designed to set the terms of political life once and for all. But contracts among groups of workers concerning the products of their labor are, in his view, common currency in a society aspiring to function without the state.

A similar reversal occurs with regard to property. It's not, as has often been stated, that Proudhon in his later years reversed his earlier convictions, worshipping what he had previously condemned, or condemning what he had worshipped. Rather than fully reinstating private property rights after having declared them untenable, Proudhon

---

[539] *L'Atelier* ("The Workshop") (1840–1850) was a newspaper founded by Philippe Buchez that considered itself the "special organ of the working class."

had, from his earliest writings, he protested that his aim was to prune the tree rather than uproot it, to prevent the abuses of "exclusive and invasive" property. His ideal was to replace absolute property with possession, which would be both guaranteed and limited: to "possessify" labor was his aspiration. Yet it's clear that in *Theory of Property*, he goes beyond merely proposing to restore possession. He indeed opens the door to *jus utendi et abutendi*,[540] the full rights of using and disposing of property. Why? Two preoccupations haunted him: the dangers posed by the state and the virtues of the peasantry. Families living off their labor on their land constitute "the miracle of politics" and act as an antidote to the political virus. In opposition to the absolute entity of the state, he proposes another absolute: the property of the soil. Here, Proudhon fully reveals preferences that have their roots in his childhood as a cowherd, favoring rural life—aligning him more closely with Quesnay than with Saint-Simon. His ruralism, one might say, lends support to his anarchism. He relies on land-owning peasants for a renewal not only of economic life but also of political life. It's understood, however, that these free peasants too should form associations, that only a mutualist organization would prevent them from falling victim to a new feudalism, and that their collectives would form the essential foundations for the agricultural-industrial federation envisioned by Proudhon—the only way to reconcile the "Marianne of the Fields" with the "Sociale of the Cities,"[541] laying the groundwork for what he termed "industrial democracy."[542]

---

[540] Latin for "the right to use and abuse," referring to Roman law on property.

[541] This is a quote from P.-J. Proudhon: *De la capacité politique des classes ouvrières*. E. Dentu, 1865, p. 30. "Marianne of the fields" and "Sociale of the cities" are symbolic representations of the rural and urban components of the ideal republic. While "Marianne," adorned in a Phrygian cap, personifies the spirit of liberty and the national symbol of the French Revolution across the countryside, "Sociale of the cities" signifies the urban workers' aspirations toward a Social and Democratic Republic, emphasizing social justice and mutual cooperation. Together, they embody the Proudhon's vision of society as an agricultural-industrial federation based on mutualist principles.

[542] "Industrial democracy" was coined by Proudhon in the his 1854 *Le manuel du spéculateur à la bourse* ("The Manual of the Stock Exchange Speculator"). See I. Harvey's translated selections from the *The Manual* in Pp. 477–484 in I. McKay (ed.): *Property is Theft!*. AK Press.

But it's important to specify that he didn't only understand this in the sense that Beatrice and Sidney Webb[543] would later interpret it in their book of the same title. He didn't just count on the actions of workers' unions. While writing *The Political Capacity of the Working Classes*, he primarily addresses urban workers; in *Theory of Property*, his other testament, he never loses sight of the peasants and the living conditions essential to them, among which the right to master their land stands paramount. He would always require associations of free cultivators to bring his vision of "industrial democracy" to life. And his socialism, which never forgets the rural communities, would remain first and foremost, as Aimé Berthod[544] suggests, a "socialism for the peasants," one that even the radicals could embrace.

In any case, through all these plans, one grasps the deep-seated reason for Proudhon's disdain for the political forms of democracy, for the kind of suffrage that atomizes individuals, and for the centralized public authorities. They are mere illusions, mere facades. The realities needed by the rightful democratic instincts of the people are within reach: in a transformation of the economic order that, starting with the free access to credit and fair trade, culminates in a mutualist and federalist organization, the only kind capable of ensuring equality without endangering freedom.

Thus, while Saint-Simonism may be seen chiefly from the producers' perspective, Fourierism from the consumers', Proudhonism

---

[543] Beatrice Webb (1858-1943) and Sidney Webb (1859-1947) were married English socialists, economists, historians, and co-founders of the London School of Economics and Political Science. The Webbs were leading members within the Fabian Society, and were also notably friends with and influenced the important economist John Maynard Keynes (1883-1946). They laid the groundwork for the British welfare state and wrote the 1897 book *Industrial Democracy* on the organization of trade unions.

[544] Adrien Aimé Berthod (1878-1944) was a philosopher of law and politician. He held various political positions, primarily during the interwar period. Berthod was a resistance fighter during the Vichy regime and was imprisoned by the Germans in 1944. He died in prison from lung disease.

might be accurately situated, as Aucuy[545] proposes, among the "socialisms of exchange." But it relies on federations of workers, not consumer groupings and certainly not the state, to achieve free credit and equitable exchange. This exchange-based socialism intends to remain a liberal socialism, opposed to collectivist centralism, precisely due to the importance it places on rural traditions and federalist aspirations.

---

[545] Marc Aucuy (1881–1948) was a was a professor who studied worker's organizations. He wrote the 1908 book *Les systèmes socialistes d'échange* ("Socialist Systems of Exchange").

Chapter X

Assessment of Proudhonism: Present

What remains of Proudhonian ideas in our current social movement, which we have attempted to classify? This inquiry has been helpfully outlined for us. Following the war, the Friends of Proudhon[546]—who embarked on republishing his works in twenty volumes—published a collection of studies under the title *Proudhon and Our Time*.[547] These studies touch on the working class, education, banking, the rural situation, federalism, and peace; they explore what advice the cherished author might offer to help us overcome the post-war disarray. On many points, we can follow the lead of these guides.

Conversely, we encounter the challenge of the variety of interpretations Proudhon's thought continues to provoke, some of which appear to starkly contradict each other. How can one reconcile the praise Proudhon receives from "revolutionary" syndicalists with the accolades from "reformists"? Even more paradoxical is the juxtaposition of left-wing Proudhonians—whether radicals or socialists—with monarchists from Action Française[548] in a shared adoration of Proudhon.

Disciples of Charles Maurras[549] have also sought to follow Proudhon, with claims that Proudhon's portrait hung in their newspaper

---

[546] *Société des amis de Proudhon* (1920-1940) was a group of Proudhonian enthusiasts, led by Bouglé, who initiated the first republication of Proudhon's complete works, known as the Marcel Rivière edition (1923-1959). Although they planned to publish 20 volumes, only 15 volumes appeared.

[547] *Proudhon et notre temps* (1920).

[548] Action Française (1899-) is a far-right monarchist movement that supported the Vichy regime. The organization advocates authoritarian monarchism and Catholic integralism and opposes democracy.

[549] Charles Maurras (1868-1952) was the leading organizer of the Action Française. He promoted royalist nationalist ideas and was the de facto leader of the Action Française in the early 20th century. Maurras was later convicted of collaborating with the Nazis and spent time in prison as a result.

offices, between the Pope and the Pretender.[550] And Dimier[551] had long since categorized him among the "Masters of the Counter-Revolution." Neo-monarchists highlight that no one has more virulently denounced the centralizing statism that democracy inevitably tends toward, nor the fundamental atomism that the system of universal suffrage imposes—each individual counting for one and no more than one. They also point out that, contrary to the democratic tradition, Proudhon found arguments to wish for the preservation of the papal temporal power. He consistently defended "the glory of the French name," and one could extract from his works on war and peace all the necessary arguments to chastise naïve pacifism. Isn't this enough to enlist our author among the ranks of the nationalists?

Each of these arguments invites serious scrutiny. Proudhon praised France fervently, but as the "homeland of the heralds of the eternal revolution," and he often warned that a modern nation must prioritize justice above all else. Proudhon extolled the virtues of war, seeing it as a necessary tool of justice in some cases. However, if war tramples legal forms, he declares it barbaric; if it erupts for economic ends, he condemns it as anachronistic. Proudhon expressed surprise that someone would begrudge the Pope a territory to reign over. But the spiritual authority that the Pope embodies had no fiercer enemy than the author of *Justice in the Revolution and in the Church*. Indeed, it was authority itself—whether of kings or Popes—that he sought to rout everywhere. In *The General Idea of the Revolution in the Nineteenth Century*, isn't it the "series" he gleefully unfolds the one that demonstrates the necessary bankruptcy of various regimes of authority? How can these views be reconciled with those that proclaim "Politics first,"[552] indicating a blind trust in the virtues of individual power?

---

[550] A reference to Maurras.

[551] Louis Dimier (1865–1943) was an early member of the Action Française and art historian. His work expressed a deep hatred of the French Revolution and an admiration of the ancien régime.

[552] "Politics First" is a slogan of Action Française.

Is "anarchist" therefore the most suitable label for our thinker? Yes, but only if we distinguish between various forms of anarchism and disentangle Proudhon's doctrine from the usual associations with the term. It's evident from the start that he cannot be categorized with violent anarchists. "I am not a disruptor,"[553] he repeatedly stated. And those who go to war against certain "bourgeois prejudices"—like family discipline, conjugal fidelity, and purity of morals—would definitely not find an ally in Proudhon. On the contrary, we know how ardently he defended the integrity of domestic morals, essential for establishing justice in the city. In this regard, Georges Sorel is very faithful to Proudhonian thought when he repeats, "The world will only become just if it becomes more chaste." In general, however, we must remember that even as Proudhon asserted the rights of human personality, he was always ready to call for order. There has been no moralist more uncompromising. Nothing could be further from his stance than the kind of amoralism associated with Stirner.[554] Proudhon's anarchistic tendencies are first limited by his concerns as a sociologist and moralist. But above all, they are subordinate to his economic plans. It is because of these plans that he was so hostile to government intervention and called for the Republic to finally become a "positive anarchy." His constant theme, as we have seen, is the "dissolution of government in the economic organism." And in this respect, his thought aligns with Saint-Simon, whom he cited and praised for opposing the remnants of the military regime with the demands of an administrative regime that would minimize political authority. Thus, the real successors to Proudhon's "anarchism" should be sought among those who aim to organize the administration of things through the voluntary agreement of groups not spawned by government power. When Maxime Leroy opposes the royalist tradition with emerging institutions of

---

[553] The full quote: "I am a revolutionary but not a disruptor."

[554] Max Stirner (1806-1856) was a German philosopher best known for writing the 1844 *The Unique and Its Property,* and the philosophy of egoism. He advocated for a radical individualism that rejected all social institutions that subordinated the individual.

professional power, he is at the intersection of the Saint-Simonian and Proudhonian traditions, which he has indeed championed. And alongside him stand all those who say not "Politics first" (which would be antithetical to Proudhon) but "Economics first," striving to rebuild, as Durkheim wanted, a series of intermediary groups capable of organizing economic life without authoritarian force.

Recall that, according to Proudhon, this order cannot be achieved without a total overhaul of the system of exchange and credit. Therefore, the primary effort of the particular groups he expects to take action should focus on these modalities. It has been aptly said that the development of mutual aid societies represents a kind of "Proudhon's revenge."[555] Indeed, they can boast of fulfilling one of the roles Proudhon envisioned for popular societies, especially when they organize credit unions for their members. He would have been particularly delighted to see this role fulfilled by the agricultural unions that have proliferated so rapidly. Peasants coming together, not only to jointly purchase fertilizer or equipment but also to avoid usurers by creating a fund for advances from which each can draw, is in perfect alignment with Proudhon's vision. But it is clear that his aspirations extended far beyond this function. The People's Bank he dreamt of would function as both a discount and deposit bank, an issuing and business bank, and provide personal property, agricultural, and mortgage credit. By conducting all these operations without charging fees on unearned income and without resorting to cash, through a sort of expansion of bills of exchange, it aims to "organize the *interchangeability* of values without the intermediary of money, just as we must organize the government of society by all citizens, without the intermediary of a monarchy, presidency, or directory." The author of the *Stock Exchange Speculator's Manual* believed that by doing this, he could not only put an end to the abuses of speculation but also abolish the "royalty of gold," making "economic democracy" possible, or

---

[555] This appears to be a reference to Edmond Lagarde's 1905 doctoral thesis, *La revanche de Proudhon, ou l'avenir du socialisme mutuelliste* ("Proudhon's Revenge, or the Future of Mutualist Socialism"), that alludes to revenge on Marxism and stresses the incompatibility between Proudhonism and Marxism.

216

as he strikingly puts it—a phrase that André Gide[556] would later echo when discussing cooperatives—prepare for the "subordination of capital to labor."

Has Proudhon's plan become a reality, at least in part? In his study "Proudhon as a banker," an article from the book *Proudhon and Our Times*[557] mentioned earlier, William Oualid[558] observes that many of Proudhon's ideas have been implemented, less because of his writings and more because of certain crisis-driven expedients. For example, during and after the war, didn't we see states increase the volume of fiduciary money in circulation, paying less and less attention to the metal reserve, and making advances to their suppliers for future deliveries? Isn't one of the effects of the "credit miracles" extolled by Émile Mireaux[559] to replace the use of cash with a more advanced bartering of goods? Hasn't it also become standard practice for banks with privileges to be required to offer loans to mutual or agricultural credit societies at significantly reduced rates? However, it's true that most of these transformations are the result of state interventions, interventions that Proudhon was quite wary of, and that they don't seem to have achieved material relief for workers or the moral purification he held in high esteem. Will we find a way to put an end to so many abuses, relying not only or primarily on the power of the state, but on the power represented by small savers in their cooperatives, unions, and mutual societies? Will this "saver's syndicalism"—to use a phrase from the editors of the new *Producer*, a phrase more Proudhonian than Saint-Simonian—manage to

---

[556] André Gide (1869-1951) was a writer and man of letters. He promoted the idea of communist individualism. In 1947, Gide won the Nobel Prize in Literature. He was the nephew of Charles Gide.

[557] "Proudhon banquier," in *Proudhon et notre temps*.

[558] William Oualid (1880-1942) was an Algerian-French philosopher of law and jurist. He worked alongside Albert Thomas, Maurice Halbwachs, and François Simiand and represented France at the Geneva Conference concerning the establishment of the International Labour Organization.

[559] Émile Mireaux (1885-1969) was an economist, politician, and supporter of economic liberalism. He was the economics editor from 1928 to 1931 for the Parisian daily newspaper *Le Temps* (1861-1942).

counterbalance what Charles Dulot,[560] the director of Social and Workers' Information, calls "economic congregations"? The outcome is uncertain. The merit remains with Proudhon for emphasizing that the social question cannot be resolved without a reorganization of credit, and that this reorganization itself presupposes a methodical participation of "economic democracy."

If we now consider the political aspect of the reforms anticipated by Proudhon in the economic order, we are confronted with an alluring concept: federalism. Proudhon believed that the 20th century must usher in the era of federations, lest humanity experience another round of torment. It is no surprise that this rallying cry has not been lost on us, particularly among those opposed to overbearing centralization. Charles-Brun,[561] one of the champions of regionalism, is reissuing *The Federative Principle.*[562] And like many of his colleagues, he believes that after the war, the book is more relevant than ever. Didn't we witness, during the conflict, the state being overwhelmed and capital threatened? Weren't consultative committees created to maximize the resources of the provinces, interfacing with groups of Chambers of Commerce? This approach was designed to curb both the effects of departmental compartmentalization and Parisian authoritarianism. Hubert Lagardelle,[563] another esteemed Proudhonian, has shown us what can be achieved with such a method, as demonstrated in the Southwest. Wouldn't it have been prudent to generalize this method when the return

---

[560] Charles Dulot (1882-19?) was a syndicalist writer. Along with François Simiand, and Albert Thomas, Dulot founded the bi-weekly syndicalist periodical *L'information ouvrière et sociale* (1921-1935).

[561] Jean Charles-Brun (1870-1946) founded the French Regionalist Federation in 1900, which still exists today, and served as its general secretary from its inception until his death. He was notably also an ardent defender of the Occitan language, a Romance language spoken in southern France.

[562] *Le principe fédératif* (1863).

[563] Hubert Lagardelle (1874-1958) was a revolutionary syndicalist who founded *Le mouvement socialiste* (1899-1914), a journal on socialism and syndicalism, of which Marcel Mauss was a contributor. Later, Lagardelle moved to the far-right, and served as the Minister of Labor under the Vichy regime. In 1946, he was sentenced to life in prison for collaborating with the Nazis but was released in 1949 due to his age.

of Alsace-Lorraine[564] to France posed unique challenges to the French unitary state? The groundwork was thus laid. Scholarly works like those by Hauser[565] methodically outlined what was necessary and possible. The results of these efforts to reconsolidate are scarcely visible so far. The state does not easily relinquish its royal and Napoleonic privileges, especially as democracy often feels the need to call on it against various local powers: another question that remains open. When we finally decide to seriously solve it, we will undoubtedly have to remember Proudhon.

Interestingly, it's perhaps on the international stage, after the war, where Proudhonian thought might find the easiest inroads. This seems paradoxical, given that the principle of nationalities, which the post-war treaties heavily favored, is exactly what Proudhon would have largely opposed. Reacting strongly against the democrats of his time, he preemptively protested against the reconstitution of Poland: he would have been no more welcoming of its independence than he was supportive of Italian unification. Undoubtedly, he would have reiterated his arguments against Czechoslovakia or Yugoslavia. In a broader sense, he opposed one of the most characteristic movements of modern Europe: the trend towards the creation of unitary, autonomous nations. But he would have undoubtedly welcomed the necessity, as proven by economic realities, for even the most independence-minded nations to acknowledge the interdependencies binding them to their neighbors. As a result, compromises, specific objective agreements, and guaranteed exchange contracts are likely to multiply: all weaving the threads of federations. And this is what the *Société Proudhon*, founded by

---

[564] Alsace-Lorraine is a region created by the German Empire in 1871 after it was seized from France during the Franco-Prussian war. The region was returned to France as part of the Treaty of Versailles (1919).

[565] Henri Hauser (1866–1946) was an economist, historian, and geographer. He held the first chair in economic history in France and later became a professor of ancient and medieval history. Hauser's 1905 book *L'impérialisme américain* predicted the rise of the United States and the decline of Europe.

Hennessy,[566] envisioned when it championed the idea of a European Federation under the auspices of the author of *The Federative Principle*—a federation intended not to challenge, but to support, and primarily to guide, the actions of the League of Nations itself.

*

* *

However, there is another form of federalism where Proudhon's thoughts survive more vividly than in regionalist or internationalist federalism: the form that Paul-Boncour[567] suggested calling economic or professional federalism, which today finds its core in the trade union movement. It is here, perhaps, that we should look for the true inheritors, the most active continuators of our author's legacy.

To fully understand this kinship, we must especially revisit *The Political Capacity of the Working Classes*. Maxime Leroy presents this book as one of the manifestos marking the history of laborers' efforts to organize.

Indeed, this testament is a fervent exhortation to worker autonomy. Proudhon believed workers have the right, and are fully justified, to form their own distinct entity, set themselves up in opposition, and constitute themselves as a class. In doing so, they will realize their own unique idea—which Proudhon naturally hoped would correspond to the mutualist idea he cherished.

---

[566] Jean Hennessy (1874-1944) was an advocate for federalism that founded the short-lived *Société Proudhon* in 1917. A section of the group turned into the *Ligue pour l'organisation de la société des nations* and participated in the League of Nations. For more information, see: C. Bouchard: Regionalism, Federalism and Internationalism in First World War France. Pp. 198-213 in J. Wright & H. S. Jones (eds): *Pluralism and the Idea of the Republic in France.* Palgrave Macmillan, 2012.

[567] Joseph Paul-Boncour (1873-1972) was a politician and Prime Minister of France from 1932 to 1933. He was a member of the Republican-Socialist Party and held several other government positions.

It is worth noting that among workers who recognized the need to organize for their emancipation, several did not merely welcome Proudhon's sympathies: they were eager to borrow some of his guiding ideas, nascent theories, and vocabulary. J.-L. Puech[568] has long detected Proudhon's influence in the preparatory meetings of the International in London, then in the first international labor congresses. The French spoke of "reciprocity" and "equal exchange," differentiated between "association" and "cooperation" (the latter better preserving individual rights), and called for mutual aid. In Geneva, in 1866,[569] it appeared that the International might be thoroughly Proudhonized. But by the Basel Congress in 1869, this influence had been expunged: Marx, who saw Proudhon as having "done much harm," had vigorously worked against this detested influence, both overtly and covertly. He now controlled the direction of the International. In the resolutions of Congresses and meetings, collectivist language began to replace mutualist language. After the German victory, which likely expanded the prestige of all things German, when socialism regained a foothold in France, it often took on a Marxist character.

At that time, one might have assumed Proudhonism was definitively dead and buried. However, it was to experience a revival in France, and this resurgence came not so much from political parties or intellectual circles but from worker groups, who sought to organize the resistance and proactive strength of their class outside the political arena. The Guesdists, who were the main importers of Marxist doctrine in France after 1870 and enjoyed contrasting determinist materialism with the traditional idealism of the French—horsepower against the *Rights of Man*, as Jules Guesde put it—had established trade unions steeped in their philosophy, which they intended to bring under their party's control.

---

[568] Jules-Louis Puech (1879–1957) was a historian of the labor movement and jurist. His 1907 doctoral thesis in law was on Proudhonism in the IWA. He later worked with Bouglé in the *Société des amis de Proudhon* to publish Proudhon's completed works. Puech also published several articles and books on socialism.
[569] The Geneva Congress of 1866 was the first General Congress of the IWA, known for making the 8-hour workday a goal of the organization.

Fernand Pelloutier,[570] the organizer of the Labor Exchanges[571] who aimed to liberate the unions from this hold and warned workers that merely seizing power—controlling the factory through laws, to borrow another phrase from Jules Guesde—would not suffice for their liberation, explicitly called upon Proudhon and his teachings to encourage them to depend on themselves. This worker autonomy, thus fostered, came to the fore in 1906 with the Charter of Amiens,[572] adopted to prevent any political school or sect's interference by a coalition of "neutrals" and "anarchists"—the latter perhaps recalling the lessons of their esteemed Proudhon. Indeed, these teachings were extensively discussed by intellectuals—Lagardelle, Sorel, and Berth[573]—who, in *The Socialist Movement* a few years before the war, strived to provide an ideology for the syndicalist ranks, distinct from those of conventional political parties. On the eve of the war, leaders of the General Confederation of Labor—including Jouhaux—were notably drawing from the same source as Pelloutier. And after the war, when the horizon opened up for reconstruction not only in material terms but also socially, morally, and intellectually, when there was anticipation for a new world free from the traditional formulas dominating the unified socialist party, it was Proudhonism that these worker leaders had in mind and relied on. I heard one of them, Marcel Laurent,[574] present to the National Committee for Social and Political Studies the plan for the Economic Council that the CGT was urgently advocating for, sketching out the potential for

---

[570] Fernand Pelloutier (1867–1901) was a revolutionary syndicalist and the leader of the *Bourses du travail* mutual exchange organization from 1895 until his death. Pelloutier promoted the idea of a general strike.

[571] The *Bourse du travail* was a form of labor council in France that encouraged mutual aid, self-organization, and education. The rise of the French Communist Party notably led to its decline.

[572] The Charter of Amiens was a proposal that was adopted by the CGT that separated the French syndicalist movement from political parties.

[573] Édouard Berth (1875–1939) was a disciple of Sorel known for co-founding the nationalist syndicalist political group *Cercle Proudhon* (1911–1925) that prefigured fascism. Initially an enthusiastic supporter of the Bolsheviks, he later became disillusioned with communism and was a critic of Stalin.

[574] Marcel Laurent (1859–1932) was a librarian, archivist, trade unionist, and socialist activist.

renewal, to complement parliamentary action, which could be achieved by drawing not only on state delegates but also on those representing consumers and, above all, producers. And Robert Pinot, listening to him, couldn't help but exclaim: "But this is pure Proudhon you're presenting to us!"

Furthermore, if one wishes to refer to a collective statement, let us revisit the motion passed at the Federal Congress of Lyon in 1918: "Labor, the creator of all wealth and the element commanding social activity, intends to be everything..."

> "This concept, realized through the workers' efforts, will be shaped according to the nature of labor itself, establishing a new order based not on authority, but on exchange; not on domination, but on reciprocity; not on sovereignty, but on the social contract."

Let's not be led astray by this term. It is not Rousseau that the militants of the CGT have in mind, but rather Proudhon: the contracts they envision are those that would be established, as Proudhon himself desired, among federated groups to enforce the law of "reciprocity" in "exchanges," and thereby secure the reign of "Labor." These expressions and concepts unmistakably reveal their origins, just as much as the phrases Jouhaux is fond of repeating: "Politics yields to economics" and "The workshop will replace the government." In this setting more than any other contemporary one, it appears that Proudhon has become the designated intellectual.

But here again, are we interpreting his teachings correctly? Are we faithful to his true spirit? Naturally, there has been debate. Don't CGT's projects since the war—despite their ultimate aim of abolishing both wage labor and the employer class through the conscious action of the organized working class—involve collaborations, or even "compromises," with representatives of the adversary classes, or at least with representatives of a state that can only be "feudal to the bourgeoisie"? These would culminate in May 1926 in an electoral program—social security, workers' control, heavier taxation on the privileged, equal access to education, and a commitment to peace—that could be signed off by both radicals and socialists. *Realism,* some claim; *reformism* would be just as fitting, if not outright *opportunism.* Where, then, is the spirit of contrarianism, of combative intransigence, that so often gleams through Proudhon's dialectic like a sword in a thicket?

Several contributors to *Socialist Movement,* whose tendencies we've previously discussed, had stressed this aspect of Proudhon's temperament. And Sorel might have thought he was being faithful to Proudhon when he penned his *Reflections on Violence*[575]—a defense of mayhem, some have said—urging workers to ruthlessly beat up the spokespeople of democracy, and relying on the "general strike," myth though it might be, to instill heroism in the hearts of the proletariat: a peculiar primer that apparently had the distinction of being a favorite read of both Lenin and Mussolini.[576] Since the war, Édouard Berth has adopted a similar stance. In his series of meditations and calls to action titled *War of States or War of Classes,*[577] the author expresses astonishment that workers would sacrifice even an inch of their flesh for national wars that have no bearing on them, wars in which they can only be victims. But, by contrast, if they brace themselves for a class war, no matter how savage, then well done: they deserve nothing but praise. And Édouard Berth, in search of a new sublime, invokes Proudhon—the Proudhon of *War and Peace*—to argue that "everything pacifist seems struck with an insurmountable dullness," and that "socialism only truly regains its grandeur when it returns to a warlike state." It's a strange amalgam that, upon analysis, reveals elements of Nietzsche, Hegel, and Bergson. But Proudhon? Scarcely, in my view. Despite his odes to war as the first revealer of rights, Proudhon, as he himself insisted, was no agitator. He didn't believe in the efficacy of revolutionary shocks—at least, this was one

---

[575] *Réflexions sur la violence* (1908).
[576] Benito Mussolini (1883-1945) was the Prime Minister of Italy from 1922 to 1943 and the Duce of the Italian Social Republic from 1943 to 1945. Originally a socialist, he founded and led the National Fascist Party, which spread fascist movements internationally. He was executed while attempting to flee Italy.
[577] *Guerre des états ou guerre des classes* (1924).

of his reasons for refusing to align with Marx in 1846.[578] To settle economic and social issues, he would place no more faith in the virtue of "class wars" than in that of "state wars." To put it bluntly, the "rationalist" that he remains—as Guy-Grand[579] clearly demonstrates in his introduction to *Justice*—would likely have been irked by the "romanticism" with which these Bergsonian intellectuals attempted to enshroud worker syndicalism. Recall that even in his work on *The Political Capacity of the Working Classes*, Proudhon opposes strikes, fearing they might devolve into a ham-fisted tactic, and he consistently cautioned against reckless behavior. This illustrates just how distant he was from those whom Sombart[580] has labeled the dilettantes of violence.

This moment also serves to remind us that *The Political Capacity of the Working Classes* illuminates just one facet of Proudhon's intellectual landscape. He was as far from being an unwavering advocate for violence as he was from embodying complete workerism. It's evident that the rural populace held a place in his considerations as significant, if not more so, than the proletariat. With their interests in mind, he championed property rights as vigorously as he did the cause of association, which allows for both radicals and socialists to draw upon his insights when formulating their platforms.

It's natural that the intricacies of such thinking might vex those inclined toward action and who might prefer more straightforward formulas to rally the masses. In this context, Marxism presents clear

---

[578] In May of 1846, Marx sent his only letter to Proudhon requesting that he join his Communist Correspondence Committee as the French correspondent for "when the moment for action comes." Proudhon replied by politely declining the invitation, which set the stage for Marx's 1847 *The Poverty of Philosophy,* sometimes referred to as "Anti-Proudhon."

[579] Georges Guy-Grand (1879–1957) was a political theorist and syndicalist who wrote several works on Proudhon, including his 1947 *La pensée de Proudhon* ("Proudhon's Thought").

[580] Werner Sombart (1863–1941) was a German historian, economist, and sociologist. His works embedded economics within a social framework and examined the historical development of capitalism.

advantages. Nonetheless, Proudhonism maintains, in my opinion, a superior virtue: it seems to be more malleable and more suitably applied to the varied realities of contemporary life.

Chapter XI

Conclusion: Outcomes and Prospects

What prospects does socialism have of materializing in the France of tomorrow, and in what forms? After the review I have undertaken and the confrontations we have engaged in, I would like to be able to answer this question.

By tracing back to the doctrines of the past to then descend to our current life, I have gained such momentum that it is difficult to abruptly halt at the present moment. I cannot help but look beyond: of the many forces of diverse origins we have discussed, which will come to dominate the others?

Socialism comes in many forms: this is one of the fundamental truths my investigation has highlighted. The primary characteristic of the French tradition in this matter is the diversity of systems it encompasses and the array of tendencies it brings together. The collectivist socialism of the Saint-Simonians, primarily concerned with the organization of producers, differs in many respects from the cooperative socialism of the Fourierists, intent on multiplying the pleasures of the consumer. Proudhon, in turn, veers towards federalism and syndicalism. And neither would have subscribed to Babeuf's revolutionary program.

But above all, neither would have accepted as-is the confluence of tendencies that we have identified as the legacy of the 18th century and the French Revolution. The philosophy that eventually prevailed, proclaiming the rights of man and of the citizen above all else, seems to pave the way for democracy. Yet it is not democracy that preoccupied our great thinkers in the first half of the 19th century: their concerns were quite different. The current that leads to socialism is initially distinctly separate from that leading to democracy. This is evident in the cases of Fourier and Saint-Simon, both of whom were troubled by the destructive convulsions of the Revolution and were disinclined to demand equality:

227

we have seen that they placed little value on political freedom and the constitutional guarantees it demands. Undoubtedly, the "Republican Defense"[581] would have held little interest for them: what does the political regime matter, provided that economic organization progresses? Proudhon himself might have almost endorsed this sentiment. However, his attitude toward democracy is markedly different from that of his predecessors, against whom he reacted, just as they reacted against the Revolution. He desired equality and liberty: two absolutes in his eyes, two irreplaceable moral values. Yet he categorically rejected any pretext of serving equality if it means a return to authority. In this sense, the Republic would represent the ideal regime to him because it is 'positive anarchy.' Thus, he positioned himself not below, but beyond traditional democratic demands. He might consider himself an ultra-democrat. The grand illusion he sought to warn democracy against is the conviction that political means could solve the economic and social problems it faces— an idea suited for Louis Blanc, attempted as best as could be in '48. The failure of this hope did not surprise Proudhon. He would have predicted it, if not desired it. And it was precisely to counteract the disappointments of democracy, ever ready to slide towards statism, that he coined the term "industrial democracy."

*

* *

From this perspective, despite their differences on certain issues, the views of Proudhon and Saint-Simon can be said to converge in support of a trend that has gained considerable favor today, and which many advocate using to tackle what they perceive as the proven ineffectiveness of political democracy in addressing economic and social challenges: the belief in syndicalism, which counts on reformed professional associations in various forms to correct the shortcomings of parliamentarism.

---

[581] The Republican Defense was a coalition supported by the Socialists that sought to put an end to the agitations against the Third Republic around the turn of the 20th century.

We've noted that Herriot, in his book *Why I Am a Radical-Socialist,*[582] highlights the influence of memories of the Revolution on the onset of his political career. It is not Robespierre or Danton,[583] but Saint-Simon and Proudhon, that H. de Jouvenel[584] discusses and analyzes in his book *Why I Am a Syndicalist.* Maxime Leroy, a theorist of professional power, also seeks to connect Saint-Simonian and Proudhonian thought. Similarly, Léon Jouhaux often quotes Proudhon's phrase, "the workshop will replace the government," when summarizing what can be expected from the syndicalist movement in France. Syndicalist leaders are thus clearly aware of a tradition upon which they can collectively rely to finally elevate economic concerns over political ones, complementing or correcting parliamentary actions with those of associated workers.

In light of this, should we conclude that one will eliminate the other, that syndicalism, having won public opinion, will lead to undervaluing the accomplishments of political democracy?

Would the establishment of "industrial democracy" imply a retreat from individualism as an end and parliamentarism as a means? This crisis might lead us back to the deficiency report that Daniel Halévy draws up when comparing the customs and methods of today's Republic with those of the past, Fournol's demonstration of the American approach's advantages in social politics over the French: a pervasive "decline of freedom."

---

[582] *Pourquoi je suis radical-socialiste* (1928).

[583] Georges Danton (1759-1794) was a lawyer, the first president of the Committee of Public Safety, and a famous orator during the French Revolution. He opposed the Reign of Terror and, in April 1794, along with other "Dantonists," was accused of treason and guillotined by the Jacobins.

[584] Henry de Jouvenel (1876-1935) was a statesman and journalist. He held various government positions, primarily during the interwar period. He was the first president of the *Union des Français de l'etranger* ("Union of French Abroad") (1927-), an association for French expatriates, from 1927 until his death. He wrote the 1928 *Pourquoi je suis syndicaliste.*

Should we accept these conclusions and believe that the progress of industrialism, valued by the Saint-Simonians, will inevitably lead to the abandonment of not only economic but also political and intellectual liberalism, cherished by the men of the Revolution? Is an inevitable seesaw effect in place, where one side can only rise by the descent of the other?

Freedom is multifaceted and can be interpreted in various ways. It encompasses numerous forms, and one would need to see all these forms and perhaps their diverging trajectories to determine if, overall, liberalism is losing or gaining ground.

Freedom, certainly for most who invoke it, means above all as complete independence as possible: the right to freely move, to choose one's profession and residence, buy and sell at will, and organize one's life without accountability to anyone. Yet even the simplest experiences soon teach us that such freedom cannot be absolute. Living in society requires individuals to accept some limits, some restrictions on their desires. Without a minimum level of regulation, communal life is impossible.

At least, if one were involved in setting these rules, if one had a voice in them, if they were somewhat under the control of those who must obey them, it would provide some compensation, some consolation. This is precisely the role of the system of political freedoms; it enables citizens to express their opinions and influence laws, both directly and indirectly, closely or from afar. The citizen then thinks as a legislator, taking part in the creation of the laws they obey. In a sense, they are obeying their own will. This is freedom as autonomy. Yet even Rousseau, the staunchest advocate for independence, warns us that in a regulated state, this kind of freedom is gained at the expense of others: "obedience to the law one has prescribed for oneself is freedom."

But does freedom not also encompass other meanings? If, unimpeded by any political authority and even dominating all political authorities, one still finds oneself unable to meet the basic needs of life—to feed, house, or clothe oneself—if one remains, in a word, powerless
230

over things, naked and defenseless, can it still be said that one is free? Formal rights seem a mockery in the face of economic destitution. This recognition leads us to affirm that without a minimum of power, freedom is merely a hollow word. This necessity for freedom-as-power is a focal point in all socialist literature. Charles Andler noted in his book *State Socialism in Germany*[585] that this concept was familiar to German thinkers who shaped socialism. However, it is not unique to them; they do not have a monopoly on this idea. Numerous thinkers in our country, between 1800 and 1848, comparing the conditions mechanization imposed on the working population with the principles proclaimed by the *Declaration of the Rights of Man*, noted that without bread, work, or guarantees of material life, a citizen is not free. And this is one of the themes elaborated by Victor Considerant in *Socialism Before the Old World*,[586] as previously by Louis Blanc in *The Organization of Labor*.[587] It is thus natural for people to want to use their freedom-as-autonomy to advocate for freedom-as-power, even if it somewhat compromises freedom-as-independence. And indeed, this is the rationale used to justify all initiatives in social policy: the protection of wages, leisure time, and insurance against accidents at work, illness, old age, and unemployment.

One might argue that it's a slippery slope. To enhance their well-being and secure their future, the masses will accept, even enforce, an increasingly restrictive web of regulations. Ultimately, they might trade their independence for a mere pittance. They might demonstrate little regard for their political rights or intellectual freedoms. As long as the economic life is in order, that's all that matters: "when the kitchen is in order, everything is in order..." Indeed, more than one conservative, disdainful of modern freedoms, has relied on social welfare policies to convince the masses to similarly disdain these freedoms. Wasn't this Bismarck's rationale when he enacted workers' laws? And isn't it, all else being equal, Mussolini's in organizing the unions? His aim is clearly to persuade the masses, through displays of prosperity, that the Rights of

---

[585] *Les origines du socialisme d'état en Allemagne* (1897).
[586] *Le socialisme devant le vieux-monde* (1848).
[587] *L'organisation du travail* (1839).

Man are superfluous, or rather dangerous—more dangerous for the people than for the rulers, because the people, by invoking these rights and claiming to use them, would impede the effective actions of the rulers themselves.

It seems unlikely that such calculations would find great success in France, if only because they conflict with a tradition that still holds power: that of the French Revolution. This tradition demands not just bread, but rights for the people, and the ability to monitor both the crafting and the application of the laws that determine their destinies. Call it a mystique if you will, but despite many disappointments, this mystique remains dear to most voters: electoral statistics are the best proof. When evaluating the political system, the mass of citizens in our country remains ready to invoke not only social utility, but also personal dignity. Efforts to convince them that a dictatorial power would better serve their interests are likely to fail. They are repelled by the notion of being treated as mere objects. They appreciate the right of each to have a say, and to form their opinions as they wish. The persistence of these sentiments is one of the defining elements of the French mindset. It is because these feelings are still palpably present that many foreign observers view France as a bastion of individualist humanism, the country least willing to be mechanized, where the people take pride in thinking for themselves—thus, logically, a country that should be relied upon to resist the advance of both American-style industrialism and German-style socialism.

Numerous recent observations support this conclusion: those of Sieburg in *Is God French?*[588] and those of André Siegfried in *A Portrait of Political Parties in France*,[589] not to mention those of Duhamel[590] in *Scenes from the Future Life*.

---

[588] *Dieu est-il français?* (1929).

[589] *Tableau des partis politiques en France* (1930).

[590] Georges Duhamel (1884-1966) was a novelist and poet. He wrote the famous 1918 novel *Civilization,* which depicted the crudeness of WWI. He was later a prominent member within the Alliance Française (1883-), an organization that promotes French culture, serving as the president from 1947 to 1949. Duhamel wrote the 1930 *Scènes de la vie future.*

*

* *

This unique climate of France is not best explained by the long-standing prestige of intellectuals and members of liberal professions, but rather by the prominence maintained by peasants. Still individualists, and mostly eager to assert their independence from both the local squire and the clergyman, they too, as Siegfried asserts, "fight on the front lines of humanism." However, the cause of liberty in France does not rest solely on the shoulders of the peasant: it would be appropriate here to mention a more general trend, which alone demonstrates how difficult it would be in our country to absorb the political into the economic: what is sometimes called secularism, the determination to defend the state against the encroachments of the Church, in order to better safeguard the rights of individual conscience. This will is found, strongly held, among urban as well as rural residents, among the proletariat as well as the bourgeoisie.

There is no need to dwell on the intensity of the struggles that this issue provokes, nor on their reverberation throughout the political life of France. Many lament these battles that divide the nation against itself. They wish to disregard them, asking for the opportunity to focus on other matters. Undoubtedly, the youth who call themselves realists and loudly demand a new kind of politics want to signify, among other things, that they are disinterested in these outdated ideological quarrels. Furthermore, many of those engaged in these disputes would also declare themselves happy to finally turn this page. We recall the anger of Jaurès against clerical intransigence that forces the Republic to defend itself, when it could be taking positive action on so many fronts to ensure real freedom for workers. But it is one of the inevitabilities of our history that this problem can never be fully resolved. The principle of secularism will always be challenged. The Church has been all-powerful for too long. It has controlled all education for too long. It feels wronged, injured by a 'liberal' regime that places the beliefs it sanctifies on the same level as others, beliefs that for so long were instruments of governance in its hands. And indeed, its clergy occasionally reiterate that the secularization

233

laws are unjust, claiming they are not truly laws (*magis sunt violentiae quam leges*[591]); they remind us that liberalism and latitudinarianism[592] are damnable errors, and moreover, that it is dangerous to believe that peoples are capable of self-governance.

In this respect, Proudhon is not mistaken: there exists a fundamental antagonism between the spirit of the Revolution and that of Catholicism. Despite the tacit understandings that allow for the compromises necessary for communal life, this conflict occasionally resurfaces. And that's why republicans—whether socialists, radicals, or even liberal-conservatives— consider it their duty to stand watch over secular schools and to explain how, while respecting all beliefs, they do not intend to allow any single one the monopoly on educating new generations. It is essential for both the unity of the nation and the freedom of the individual that the seeds of division and methods of authority remain outside public school doors. The life philosophy one settles upon is only valuable if it is freely chosen. From this viewpoint, the critical spirit—so odious to the Saint-Simonians—takes on renewed value and a social function. It is considered the salt of democracy, promising the individual a sort of perpetual rebuke to authority.

The disadvantage, the peril of the situation spawned by this tradition has been pointed out time and again. It not only makes the task of the 'organizers' detested by Proudhon more difficult because, far from promoting subservience to men, it would suggest resistance, or at the very least, endorse universal critique and constant vigilance. But it also risks perpetuating a sort of latent intellectual conflict between supporters of Catholic authority and proponents of secular freedom. Conversely, as Romier has astutely observed, this perennially thorny issue keeps minds from becoming complacent, encourages them to coalesce under banners other than those of mere interests, and ultimately fuels a kind of public spiritual life in France that transcends the economic sphere.

---

[591] Latin for "acts of violence rather than laws." This quote is from Thomas Aquinas' (1225-1274) *Summa Theologiae*, 21, 96, 4.

[592] *Latitudinarianism* indicates a philosophy of tolerance to other beliefs.

It is also worth noting that in practice, these antagonisms are often less severe than they might seem when principles are directly confronted. They do not preclude collaboration on numerous fronts. When the nation is threatened, it goes without saying, Catholics and secularists demonstrate their ability to come together instantly. Here, the sense of national identity retains its dominating force. But social issues are also capable of prompting such alignments. Haven't we seen, before the war, on the same public platform, an Archbishop and a Secretary of the General Confederation of Labor jointly advocating for Sunday rest? Since then, numerous social Catholics have joined their voices with those of radicals and socialists to demand the eight-hour workday or social security. From Lamennais[593] to De Mun,[594] via Buchez, they can cite a great tradition that advises them not only to organize private charity but also to accept state intervention, and above all, to support the action of workers' associations. This means that when it comes to passing laws with a socialist orientation—the very laws to which Saint-Simonian reflections have sensitized minds—democrats will increasingly find support from Catholics.

Nevertheless, a significant disagreement remains between them. And it pertains to democracy itself, a principle that the Catholic tradition seems to have difficulty accepting.

We are certainly aware that there are many ardent Catholic democrats, and they are highly active in areas of international politics as well as social policy. The support of this force is far from negligible. Nevertheless, it is also well-known—and experience has shown—that these

---

[593] Félicité Robert de La Mennais, or Lamennais (1782–1854) was an influential priest and philosopher. He originally advocated for the dominance of the Catholic Church over the state but moved towards more liberal positions. Lamennais was excommunicated by Pope Gregory XVI, which led to him renouncing Catholicism.

[594] Adrien Albert Marie de Mun (1841–1914) was a Catholic politician and social reformer. After being a prisoner of war during the Franco-Prussian War, he promoted Catholic Social Teaching and supported the working class. Nonetheless, De Mun was a prominent anti-Dreyfusard and antisemite.

democrats can be called to order at any moment, and to respect the Catholic hierarchy, by the authority of the Pope. The distinction between opinions that are and those that are not within his purview holds little value when a decisive stroke of his crozier falls upon bowed heads. And if, for instance, he commands his faithful to renew their battle against secular laws, the entire republican structure is once again shaken. As long as such possibilities remain open, the syndicalist aspiration we've identified, stemming from the theories of the great French socialists between 1800 and 1848, will not be fulfilled: politics will not be confined to the "science of production," and it will continue to address issues beyond purely economic concerns, thereby affirming that politics, outside of economics, will retain its raison d'être.

*
* *

Moreover, setting aside the issue of secularism, it will be difficult to convince the majority of French people that economic and social issues are purely technical matters that should be left to experts without the masses having their say. As Guy-Grand aptly pointed out in *Proudhon and Our Time*, a vote always indirectly reflects a metaphysical preference. Do you support or oppose a measure of social legislation? Ultimately, this depends on your worldview, the values you prioritize, and for instance, the standard of living or the degree of control you deem just to grant the masses. These value judgments, whether optimistic or pessimistic, are the very soul of political parties. And the effort to make one or another of these visions prevail in a country's legislation and administration indeed requires political parties, public discussions, and the deliberations of assemblies where the majority rules and directs government intervention.

If these observations hold true and this sentiment continues to resonate strongly in France, then it is premature, despite numerous critical voices, to declare the end of political thought in the nation. The French are likely to long retain the habit of squabbling over abstractions. Perhaps, to further explain this persistence of politics, one must once again consider the rural masses, whose significance we have previously noted. If industrial democracy is to establish itself here, it must make ample room for rural democracy. Proudhon, would be the first to remind us of this, adapting the Physiocratic tradition to a new context. However, contrary to what Proudhon himself might have thought, rural democracy could be the last to dismiss the methods of political democracy: not only because peasants, in many regions, remember the pressure exerted on them by local powers, and would likely call on central government support against them, but also because, to safeguard their living conditions, to ensure fair prices for crops, and to defend against the abuses of speculation or the excesses of imports, they need the law: their unions ultimately depend on state intervention. According to an astute observer—Marcel Déat in *Socialist Perspectives*—peasant thinking here may take a path opposite to that of worker thinking: the latter tends to move from the political to the economic, the former from the economic to the political. The myriad practical problems that daily life poses for farmers might prompt them to turn to the state, renewing their desire every day to influence government action through their representatives. Conversely, workers, faced with imperfect labor laws that fail to adequately address the diversity and complexity of their conditions in factories, increasingly recognize the need to supplement, if not at times replace, parliamentary activity with union activity.

However, as the same observer notes, this doesn't mean they are prepared to abandon the democratic ideal. What Sidney and Beatrice Webb have studied under the name of *industrial democracy*, namely the organization of trade unions, reflects a defensible thesis. Doesn't syndicalism offer workers the best means of representation and the most effective tool for collective action? It advocates—not only in our country but as its adopted motto suggests—not only for welfare but also for freedom. It provides the working masses with various ways to oversee employers and to exert pressure on the state. Through these new channels, the democratic spirit continues to make gains. Consequently, it is unsurprising that, following the workers' example, other social groups such as civil servants seek the power of union solidarity to bring their grievances before public authorities and public opinion, thereby

237

accelerating and enlightening parliamentary action. Understood in this way, syndicalism is not a negation but an extension of democracy: it builds a bridge between political and industrial democracy, enabling us to collectively harness both the legacy of the French Revolution and that of Saint-Simonian and Proudhonian socialism.

Moreover, the democratic spirit might also find a home in many other institutions that yet to be explored, not among trade unions per se, but within cooperative associations, which we have noted embody a part of Fourierist thought. As previously mentioned, the workers' production associations did not fulfill all expectations set in '48. Despite the 210 million in transactions conducted in 1930, using state funds, by the 340 cooperatives affiliated with the advisory chamber, they seem incapable of imposing significant transformations on the economic landscape. This does not mean that they no longer have a role to play. By elevating employees to the status of co-managers of workshops, they engage in an educational mission that an industrial democracy would logically seek to generalize. And if, at present, they struggle to compete with larger, well-capitalized companies, perhaps by limiting their aspirations to collaborating to create work that they remain free to organize as they see fit, workers might preserve a degree of autonomy that should not be underestimated. Isn't this sort of arrangement what H. Dubreuil, the author of *Industrial Republic*, places most of his hopes in?

Furthermore, consumer cooperatives, which currently have a much broader scope than production cooperatives, can also boast fidelity to the democratic spirit. Unlike joint-stock corporations where one individual can control as many votes as shares they purchase, nullifying the influence of smaller shareholders, each member of a consumer cooperative has one and only one vote at meetings where that decide on purchases or resource distribution. If these cooperatives, by banding together, not only push back against profit-driven private commerce but also extend their control over an increasing number of industrial establishments that become their regular suppliers, and if they manage to limit, by pooling their savings, the dominance of investment banks, one could argue that the new world they are trying to build aligns well with what Poisson calls a "cooperative republic."

The tradition of the French Revolution, which insists that individuals retain some control over institutions, finds ample means to persist in today's economic and social realities. It is not confined solely to parliamentarism. Even if parliamentarism's role were somehow reduced in national life, industrial democracy might not necessarily be diminished simultaneously.

*
* *

At present, decisions that impact the entire nation are deliberated in assemblies whose members are elected by universal suffrage; without their consent, these decisions cannot become law. This safeguard is widely regarded by public opinion as one of the most reliable protectors of freedom. Should this safeguard be weakened—if, with the support of syndicalism, parliamentarism were reduced to a mere formality—it would mark a significant shift. It would then become evident that an ideological movement, which claims its roots in the legacy of great French socialists, might destabilize one of the central institutions born from the spirit of the French Revolution. Therefore, the ongoing duel that we are witnessing between parliamentarism and syndicalism deserves our close attention.

Syndicalism often critically assesses the methods of the republican state, highlighting that the state, due to the growth and complexity of industry and its significant influence on national life, tends to take on roles for which it is ill-equipped. The rapid expansion of modern enterprises continuously presents complex challenges, whether in their interactions with the consumer mass or the working class. Questions such as which product categories should be protected by tariffs and to what extent, or how to ensure workers have adequate leisure time without stalling the factory's momentum or reducing its output, are persistent and unavoidable. However, addressing these issues with the traditional tools available to the democratic state leads to various difficulties, exposing the system to numerous disappointments and defects. Parliamentarians lack expertise, ministers lack time, and bureaucrats lack flexibility. Politicians, whom René Giraud coldly labels as the last idealists of this century in his study *Towards an Economic International*,[595] are almost by definition the least equipped to solve the overriding economic issues. "We live in the era of the machine," observes Charles Albert in *The Modern State*.[596] "Yet politically, we have not adapted to the presence of the machine. It's in our workshops, factories, and on our roads, even in the homes of our peasants, but it is not yet reflected in our laws." There's an excess of speeches, partisan squabbles, words, and an undue reverence for doctrines, along with too many concessions to electoral appetites. The contributors to the *Syndicalist Library*[597] repeatedly paint this bleak picture, which ostensibly justifies the youthful ambition attributed to Paul-Boncour, de Monzie,[598] and Henry de Jouvenel: "To modernize France by syndicalizing the Republic."

One of the key arguments among syndicalist reformers is the observation of the state's impotence in handling economic issues. "Today, resentment towards the state stems more from its powerlessness than from its tyranny," remarks Pierre Loewel[599] in *Inventory 1931*. But another notable fact that warrants emphasis, providing an additional argument, is the growing power of forces organized for the service of economic life set against the backdrop of a helpless state. "It is no longer in the national assemblies and councils that the nation's affairs are decided," we are assured. "It is at the Committee of Steelmakers, the

---

[595] *Vers une internationale économique* (1931).

[596] Charles Albert (1869–1957) was a journalist and syndicalist who wrote *L'état moderne* (1929). He later became a member of the neo-socialist party.

[597] *Bibliothèque syndicaliste* (1928–1932).

[598] Anatole de Monzie (1876–1947) was a political theorist and politician. He was a friend of Henry de Jouvenel and is credited with introducing philosophy into France's high school curriculum.

[599] Pierre Loewel (1890–1955) was a historian who wrote the 1931 book *Inventaire 1931*.

Board of Directors of Le Creusot,[600] the Consortium of Large Banks,[601] the Union of Economic Interests,[602] or the Federation of Chambers of Commerce."[603] Furthermore, at the other end of the battle line, the power of the unions is evident: civil servant unions, worker unions advocating for pay rises or resisting pay cuts, and exerting influence over ministers and parliament, reveal that the state has largely been reduced to a façade. To quote de Jouvenel once more, "Everything is organized against the state, which should be presiding over the organization of everything."

This provides another incentive to attempt to 'decongest' the republican state, to encourage it to delegate as many of its functions as possible to competent and relatively autonomous bodies, and to finally accept a degree of professional decentralization without which there is no longer any salvation. At stake is not solely the nation's prosperity, but also the vitality of the state itself. If better oversight is desired, it is crucial for the state to act less on its own initiative. In any case, it is high time it defined roles and simultaneously set limits for the economic forces that have spontaneously formed within what Hegel called 'civil society': to acknowledge, incorporate, and integrate them—lest it be overwhelmed by them.

*

*　*

One of the key institutions that syndicalists rely on to initiate this regeneration of the state is naturally the National Economic Council. There is a widespread desire to see this council more inclusively staffed and granted broader powers than it currently possesses. By bringing together representatives from public administrations, various categories of producers, and representatives of the consumer masses, it would be tasked with reconciling the realms of production and politics. This body

---

[600] *Conseil d'administration du Creusot.* Le Creusot is an industrial town and the site of ore mines and forges.
[601] *Consortium des grandes banques.*
[602] *Union des intérêts économiques.*
[603] *Fédération des chambres de commerce.*

would act as a conduit through which political France could, when necessary, issue directives for the public good to economic France, and through which economic France could communicate its ideas, plans, and needs to political France.

However, the extent to which the powers of such a council should be expanded raises significant questions. Should it evolve into a true professional parliament? What would those who are concerned about preserving the sovereignty of the political parliament say? And on the other hand, will the economic forces we're trying to integrate acquiesce to this integration, or will they resist being tamed? The momentum we thus describe could thus encounter two forms of resistance: one from the side of "democracy," the other from "syndicalism." The concept of a professional parliament endowed with decision-making power doesn't seem to be readily embraced by French public opinion. It would be futile to argue that a nation is merely an organism. The constituent elements of society are not atomized individuals; rather, the entities developed for and by economic life also represent legitimate representative bodies. Therefore, it is essential to pay close attention to the tendencies they express. Such ideas might find more resonance in Germany, where, since Hegel, there is a longstanding tradition of organicism.[604] According to Vermeil, it would be challenging for Germany to abandon this mindset in favor of a democratic system that allows individuals to vote *viritim*, as Proudhon said, where each counts as one and only one. The tradition in France is quite different. Although the validity of syndicalist criticisms of parliamentarianism is recognized, they are welcomed with a sort of relief. Yet those who attempt to demonstrate that the Chambers have undertaken the most useful initiatives since and during the war face a steep challenge. Is this reason enough to encourage Parliament to cede its place to councils of professionals or experts? Firstly, it is not clear how the system would function, nor is it certain that all economic categories would be fairly represented in these new types of deliberating assemblies. How could one set, without arbitrariness, the number of votes each

---

[604] Organicism is a philosophical stance that holds that human societies, and the universe more generally, ought to be considered akin to a living organism.

242

category could wield when decisions that requiring a majority are made? Most importantly, isn't there a risk that that each professional group represented might vote based its own interests rather than the general interest, succumbing to what Jaurès called corporate greed? To encourage solutions aligned with the general interest, it might be simpler and wiser to consult the sentiments of individuals, considered as citizens and consumers, rather than dividing them into various categories of producers. These reasons hold significant weight in the minds of many French, even those drawn to the syndicalist program, leading to a preference for the National Economic Council to remain an advisory body, not a decision-making one. There might be calls for the Council to be mandatorily consulted on economic and social laws to address parliamentary 'incompetence,' but extending its role further would infringe on the institution through which the sovereignty of the people is expressed, albeit imperfectly. No one wishes to take such a step. They are ready to offer a crutch to Parliament, but wouldn't want to trip it up.

To understand this mindset, let's consider the shifts in democratic opinion within a particularly representative league tasked with defending the tradition of human rights. This league unites an increasing number of republican, radical, and socialist activists committed to maintaining principled positions. At its latest Congress, the topic of discussion was Syndicalism and the State. The Congress members favorably received critiques of parliamentary inertia and applauded the arguments of the rapporteur, Mr. Oualid, who demonstrated potential improvements in assembly work efficiency, not just through better techniques but also by involving specialists, citing the practices of the International Labor Office as an example. However, he was cautious not to suggest that elected representative assemblies should be replaced. The Congress supported his proposal for a resolution stating, "National sovereignty, singular, inalienable, and perpetual, must remain the exclusive domain of the entire nation, composed of individual citizens of a political state; therefore, the legislative process, as an expression of the national will, should be reserved for Parliament, freely elected by universal suffrage."

This language and these ideas recall those of the French Revolution. Democratic league members intend to preserve, and declare their readiness to defend, national sovereignty, continuing to believe that decisions made by a majority in a universally elected assembly provide the best safeguard for the protection of rights.

However, as discussions progressed, another sentiment emerged, reminiscent of socialism and even revolutionary socialism, showing resistance to the integrations envisioned by syndicalist reformers. The rapporteur had noted that for the new system to be well-balanced and for tasks to be rationally allocated between Parliament and the National Economic Council, the trade union body, the Council's powers, rights, and duties must be clearly defined. This would be the most reliable way to set boundaries for syndicalism, effectively saying, "This far, but no further." At this juncture, there was a palpable sense of unease among the audience, and some resistance emerged. Several Congress members, affiliated with workers' unions, voiced their opposition to integrating syndicalism into the current state apparatus, almost critiquing what they saw as its taming. For them, the union, especially the workers' union, is not just a coalition of interests but a beacon of idealism. It earns the devotion of its members because it promises that through their actions, both defensive and constructive, they are part of building a new world where justice will finally prevail.

In that regard, Victor Basch,[605] president of the League, suggested that it would be better if syndicalism did become a cog in the state machinery. If it must influence the formulation and application of laws, it should do so from outside the state structure, running parallel but not in conjunction. This approach would best "preserve its full offensive power."

The final word, "offensive," is revealing. It resonates with a revolutionary spirit, a readiness to fight. From this perspective, the

---

[605] Victor Basch (1863–1944) was a philosopher and the President of the *Ligue des droits de l'homme* from 1926 to 1944. Notably, Basch a fervent anti-Nazi, was assassinated under the Vichy regime.

244

primary mission of the unions is to continually challenge a political-economic system that produces or tolerates numerous injustices. They are urged not to look too far ahead, not to detail their plans for the future or their current strategies too finely. The directive is simply to charge ahead. This approach echoes the philosophy long championed by Georges Sorel, author of *Reflections on Violence*, and his followers. For them, the most crucial aspect was to sustain the flame of heroism in the hearts of the proletariat, even if it meant relying on "myths" such as the general strike. Drawing on the distinction made by Charles Péguy[606] between mysticism and politics, they argued that what mattered most was a mystique, specifically a workerist mystique. They viewed Jaurès, who argued that the "reasons of the majority" should not be disregarded since the producer must always consider the voter, with a certain disdain.

Today, do the workers' unions within the General Confederation of Labor lean more toward Jaurès or toward Sorel? Since the war, influenced by Léon Jouhaux—himself an admirer of Proudhon—they have championed the primacy of labor and highlighted the need to expand the role of technology in the social economy. Their leaders strongly pushed for the creation of the National Economic Council. Furthermore, by repeatedly calling for nationalizations, albeit industrialized ones, they have shown that they would be the first to distrust a statist collectivism; the omnipotence of bureaucracy, often synonymous with incompetence, is as abhorrent to them as to anyone. They rely on the action of their unions to correct errors and modernize administrative methods. But they also introduce a new concept, unprecedented in the history of worker syndicalism: the general interest, of which they claim to be the most informed advocates. Isn't this concern, coupled with their experience of worker life, what pushed them to draft a minimal political action program, which left-wing parties were eager to endorse? Clearly, syndicalism as understood today accommodates a role for

---

[606] Charles Péguy (1873-1914) was an influential essayist, poet, and socialist strongly influenced by Catholicism. Péguy's works expressed mystical inspiration, often evoking the Joan of Arc, which is a French symbol of heroism in dark times. He was killed in battle during WWI.

parliamentarism. It would be prepared to use, with necessary additions, the framework built by democracy for its preservation.

How long will this mindset persist? At the latest Congress of the CGT, it was evident that several trade unionists, lamenting the split between the CGT and the CGTU[607]—the latter influenced by Moscow— were questioning whether by presenting itself as a defender of the general interest, by allowing itself to be assimilated, by accepting roles for its members in mixed councils, both national and international, syndicalism was becoming tepid, losing its fervor. Jouhaux countered by emphasizing the timeliness and effectiveness of practicing a policy of engagement, both in Paris and Geneva, which he argued brings appreciable results today while leaving all hopes for the future intact for workers. Nonetheless, the argument persists, stirring considerable emotion among delegates, that accepting collaborations is a slippery slope toward compromises, ultimately propping up a system that should be toppled. In essence, the suggestion is from all sides is that worker syndicalists might once again need an infusion of combative spirit.

These debates are highly instructive; they shine a bright light on the conditions necessary for social action aimed at fundamentally transforming the institutions of the economic regime. Both mystique and technique are required: technique to rationally organize, for instance, relationships between different categories of producers or between producers and consumers, and to achieve optimal output from a transformed factory; mystique to provide the driving force for the mill wheel, to mobilize the essential moral forces needed for success. Between these two poles, technique and mystique, the sentiments of those involved oscillate, shifting with the times, the crises faced, and the outcomes recorded, sometimes leaning one way and sometimes another.

---

[607] The *Confédération générale du travail unitaire* (1922-1936) was a confederation of anarcho-syndicalist unions that were expelled from the CGT and became affiliated with the French Communist Party.

Ultimately, it's impossible to do without either of these elements if one truly aims to foster a thriving industrial democracy.

The doctrines we've summarized, as observed, cater to both the need for ideals and the need for tangible "materializations." Moreover, they exhibit tendencies that in some aspects align and complement each other, while in others they limit and counterbalance each other. The choices of French public opinion—or rather, the varied opinions across France—faced with this array of possibilities, will largely depend on the circumstances we encounter, the experiments we conduct or endure. For instance, if top-down organization—dominated by bankers and captains of industry favored by the Saint-Simonians—fails to address the post-war disorder, the alarming spread of unemployment among workers, the downturns that impoverish farmers, or the crippling cost of living that plagues small consumers, then revolutionary mystique will likely gain traction. Conversely, if the opponents of the current economic regime were to seize power, in one way or another, without achieving clearly beneficial outcomes for the nation's masses, both consumers and worker-producers, and if their laws and decrees primarily resulted in increased economic chaos, then we might witness a political backlash. In such cases, there would likely be a call for technical expertise to intervene, tasked with "transforming the station without stopping the traffic." This serves as a reminder that the state, even under the pressure of disgruntled masses, might fail to achieve any viable economic or social outcomes if a cadre of experienced technicians does not emerge within the cooperatives inspired by Fourier, or the worker and peasant federations envisioned by Proudhon—personnel that an industrial democracy, more than any other regime, desperately needs.

Appendices to the English Edition

Two Resurrections:
Saint-Simonism and Proudhonism
By Célestin Bouglé (1918)

* Originally published as: C. Bouglé: Deux Résurrections: Saint-Simonisme et Proudhonisme. Pp. 2005-2007 in *L'Europe nouvelle*, 1(42), October 24, 1918.

Seemingly abandoned in favor of foreign doctrines, old French socialist thought nonetheless continued to shape the mindset of the working class and its activists. In recent years, we have seen its resurgence, more or less consciously, but distinctly.

It falls to the author of The Sociology of Proudhon[608] *and an upcoming volume that will take us* Among the Socialist Prophets[609] *to specify for the readers of* New Europe[610] *the signs that mark this resurrection of the doctrines of '48.*

Anyone who combines a curiosity about present realities with some knowledge of the classical systems of social philosophy cannot help but seek a connection between these two domains. Among the doctrines developed by our great socialist innovators, don't some resonate with the economic facts we are witnessing today? Could their resurrected ideas serve as focal points for coordinating the many transformations that are spontaneously emerging before our eyes? It appears that such principles, capable of being revived to organize life, might be found in Saint-

---

[608] Bouglé published *La sociologie de Proudhon* in 1911.
[609] *Chez les prophètes socialistes* (1918).
[610] *Europe nouvelle* (1918-1940).

Simonism and others in Proudhonism, with one possibly complementing or correcting the other.

*
* *

Charles Rist recently wrote in the *Political Economy Review*,[611] "What we need is neo-Saint-Simonism." Is this merely wishful thinking? There is more to the economist-historian's words. He recognizes that facts are shaping the resurgence he envisions by the very force of things— by the necessities of war—there is, now more than ever, a hint of Saint-Simonism in the air.

Indeed, it's one of the current paradoxes: the war, which they detested more than anything in the world, has dragged these great pacifists behind its chariot, reopening paths to their program.

They believed in peace, made nearly inevitable by the very progress of industry. They didn't foresee that a nation would synthesize two elements they considered irreconcilably hostile to each other: militarism and industrialism. This unexpected synthesis set the stage for a formidable explosion, potent enough to shatter the faith of the Saint-Simonians.

Yet if they were profoundly mistaken in this regard, how often did they speak a language that is only today becoming common?

Their brand of industrialism stands against what they call constitutionalism. And their socialism prioritizes the importance of production.

This implies that two issues lose their interest in their view: the forms of government forms and the modalities of distribution.

Many today, coming from very different perspectives, would agree that we've been too fixated on these two sets of issues. "Less politics"—to

---

[611] *Revue d'économie politique* (1887–).

embrace this motto is to recall, in line with the Saint-Simonian tradition, that what matters above all is the development of the nation's resources. To succeed in this mission, to prepare what Herriot terms the economic reorganization of the nation, it's crucial to diminish the significance of the very doctrines that could still divide parties yesterday. In our battle with nature, we must maintain some of the united front that was necessary to resist the enemy. Audibert[612] recently asked if we could establish a party above all parties, a productivist party?

Productivist—this new term signifies not so much a birth as a rebirth: the rebirth of the mindset of the forefathers of *producers*. Lysis[613] repeats in all tones: "Intensify production: distribution will take care of itself. That is the true formula of the new democracy." To establish his thesis, he willingly denounces what he calls the French error. He overlooks just one thing: the concept he's embracing is a long-established French idea. The ground he's rediscovering is, in fact, venerable French soil.

Transforming the nation into a vast workshop, and ensuring that one person is less exploited by another by first better exploiting the earth—this is indeed the supreme ideal for the Saint-Simonians. Their thought would progress in stages from liberalism to socialism. But their brand of socialism, as noted by one of their best historians, Elie Halévy, would always remain a socialism centered on production.

To achieve this ideal, some of the methods extolled by the Saint-Simonians coincide precisely with those imposed by the necessities of war.

The state had to intervene in nearly everything, but not without changing its ways. To the joy of Maxime Leroy, a lawyer eager to embrace

---

[612] Marcel Audibert (1883-1967) was a journalist, jurist, and writer.
[613] Eugène Letailleur (1869-1927), who went by the alias Lysis, was a banker and writer who opposed modern finance. He published several articles in *L'humanité*.

new developments, administrative action has taken unprecedented forms. Faced with shrinking supplies and growing demands, it became necessary to purchase for the nation, and to distribute goods among provinces and raw materials among factories.

Immense and complicated tasks that could not possibly be accomplished without the collaboration of seasoned professionals.

Thus, industrialists, merchants, bankers, and engineers were brought into regional committees, interministerial offices, and government councils. This is what Maxime Leroy refers to as "the administrative ascent of the producers." But isn't this rise precisely what the author of the *Letters from an Inhabitant of Geneva* was advocating? In the various "Chambers" he proposed, to finally make politics truly industrial—chambers of invention, examination, and execution—he envisioned a means to grant political influence to those who had demonstrated economic prowess. He carved out steps for the rise of expertise.

However, it's not merely the consultation with industrial experts that lends a unique character to the renewal efforts we are witnessing. The movement is broader. It is a movement toward general convergence, a sort of universal syndicalization. Willingly or not, it's impossible to work in different directions. The state itself, because of the requests it makes to allied nations, must remind the factory, trading post, and bank owners that operating in a scattered fashion is no longer viable.

Due to limitations on available freight and tightening credit, agreements must be made today on quantities to import or export, just as tomorrow agreements must be made on the order of priority for restocking and rebuilding. Whether intended or not, the war has taught the business world solidarity. And it is perhaps in this aspect that the war has most advanced us toward Saint-Simonism.

For that was indeed their obsession: to organize. We should not be misled into thinking that the formula was invented by Ostwald.[614] The Saint-Simonians, nearly a century ago, reiterated this theme in every way. When the Péreire brothers worked on consolidating credit companies as well as railroad companies, they were merely implementing, in their way, an idea dear to their school. "The real purpose of political economy," Enfantin proclaimed, "is the coordination of efforts." To achieve this coordination, which aims to limit the drawbacks of anarchic competition, there must also be an understanding among bankers, who act as the generals of industry, and whose banks ought to serve as "representative chambers of workers, constantly striving to procure for them the materials of production at the lowest possible cost."

This illustrates that many of the "reforms" now demanded as necessitated by circumstances are precisely those anticipated and prepared for by the great social innovators, the Saint-Simonians.

Post-war France could, without diminishing its stature, return to their teachings.

*

* *

Yet something essential is lacking in this school, something that might be dangerous to discard: and that is nothing less than the democratic spirit.

The disciples of the gentleman-messiah may turn to socialism, but they will not revert to democracy. They approach the people, but always with the underlying intent to lead them. The sentiment they most willingly instill is not merely confidence in talent, but reverence for superiors. Thus, they remain, as was said at the time, hierarchs. The notion that the

---

[614] Wilhelm Ostwald (1853–1932) was a German chemist and philosopher. He is considered one of the founders of physical chemistry and received the Nobel Prize in Chemistry in 1909. One of his long-standing interests was unification through systematization, which extended from chemistry to labor organization.

people might wish to act independently, or even to critique and oversee, is difficult for them to accept, while the potential for those with abilities to abuse power concerns them very little.

And it is precisely here that Saint-Simonian tendencies could be beneficially supplemented or corrected by Proudhonian tendencies. To remind us of the rights of the people and the "capacity" of the working class, there is no equal to the former typographer turned economist. Born of the people, he stayed true to his roots; he was a democrat as naturally as one breathes.

And I'm well aware that shortly before the war, there were attempts to conscript his defiant spirit into the ranks of the anti-democrats.[615] Few intellectual co-optations were more paradoxical than this one. What Proudhon absolutely opposed was the promotion of statism in the name of democracy, the strengthening of authoritative institutions. That's why he launched such a fervent attack against someone like Louis Blanc. But he was the first to advocate for what he termed, before Sidney Webb, industrial democracy. He insisted that to truly establish a stable order—an order stable because it is egalitarian—control by the producers in economic life is essential. And by producers, he didn't mean the captains of industry, but rather the industrial army, the mass of workers. Only they can harmonize "the Marianne of the fields with the Sociale of the cities."

Thus, they will act in unison on the rates of exchange. They will restore the true value to the products of labor by liberating them from the tolls imposed by financial speculation in all its forms. They will ultimately make credit accessible to workers. If Saint-Simonian socialism is centered on production, Proudhonian socialism focuses on exchange. It is primarily through the reformation of the People's Banks that he envisions the salvation of the world. However, it is self-evident that the workers' cooperatives he envisions, aimed at forming an egalitarian agro-industrial

---

[615] Alluding to the national syndicalist political party *Cercle Proudhon.*

federation, could not influence exchange rates without first addressing the conditions of production.

Therefore, it's not only cooperatives but also trade unions that can claim allegiance to the Proudhonian tradition. Anyone who believes that the primary requirement for the rejuvenation of economic life is the direct involvement of workers in governance is, at heart, a Proudhonist.

"The maximum production for the maximum wage in the shortest amount of time," that's our agenda, Jouhaux declared in a session that has since become renowned. For his part, Albert Thomas in *Workers' and Social Information*[616] encapsulated the sentiment of today's working class with the phrase: "everything that is produced belongs to us." These declarations are sure to please the neo-Saint-Simonians. But for this grand scheme to be fully realized, is it sufficient to place our trust in the "superiors"? Wouldn't it be prudent to suggest, or even imperative to enforce, certain measures that prevent industry from neglecting the human element for the sake of objects? This implies that we might need to call upon Proudhon for support...

Indeed, those who aim to rejuvenate syndicalist doctrines, considering the very lessons learned from the war—the editors of *The Clearing*[617] for instance—are not misguided: they constantly revisit the concept of a *return to Proudhon*...

*
* *

Thus, alongside Saint-Simonism, Proudhonism is being revived before our eyes—both seemingly invigorated in an unexpected manner by the great shock.

---

[616] *Information ouvrière et sociale* (1918-1920).
[617] *La clairière* (1917-1919).

Revived—to clash once more as in the past, or to cooperate by mutually imposing limits? In short, are we on the verge of witnessing a renewed confrontation, or a pragmatic union?

Should the reorganization of industry, which is universally acknowledged as necessary, proceed top-down, in the Saint-Simonian manner, or could it make significant room for grassroots aspirations, in the way Proudhon would have preferred?

It's a weighty question, as one might surmise. The observer might be able to respond, perhaps in a few years' time...

Variations of Marxism
By Célestin Bouglé (1938)

* Originally published as: C. Bouglé: Variations sur le Marxisme. *Marianne*, 286, April 13, 1938.

The philosophy of Marxism during my student days was exceedingly straightforward, or rather, oversimplified. It was marked by vehement denials: the repudiation of anything resembling spiritualism, the rejection of idealism, the refusal to assign any significance or effectiveness to doctrines, beliefs, or emotions.

Should the *Rights of Man* or immanent justice be mentioned, Paul Lafargue,[618] Karl Marx's son-in-law, would stand up to dismiss these "metaphysical charlatans." And he would sharply reprimand Jaurès, the mediator, for attempting to drape idealism alongside materialism in the folds of his orator's robe, for daring to summon Plutarch or Michelet in the same breath as Karl Marx. Hadn't Marx himself assertively stated: "It is not the consciousness of men that determines their existence, but on the contrary, their social existence that determines their consciousness"?[619] From such a premise, what grand constructs might be imagined!

We must delve into the modes of production that sustain life for the underlying reason, not only for ways of governance or for legislating, but for modes of thought: not only must law and religion be explained, but literature and philosophy must also now be interpreted as material

---

[618] Paul Lafargue (1842–1911) was a Cuban-born French Marxist who married Karl Marx's daughter, Laura Marx (1845–1911), with whom he committed suicide. Along with Jules Guesde, Lafargue, found and lead the *Parti ouvrier français* ("French Workers' Party") from 1880 to 1902 and played a significant role in popularizing Marxism in France.

[619] K. Marx: *A Contribution to the Critique of Political Economy.* Translated by S. W. Ryazanskaya. Progress Publishers, 1977, p. 21.

byproducts, rooted in the advancements of industrial technology and the class struggle.

Take note: if the mathematical physicists of the century have embraced the concept of a natural law of absolute value, it's because of the advancements in royal absolutism observed in their era. As for the hypothesis of the unity of cosmic forces, it likely emerged from the salons of the 17th century, where the bourgeoisie leisure class amused themselves with clever comparisons.

These examples are sufficient. They serve as cautionary signposts, warning of the peril in attempting to attribute the highest achievements of the human spirit—religion, science, art—to the solitary influence of the productive forces of economic life. The mismatch between the single cited cause and the value, complexity, and diversity of the outcomes is blatantly apparent. The interpreter, persisting in his reductionism, assumes the guise of an inept Sisyphus.[620]

From this emerges a reticence among Marxist philosophers, a step back from the precipice. They revisit their foundational texts and recognize that indeed, the theories have been excessively simplified. Even Marx himself didn't endorse such a narrow view.[621] Did he ever truly intend to banish all forms of idealism from the philosophy of history? He set a goal for himself, striving to replace the dominion of necessity with that of freedom, and as Saragat[622] noted, remained a "humanist." Without

---

[620] In Greek mythology, Sisyphus was a tyrant who angered the gods and was thereby punished for eternity to roll an enormous boulder up a hill that would roll back down anytime he approached the top.

[621] Not long before his death, Marx accused Guesde and Lafargue of "revolutionary phrase-mongering" and famously confided to Engels that if their stances were considered Marxist, then "I myself am not a Marxist."

[622] Giuseppe Saragat (1898–1988) was an Italian socialist who became the first socialist president of Italy from 1964 to 1971. Leading up to WWII, he notably opposed Mussolini and was forced into exile. Saragat also helped forge ties between Italian socialists and other European socialist groups.

a doubt, he would have concurred with Engels that the economic factor only comes into play "in the last instance."[623]

Ultimately, we encounter a Marxism that should not be labeled as diluted, but rather as enriched and made more flexible, open to tolerating, embracing, and seeking out nuanced explanations that would have once sent shivers down the spine of Paul Lafargue in my student days.

What is most intriguing is that Russia itself, Soviet Russia, is contributing to this intellectual enrichment and mellowing.

This is at least the impression given in G. Friedmann's[624] thoroughly informed and nuanced book, *From Holy Russia to the USSR*.

He recounts an anecdote attributed to Stalin.[625] When questioning his son about the history of England, Stalin was surprised to hear references to "merchant capital" and "the third phase of conflict between the landed gentry and the urban bourgeoisie" but not a word about Cromwell.[626] The call was for Russian children to be given a more tangible, animated history, where individuals are seen living and taking action. It

---

[623] F. Engels to J. Bloch. September 21, 1890.

[624] Georges Friedmann (1902-1977) was an influential sociologist known for his research on industrialism and the sociology of work. He is considered one of the founders of industrial sociology. Friedmann's work examined how technology shapes organizations and the experience of work itself. He wrote the 1938 book *De la Sainte Russie à l'U.R.S.S.*

[625] Joseph Stalin (1878-1953) was a Marxist politician born in modern-day Georgia. Following Vladimir Lenin's (1870-1927) death, Stalin was the leader of the Soviet Union from 1924 until his death. Under Stalin, the Soviet Union rapidly industrialized and became a world power. He implemented the Great Purge in the 1930s, leading to mass imprisonment and executions of millions of Soviet citizens.

[626] Oliver Cromwell (1599-1658) was an influential English politician and military leader. Following the execution of King Charles I (1600-1649) and the exile of his son Charles II (1630-1685), Cromwell ruled as Lord Protector of the Commonwealth of England (1649-1660) from 1653 until his death.

was time to put an end to the repetitive invocation of merchant capital, a staple in the early works of Pokrovsky.[627]

It's also time to cease the excessive efforts to pigeonhole great writers into a class, to label them as incapable of looking beyond the economic interests of their cohorts, as if they were mere automatons speaking on behalf of their class.

Perusing our latest literature textbooks, one might conclude from Yermilov's[628] statements in *Pravda*[629] that the Russian classics were nothing more than zealots preoccupied with the material welfare of their social stratum. It is high time to acknowledge that they have often, through the strength of their personal intellect, broken free from this vicious cycle to touch upon humanistic values. It is high time to assert that the unionized workers of the USSR have the right to derive intellectual and moral sustenance from more than just a single author of Holy Russia.

Bravo. And thanks for the breath of "humanism." In France as well—and Georges Friedmann is more aware of this than anyone—a similar clearing of the remnants of "vulgar sociology" would be most beneficial.

---

[627] Mikhail Pokrovsky (1868-1932) was an influential Soviet Marxist historian. He rejected the focus on "great men" in history and instead focused on economic forces that drove historical change and developments.

[628] Vladimir Yermilov (1904-1965) was a Soviet literary critic known for harassing the famous Soviet poet Vladimir Mayakovsky (1893-1930), ultimately leading to his suicide. Yermilov is remembered for being severely critical of other writers.

[629] *Pravda* (1912-) is a Russian newspaper that was the official paper of the Central Committee of the Communist Party of the Soviet Union (1912-1991).

Afterword to the English Edition

By Cayce Jamil

Following the 1932 publication of this book, France, which had initially been resilient to the Great Depression compared to the US, Britain, and Germany, became increasingly afflicted by the economic downturn, reaching its low point by 1935. With Adolf Hitler (1889-1945) rising to power in Germany in 1933 and fascism gaining traction in France, radicals, socialists, and communists signed a pact in July 1935, forming what became known as The Popular Front. Their program sought significant reforms including a state unemployment insurance fund, a reduction working hours in the week without wage cuts, large-scale public works, recognition of women's right to work, and defense measures against fascist groups. The Popular Front won the 1936 legislative election, leading to the formation of the first government headed by the SFIO. In the same month, France saw the largest strike wave of the Third Republic, with roughly 2.4 million workers participating. Employers made substantial concessions, agreeing to collective contracts, raising wages for lower-paid workers, recognizing union shop stewards, and enshrining workers' rights such as allowing for private spaces free from company control.[630]

Following the gains from the strike wave, the Popular Front government initiated major public works, nationalized the arms industries and rail companies, created a Grain Board to stabilize prices, implemented democratic reforms in the Bank of France, and dissolved fascist groups. No other government within the Third Republic had acted so decisively, and notably while working within the law. However, the wage increases and the implementation of a 40-hour workweek compelled France to devalue their currency, inadvertently reducing the real value of wages. By early 1937, the social reforms were put on hold,

---

[630] C. Sowerwine: *France Since 1870: Culture, Politics, & Society*. Palgrave Macmillan, 2001, pp. 148-156.

and the coalition soon ran out of steam.[631] When the radical Édouard Daladier (1884–1970) came to power in 1938, he reversed many of the Popular Front's policies by cutting expenditures, reinstating a 48-hour workweek, and severely repressing strikes. Fascist groups reemerged stronger than ever. Concurrently, Daladier signed the Munich Agreement in September 1938, granting the Nazis control over the Sudetenland. [632]

A year later, when the Nazis invaded Poland, France, alongside Britain, was obliged to declare war on Germany to curb their aggression. However, in May 1940, the German army drove through Northern France and defeated France within a month. The Armistice with Germany led to the installation of the notorious Vichy regime (1940–1944), which effectively ended the Third Republic and resulted in collaboration with the Nazis. Panic spread among civilians, with some 10 million fleeing. The government increased police powers, abolished political parties, banned political meetings, and revised school curriculums. Additionally, the Vichy regime implemented antisemitic policies and was responsible for the deaths of roughly 72,000 French citizens in concentration camps.[633]

Following France's liberation in 1944 and the establishment of the Fourth Republic (1946–1958), the socialist and communist parties initially enjoyed a majority within the Assembly. However, from late 1946 until 1954, France went to war against the Communist Party of Vietnam in a bid to maintain control of their colony. Due to escalating Cold War tensions and concerns about the Soviet Union's influence over the French Communist Party (PCF), the party was excluded from the government. The PCF, which was the dominant leftist political party throughout the Fourth Republic, advocated a pro-Stalinist stance and became politically isolated. Moreover, the US exerted significant influence over France, further dividing public opinion. Consequently, socialist ideas were largely subordinated to the demands of an increasingly bipolar world. When the Algerian War (1954–1957) erupted, public

---

[631] *Ibid.,* pp. 157–160.
[632] *Ibid.,* pp. 181–185.
[633] *Ibid.,* pp. 195–202.

opinion further fragmented, leading to the demise the Fourth Republic and the establishment of the Fifth Republic (1958–).[634]

The devastation of World War II and the social fragmentation of the post-war era, not to mention Bouglé's death in 1940, led to the near-complete neglect of classical French socialist thought. During this fragile and uncertain period, the exiled Russian sociologist Georges Gurvitch (1894–1965) emerged as a prominent figure in reviving interest in classical socialism. Gurvitch was prolific, contributing numerous articles on the French socialists. He authored several significant books, including *The French Founders of Contemporary Sociology: Saint-Simon and P.-J. Proudhon,*[635] which underscored the importance of the French socialists in the development of contemporary sociology. His other notable works include *For the Centenary of the Death of Pierre-Joseph Proudhon: Proudhon and Marx, a Confrontation,*[636] and *Proudhon: His Life, His Work, with an Exposition of His Philosophy.*[637] Additionally, he curated a collection of Saint-Simon's writings, titled *Social Physiology.*[638] Furthermore, Gurvitch exhibited a keen engagement with Marx's early writings, especially the 1932 publications of the *Economic and Philosophic Manuscripts of 1844,* and *The German Ideology,* which shed light on Marx's intellectual exchanges with the French socialists. Following in Gurvitch's footsteps, his former student Pierre Ansart (1922–2016) continued to explore the intricate intellectual interplay between Marx and the French socialists through a series of articles and books, especially his *Marx and Anarchism: Essay on the Sociologies of*

---

[634] *Ibid.,* pp. 238–306.
[635] *Les fondateurs français de la sociologie contemporaine: Saint-Simon et P.-J. Proudhon* (1955).
[636] *Pour le centenaire de la mort de Pierre-Joseph Proudhon: Proudhon et Marx, une confrontation* (1964).
[637] *Proudhon: sa vie, son œuvre, avec un exposé de sa philosophie* (1965).
[638] *La physiologie sociale* (1965).

Saint-Simon, Proudhon, and Marx,[639] which further delved into this rich academic terrain.

However, in the post-war era, interest in Marxism eclipsed the various French socialist schools of thought. This period marked a "golden age" for Marxist publications in France and saw the emergence of diverse interpretations of Marx's doctrine.[640] It was not until the civil unrest of May 1968 that a modest revival of French socialist thought, emphasizing the social economy, begin to gain traction. For example, in the 1970s, *autogestion,* or self-management, became a focal point of the Left in France, including by trade union federations, the Socialist Party, and even the PCF.[641] Coined in the late 1950s, *autogestion* encompasses the concepts of *self-creation, self-control,* and *self-provisioning,* embodying the ideals of *self-reliance* and *self-determination.*[642] The concept gained momentum with the publication of the journal *Autogestion* in 1966, which continued to disseminate ideas on the subject until 1986. The journal played a pivotal role in popularizing *autogestion* and was significantly influenced by the work of the late sociologist Georges Gurvitch, to whom its first issue was dedicated.[643]

In fact, the Socialist President François Mitterrand (1916–1996), who ran the first authentically socialist government in France since the Popular Front of the 1930s from 1981 to 1995, championed *autogestion* in his original political campaigns, but once in office made no serious

---

[639] *Marx et l'anarchisme: essai sur les sociologies de Saint-Simon, Proudhon et Marx* (1969).

[640] J. Hage: A Golden Age for Marxist Publishing? The 1960s and 1970s. Pp. 137–148 in J.-N. Ducange & A. Burlaud (eds.): *Marx, a French Passion.* Translated by D. Broder. Brill Publishing.

[641] D. Sassoon: *One Hundred Years of Socialism: The West European Left in the Twentieth Century.* I.B. Tauris & Co Ltd, 2010, p. 403, 538.

[642] M. Vieta: The Stream of Self-Determination and *Autogestión:* Prefiguring Alternative Economic Realities. Pp. 781–809 in E*phemera: Theory and Politics in Organization,* 14(4), 2014.

[643] M. Tyldesley: *Liberate and Federate: Three Proudhonian Socialists in an Age of Fascism, Stalinism and War.* Irene Publishing, 2024, pp. 165–168.

attempt to implement it.[644] Nonetheless, Mitterrand did legally recognize the social economy as well as stimulated academic research on the topic. Following these developments, a series of laws aimed at supporting France's social economy have been enacted.[645] Moreover, the concept of *autogestion* transcended French borders, inspiring movements globally. Examples of *autogestion* manifesting worldwide include Brazil's landless peasants' and workers' movement, Argentina's worker-recovered enterprises, Quebec's solidarity cooperatives, Bolivia's campesino-indigena movement, urban guerrilla gardening initiatives, community cash systems, the DIY movement, and the burgeoning worker-cooperative sector.[646]

Although the nuanced legacy of French socialist thinkers has remained relatively marginalized in the public consciousness over the past century and a half, a dedicated contingent of researchers, particularly within Francophone academic circles, has sustained an interest in their ideological contributions. Scholarly endeavors such as the *Cahiers Saint-Simon* (1973-2019), *Cahiers Charles Fourier* (1990-), and the *Archives Proudhoniennes / Revue d'etudes Proudhonnienes* (1995-) have all continued to shed light on the relevance of French socialist thought for contemporary analysis. Furthermore, in the English-speaking world, initiatives such as Shawn Wilbur's *The Libertarian Labyrinth* (2005-) have been instrumental in translating and disseminating the works of French socialist thinkers, thereby expanding their accessibility and potential impact. In other words, after a 25-year lull following WWII, the revival of French socialisms reemerged in 1968 and quietly continues up to the present day.

In the following analysis, I intend to outline, in a non-exhaustive manner, the present-day significance outside of France of the ideas put

[644] Sassoon: *One Hundred Years of Socialism*. I.B. Tauris & Co Ltd, 2010, pp. 536-540.
[645] R. McIntyre: The Development of Social Economy in France Since 1945. Pp. 253-261 in *Forum for Social Economics,* 47(2), 2018.
[646] Vieta: The Stream of Self-Determination and *Autogestión*. 2014, p. 798.

forth by the French socialists. Based on Bouglé's analysis, I examine how the ideas of the French socialists have implicitly shaped society in the post-WWII period, especially in the context of Marxism's decline as the predominant theory of socialism following the dissolution of the Soviet Union. In particular, I analyze the Saint-Simonian spirit with its emphasis on production and large-scale industry, the Fourierist spirit with its stress on consumption and cooperatives, and the Proudhonian spirit with its underscoring of exchange and syndicalism. Additionally, I discuss some of the major structural changes over the 20th century. Finally, utilizing some of the insights from Bouglé, Marcel Mauss, and Georges Gurvitch, the exploration will conclude with an attempted synthesis of the insights of the French socialist ideologies and what it might offer for contemporary society.

Saint-Simonism in the Post-War Era

A century after the death of Saint-Simon in 1825, there was a marked resurgence of interest in Saint-Simonian ideas. For example, Saint-Simon's innovative blend of science and Christianity, along with an emphasis on rational administration, played a pivotal role in the development and international diffusion of 'scientific management.' In France, this movement became known as Fayolism, while in the United States it was referred to as Taylorism, and was notably linked to the anti-sweatshop campaigns, advocating for better working conditions. During the interwar period, when companies grew in size and capital concentration intensified, a growing disconnect between workers and owners emerged and the Saint-Simonian model of elite, hyper-rationalized management became particularly pertinent.[647]

Consequently, many owners introduced a new managerial stratum within their organizations, aligning managerial interests more closely with state power. The managerial class that took the reins of 'scientific management' favored positive reinforcement over punitive

---

[647] J. A. Merkle. *Management and Ideology: The Legacy of the International Scientific Management Movement.* University of California Press, 1980, pp. 130–171.

measures. Scientific management aimed to refine performance evaluation processes, not only to boost efficiency but also to impart greater respect to the labor force and reduce the perceived need for unionization. Despite its initial aims and widespread implementation, the elitist bent of the Saint-Simonian movement encountered significant resistance from workers. Nonetheless, its influence endured, fundamentally altering the relationship between the knowledge of production processes and their actual execution. It also ingrained the concept of performance standards within corporate structures, leaving a lasting imprint on the organization of work.[648]

Moreover, Edward S. Mason (1899–1992), a pivotal figure in the development of the field of industrial organization in the United States, showed a keen interest in Saint-Simonism starting in the 1920s. As a member of the influential Harvard Economics department, Mason proposed the idea that a society could be both unequal and just, provided that its economic system was capable of allocating roles based on individual capacities.[649] Mason's perspective was shared and further developed by colleagues at Harvard, particularly his co-author Carl Friedrich (1901–1984). Friedrich highlighted the concept of "responsible elites," suggesting that democracy would function most effectively under the administration of technocrats—specialists with the skills and knowledge to make informed decisions for the public good.

During the administration of Franklin D. Roosevelt (FDR), particularly throughout World War II, these academic ideas were not merely theoretical but had practical implications. The wartime context necessitated an unprecedented level of government intervention in the economy. Mason, Friedrich, and their Harvard colleagues became an integral part of the intellectual backbone for FDR's administration during

---

[648] R. Edwards. *Contested Terrain: The Transformation of the Workplace in the Twentieth Century.* Basic Books, 1979, pp. 72–104.
[649] L. Frobert: Industrialism in the Mirror: Edward S. Mason, Reader of the Saint-Simonians. Pp. 410-427 in *The European Journal of the History of Economic Thought,* 27(3), 2020.

this period. Their advocacy for technocratic governance dovetailed with the needs of a wartime economy, where efficient and effective management of resources was crucial.[650]

Relatedly, the promotion of international peace by the Saint-Simonians gained renewed urgency in the aftermath of World War II, the deadliest military conflict in history, with an estimated 65 million fatalities, two-thirds of whom were civilians. For comparison, WWI resulted in approximately 25 million deaths, with civilians accounting for about one-third. WWII was also marked by the first factory-style mass killings, carried out in Nazi concentration camps.[651] In light of the extensive devastation, the international community recognized the need for a new peacekeeping organization. This led to the establishment of the United Nations (UN), which held its inaugural meeting in January 1946, succeeding the ineffective League of Nations. In 1948, the UN adopted the Universal Declaration of Human Rights, distinguishing itself from its predecessor. While initially overlooked, this declaration, inspired by the *Declaration of the Rights of Man and of the Citizen*, has become a seminal text underpinning the global recognition of human rights.[652] The UN learned from the League's shortcomings; it refrained from enforcing peace treaties, established its own peacekeeping forces, and succeeded in attracting a broader membership, including the United States, which had notably abstained from joining the League. The UN also created the Economic and Social Council, the International Court of Justice, and various specialized agencies such as the International Labour Organization, the World Health Organization, and UNESCO. By 2011,

---

[650] S. Turner: Carl Friedrich and the Cancellation of Pareto. Pp. 145–160 in C. Adair-Toteff (ed.): *Vilfredo Pareto's Contributions to Modern Social Theory: A Centennial Appraisal.* Routledge, 2023.
[651] S. Malešević: *The Rise of Organised Brutality: A Historical Sociology of Violence.* Cambridge University Press, 2017.
[652] S. Moyn: *Not Enough: Human Rights in an Unequal World.* The Belknap Press, 2018, pp. 57–67.

268

the UN had expanded to include 193 member nations, encompassing nearly all recognized nations worldwide.[653]

In spite of the UN, the Cold War era, spanning from 1946 to 1991, was characterized by an ongoing state of military readiness, especially between the ideologically opposed superpowers: the United States and the Soviet Union. During this half-century, the United States was seen as the bastion of capitalism, while the Soviet Union was the standard-bearer for socialism. Both nations engaged in extensive foreign interventions to curb the influence of the other, leading to numerous revolutions against colonial regimes and widespread civil disturbances. This period of geopolitical tension also overlapped with what has been termed "the golden age of capitalism," lasting from 1945 to 1973, a time of remarkable economic growth for the world's leading economies. During the 1970s, a pivotal shift occurred that shaped the global economic landscape: the rise of neoliberalism and a concurrent slowdown in economic growth in both the Soviet Union and the United States. This period was also marked by a revolution in information technology and transportation, which further globalized manufacturing processes.[654] The substantial allocation of resources to the military sector, coupled with the depletion of natural resources and the failure to enact adaptive policies, ultimately took a toll on the Soviet Union, setting the stage for its collapse.[655]

Although he died just before the outbreak of the Cold War, John Maynard Keynes (1883–1946), who was not only influenced by the French socialist tradition—particularly Proudhon's exchange theories[656]—

[653] Growth in United Nations Membership. *United Nations*. Available at: www.un.org/en/about-us/.
[654] M. Mason: *Turbulent Empires: A History of Global Capitalism Since 1945.* McGill-Queen's Press, 2018.
[655] R. C. Allen: The Rise and Decline of the Soviet Economy. Pp. 859–881 in *Canadian Journal of Economics,* 34(4), 2001.
[656] D. Dudley: Keynes and Proudhon. Pp. 63–76 in *The Journal of Economic History,* 2(1), 1942.

but also described himself as a "non-Marxist socialist,"[657] was integral in shaping the "first-world" economies following WWII. Keynes' education in economics was deeply rooted in the Marshallian tradition, named after Alfred Marshall (1842–1924), who himself held the French socialists in high regard and acknowledged their significant impact on his work.[658] Similarly, at Cambridge University, Keynes was a member of the Apostles, an influential secret society that adopted increasingly socialist views during the interwar period.[659] Their collective stance against the punitive measures of the Treaty of Versailles and the call for an internationalist approach to organize the globalized economy and avoid further global conflict paralleled the Saint-Simonian emphasis on cooperation and the rational organization of society.[660]

Furthermore, Keynes played a significant role in designing the Bretton Woods system in 1944, which led to the establishment of key financial institutions like the International Monetary Fund and the World Bank.[661] By pegging currencies to the US dollar, which in turn was fastened to gold, this system aimed to secure economic stability across the "first-world" economies dominated by the US. While the system was designed to favor American interests, it also succeeded in creating a

---

[657] E. W. Fuller: Was Keynes a Socialist? Pp. 1653–1682 in *Cambridge Journal of Economics,* 43(6), 2019.

[658] K. Caldari: Alfred Marshall and François Perroux: The Neglected Liaison. Pp. 134–174 in *The European Journal of the History of Economic Thought,* 25(1), 2018: 156.

[659] D. Macciò: The Apostles' Justice: Cambridge Reflections on Economic Inequality from Moore's "Principia Ethica" to Keynes's "General Theory" (1903–36). Pp. 701–726 in *Cambridge Journal of Economics,* 40(3), 2016.

[660] D. Macciò: Ethics, Economics and Power in the Cambridge Apostles' Internationalism Between the Two World Wars. Pp. 696–721 in *The European Journal of International Relations,* 22(3), 2016: 702–703.

[661] R. Skidelsky: Keynes, Globalisation and the Bretton Woods Institutions in the Light of Changing Ideas About Markets. Pp. 15–30 in *World Economics,* 6(1), 2005.

framework for global economic stability, which, in turn, promoted social mobility and curtailed financial speculation.[662]

In response to the post-World War II prevalence of Keynesian and Marxist ideologies, the Mont Pèlerin Society (MPS) was established in 1947. Supported by generous funding from various chambers of commerce, the society coalesced around the ideas of Friedrich Hayek (1899–1992), who was the inaugural president and served until 1961. The MPS is renowned for advocating what is now widely known as "neoliberalism." The members of the MPS claimed to defend the "central values" of Western society, such as liberty and property rights. They aimed to reshape the state's role in the market and mobilize state power in order to expand and perpetuate a (quasi-)marketocracy.[663]

Shortly after its inaugural conference, Hayek published *The Counter-Revolution of Science*, which critiqued Saint-Simonism, Positivism, sociology, and, more broadly, French socialisms. He accused these schools of thought of "scientism," or a "slavish imitation of the method and language of Science..."[664] Hayek recognized Saint-Simon as a crucial socialist theorist, whose influence he believed had been underestimated. He identified Saint-Simon as a principal intellectual adversary, particularly criticizing his preoccupation with systematic organization. Hayek went on to label both Saint-Simon and Auguste Comte as "false individualists," alleging that they presumed to have the authority to impose regulations on society.[665]

---

[662] P. Mason: *Postcapitalism: A Guide to Our Future.* Farrar, Strauss and Giroux, 2015, pp. 79–83.

[663] A. Tickell & J. Peck: Making Global Rules: Globalization or Neoliberalization. Pp. 163–181 in J. Peck & H. W.-C. Yeung: *Remaking the Global Economy: Economic-Geographical Perspectives.* Sage, 2003: 166.

[664] F. A. Hayek: *The Counter-Revolution of Science.* The Free Press, 1952, p. 18, pp. 163–164.

[665] F. A. Hayek: Individualism: True and False. Pp. 1–32 in *Individualism and Economic Order.* University of Chicago Press, 1948.

Contrary to the Durkheimians' "anarchistic" interpretation, Hayek viewed Saint-Simon's doctrine through an authoritarian lens, and crafted a narrow definition of socialism that emphasized central planning and state ownership.[666] For example, Hayek asserted, "[t]he French writers who laid the foundations of modern socialism had no doubt that their ideas could be put into practice only by a strong dictatorial government."[667] Hayek extended this authoritarian assumption to Comte and the origins of sociology, characterizing Comte as even more autocratic and misguided than Saint-Simon. According to Hayek, both Saint-Simon and Comte aimed to foist the outcomes of scientific inquiry onto an unwitting public.[668]

In reality, Hayek's criticisms are more applicable to the stances of the "logical positivists" rather than those of the "classical positivists," who saw governmentalism as the root of the social problem.[669] In fact, critics have noted that Hayek might not have directly engaged with Comte's writings, relying instead on John Stuart Mill's (1806–1873) well-known and potentially distorted interpretations, as well as echoing Mill's selected quotes from Comte, in order to attack "positivism."[670] As a result, Hayek doesn't appear to have explored the French socialists' ideas independently but, instead, through the prevailing frameworks of logical positivism and orthodox Marxism.[671] Ironically, despite his advocacy for liberty and choice, Hayek played a role in promulgating his own normative vision globally. Notoriously, he personally consulted with the

---

[666] J. Bockman: *Markets in the Name of Socialism: The Left-Wing Origins of Neoliberalism*. Stanford University Press, 2011, pp. 31–32.

[667] F. A. Hayek: *The Road to Serfdom*. Routledge, 1944 / 2001, p. 24.

[668] Hayek: *The Counter-Revolution of Science*. 1952, p. 183.

[669] R. Vernon: Auguste Comte and the Withering-Away of the State. Pp. 549–566 in *Journal of the History of Ideas*, 45(4), 1984.

[670] M. Gane: Comte and His Liberal Critics: From Spencer to Hayek. Pp. 205–225 in A. Wernick (ed.): *The Anthem Companion to Auguste Comte*. Anthem Press, 2017.

[671] N. Gane: Sociology and Neoliberalism: A Missing History. Pp. 1092–1106 in *Sociology*, 48(6), 2014.

Chilean dictator Augusto Pinochet (1915–2006), while notably refraining from commenting on Pinochet's crimes and human rights abuses.[672]

Following the inaugural MPS conference in 1947, a wave of like-minded organizations emerged, including the Institute of Economic Affairs (1955–) and the Trilateral Commission (1973–). During the 1970s, the Chicago School of Economics became the epicenter for championing neoliberal policies. In this period, Hayek was awarded the Nobel Prize in Economics in 1974, followed two years later by Milton Friedman (1912-2006), a leading figure within the Chicago School. These institutions and individuals played a crucial role in disseminating neoliberal ideas, which gained the endorsement of influential policymakers such as Margaret Thatcher (1925-2013) in the UK and Ronald Reagan (1911-2004) in the US.[673] Several factors facilitated the adoption of neoliberal policies: the US' fiscal pressures from the Vietnam War, the costs associated with welfare reforms in the 1960s, and rising productivity in foreign economies. This set the stage for US President Richard Nixon's (1913-1994) decision in August 1971 to suspend the dollar's convertibility into gold, which effectively marked the end of the Bretton Woods system. The Keynesian economic framework suffered another significant setback in October 1973 when oil-exporting countries in the Middle East, reacting to the conflict with Israel, imposed an embargo that led to a fourfold increase in oil prices.[674] The economic stability and growth that had characterized the previous decades were abruptly undermined. The subsequent rapid deregulation and expansion of the financial sector contributed to deindustrialization in Western economies.[675]

---

[672] Gane: Comte and His Liberal Critics. 2017.

[673] K. Birch: Neoliberalism: The Whys and Wherefores... and Future Directions. Pp. 571–584 in *Sociology Compass,* 9(7), 2015.

[674] Mason: *Postcapitalism.* 2015, p. 87.

[675] A. L. Kalleberg: *Good Jobs, Bad Jobs: The Rise of Polarized and Precarious Employment Systems in the United States, 1970-2000s.* Russell Sage Foundation, 2011.

Although the influence of Saint-Simonism on public policy has diminished with the rise of neoliberalism, its focus on economic organization retained relevance in modern times, particularly through the proliferation of nongovernmental organizations (NGOs). Immediately following World War II, NGOs faced institutional challenges, with their growth and effectiveness often hampered by the geopolitical climate of the Cold War. Since the dissolution of the Soviet Union, NGOs have surged to the forefront of humanitarian efforts, environmental activism, international development, and public engagement. They have also begun to assume a more influential role within the United Nations framework.[676] While estimates vary, some suggest that there are around a million NGOs operating globally, with a presence in every nation. These organizations range widely in their missions and operations. World Vision International, for example, concentrates on the welfare of children, while the Association of Sarva Seva Farmers in India advocates for self-reliance among farmers. Despite the diversity in their objectives and methods, NGOs have become a crucial element of the evolving civil society and social economy. Nevertheless, the expectations for NGOs to drive social change have been exceedingly high and not entirely realistic. While they have made positive contributions, the anticipated social transformation attributed to these organizations has not been fully realized.[677]

Putting it together, Saint-Simonian ideas subtly permeated various facets of society, influencing not only large-scale industry and international peace but also the formulation of public policies, notably FDR's New Deal and the Bretton Woods agreement. However, the ascent of financialization starting in the 1970s dealt successive, critical blows to Saint-Simonism. This decline became particularly evident as profits increasingly stemmed from labor cutbacks and financial speculation, rather than from the traditional production and exchange of

---

[676] S. Charnovitz: Two Centuries of Participation: NGOs and International Governance. Pp. 183–286 in *Michigan Journal of International Law,* 18(2), 1997.

[677] D. Lewis: Nongovernmental Organizations, Definition and History. Pp. 1056–1062 in *International Encyclopedia of Civil Society,* 41(6), 2010.

commodities. Interestingly, the governments that most staunchly defied the prescriptions of neoliberal institutions by consistently applying state-led interventions in their economies have emerged as rapidly growing economies. Specifically, Brazil, Russia, India, China and South Africa, often referred to collectively as the BRICS countries, demonstrated resilience and experienced minimal negative impact from the 2008 financial crisis.[678] Nonetheless, the legacy of Saint-Simonism remains alive, particularly through international organizations like the UN and its related institutions as well as NGOs.

Fourierism in the Post-War Era

Fourierism is often recalled as a tradition associated with utopian communities, yet it more accurately represents a movement that defined itself in opposition to the prevailing "civilized" political order of its time. Fourierism's legacy extends far beyond a mere historical curiosity of the 20th century; it established the foundations for challenging the emotional disturbances fostered by civilization and advocated for an alternative societal model that places a higher value on emotional well-being. Significantly, Fourierism's influence permeated cultural movements such as surrealism, which drew inspiration from Fourier's ideas.[679] Moreover, contemporary strands of occultism also find their roots in Fourier's works, indicating the movement's broad and enduring impact on various aspects of modern thought and culture.[680] The quest for emotional stability, a fundamental psychological necessity, has not been adequately addressed by market mechanisms or state interventions. This deficiency

---

[678] M. Chatterjee & I. Naka: Twenty Years of BRICS: Political and Economic Transformations Through the Lens of Land. Pp. 2–13 in *Oxford Development Studies,* 50(1), 2022.

[679] K. White: Introduction. Pp. 1–19 in A. Breton: *Ode to Charles Fourier.* Translated by K. White. Cape Goliard Press, 1970.

[680] J. Strube. Socialist Religion and the Emergence of Occultism: A Genealogical Approach to Socialism and Secularization in 19th-Century France. Pp. 359–388 in *Religion,* 46(3), 2016.

has propelled social actors to explore experimental forms of relationships and organization.[681]

The Fourierist ethos resonates within what is often referred to as "the third sector" or "the solidarity economy," which diverges from the traditional hierarchical firms governed by external investors or bureaucrats. This sector encompasses a variety of member-controlled cooperatives, non-profits, commons, and commons-based peer production entities. These organizations are characterized by mutualistic practices that emphasize reciprocity and social engagement over hierarchy and compliance. Significantly, the formation of alternative economic organizations such as cooperatives is frequently a reaction to increased employment instability and joblessness within the broader economy. These entities arise as a means to provide economic agency and security in an environment where traditional employment structures may fail to do so.[682]

Collectivist enterprises within the third sector typically position themselves as alternatives to the hierarchically controlled and resource-abundant organizations that dominate the traditional economic landscape. The social practices inherent in these third-sector entities are observed to foster enhanced group solidarity, standing in contrast to the more stratified structures of hierarchical organizations. Furthermore, these collectivist forms of organization often contribute to the advancement of civil rights and the affirmation of human dignity. They seek to create environments where the value of each individual is recognized, and collaborative efforts are made to address the needs and rights of all members, reflecting a commitment to a more equitable and inclusive approach to economic and social engagement.[683] It is not surprising that these alternative organizational forms are not only aligned

---

[681] C. J. Guarneri: The Americanization of Utopia: Fourierism and the Dilemma of Utopian Dissent in the United States. Pp. 72–88 in *Utopian Studies,* 5(1), 1994.

[682] V. Pérotin: Entry, Exit, and the Business Cycle: Are Cooperatives Different? Pp. 295–316 in *Journal of Comparative Economics,* 34(2), 2006.

[683] K. Hart, J.-L. Laville & A. D. Cattani (eds): *The Human Economy: A Citizen's Guide.* Polity Press, 2010.

with social movements but also garner support from diverse professional communities. These entities often embody the values and goals of social change, attracting the endorsement and collaboration of professionals who seek to contribute to societal progress and innovation beyond the confines of traditional corporate structures.[684]

In recent decades, the third sector has gained considerable ground, becoming a significant force in the global economy. For instance, data from 2017 indicates that there were approximately 3 million cooperatives operating across 156 countries, collectively boasting a membership of at least one billion individuals. These cooperatives are substantial employment engines, providing jobs for nearly 300 million people, which equates to about 10% of the global workforce. This underlines the growing impact and reach of cooperative models in the worldwide economic landscape.[685] The International Cooperative Alliance (1895-), a prominent non-governmental organization that was among the first to be granted "consultative status" by the United Nations—despite having no affiliation with the League of Nations—represents more than 300 cooperative federations from 107 countries. The third sector's significance in promoting sustainability has not gone unnoticed by the UN, which has not only advocated for cooperatives but, in 2023, also adopted resolutions that endorse the social and solidarity economy. These resolutions reflect the UN's recognition of the vital role that cooperatives and similar organizations play in achieving sustainable development goals and fostering a more inclusive global economy.[686]

Consumer activism has been another integral yet often overlooked component of social movements throughout the 20th century.

---

[684] J. Rothschild & J. A. Whitt: *The Cooperative Workplace: Potentials and Dilemmas of Organizational Democracy and Participation.* Cambridge University Press, 1986, pp. 116–136.

[685] H.-S. Eum: *Cooperatives and Employment: Second Global Report.* CICOPA.

[686] International Cooperative Alliance: About us. *International Cooperative Alliance.* Available at: www.ica.coop/en/about-us/international-cooperative-alliance.

Prior to World War I, consumer activism was already evident through the anti-sweatshop movement, campaigns for fair worker wages, and boycotts of stores that were publicized by organizations such as the National Consumers League (1899-). The interwar period saw the formation of additional consumer activist groups, including the League of Women Shoppers (1935-1949), which played a significant role in mobilizing activists. The modern consumer movement gained momentum as academics began to scrutinize consumer societies more closely, leading to the establishment of the Consumer's Research nonprofit in 1928. This organization was pioneering in its comparative testing of branded goods. In the United States, the influence of consumer activism was recognized to the extent that consumer representatives were incorporated into New Deal agencies. A parallel development occurred in India, where Mahatma Gandhi (1869-1948) drew global attention by leading a boycott of British goods in the 1930s, demonstrating the power of consumer activism as a tool for social change.[687]

After a period of relative quiet following World War II, consumer associations began to proliferate across Europe, Asia, and Australia starting in the mid-1950s. The year 1960 marked the establishment of a global federation of consumer organizations, the International Organization of Consumers Unions (IOCU). The IOCU has been instrumental in advocating for a suite of consumer rights, including the right to be informed about the collection and use of personal data, and has launched several significant global initiatives. These include the International Baby Food Action Network in 1979, Health Action International in 1981, and the Pesticide Action Network in 1982. By the 1990s, consumer movements had expanded into South America and Africa. As consumer organizations formed in developing countries, issues of basic needs and poverty increasingly came to the forefront of the movement's agenda. The IOCU, with over 250 member organizations across 120 countries, now holds General Consultative

---

[687] R. A. Hawkins: Boycotts, Buycotts and Consumer Activism in a Global Context: An Overview. Pp. 123-143 in *Management & Organizational History*, 5(2), 2010.

Status with the United Nations Economic and Social Council. Through its engagement with the UN, the IOCU has been a key player in implementing consumer protection frameworks worldwide.[688]

The resurgence of neoliberal policies marked a turning point for consumer activism and regulation. During this era, the business community, revitalized by the neoliberal agenda, mounted significant resistance against consumer advocacy and regulatory measures. A case in point is the experience of the 1970s in the United States, where President Jimmy Carter (1924-) concurred with the establishment of a federal consumer protection agency. However, due to escalating pressure from business leaders, the proposed agency never came to fruition.[689] In a similar vein, the IOCU collaborated with other NGOs through the United Nations to establish a Code of Conduct for Transnational Corporations during the 1980s. Despite these efforts, the initiative was ultimately unsuccessful, largely due to intense lobbying by multinational corporations. Additionally, delegates from the US government played a significant role in opposing the enactment of the code.[690]

Since the 1990s, the consumer movement has shifted its focus from advocating for government regulation to fostering change directly within the marketplace, a phenomenon often referred to as the "certification revolution." Independent non-governmental organizations began to offer labeling schemes that provide consumers with information about fair trade practices, organic food, ecological impacts, sustainable forestry, and marine conservation associated with products. Concurrently, issues pertaining to human and animal rights have become increasingly entwined with personal consumption choices.

---

[688] M. Hilton: Social Activism in the Age of Consumption: The Organized Consumer Movement. Pp. 121-143 in *Social History,* 32(3), 2007.
[689] G. Schwartz: The Successful Fight Against a Federal Consumer Protection Agency. Pp. 45-57 in *MSU Business Topics,* 27(3), 1979.
[690] T. G. Weiss: The UN Code of Conduct for Transnational Corporations. Pp. 86-97 in D. P. Forsythe (ed.): *The United Nations in the World Political Economy.* Palgrave Macmillan, 1989.

In response to these NGO-certified labeling schemes, multinational corporations have introduced their own labels, which critics argue may dilute rights standards and obscure information. As a countermeasure to such corporate strategies, consumer movements have embraced tactics such as culture jamming, exemplified by groups like Adbusters (1989–), which aim to subvert corporate advertising. Additionally, the principles of voluntary simplicity, which advocate for reduced spending and more modest lifestyles, have gained traction. These movements represent a growing trend toward challenging consumerism and promoting more conscious and sustainable consumption habits.[691]

To Marcel Mauss, who regularly advocated for the empowerment of consumers through cooperatives, there remained a dual movement within globalized society. On one side, there was the trend of modern nation-states increasingly centralizing their roles, taking on economic services such as monetary policy and business regulation. On the opposite side, Mauss identified a grassroots movement, which he described as "half-voluntary and half-obligatory, half-economic and half-moral... it is the fact of citizens becoming aware of new interests, new legal forms and imposing them consciously and voluntarily on the state."[692]

Despite his support for consumer empowerment, Mauss maintained a critical view of the solidarity economy. He argued that cooperatives, as they existed, were "more akin to the present regime than to the future regime of society. In fact, they are above all associations of small capitalists within a cooperative legal form..."[693] The third sector, while embodying the mutualistic ideal, often finds itself constrained by political dependencies and the need to make compromises that can stray from its foundational principles. These systemic forces, coupled with the absence of a cohesive and explicit ideology, significantly limit the sector's

---

[691] W. A. Wiedenhoft-Murphy: Consumer Movements, Contemporary. Pp. 1–6 in *The Wiley Blackwell Encyclopedia of Consumption and Consumer Studies.* Wiley, 2015.
[692] Mauss: *La nation.* 2013, p. 296.
[693] *Ibid.*, p. 371.

potential for impact. If social cooperation is to transcend the entrenched state-corporate nexus, it will be, according to Mauss, "when cooperation leaves the commercial, industrial and financial world and enters into the moral world. It is why... I stay a socialist..."[694] Indeed, the emergence of a grassroots movement advocating for consumer rights, among other issues, suggests a spontaneous collective action. However, this movement seems to lack a fully articulated moral framework or a "collective conscience" that clearly defines its ethical underpinnings and objectives, and lacks a unifying ideology to position itself in opposition to the status quo.

Proudhonism in the Post-War Era

The 20th century was marked by the rise and fall of the global labor movement. Generally speaking, the labor movement saw its zenith in the decade subsequent to the original 1932 publication of this book. For example, in the United States, labor union membership stood at approximately 11% in 1929, a figure that remarkably echoes the membership levels as of 2024. By 1939 though, union membership in the U.S. had surged to 29%, reaching its apex at 35.4% by the end of World War II in 1945. This period marked a significant era of growth and power for labor unions, reflecting a stark contrast to the labor movement's position in both the early and later parts of the 20th century.[695] The fluctuation in union membership experienced in the United States during the mid-to-late 20th century mirrored a global trend.[696]

---

[694] M. Mauss: Note préliminaire sur le mouvement coopératif et spécialement sur le mouvement coopératif de consommation, plus spécialement sur le mouvement coopératif français (1936). Pp. 758–763 in Mauss: *Ecrits politiques,* 1936. Quoted in S. Celle: The Metamorphosis of the Cooperative Ideologies in French Capitalism During the Interwar Period (1919-1939). *The 28th Annual EAEPE Conference,* 2016: 14.
[695] G. Mayer: *Union Membership Trends in the United States.* CRS Report for Congress, 2004.
[696] J. Visser: Union Membership Statistics in 24 Countries. Pp. 38–49 in *Monthly Labor Review,* 129, 2006.

The 1929 Great Depression had profound effects on the global workforce, leading to widespread unemployment, wage reductions, and cuts in social welfare. These hardships galvanized labor movements around the world as workers sought to protect their rights and livelihoods. The response to this empowerment of labor varied internationally, with some nations experiencing severe repression at the hands of nationalist movements. In Spain, the conflict between labor and nationalism culminated dramatically. General Francisco Franco's (1892-1975) regime waged a brutal campaign against organized labor during the Spanish Civil War from 1936 to 1939. This conflict resulted in tragic losses, with estimates of up to half a million people killed. The labor movement in Spain at this time was notably robust; the Confederación Nacional del Trabajo (CNT) (1910-), a syndicalist union, was one of the most significant in history, boasting around 1.5 million members. The CNT was so influential that it managed to take control of parts of Catalonia during the civil war, before being brutally suppressed.[697]

In the United States, the New Deal of the 1930s significantly bolstered the position of organized labor, leading to its integration within the framework of the state. The establishment of the National Labor Relations Board (NLRB) in 1933 marked a pivotal moment, as it was designed to address unfair labor practices and safeguard the right to collective bargaining. By the end of the 1930s, trade unions had emerged as influential players in U.S. politics, a status that was further reinforced by the economic demands of WWII. The war effort effectively mobilized the American workforce, drastically reducing unemployment from 17% in 1939 to a mere 2% by 1943. This period saw an unprecedented level of union growth and a significant decrease in income inequality. The 1940s stand out as the sole decade in U.S. history where income disparity narrowed rather than widened, briefly positioning the United States as having the most equal income distribution in the world. However, the alliance between unions and political parties had unintended consequences. The unions became increasingly bureaucratic and

---

[697] L. van der Walt: Syndicalism. Pp. 249-263 in *The Palgrave Handbook of Anarchism*. Palgrave, 2019.

centralized, which in turn led to a membership that was less actively engaged.[698]

At the conclusion of World War II, the military, business, and political elites in the United States found themselves in a position of substantial influence over the government. The onset of the Cold War provided a rationale for continued military expansion, which garnered support from both business and political elites. The patriotic fervor of the wartime period also exerted pressure on union leaders to refrain from strikes, which were often perceived as unpatriotic. Meanwhile, the bureaucratization of major unions led to a backlog of unaddressed member grievances. This tension culminated in 1946 with the largest strike wave of the 20th century in the United States, involving nearly 5 million workers. These strikes ultimately achieved wage increases for the participants. In response to this labor unrest and spurred by the interests of big business, Congress passed the Taft-Hartley Act of 1947. This legislation introduced significant restrictions on labor activities, including banning jurisdictional strikes, closed shops, and secondary boycotts. It also barred supervisors from union membership and allowed states to enact right-to-work laws, all measures designed to curtail union power. The impact of the Taft-Hartley Act was profound, and unions in the United States began a steady decline, particularly within the private sector.

The onset of neoliberalism marked a further regression for trade unions. In the US, President Reagan's dismissal of over 11,000 striking air traffic controllers, coupled with his appointments to the National Labor Relations Board of individuals who were openly antagonistic toward unions, dealt a severe blow to the labor movement.[699] The decline of the labor movement, already underway, was hastened by the increasing dominance of finance in the marketplace, a trend that accompanied the rise of neoliberalism. This economic philosophy, which emphasizes

---

[698] M. Mann: *The Sources of Social Power. Volume 4: Globalizations, 1945–2011.* Cambridge University Press, 2013, pp. 37–38.
[699] Mann: *The Sources of Social Power. Volume 4.* 2013, pp. 49–66.

deregulation, free trade, and the privatization of industry, has persistently undermined the labor landscape across the globe.[700]

Although the syndicalist movement today is small and fragmented, there are signs of life and rapprochement. For example, the New Left has promoted syndicalist themes, which has engendered new concepts like 'student syndicalism' that emerged from the Students for a Democratic Society (1960–1974). Organizations like the International Workers' Association (1922–) and the Industrial Workers of the World (1905–) saw revivals in the 1980s and 1990s, particularly in Africa and Eastern Europe. Today, the largest syndicalist unions appear to be Spain's CNT and the Confederacion General del Trabajo (1930–), which in 2018 claimed 50,000 and 100,000 members respectively.[701] Therefore, while syndicalism declined over the course of the 20th century, there remains the possibility of it reproliferating in the 21st century.

In the realm of exchange theories, credit unions—a form of member-owned financial cooperative—flourished throughout the 20th century as alternatives to commercial banks. By 2009, the global presence of credit unions was significant, with an estimated 50,000 credit unions serving 184 million members across nearly 100 countries. While economic theories typically portray firms as profit-maximizers, credit unions operate under a different paradigm, aiming to serve the interests of their members by providing favorable rates and financial services. However, the landscape for credit unions has evolved in the context of deregulated markets. In such an environment, where they compete directly with commercial banks, credit unions have sometimes adopted more commercial behaviors in order to remain viable.[702] Relatedly, as mentioned earlier, Proudhon's exchange theories appear to have implicitly inspired Keynes' thought in that they both sought to affirm the

---

[700] Visser: Union Membership Statistics in 24 Countries. Pp. 38–49 in *Monthly Labor Review,* 129, 2006.
[701] A. Pascual: Del 8M a Amazon: CNT y CGT resucitan a costa de los dinosaurios sindicales. *El Confidencial,* March, 23, 2018.
[702] D. McKillop & J. O. S. Wilson: Credit Unions: A Theoretical and Empirical Overview. Pp. 79–123 in *Financial Markets, Institutions, and Instruments,* 20(3), 2011.

sovereignty of producers over the monetary system. This theoretical legacy has inspired local monetary systems in existence today such as the Swiss WIR Bank (1934–) and the Italian Sardex (2010–).[703]

Nevertheless, alongside the simultaneous decline of syndicalism and the spread of financialization, the late 20th century witnessed an unprecedented surge in communication technologies, catalyzing the formation of a networked global economy. This technological revolution, characterized by the advent of the internet and the widespread adoption of smartphones, has brought about a seismic shift in social practices and economic interactions. The rapid exchange of communication and information has notably challenged the supremacy of traditional centralized bureaucracies, giving rise to distributed networks that often operate on a horizontal structure. This shift resonates with Pierre-Joseph Proudhon's skepticism toward centralized commerce and banking. Modern peer-to-peer networks, for instance, embody the Proudhonian ethos by facilitating financial transactions that bypass traditional intermediaries and middlemen.[704] Despite the control of cultural transmission largely being in the hands of the elite throughout the 20th century, the advent of rapid and global communication networks has begun to shift this dynamic. These networks, alongside grassroots social movements, have played a crucial role in shaping the modern collective conscience—a term that resonates with both Proudhonian and Durkheimian sociological theory. These movements have left an indelible mark on the spirit of modernity, even if their philosophical roots in Proudhon's ideas remain largely uncelebrated.

Furthermore, the influence of Proudhonism on the proliferation of civil disobedience in the 20th century, while often overlooked, is significant. Alex Prichard, in his introduction to Proudhon's recently

[703] S. Papaud: Libertarian Economic Thought and Non-Capitalist Money: Pierre-Joseph Proudhon (1809–1865) and Silvio Gesell (1862–1930): A "Monetary Analysis Socialism"? Hal Science, 2022, p. 26.
[704] K. Carson: *The Homebrew Industrial Revolution: A Low-Overhead Manifesto.* BookSurge, 2010.

translated 1861 *War and Peace*, highlights this connection, particularly through the work of Leo Tolstoy (1828-1910). Tolstoy, who had personal interactions with Proudhon, is believed to have written his celebrated novel 1869 *War and Peace* as a tribute to the French social theorist. Tolstoy's development of a pacifistic form of civil disobedience that emphasized the conscience had profound implications for future social movements. Tolstoy's philosophy of nonviolent resistance had a deep impact on Mahatma Gandhi,[705] who adapted these ideas in his struggle for Indian independence. Gandhi's approach, in turn, influenced Martin Luther King, Jr. (1929-1968), who became a pivotal figure in the American civil rights movement.[706] Through these figures, a thread of Proudhonian thought can be traced through some of the most transformative social movements of the century.

Moreover, the proliferation of civil disobedience throughout the 20th century played a significant role in nurturing the youth counterculture. The counterculture movement's roots can be traced back to the increased accessibility of the automobile among elite youth in the 1920s. The automobile became a symbol of independence, providing young people with the means to broaden their social horizons and interact with a more diverse range of people outside of their immediate communities. As automobiles facilitated mobility, there was a noticeable shift away from home- and family-centered activities. Public spaces such as restaurants, bars, sports arenas, movie theaters, and nightclubs grew in popularity as the preferred venues for socializing. By the mid-20th century, the mass consumption culture associated with automobiles had permeated the middle class, with young people from these backgrounds emulating the lifestyle of their wealthier counterparts. The increased casualness in social interactions and a move towards more egalitarian

---

[705] A. Prichard: Introduction. Pp. 1–37 in P.-J. Proudhon: *War and Peace: On the Principle and Constitution of the Rights of People.* Translated by P. Sharkey. AK Press, 2022: 27–30. Also, see D. Matual: The Gospel According to Tolstoy and the Gospel According to Proudhon. Pp. 117–128 in *Harvard Theological Review,* 75(1), 1982.
[706] B. Chakrabarty: *Confluence of Thought: Mohandas Karamchand Gandhi and Martin Luther King, Jr.* Oxford University Press, 2013.

rituals reflected a broader erosion of traditional hierarchies and deference.[707] In turn, the counterculture movement, with its challenge to conventional norms and authorities, can be seen as a spontaneous rekindling of anarchist ideas among Western youth.[708]

From the anti-authoritarian youth counterculture and the civil rights movement to the widespread use of social protest, where the Proudhonists failed politically, they succeeded culturally. As Jesse Cohn suggests, "their politics translated nicely into the aesthetic realm, where it came to mean a kind of individualist stance, a willful refusal to make sense to a mass audience..."[709] This ethos has become particularly pervasive with the advent of the internet in the 21st century, facilitating the spread of an anti-authoritarian cultural movement on a global scale.[710] This movement has given rise to a new kind of anti-establishment populism, one that is less reliant on formal member-based organizations and more on decentralized networks of online users. These networks have become catalysts for open-source economics and online piracy, challenging traditional models of intellectual property. A vast array of creative content, from music and films to books and academic articles, is now shared freely online, despite persistent efforts by corporations and governments to control such exchanges. Technological advancements have drastically reduced production costs and have made networked, small-scale production more viable and efficient. In this new landscape, the role of capital as the guiding force of society, a hallmark of industrialism, is increasingly viewed as parasitic, inefficient, and superfluous. The shift toward a more egalitarian and decentralized production and distribution model reflects a significant cultural

---

[707] R. Collins: *Conflict Sociology: Toward an Explanatory Science.* Academic Press, Inc., 1975, pp. 210–224.
[708] M. Lerner: Anarchism and the American Counter-Culture. Pp. 430–455 in *Government and Opposition,* 5(4), 1970.
[709] J. Cohn: *Underground Passages: Anarchist Resistance Culture 1848–2011.* AK Press, 2011, Introduction.
[710] N. Witoszek: *The Origins of Anti-Authoritarianism.* Routledge, 2019.

transformation, one that continues to challenge and redefine the relationship between capital, government, and society.[711]

French Socialisms Today

The late 20th century was marked by significant developments, among which the decolonization movement stands out as a key historical process. This movement catalyzed the emergence of numerous independent nation-states, particularly following World War II. The principle of national self-determination, which gained prominence during this period, propelled the movement and influenced colonial territories to assert their sovereignty. In India and Indochina, for instance, nationalistic fervor challenged and eventually eroded the established colonial order. The decline of imperialism was further hastened by the financial strains and overextension faced by colonial powers. This period also witnessed the disintegration of the Soviet Union, leading to the independence of its various constituent republics. These shifts contributed to the evolution of a global international order, one predicated on the concept of sovereign nations. Despite the aim of universal equality, this new order is characterized by significant disparities and a hierarchical structure. Within this framework, each state maintains authority through its monopoly on violence, which it employs to regulate its population, natural resources, and economic activities. As a result, a somewhat homogeneous set of social structures and norms has become pervasive, shaping the interactions and governance of societies worldwide.[712]

Concurrently, the United Nations recognized the concept of the "right to nationhood" as an essential human right, and this principle is enshrined in the UN Charter. This acknowledgment has elevated nationhood to a central ideology in modern times.[713] However, there

---

[711] A. Negri & M. Hardt: *Multitude: War and Democracy in the Age of Empire.* Penguin Books, 2004, p. 336.
[712] M. Collins: Decolonization. In *The Encyclopedia of Empire.* Wiley Online Library, 2016.
[713] S. Maleševic: *Nation-States and Nationalisms: Organization, Ideology and Solidarity.* Polity Press, 2013.

288

remains a prevalent conflation of nationhood with the state and nationalism. Despite this association, a closer examination suggests that nationhood can be seen as distinct to, and perhaps even in opposition to, the state and nationalism.

Marcel Mauss offers an illuminating perspective in his largely overlooked seminal work on nationhood, *The Nation.* In the work, Mauss traces the origins of modern nationhood to the American and French revolutions of the late 18th century, asserting that it arose independently of the state. Nations, as conceptualized by Mauss, differ from previous social arrangements in that they lack intermediate bodies between the state and citizens. Instead, the nation is constituted through the integration of its citizens, bound together by shared rights, duties, norms, and practices, thus forging a new form of political society. Mauss highlights the "rituals of pact" observed during revolutionary movements that he describes as collective effervescent moments, which are intense shared emotional experiences, that contributed to the creation of the social reality of nationhood. These collective experiences redefined the individual's relationship to society, transforming subjects into citizens and endowing them with inherent dignity. Nationhood, as it evolved through these transformative moments, individualized societies and conferred a sense of sacredness upon the social collective. Consequently, it shifted the locus of power from the state apparatus to the social fabric, positioning the latter as the primary force for integration. In this way, Mauss's analysis suggests that the essence of nationhood lies less in the institutional structures of the state and more in the collective consciences and social bonds that unite individuals within a shared political identity.[714]

However, the concept of nationhood, particularly after its manifestation in revolutionary France with the creation of the "national army," led to a transformation in the nature of warfare. The notion of the nation as a total social entity meant that wars were no longer merely skirmishes between select groups; they became existential conflicts

---

[714] F. Callegaro: The Gift of the Nation: Marcel Mauss and the Intersocial Turn of Sociology. Pp. 49–77 in *Durkheimian Studies*, 25, 2021.

involving entire societies. This totalization of social identity in conflict set the stage for the total wars that characterized the 20th century. In these total wars, the distinction between combatants and non-combatants were blurred, as entire populations were mobilized for the war effort and became legitimate targets. This stands in stark contrast to the warfare of traditional societies, where small, often clan-based groups would engage in limited conflicts with clear boundaries and specific objectives. The rise of nationhood inadvertently fostered nationalist movements that, according to Mauss, were a corruption of the original concept of the nation. These movements often harbored aggressive ambitions for conquest and domination, distorting the spirit of what a nation was intended to represent. As state interests aligned with capitalist ambitions, imperialism became a force that drove nations to extend their influence through war, justified by a supposed "civilizing" mission. Such imperialist endeavors involved the subjugation and colonization of weaker states, often obliterating their collective identities and imposing the colonizer's own national framework. In this way, nations, under the guise of spreading civilization, often engaged in acts of barbarism.[715]

Mauss postulated that the rise of public opinion and the increasing interconnectedness of nations would eventually temper imperialist and nationalist tendencies. In opposition to both nationalism, which prioritizes the interests of one nation over others, and globalism, which overlooks the distinct realities of different groups, Mauss emphasized the socialist character of *internationalism* that emphasized mutual recognition and respect between groups and nations. He drew parallels between the international order he believed was slowly and painfully coming into fruition, and the associative dynamics observed in poly-segmental societies, such as those comprised of clans and tribes. These societies, which historically engaged in practices like gift-giving, managed to maintain balance and peace, without the need for complete integration, through a system that allowed for the coexistence of relatively independent parts within a federated structure. As such, these societies were able to maintain distinct identities and peaceful relations with each

---

[715] *Ibid.*

other without merging into a singular, non-segmented society like an empire or nation.[716]

From his analysis of poly-segmental societies, Mauss inferred that for nations, "the spirit of peace is, above all, a spirit of federation; it is possible only through federation, which one must create to have peace..."[717] He argued that a stable international consensus would not arise from precarious agreements made in a state of constant conflict, in the vein of a Hobbesian worldview, but rather through the decline of the absolutist state, economic interdependence among nations, and mutual recognition and respect for the sovereignty and unique character of each nation. Mauss contended that such a federated approach would facilitate exchanges of gifts and services between nations, similar to those that occurred in clan-based societies, thereby promoting a spirit of cooperation and mutual aid.

Furthermore, Mauss anticipated that once the "popular classes" recognized the alignment of their nation's ideals with their own interests, they would self-organize, undermining capitalist interests that often underpin imperialism. This self-organization would simultaneously lead to the creation of communities of citizen-workers who would manage their resources collectively and share surpluses through a system of mutual gift exchange. Ultimately, Mauss envisioned this process as a pathway to an internationalist form of socialism, one in which nations would cooperate and exchange on the basis of equality and solidarity, rather than competition and domination. He saw the potential for nations to evolve into communities that not only respect each other's independence but also support each other's prosperity through a system that echoes the ancient practices of gift exchange, updated to the scale of modern international relations.[718]

---

[716] *Ibid.*
[717] M. Mauss: *La nation.* 2013, p. 181.
[718] Callegaro: The Gift of the Nation. *Durkheimian Studies*, 2021.

Turning from Mauss' analysis of the spread of nationhood, another significant development has been the emergence and proliferation of human rights as a central theme in international discourse since the 1970s, especially as the influence of traditional leftist ideologies (the "Old Left") began to wane. This period saw human rights being championed across various regions and through numerous movements, highlighting the universal, moralistic, and anti-totalitarian nature of these rights, which are understood as essential to safeguarding human dignity. In the post-WWII era, an international network of non-governmental organizations dedicated to human rights has developed. These organizations, such as Amnesty International (1961–), Human Rights Watch (1978–), Center for Economic and Social Rights (1993–), and the Open Society Foundation (1993–), work to monitor, report, and advocate for human rights around the world. The first international human rights organization, the International Federation for Human Rights (FIDH), which formed in 1922, now contains around 190 other organizations across 112 countries.[719] Moreover, the United Nations has been instrumental in embedding human rights within political and economic institutions at both local and international levels. Even the International Labor Organization, which long stayed silent on the issue of human rights, finally began promoting transnational labor rights as the Soviet Union began to fall in 1989.[720]

However, the current approach to human rights continues to be deeply rooted in the liberal tradition, appealing to governments to enforce these rights on populations that tend to be perceived as passive and fragmented. The initial friction between the protection of human rights and the interests of the nation-state has advanced, with these latter entities increasingly co-opting human rights rhetoric. Consequently, the language of human rights is often utilized as a façade to advance their own agendas. Sociologists Lea David and Siniša Malešević have articulated this tension, noting that "human rights doctrine clashes with the nation-state apparatus

---

[719] J. Eckel. The International League for the Rights of Man, Amnesty International, and the Changing Fate of Human Rights Activism from the 1940s through the 1970s. Pp. 183–214 in *Humanity*, 4(2), 2013.
[720] Moyn: *Not Enough*. 2018, pp. 173–211.

and nationalist ideologies, and though often nominally being institutionalized and adopted on the state level, in reality, their doctrinal power, being filtered through [the] nation-state, becomes less potent and put in service of nationalist ideology."[721] Although the ideology of human rights has reached a global stage, becoming part of the world polity, it has done so at the cost of being appropriated by the intertwined interests of states, corporations, and nationalist movements. This co-optation raises critical questions about the efficacy and integrity of human rights in a world where they are at risk of being subsumed by the very powers they are meant to regulate.

The contrast between liberal and socialist traditions in the understanding of human rights is rooted in fundamentally different philosophical and ideological assumptions about the nature of rights and how they come to be recognized and enacted. In the liberal tradition, human rights are often seen as transcendent universals—pre-existing, inherent, and applicable to all individuals regardless of their social or historical context. This perspective either tends to posit that human rights are a natural part of human existence, which states are obligated to protect, or alternatively, it strips the individual of their group memberships and places rights above their social context. The socialist tradition, conversely, views human rights as a product of social groups and historical processes. For example, in opposition to the liberal approach, the socialist approach to human rights identifies the following properties:

- *Socially Constructed*: From a socialist viewpoint, rights emerge from social movements with a strong collective effervescence and are animated by consensus. They are not understood as inherent or timeless but as developments that arise from the collective actions of groups.

---

[721] L. David & S, Malešević: Ideology and Nation-States: Between Nationalism and Human Rights. Pp. 23–39 in *The Routledge Handbook of Ideology and International Relations*. Routledge, 2022: 32.

- *Radical Pluralism*: This conception acknowledges a pluralistic origin of rights, where different groups may conceive and prioritize different sets of rights based on their specific contexts and struggles.

- *Group Immanence and Social Obligation*: Rights are seen as grounded in the collective identity and goals of social groups. These groups, through their collective action, are responsible for upholding and protecting the rights that they have deemed essential for their members' dignity.[722]

- *Tendency Toward Unification*: Despite the diversity of origins and conceptions of rights, there is a tendency for rights and duties to become more unified and standardized through interactions between different peoples and societies.[723]

- *Primacy of Economic Rights*: In the socialist tradition, political and civil rights cannot be effectively realized without economic rights. True freedom and participation in society require economic security and equality, which can only be achieved through the universalization of property and for the products of collective labor to be owned by the group/s who produced it.[724]

Alongside the proliferation of nations and the emergence of the international discourse on rights, another significant development to take into account was the decline of the "Old Left" and the ascendancy of the "New Left." During the early part of the 20th century, the Old Left was politically peripheral, but in the aftermath of World War II, its influence surged, particularly as Marxist parties gained control in about a third of the world's nations. The Old Left was characterized by its commitment to a disciplined, organized mass movement with the ultimate aim of capturing state power. This focus led to a concentration on working-class issues to the exclusion of other social concerns. Furthermore, the Old

---

[722] G. Gurvitch: Proudhonian Synthesis. Translated by S. Murdock. The Anarchist Library, 2023.
[723] J. Terrier: The National and the Transnational: Marcel Mauss. Pp. 145–173 in *Visions of the Social: Society as a Political Project in France, 1750–1950*. Brill, 2011.
[724] G. Gurvitch: *The Bill of Social Rights*. International Universities Press, 1946.

Left equated large-scale industry with efficiency, prioritizing grand industrial projects.[725] For instance, Vladimir Lenin admired the German bureaucracies of their era and argued that once they had been "freed from the 'parasite'" they would serve as "an example of the socialist economic system."[726] In essence, the Old Left championed a model of coordination based on hierarchical structures, while often dismissing the viability of pluralism and smaller-scale, use-oriented production.

The "world-revolution of 1968" is often cited as a pivotal moment in the shift from the Old Left's vanguardist approach to the more democratic and pluralistic orientation of the New Left. The 1960s were marked by social upheaval and anti-colonial struggles, but 1968 distinguished itself as "the very first trans*continental* revolt."[727] This wave of protests spanned across various geopolitical divides, from the "first-world" nations of France, West Germany, and the United States, through the "second-world" across the Iron Curtain to Soviet-aligned states like Yugoslavia, Czechoslovakia, and Poland, and reaching into "third-world" countries such as Senegal, South Africa, and Pakistan.

The year 1968 marked a turning point for social movements for several reasons. First, there was a growing disillusionment with the United States as a guarantor of world order; instead, it was increasingly viewed as a colonial power masking its political hegemony behind the Cold War. Second, the inability of Marxist-Leninist and social democratic parties, which had risen to power in various parts of the globe during the mid-20th century, to deliver on their revolutionary promises led to a rising sense of disappointment and a loss of faith in the Old Left. Lastly, the Old Left's singular focus on the workers' movement fractured as "the forgotten

---

[725] W. J. Morgan: Marxism-Leninism: The Ideology of Twentieth-Century Communism. Pp. 656–662 in J. D. Wright (ed.): *International Encyclopedia of the Social and Behavioral Sciences, Vol 14.* Oxford, 2015.
[726] V. Lenin: *The State and Revolution: The Marxist Theory of the State and the Tasks of the Proletariat in the Revolution.* Lenin Internet Archive, 1999, p. 36.
[727] G.-R. Horn: 1968: A Social Movement *Sui Generis.* Pp. 515–541 in S. Berger & H. Nehring (eds.): *The History of Social Movements in Global Perspective: A Survey.* Springer, 2017: 516.

peoples" began to assert their presence, bringing to the forefront a diverse array of issues including gender, race, ethnicity, sexuality, prisoners' rights, housing rights, anti-colonialism, ecology, and animal rights. Although the revolutions of 1968 were largely politically suppressed and didn't achieve their immediate objectives, they left an indelible social legacy. Some theorists posit that there "have only been two world revolutions. One took place in 1848. The second took place in 1968. Both were historic failures. Both transformed the world."[728]

While contemporary scholarship often emphasizes the unprecedented nature of post-1968 social movements, a closer examination suggests they are more accurately viewed as an extension of the initiatives spearheaded by classical French socialisms. As previously noted, there has been a tendency among academics and the public to overlook the contributions of the classical French socialist movements, particularly their engagement with spirituality and pluralism, in favor of more formally organized social movements such as Marxism-Leninism, which are perceived as "serious" and "real." The sociologist Craig Calhoun has critiqued this oversight, noting that "social scientists lost sight of the traditions of direct action, fluid and shifting collective identities, and communitarian and other attempts to overcome the means/ends division of more instrumental movement organization."[729] Feminism serves as a pertinent example of this trend: it garnered minimal academic attention until the resurgence of a vibrant feminist movement around 1968, which effectively brought it back into the spotlight. The French socialists of the 19th century, who could arguably be termed the "Old New Left," shared similarities with the post-1968 New Left in their international orientation and their emphasis on social rather than political practices. In contrast, the Old Left was often preoccupied with conventional politics and was largely nationalist in orientation. Therefore,

---

[728] G. Arrighi, T. K. Hopkins, & I. Wallerstein: *Antisystemic Movements.* Verso, 1989, p. 97.

[729] C. Calhoun: "New Social Movements" of the Early Nineteenth Century. Pp. 385–427 in *Social Science History,* 17(3), 1993: 388.

the practices of the New Left can be seen as a tacit revival of the approaches championed by the French socialists.

As a whole, the 20th century, marked by an estimated quarter of a billion casualties from approximately 250 conflicts, stands as the most devastating in recorded history.[730] The end of this century witnessed profound transformations on a global scale. Following the disbanding of the Soviet Union in 1991, the United States military emerged as an unrivaled force, signifying a new era of geopolitical dynamics. Concurrently, the financialization that began in the 1970s, characterized by increased economic volatility and insecurity, has now become a global phenomenon. In this shifting economic landscape, nations previously categorized as "developing," such as China, Brazil, India, Russia, and South Africa, have experienced significant advancements, challenging the economic dominance of "developed" powers.

Moreover, the issue of climate change, with human activity as a central contributing factor, has gained unprecedented attention since the 1980s. The relentless progression of climate change is anticipated to exacerbate CO_2 emissions, leading to rising sea levels, and sparking water and food scarcities. It is also expected to increase the frequency of extreme weather events, such as hurricanes and heatwaves, potentially triggering mass migrations.[731] Similarly, the recent Covid-19 pandemic has strained the fabric of societies worldwide. The economic and health impacts of the pandemic have disproportionately affected the poor, exacerbated unemployment, and widened social inequalities. Given the virus's unpredictable nature, its long-term consequences remain uncertain, casting a shadow on the future of global health and economic stability.[732] Lastly, the 2022 Russian invasion of Ukraine and the Israeli-

---

[730] M. White: *Atrocitology: Humanity's 100 Deadliest Achievements*. Norton, 2012.

[731] Intergovernmental Panel on Climate Change: *Climate Change 2023 Synthesis Report*. 2023. Available at: www.ipcc.ch/report/ar6/syr/.

[732] International Labour Organization: *World Employment and Social Outlook Trends 2022*. Available at: www.ilo.org/global/research/global-reports/weso/trends2022/WCMS_834081/lang--en/index.htm .

Palestinian conflict that flared up again in October 2023 raise serious concerns about the possibility of a Third World War in the near future.[733]

At the same time, with the proliferation of a networked international order, especially in the wake of the internet, which is essentially a "network of networks," non-hierarchical and self-regulatory social practices have been called into fruition. In many ways, Saint-Simon's prophecy that the governing of people will be replaced by the administration of things appears to be emerging.[734] However, alongside these spontaneous mutualistic practices, there remain entrenched hierarchical social practices and external surveillance associated with the governmental state that seek to coopt it, leaving the "feudalization of networks" a possibility. As Bouglé suggested, "before the Saint-Simonian notion of the producer could play a significant role in social life today, [it is necessary] that this idea take a dip in the rapids of Proudhonism."[735] While the Saint-Simonian spirit has seemingly been fulfilled with the creation of truly networked global civilization and the Fourierist spirit has proliferated internationally with its focus on horizontal economic institutions, the Proudhonian spirit has yet to be fully realized. The fulfillment of the Proudhonian spirit implies to simultaneously escape hierarchical social structures and to "enter the network."[736] Arguably only by organizing themselves from the bottom-up, through voluntarily-endorsed agreements, as well as linking themselves to existing federations and confederations, can the governmental state based on coercion be made obsolete and overcome.

In summary, society is experiencing a dual movement: one veering toward internationalism and the strengthening of the social

---

[733] T. Turi, I. Warka, & A. Sudiarto: The Potential of a Third World War as the Implication of the War Between Russia and Ukraine. *International Journal of Humanities Education and Social Sciences*, 3(4), 2024.

[734] G. Balandier: *Le grand système*. Fayard, 2001, p. 254.

[735] C. Bouglé: *De la sociologie à l'action sociale: pacifisme, féminisme, coopération*. PUF, 1923, p. 17. Quoted in Humphreys: 1999, p. 128.

[736] P. Musso: Network Ideology: From Saint-Simonianism to the Internet. Pp. 19–66 in J. L Garcia (ed.): *Pierre Musso and the Network Society: From Saint-Simonianism to the Internet*. Springer, 2016, p. 33.

economy and the other toward nationalism and totalitarianism. The former movement appears to lead to an international order concerned with mutual recognition, while the latter movement appears to be pushing humanity toward another catastrophic world war. As Georges Gurvitch astutely pointed out, there is a "successive deepening of the disequilibrium between the legal order of the State and the jural framework of economic society. In the contemporary legal system... there are... contradictory tendencies towards pluralistic democracy and towards totalitarianism."[737] Although social science can elucidate the values inherent in internationalism, such as pluralism, the recognition of social rights, and human dignity, it fundamentally lacks the capacity to enforce these values upon society. The direction humanity chooses will depend on the actions and interactions of each society's members.[738] In other words, by fostering the expansion of networks and acknowledging the immanent collective conscience within the social fabric, societies can arguably organize themselves in a manner that engenders both freedom and equality.

In conclusion, the influence of French socialist thinkers has been profound, shaping contemporary societies in ways that are not always consciously recognized. Despite a seeming disregard for French socialist theories in academic discourse, their insights are perhaps more pertinent to current societal challenges than ever before.

---

[737] G. Gurvitch: *Sociology of Law.* Routledge & Kegan Paul ltd., 1947, p. 230.
[738] C. Bouglé: *The Evolution of Values: Studies in Sociology with Special Applications to Teaching.* Translated by H. S. Sellars. Henry Holt and Company, 1926, pp. 211-225.

Bibliography / Further Reading

* *The below paragraph and the French reading lists were written by Bouglé. All resources in English at the end of each section were provided by the editor.*

The books that I have used in preparing my work and that I cite in this bibliography are for the most part collected at the Centre de documentation sociale at the École Normale Supérieure, and whose resources have been very valuable to me. The Centre's staff have also been of great help to me: I owe special thanks to Ms. Poré and Mr. Maurice Le Lannou.[739]

I. - The 18th Century and Socialism.

G. Adler: *Geschichte des Sozialismus und Kommunismus bis 1789.* Leipzig, Hirschfeld, 1899, 281 p.

Baldensperger, Beaulavon, Benrubi, Bouglé, etc.: *J.-J. Rousseau.* Chapter 7: *Rousseau et le socialisme,* by C. Bouglé. Paris, Alcan, 1912, pp. 171-186.

L. Cahen: *L'idée de lutte de classes au XVIIIème siècle.* Revue de Synthèse historique, 1906, t. XII, pp. 214 et seqq.

J. Charmont: *La renaissance du droit naturel.* Montpellier, Coulet, 1910, 218 p.

A. Cresson: *Les grands courants de la pensée philosophique en France.* Paris, A. Colin, 1927, 2 vol, 208 & 210 p.

L. Ducros: *Les Encyclopédistes.* Paris, Champion, 1900, 376 p.

---

[739] Maurice Le Lannou (1906-1992) went on to become a geographer who specialized in the Mediterranean region.

A. Espinas: *La philosophie sociale au XVIIIème siècle et la Révolution.* Paris, Alcan, 1898, 412 p.

A. Lichtenberger: *Le socialisme au* XVIIIème *siècle.* Paris, Alcan, 1895, 470 p.

P. Mantoux: *La révolution industrielle au XVIIIe siècle.* Paris. Cornely, 1906, 544 p.

H. Michel: *L'idée de l'État.* Paris, Hachette, 1896, 655 p.

D. Mornet: *La pensée française au XVIIIe siècle.* Paris, A. Colin, 1926, 215 p.

R. Picard: *L'idée de lutte des classes au XVIIIe siècle.* Revue d'Économie politique, tome 5, 1891, pp. 628 et seqq.

M. Roustan: *Les philosophes et la société française au* XVIIIème *siècle.* Lyon, Rey; Paris, Picard; 1906, 455 p.

H. Sée: *La vie économique et les classes sociales en France au X VIIIe siècle.* Paris, Alcan, 1924, 231 p.

La France économique et sociale au X VIIIe siècle. Paris, A. Colin, 1925, 188 p.

Resources in English.

C. Adams, J. R. Censer, & L. J. Graham (eds.): *Visions and Revisions of Eighteenth Century France.* The Pennsylvania State University Press, 1997.

G. Atkinson & A. C. Keller: *Prelude to the Enlightenment: French Literature 1690–1740.* George Allen & Unwin Ltd, 1971.

E. Barber: *The Bourgeoisie in 18th-Century France.* Princeton University Press, 2015.

D. A. Bell: *The Cult of the Nation in France: Inventing Nationalism, 1680–1800.* Harvard University Press, 2009.

E. A. Bond: *The Writing Public: Participatory Knowledge in Enlightenment and Revolutionary France.* Cornell University Press, 2021.

Y. Cheng: *Creating the "New Man": From Enlightenment Ideals to Socialist Realities.* University of Hawai'i Press, 2009.

R. Darnton: *The Business of Enlightenment: A Publishing History of the Encyclopédie, 1775–1800.* Harvard University Press, 1979.

É. Durkheim: *Montesquieu and Rousseau: Forerunners of Sociology.* Translated by R. Manheim. The University of Michigan Press, 1960.

A. G. Enciso: *War, Power and the Economy: Mercantilism and State Formation in 18th-Century Europe.* Routledge, 2016.

F. Furet: *Revolutionary France, 1770–1880.* Translated by A. Nevill. Blackwell, 1992.

A. J. Gabay: *The Covert Enlightenment: Eighteenth-Century Counterculture and its Aftermath.* Swedenborg Foundation Publishers, 2005.

P. Gay: *The Enlightenment: An Interpretation.* Knopf, 1966.

D. Goodman: *A Cultural History of the French Enlightenment.* Cornell University Press, 1994.

W. B. Guthrie: *Socialism Before the French Revolution.* Macmillan, 1907.

J. R. Harris. *Industrial Espionage and Technology Transfer: Britain and France in the 18th Century.* Taylor & Francis, 2018.

M. Kwass: *Privilege and the Politics of Taxation in Eighteenth-Century France: Liberté, Égalité, Fiscalité.* Cambridge University Press, 2006.

S. Lukes & N. Urbinati (eds): *Condorcet: Political Writings.* Cambridge University Press, 2012.

J. Israel: *The Enlightenment that Failed: Ideas, Revolution, and Democratic Defeat, 1748–1830.* Oxford University Press, 2019.

P. Mantoux: *The Industrial Revolution in the Eighteenth Century: An Outline of the Beginnings of the Modern Factory System in England.* Translated by M. Vernon. J. Cape, 1928.

S. C. Maza: *Servants and Masters in 18th Century France: The Uses of Loyalty.* Princeton University Press, 2014.

R. Darnton: *Poetry and the Police: Communication Networks in Eighteenth-Century Paris.* Harvard University Press, 2012.

D. Mornet: *French Thought in the Eighteenth Century.* Translated by L. M. Levin. Prentice-Hall, 1929.

R. R. Palmer: *Catholics and Unbelievers in 18th Century France.* Princeton University Press, 1939.

A. H. Pasco: *Revolutionary Love in Eighteenth- and Early Nineteenth-Century France.* Routledge, 2016.

J. Riskin: *Science in the Age of Sensibility: The Sentimental Empiricists of the French.* University of Chicago Press, 2002.

D. Roche: *France in the Enlightenment.* Translated by A. Goldhammer. Harvard University Press, 1998.

M. Roustan: *The Pioneers of the French Revolution.* Translated by F. Whyte. Little Brown and Co., 1926.

H. Sée: *Economic and Social Conditions in France during the Eighteenth Century*. Translated by E. H. Zeydel. Alfred A. Knopf, 1927.

"The Economic and Social Origins of the French Revolution." Pp. 1-15 in *The Economic History Review* 3(1), 1931.

J. Shovlin: *Trading with the Enemy: Britain, France, and the 18th-Century Quest for a Peaceful World Order*. Yale University Press, 2021.

R. Wuthnow: *Communities of Discourse: Ideology and Social Structure in the Reformation, the Enlightenment, and European Socialism*. Harvard University Press, 1989.

II. - Physiocrats and Rural Landowners.

M. Augé-Laribé: *Grande et petite propriété*, Montpellier, Coulet, 1902, 217 p.

Le problème agraire du socialisme. La viticulture industrielle du Midi de la France. Paris, Giard et Brière, 1907, 356 p.

L'évolution de la France agricole. Paris, A. Colin 1912, 300 p.

Le paysan français après la guerre. Paris, Garnier, 1923, 292 p.

Syndicats et coopératives agricoles. Paris, A. Colin, 1926, 205 p.

A. Compère-Morel: *La question agraire et le socialisme en France*. Paris, Rivière, 1912, 172 p.

H. Denis: *Histoire des systèmes économiques et socialistes*. Paris, Giard et Brière, 1904, 2 vol., 365-560 p.

C. Gide & C. Rist: *Histoire des doctrines économiques*. Book 1, ch. 1, Paris, Sirey, 5th ed., 1926, 814 p.

J. Méline: *Le salut par la terre et le programme économique de l'avenir*. Paris, Hachette, 1919, 270 p.

A. Oncken: *Geschichte der Nationalökonomie.* 1ª Teil: Die Zeit vor Adam Smith. Leipzig, Hirschfeld, 1902, 516 p.

E. Richner: *Le Mercier de la Rivière. Ein Führer der physiokratischen Bewegung in Frankreich.* Zurich, Girsberger, 1931, 288 p.

H. Truchy: Le libéralisme économique dans les oeuvres de Quesnay. *Revue d'Économie politique*, 1889.

G. Weulersse: *Le mouvement physiocratique en France (de 1756 à 1770).* Dissertation. Paris, Alcan, 1910, 784 p.

Les physiocrates. Paris, Doin, 1931, 321 p.

Resources in English.

J. G. Backhaus (ed.): *Physiocracy, Antiphysiocracy, and Pfeiffer.* Springer, 2011.

A. R. Baker: *Fraternity Among the French Peasantry: Sociability and Voluntary Associations in the Loire Valley, 1815–1914.* Cambridge University Press, 2004.

M. Beer: *An Inquiry into Physiocracy.* George Allen and Unwin, 1939.

J. Blum: *The End of the Old Order in Rural Europe.* Princeton University Press, 1978.

E. Fox-Genovese: *The Origins of Physiocracy.* Cornell University Press, 1976.

J. G. Gagliardo: *From Pariah to Patriot: The Changing Image of the German Peasant, 1770–1840.* University of Kentucky Press, 2014.

P. Goubert: *The French Peasantry in the Seventeenth Century.* Cambridge University Press, 1986.

H. Higgs: *The Physiocrats: Six Lectures on the French Economists of the 18th Century.* Macmillan and Company, 1897.

P. T. Hoffman: *Growth in a Traditional Society: The French Countryside, 1450-1815.* Princeton University Press, 1996.

P. M. Jones: *The Peasantry and the French Revolution.* Cambridge University Press, 1988.

S. L. Kaplan & S. A. Reinert (eds.): *The Economic Turn: Recasting Political Economy in Enlightenment Europe.* Anthem Press, 2019.

S. C. Maza: *Servants and Masters in 18th-Century France: The Uses of Loyalty.* Princeton University Press, 1983.

R. L. Meek: *The Economics of Physiocracy.* Harvard University Press, 1963.

A. Moulin: *Peasantry and Society in France since 1789.* Cambridge University Press, 1991.

N. Plack: *Common Land, Wine and the French Revolution: Rural Society and Economy in Southern France, c. 1789-1820.* Routledge, 2009.

H. L. Root: *Peasants and King in Burgundy: Agrarian Foundations of French Absolutism.* University of California Press, 1987.

E. C. Spary: *Feeding France: New Sciences of Food, 1760-1815.* Cambridge University Press, 2014.

G. Vaggi: *The Economics of François Quesnay.* Duke University Press, 1987.

L. Vardi: *The Physiocrats and the World of the Enlightenment.* Cambridge University Press, 2012.

307

The Land and the Loom: Peasants and Profit in Northern France, 1680–1800. Duke University Press, 1993.

A.S. Wyngaard: *Urban Itineraries: Representations of the Peasant in Eighteenth-Century French Literature and Painting.* Dissertation at University of Pennsylvania, 1998.

III. - The French Revolution and Socialism.

V. Advielle: *Histoire de Gracchus Babeuf et du Babouvisme.* Paris, 1884, 2 vol., 543 & 319 p.

A. Aulard: *La Révolution française et le régime féodal.* Paris, Alcan, 1919, 283 p.

Histoire politique de la Révolution française. Paris, Colin, 804 p.

F. Buisson: *Condorcet.* Paris, Alcan, 1929, 137 p.

P. Buonarroti: *Histoire de la conspiration pour l'égalité dite de Babeuf.* Paris, Le Chevalier, 1869, 209 p.

L. Cahen: *Condorcet et la Révolution française.* Paris, Alcan, 1904, 592 p.

E. Champion: *Esprit de la Révolution française.* Paris, A. Colin, 1887, 300 p.

La France d'après les Cahiers de 1789. Paris, A. Colin, 1897, 257 p.

G. Davy: *Le droit, l'idéalisme et l'expérience.* Paris, Alcan, 1922, 165 p.

M. Dommanget: *Babeuf et la conjuration des Égaux.* Paris, Librairie de l'Humanité, 1922, 102 p.

E. Faguet, A. Lichtenberger, M. Wolff, P. Sagnac, L. Cahen and Levyschneider: *L'œuvre sociale de la Révolution française.* Paris, Fontemoing, n.d., 460 p.

M. Jaffé: *Le mouvement ouvrier à Paris pendant la Révolution française, 1789-1791.* Paris, Presse Universitaire, 1924, 207 p.

J. Jaurès: *Histoire socialiste de la Révolution française.* Paris, Librairie de l'Humanité, 1923-1924, 8 vol., from 400 to 450 p.

K. Kautsky: *La lutte des classes en France en 1789.* Paris, Jacques, 1901, 130 p.

E. Lavisse: *Histoire de France contemporaine.* Paris, Hachette, n. d.

  I. Sagnac: *La Révolution (1789-1792),* 1932, 436 p.

  II. Pariset: *La Révolution (1792-1799),* 1910, 433 p.

G. Lefebvre: *Les recherches relatives à la répartition de la propriété et de l'exploitation foncières, à la fin de l'ancien régime;* and *Les études relatives à la vente des Biens Nationaux.* Revue d'Histoire moderne, 1928, pp. 103-130 and pp. 188-219.

  La place de la Révolution dans l'histoire agraire de la France. Annales d'Histoire économique et sociale, t. 1, 1929, pp. 506-523.

Lefebvre-Sagnac-Guyot: *La Révolution française.* Paris, Alcan, 1930, 577 p.

A. Lichtenberger: *Le socialisme et la Révolution française.* Paris, Alcan, 1899, 307 p.

P. Louis: *Histoire du socialisme en France depuis la Révolution jusqu'à nos jours.* Paris, Rivière, 1925, 408 p.

A. Mathiez: *La Révolution française.* Paris, A. Colin, 1922-1927, 3 vol. in-12.

  La vie chère et le mouvement social sous la Terreur. Paris, Payot, 1927, 613 p.

La réaction thermidorienne. Paris, A. Colin, 1929, 324 p.

G. Morin: *La révolte des faits contre le code.* Paris, Grasset, 1920, 249 p.

G. Perreux: *La propagande républicaine au début de la monarchie de juillet.* Paris, Hachette, 1930, 92 p.

R. Picard: *Les cahiers de 1789 et les classes ouvrières.* Paris, Rivière, 1910, 276 p.

P. Robiquet: *Buonarroti et la secte des Égaux.* Paris, Hachette, 1910, 328 p.

G. Sencier: *Le babouvisme après Babeuf.* Paris, Rivière, 1912, 348 p.

A. Thomas: *G. Babeuf. La doctrine des Égaux.* Paris, Cornély, 1909, 96 p.

Resources in English.

F. Aftalion: *The French Revolution: An Economic Interpretation.* Cambridge University Press, 1990.

N. Aston: *Religion and Revolution in France, 1780-1804.* Catholic University of America Press, 2000.

A. Aulard: *The French Revolution: A Political History 1789-1804.* 4 volumes. Translated by B. Miall. T. F. Unwin, 1913.

E. B. Bax: *The Last Episode of the French Revolution: Being a History of Gracchus Babeuf and the Conspiracy of the Equals.* Grant Richards Limited, 1911.

J. Beecher: *Writers and Revolution: Intellectuals and the French Revolution of 1848.* Cambridge University Press, 2021.

J. Bergman: *The French Revolutionary Tradition in Russian and Soviet Politics, Political Thought, and Culture.* Oxford University Press, 2019.

G. Best (ed.): *The Permanent Revolution: The French Revolution and its Legacy, 1789-1989.* Fontana Press, 1988.

I. H. Birchall: *The Spectre of Babeuf.* Macmillan Press Ltd, 1997.

M. Broers: *Europe under Napoleon 1799-1815.* St. Martin's Press, 1996.

H. G. Brown: *Ending the French Revolution: Violence, Justice, and Repression from the Terror to Napoleon.* University of Virginia Press, 2006.

P. Buonarroti: *Babeuf's Conspiracy for Equality.* Translated by Bronterre. H. Hetherington, 1836.

T. Carlyle: *The French Revolution: A History.* James Fraser, 1837.

R. Chartier: *The Cultural Origins of the French Revolution.* Duke University Press, 1991.

G. C. Comninel: *Rethinking the French Revolution: Marxism and the Revisionist Challenge.* Verso, 1987.

I. Davidson: *The French Revolution: From Enlightenment to Tyranny.* Profile Books Ltd, 2016.

S. Desan: *Reclaiming the Sacred: Lay Religion and Popular Politics in Revolutionary France.* Cornell University Press, 1990.

W. Doyle: *The Oxford History of the French Revolution.* Oxford University Press, 1989.

Origins of the French Revolution. Oxford University Press, 1999.

The French Revolution: A Very Short Introduction. Oxford University Press, 2001.

Aristocracy and Its Enemies in the Age of Revolution. Oxford University Press, 2009.

Napoleon at Peace: How to End a Revolution. Reaktion Books, 2022.

E. L. Einstein: *The First Professional Revolutionist: Filippo Michele Buonarroti (1761–1837).* Harvard University Press, 1959.

F. Fehér (ed.): *The French Revolution and the Birth of Modernity.* University of California Press, 1990.

F. Furet: *Interpreting the French Revolution.* Translated by E. Forster. Cambridge University Press, 1981.

Marx and the French Revolution. Translated by D. Furet. University of Chicago Press, 1988.

The French Revolution 1770–1814. Translated by A. Nevill. Blackwell, 1992.

Revolutionary France, 1770–1880. Translated by A. Nevil. Oxford University Press, 1995.

W. Geer: *The French Revolution: A Historical Sketch.* The Plimpton Press, 1922.

J. Goldstein: *The Post-Revolutionary Self: Politics and Psyche in France, 1750–1850.* Harvard University Press, 2005.

H. Gough: *The Terror in the French Revolution.* Bloomsbury Publishing, 2010.

J. N. Heuer: *The Family and the Nation: Gender and Citizenship in Revolutionary France, 1879–1830.* Cornell University Press, 2007.

J. Israel: *Revolutionary Ideas: An Intellectual History of the French Revolution from the Rights of Man to Robespierre.* Princeton University Press, 2015.

J. Jaurés: *A Socialist History of the French Revolution.* Translated by M. Abidor. Pluto Press, 2015.

R. M. Johnston: *The French Revolution.* Henry Holt and Company, 1909.

C. Jones: *The Longman Companion to the French Revolution.* Taylor & Francis, 1988.

J. Klaits & M. H. Haltzel (eds.): *The Global Ramifications of the French Revolution.* Cambridge University Press, 1994.

G. Lefebvre: *The Coming of the French Revolution.* Translated by R. R. Palmer. Princeton University Press, 1947.

The French Revolution. 2 volumes. Translated by J. H. Stewart & J. Friguglietti. Columbia University Press, 1964.

The Thermidorians and the Directory: Two Phases of the French Revolution. Translated by R. Baldick. Random House, 1964.

C. Lucas (ed.): *Rewriting the French Revolution.* Clarendon Press, 1991.

M. Lyons: *Napoleon Bonaparte and the Legacy of the French Revolution.* St. Martin's Press, 1994.

J. Markoff: *Abolition of Feudalism: Peasants, Lords, and Legislators in the French Revolution.* Penn State Press, 2010.

L. Mason: *The Last Revolutionaries: The Conspiracy Trial of Gracchus Babeuf and the Equals.* Yale University Press, 2022.

A. Mathiez: *The Fall of Robespierre, and Other Essays.* Alfred A. Knopf, 1927.

313

The French Revolution. Translated by C.A. Phillips. Alfred A. Knopf, 1928.

After Robespierre: The Thermidorian Reaction. Translated by C. A. Phillips. Alfred A. Knopf, 1931.

J. McManners: *The French Revolution and the Church.* S. P. C. K., 1969.

P. McPhee: *A Social History of France, 1780–1914.* Routledge, 1992.

S. E. Melzer & L. E. Rabine (eds.): *Rebel Daughters: Women and the French Revolution.* Oxford University Press,1992.

F.-A. Mignet: *History of the French Revolution from 1789 to 1814.* Henry G. Bohn, 1856.

D. Moggach & G. S. Jones (eds): *The 1848 Revolutions and European Political Thought.* Cambridge University Press, 2018.

D. Outram: *The Body and the French Revolution: Sex, Class and Political Culture.* Yale University Press, 1989.

M. Ozouf: *Festivals and the French Revolution.* Harvard University Press, 1991.

R. R. Palmer: *The World of the French Revolution.* George Allen & Unwin Ltd, 1971.

J. B. Peixotto: *The French Revolution and Modern French Socialism: A Comparative Study of the Principles of the French Revolution and the Doctrines of Modern French Socialism.* TY Crowell, 1901.

D. H. Pinkney: *The French Revolution of 1830.* Princeton University Press, 1972.

J. D. Popkin: *A New World Begins: The History of the French Revolution.* Basic Books, 2021.

R. B. Rose: *Gracchus Babeuf: The First Revolutionary Communist.* Stanford University Press, 1978.

S. Schama: *Citizens: A Chronicle of the French Revolution.* Random House, 1989.

W. H. Sewell: *Work and Revolution in France: The Language of Labor from the Old Regime to 1848.* Cambridge University Press, 1980.

D. M. G. Sutherland: *France, 1789–1815: Revolution and Counter-Revolution.* Oxford University Press, 1986.

B. Stone: *The Genesis of the French Revolution: A Global-Historical Interpretation.* Cambridge University Press, 1994.

L. A. Thiers: *The History of the French Revolution 1789–1800.* 5 volumes. Translated by. F. Shoberl. Richard Bently and Son, 1895.

A. de Tocqueville: *The Old Regime and the Revolution.* Translated by J. Bonner. Harper & Brothers Publishers, 1856.

Recollections: The French Revolution of 1848. Translated by G. Lawrence. Transaction Publishers, 1987.

N. H. Webster: *The French Revolution: A Study in Democracy.* Constable & Company, 1926.

D. Williams: *Condorcet and Modernity.* Cambridge University Press, 2004.

IV. - Socialist Systems in General.

C. Andler: *Le manifeste communiste.* Paris, Rieder, 1902, 209 p.

C. Bouglé: *Chez les prophètes socialistes.* Paris, Alcan, 1918, 246 p.

H. Bourgin: *Les systèmes socialistes.* Paris, Doin, 1923, 417 p.

G. and H. Bourgin: *Le socialisme français de 1789 à 1848.* Paris, Hachette, 1912, 109 p.

M. Bourguin: *Les systèmes socialistes et l'évolution économique.* Paris, A. Colin, 1904, 519 p.

J. Delevsky: *Les antinomies socialistes et l'évolution du socialisme français.* Paris, Giard,1930, 524 p.

J.-C. Demarquette: *Les idées de Sismondi.* Paris, "Le Trait d'union," 1930, 180 p.

É. Durkheim: *Le socialisme, sa définition, ses débuts. La doctrine saint-simonienne.* Paris, Alcan, 1928, 352 p.

F. Engels: *Socialisme utopique et socialisme scientifique* (Translated by P. Lafargue). Paris, Jacques, 1902, 35 p.

E. Fournière: *Les théories socialistes au XIXème siècle, de Babeuf à Proudhon.* Paris, Alcan,1904, 415 p.

C. Gide & C. Rist: *Histoire des doctrines économiques depuis les physiocrates jusqu'à nos jours.* Paris, 1909, 2 vol.

K. Grün: *Die soziale Bewegung in Frankreich und Belgien.* Darmstadt, 1845.

J. Guillaume: *L'Internationale. Documents et souvenirs.* Paris, Société nouvelle, 1905-10, 4 vols.

G. Gurvitch: *L'idée du droit social. Notion et système du droit social. Histoire doctrinale depuis le XVII° siècle jusqu'à la fin du XIXème siècle.* Paris, Sirey, 1931, 710 p.

G. Isambert: *Les idées socialistes en France de 1815 à 1848*. Paris, Alcan, 1905, 426 p.

P. Keller: *Louis Blanc und die Revolution von 1848*. (Research published by Saitzew). Zurich, Girsberger, 1926, 232 p.

H. Louvancour: *De Henri de Saint-Simon à Charles Fourier*. Paris, dissertation, 1913, 452 p.

A. Merger: *Le droit au produit intégral du travail*. (Translated by Bonnet). Paris, Giard, 1900, 244 p.

J. Prudhommeaux: *Icarie et son fondateur Étienne Cabet*. Paris, Cornély, 1907, 664 p.

J.-L. Puech: *La vie et l'oeuvre de Flora Tristan*. Paris, Rivière, 1925, 514 p.

La tradition socialiste en France et la Société des Nations. Paris, Rivière, 1921, 228 p.

L. Reybaud: *Études sur les réformateurs, ou socialistes modernes*. Paris, Guillaume, 7th ed., 1864, 2 vol., 472 & 456 p.

G. Richard: *La question sociale et le mouvement philosophique au XIXème siècle*. Paris, A. Colin, 1914, 363 p.

W. Sombart: *Le socialisme et le mouvement social au XIXème siècle*. Paris, Giard et Brière, 1898, 187 p.

L. Von Stein: *Der Socialismus and Communismus des heutigen Frankreichs*. Leipzig, 1842, 475 p.: 2nd ed. 1848, 590 p.

G. Weill: *Histoire du mouvement social en France 1852-1924*. Paris, Alcan, 1924, 490 p.

Resources in English.

D. E. Barclay & W. D. Weitz (eds): *Between Reform and Revolution: German Socialism and Communism from 1840 to 1990.* Berghahn Books, 1998.

J. H. Billlington: *Fire in the Minds of Men: Origins of the Revolutionary Faith.* Basic Books, 1980.

M. J. Buhle: *Women and American Socialism, 1870–1920.* University of Illinois Press, 2023.

E. Cabet: *Travels in Icaria.* Translated by L. J. Roberts. Syracuse University Press, 2003.

B. Clift: *French Socialism in a Global Era.* Continuum International Publishing Group, 2005.

G. D. H. Cole: *A History of Socialist Thought.* 5 volumes. Macmillan & Co, 1953–1960.

Towards a Libertarian Socialism: Reflections on the British Labour Party and European Working-Class Movements. AK Press, 2021.

V. Considerant: *Principles of Socialism: Manifesto of Nineteenth Century Democracy.* Translated by J. Roelofs. Maisonneuve Press, 2006.

B. D. Denitch: *Limits and Possibilities: The Crisis of Yugoslav Socialism and State Socialist Systems.* University of Minnesota Press, 1990.

R. T. Ely: *French and German Socialism in Modern Times.* Harper & Brothers, 1883.

W. Eckhardt: *The First Socialist Schism.* Translated by R. M. Homsi, J. Cohn, C. Lawless, N. McNab, & B. Moreel. PM Press, 2016.

F. Engels: *Socialism: Utopian and Scientific.* Translated by E. Aveling. Progress Publishers, 1970.

A. Fried & R. Sanders: *Socialist Thought: A Documentary History.* Anchor Books, 1964.

C. Gide & C. Rist: *A History of Economic Doctrines: From the Time of the Physiocrats to the Present Day.* Translated by R. Richards. D.C. Heath and Company, 1947.

S. K. Grogan: *French Socialism and Sexual Difference: Women and the New Society, 1803-44.* Palgrave Macmillan, 1992.

G. Gurvitch: *Sociology of Law.* Routledge & Kegan Paul ltd, 1947.

The Bill of Social Rights. International Universities Press, 1946.

G. Hodgson: *Is Socialism Feasible? Towards an Alternative Future.* Edward Elgar Publishing, 2019.

A. Honneth: *The Idea of Socialism: Towards a Renewal.* Translated by J. Ganahl. Polity Press, 2017.

G. S. Jones: *Languages of Class: Studies in English Working Class History 1832-1982.* Cambridge University Press, 1983.

An End to Poverty? A Historical Debate. Columbia University Press, 2004.

G. S. Jones & G. Claeys (eds): *The Cambridge History of the Nineteenth-Century Political Thought.* Cambridge University Press, 2011.

T. Kirkup: *A History of Socialism.* Adam and Charles Black, 1913.

D. Lane: *The Socialist Industrial State: Towards a Political Sociology of State Socialism.* Taylor & Francis, 2023.

J. H. Laslett & S. M. Lipset (eds.): *Failure of a Dream? Essays in the History of American Socialism.* University of California Press, 1974.

A. Lipow: *Authoritarian Socialism in America: Edward Bellamy and the Nationalist Movement.* University of California Press, 1982.

J. Mark & P. Betts (eds.): *Socialism Goes Global: The Soviet Union and Eastern Europe in the Age of Decolonization.* Oxford University Press, 2022.

L. Martell: *Alternative Societies: For a Pluralist Socialism.* Bristol University Press, 2023.

F. E. Manuel: *The Prophets of Paris.* Harvard University Press, 1962.

F. E. Manuel & F. P. Manuel: *Utopian Thought in the Western World.* Harvard University Press, 1979.

A. Menger: *The Right to the Whole Produce of Labour.* Translated by M.E. Tanner. Macmillan and Co. Ltd, 1899.

B. H. Moss: *The Origins of the French Labor Movement, 1830–1914: The Socialism of Skilled Workers.* University of California Press, 1976.

M. Newman: *Socialism: A Very Short Introduction.* Oxford University Press, 2020.

J. B. Peixotto: *The French Revolution and Modern French Socialism.* Thomas Y. Crowell & Company Publishers, 1901.

P. M. Pilbeam: *French Socialists before Marx: Workers, Women and the Social Question in France.* McGill-Queen's University Press, 2000.

B. Russell: *Roads to Freedom: Socialism, Anarchism, and Syndicalism.* Allen & Unwin, 1918.

H. P. Segal: *Utopias: A Brief History from Ancient Writings to Virtual Communities.* Blackwell Publishing, 2012.

W. Sombart: *Socialism and the Social Movement in the 19th Century.* Translated by A. P. Atterbury. G. P. Putnam's Sons, 1898.

K. Taylor: *Political Ideas of the Utopian Socialists.* Routledge, 1982.

M. I. Tugan-Baranowsky: *Modern Socialism in its Historical Development.* Translated by M. I. Redmount. Swan Sonnenschein & Co., 1910.

L. Von Stein: *The History of the Social Movement in France, 1789-1850.* Translated by K. Mengelberg. Bedminster Press, 1964.

V. - Saint-Simonism.

H. R. d'Allemagne: *Les Saint-Simoniens, 1827-1837.* Paris, Gründ, 1930, 442 p.

C. Bouglé & E. Halévy: *Doctrine de Saint-Simon.* New edition Paris, Rivière, 1924, 501 p.

M. Bourbonnais: *Le Néo-Saint-Simonisme et la vie sociale d'aujourd'hui.* Paris, Presse Universitaire, 1923, 126 p.

G. Brunet: *Le mysticisme social de Saint-Simon.* Paris, Presses françaises, 1925, 125 p.

E.-M. Butler: *The Saint-Simonian Religion in Germany.* Cambridge University Press, 1926, 446 p.

H. Carnot: *Sur le Saint-Simonisme.* Séances et travaux de l'Académie des Sciences morales, 1887.

S. Charléty: *Essai sur l'histoire du Saint-Simonisme.* 1st ed., Paris, Hachette, 1896, 498 p. 2nd ed., Paris, Hartmann, 1930, 379 p.

Enfantin. Textes choisis précédés d'une introduction. Paris, Alcan, 1930, 108 p.

G. Dumas: *Psychologie de deux messies positivistes : A. Comte et Saint-Simon.* Paris, Alcan, 1905, 314 p.

G. Eckstein: *Der alte und der neue Saint-Simonismus.* Archiv für die Geschichte des Sozialismus and der Arbeiterbewegung, t. II, 1912, pp. 425–441.

G. Gignoux: *L'industrialisme, de Saint-Simon à Walther Rathenau.* Revue d'histoire des Doctrines économiques et sociales, Paris, 1923.

G. Salomon: *Saint-Simon und der Sozialismus. Wege zum Sozialismus.* Berlin, 1919.

M. Leroy: *Le socialisme des producteurs. "Henri de Saint-Simon."* Paris, Rivière, 1924, 188 p.

La vie du Comte de Saint-Simon. Paris, Grasset, 1925, 336 p.

F. Muckle: *Henri de Saint-Simon, die Persönlichkeit und das Werk.* Iéna, Fischer, 1908, 384 p.

A. Péreire: *Autour de Saint-Simon.* Paris, Champion, 1912, 221 p.

Écrits de Isaac et Émile Péreire, 8 tomes. Librairie des imprimeries réunies, 1900–1905.

J. Plenge: *Die erste Gründung und Geschichte des Credit Mobilier.* Tübingen, 1911, 184 p.

W. Spuhler: *Der SaintSimonismus. Lehre and Leben, von Saint-Amand Bazard,* Zürcher Volkswirtschaftliche Forschungen, 1926.

M. Thibert: *Le rôle social de l'Art d'après les Saint-Simoniens.* Paris, Rivière, 1926, 73 p.

J.-B. Vergeot: *Le crédit comme stimulant et régulateur de l'industrie; la conception saint-simonienne*. Paris, Jouve, 1918, 300 p.

M. Wallon: *Les Saint Simoniens et les chemins de fer*. Paris, Pedone, 1908,171 p.

G. Weill: *Un précurseur du socialisme. Saint-Simon et son oeuvre*. Paris, Perrin, 1894, 247 p.

L'école Saint-Simonienne. Paris, Alcan, 1896, 319 p.

E. de Witt: *Saint-Simon et le système industriel*. Paris, dissertation, 1902, 187 p.

Le producteur. 1ª year, 1920. Special issue devoted to Intellectual Credit ("Crédit intellectual") (Volume 5, August-September 1921).

Revue d'histoire économique et sociale. Special issue devoted to Saint-Simon, 1925.

Resources in English.

O. W. Abi-Mershed: *Apostles of Modernity: Saint-Simonians and the Civilizing Mission in Algeria*. Stanford UP, 2010.

S. Bazard & B. Enfantin: *The Doctrine of Saint-Simon: An Exposition, First Year, 1828-1829*. Translated by G. I. Iggers. Beacon Press, 1958.

J. B. Briscoe: *Saint-Simonism and the Origins of Socialism in France, 1816-1832*. Dissertation at Columbia University, 1980.

A. J. Booth: *Saint-Simon and Saint-Simonism: A Chapter in the History of Socialism in France*. Longmans, Green, Reader, and Dyer, 1871.

E. M. Butler: *The Saint-Simonian Religion in Germany: A Study of the Young German Movement*. Cambridge University Press, 1926.

R. B. Carlisle: *The Proffered Crown: Saint-Simonianism and the Doctrine of Hope.* John Hopkins University Press, 1987.

D. B. Cofer: *Saint-Simonism in the Radicalism of Thomas Carlyle.* Von Boeckmann-Jones, 1931.

C. Crossley: *French Historians and Romanticism: Thierry, Guizot, the Saint-Simonians, Quinet, Michelet.* Routledge, 2002.

G. d'Eichthal: *A French Sociologist Looks at Britain: Gustave d'Eichthal and British Society in 1828.* Trans. by B. Ratcliffe & W. Chaloner. Manchester University Press, 1977.

M. Dondo: *The French Faust: Henri de Saint-Simon.* Philosophical Library, 1955.

É. Durkheim: *Socialism.* Translated by C. Sattler. Collier Books, 1962.

A. Essinger: *Goethe and Saint-Simon.* Thesis at the University of Wisconsin, 1917.

J. L. Garcia (ed): *Pierre Musso and the Network Society: From Saint-Simonianism to the Internet.* Springer, 2016.

F. A. Hayek: *The Counter-Revolution of Science: Studies on the Abuse of Reason.* The Free Press, 1952.

G. Ionescu: *The Political Thought of Saint-Simon.* Oxford University Press, 1976.

G. Iggers: *The Social Philosophy of the Saint-Simonians (1825–1832).* Dissertation at the University of Chicago, 1951.

The Cult of Authority: The Political Philosophy of the Saint-Simonians. Martinus Nijhoff, 1970.

G. Jacoud (ed.): *Political Economy and Industrialism: Banks in Saint-Simonian Economic Thought.* Routledge, 2010.

D. N. Lindley: *The Saint-Simonians, Carlyle, and Mill: A Study in the History of Ideas.* Dissertation at Columbia University, 1958.

R. P. Locke: *Music, Musicians, and the Saint-Simonians.* University of Chicago Press, 1986.

F. E. Manuel: *The New World of Henri Saint-Simon.* Harvard University Press, 1956.

F. M. H. Markham (ed.): *Henri Comte de Saint-Simon (1760–1825).* Basil Blackwell, 1952.

M. P. Murphy: *Envisioning Romantic Political Economy: The Formative Years of Michel Chevalier (1806–1879).* Dissertation at the University of California, Santa Cruz, 2011.

P. Musso: Religion and Political Economy in Saint-Simon. Pp. 809–827 in *The European Journal of the History of Economic Thought,* 24(4), 2017.

Violence in the Philosophy of Saint-Simon. Pp. 125–143 in *Violence and Non-Violence across Time.* Routledge India, 2018.

E. L. Ortiz & S. Altmann: *Mathematics and Social Utopias in France: Olinde Rodrigues and His Times.* American Mathematical Society, 2013.

R. K. P. Pankhurst: *The Saint-Simonians, Mill and Carlye: A Preface to Modern Thought.* Norwood Editions, 1976.

M. A. Perlberg: *Men and Women in Saint-Simonianism: The Union of Politics and Morals.* Dissertation at the University of Iowa, 1993.

B. M. Ratcliffe. *Saint-Simonism and Railways, 1825–1848: A Study of the Early Intellectual and Entrepreneurial Careers of Émile and Isaac Péreire.* Dissertation at University of Manchester, 1969.

H. Shine: *Carlyle and the Saint-Simonians: The Concept of Historical Periodicity.* The John Hopkins Press, 1941.

K. Taylor: *Henri Saint-Simon 1760–1825: Selected Writings on Science, Industry, and Social Organisation.* Croom Helm Ltd., 1975.

S. Walsh: *Pragmatic Utopia and Romantic Science: Colonial Identities and Saint-Simonian Influences in the Writings of Thomas Ismaÿl Urbain (1812–1884) and Henri Duveyrier (1840–1892).* Dissertation at the National University of Ireland, Galway, 2013.

Y. Yook: *Continuity and Transformation: Emile Barrault and Saint-Simonianism.* Dissertation at the University of Washington, 1995.

A. Zouache (ed): *The Political Economy of Saint-Simonism.* Fabrizio Serra, 2009.

The European Journal of the History of Economic Thought. Volume 27, issue 3, special issue titled "Economists and Saint-Simonism," 2020.

VI. - Fourierism.

H. Bourgin: *Fourier, contribution à l'étude du socialisme français.* Paris, Bellais, 1905, 608 p.

Victor Considerant, Lyon, Imprimeries réunies, 1909, 126 p.

E. Dessignole: *Le féminisme d'après la doctrine sociale de Charles Fourier.* Lyon, Stock, 1903, 148 p.

M. Dommanget: *Victor Considerant.* Paris, Éditions sociales internationales, 1929, 218 p.

M. Friedberg: *L'influence de Charles Fourier sur le mouvement social contemporain en France.* Paris, Giard, 1926, 174 p.

J. Gaumont: *Histoire abrégée de la coopération en France et à l'étranger.* Paris, Rieder, 1921, 194 p.

Histoire générale de la coopération en France. Paris, Fédération nationale des coopératives de consommation, 1923, 2 vol.

I. Précurseurs et prémices, 630 p.

II. Formation et développement de l'Institution coopérative moderne, 735 p.

C. Gide: *Fourier, précurseur de la coopération.* Paris, Association pour l'enseignement de la coopération, 1922–1923, 203 p.

Cours professé au Collège de France sur la coopération. Paris, Association pour l'enseignement de la coopération, 1922–1924.

Les sociétés coopératives de consommation. Paris, Sirey, 4th ed., 1924, 338 p.

Les colonies communistes et coopératives. Paris, Association pour l'enseignement de la coopération, 1927–1928, 288 p.

M. Lansac: *Les conceptions méthodologiques et sociales de Charles Fourier, leur influence.* Paris, Vrin, 1926, 134 p.

B. Lavergne: *Les coopératives de consommation en France.* Paris, A. Colin, 1923, 210 p.

L'ordre coopératif. Tome 1, Paris, Alcan, 1926, 601 p.

E. Poisson: *La république coopérative.* Paris, Grasset, 1920, 256 p.

Socialisme et coopération. Paris, Rieder, 1922, 126 p.

M. Thibert: *Le féminisme dans le socialisme français.* Dissertation, Paris, 1920.

Resources in English.

J. Beecher: *Charles Fourier: The Visionary and His World.* University of California Press, 1986.

Victor Considerant and the Rise and Fall of French Romantic Socialism. University of California Press, 2001.

J. Beecher & R. Bienvenu (eds): *The Utopian Vision of Charles Fourier: Selected Texts on Work, Love, and Passionate Attraction.* Beacon Press, 1971.

M. P. Bowman: *Laboring for Global Perfection: The International Dimension of Mid-Nineteenth-Century Fourierism.* Dissertation at the University of California, Santa Barbara, 2013.

W. H. Brock: *Phalanx on a Hill: Responses to Fourierism in the Transcendental Circle.* Dissertation at Loyola University, 1995.

J. T. Codman: *Brook Farm: Historic and Personal Memoirs.* Arena, 1894.

M. F. Cross: *In the Footsteps of Flora Tristan: A Political Biography.* Liverpool University Press, 2020.

J. Curl: *For All the People: Uncovering the Hidden History of Cooperation, Cooperative Movements, and Communalism in America.* PM Press, 2012.

S. Dijkstra: *Flora Tristan: Feminism in the Age of George Sand.* Pluto Press, 1992.

C. Fourier: *Selections from the Works of Fourier.* Translated by J. Franklin. Swan Sonnenschein & Co., 1901.

E. Furlough: *Consumer Cooperation in France: The Politics of Consumption, 1834–1930.* Cornell University Press, 1991.

E. Furlough & C. Strikwerda (eds.): *Consumers against Capitalism? Consumer Cooperation in Europe, North America and Japan, 1840–1990.* Rowman & Littlefield Publishers, 1999.

C. Gide: *Consumers' Co-operative Societies.* Translated by the staff of the co-operative reference library. Alfred A. Knopf, 1922.

Communist and Co-operative Colonies. Translated by E. F. Row. George G. Harrap & Company, 1930.

Productive Co-operation in France. Pp. 30–66 in *The Quarterly Journal of Economics,* 14(1), 1899.

P. Godwin: *A Popular View of the Doctrines of Charles Fourier.* JS Redfield, 1844.

C. Guarneri: *The Utopian Alternative: Fourierism in Nineteenth-Century America.* Cornell University Press, 1991.

A. Hart: *Fourierist Communities of Reform: The Social Networks of Nineteenth-Century Female Reformers.* Springer Nature, 2021.

A. Hemmens: *The Critique of Work in Modern French Thought: From Charles Fourier to Guy Debord.* Springer, 2019.

A. Loman. *Somewhat on the Community System: Representations of Fourierism in the Works of Nathaniel Hawthorne.* Routledge, 2014.

A. J. Mortenson: *The Wisconsin Phalanx: An Experiment in Fourierism in America.* Thesis at the University of Wyoming, 1967.

G. Patmore & N. Balnave: *A Global History of Co-operative Business.* Routledge, 2018.

C. Pellarin: *The Life of Charles Fourier.* William H. Graham, Tribune Buildings, 1848.

G. Pente: *Transatlantic Fourierism: Albert Brisbane and the Democratic Politics of Visionary Socialism, 1828–1898.* Dissertation at the University of Colorado at Boulder, 2020.

R. N. Pettitt: *Albert Brisbane: Apostle of Fourierism in the United States, 1834–1890.* Dissertation at Miami University, 1982.

J. Pratt: *Sabotaged: Dreams of Utopia in Texas.* University of Nebraska Press, 2020.

N. V. Riasanovsky: *The Teaching of Charles Fourier.* University of California Press, 1969.

A. D. Roberts: *Zola and Fourier.* Dissertation at the University of Pennsylvania, 1959.

N. Robertson: *The Co-operative Movement and Communities in Britain, 1914–1960: Minding Their Own Business.* Ashgate Publishing, 2010.

J. Rothschild & J. A. Whitt: *The Cooperative Workplace: Potentials and Dilemmas of Organizational Democracy and Participation.* Cambridge University Press, 1986.

K. M. Tomasek: *"The Pivot of the Mechanism": Women, Gender, and Discourse in Fourierism and the Antebellum United States.* Dissertation at the University of Wisconsin-Madison, 1995.

Urban Homesteading Assistance Board: *Building for Us: Stories of Homesteading and Cooperative Housing.* Interference Archive, 2019.

S. Webb & B. Webb: *The Consumers' Co-operative Movement.* Longmans, Green, & Co., 1921.

R. C. Williams: *The Cooperative Movement: Globalization from Below.* Routledge, 2016.

D. Zeldin: *The Educational Ideas of Charles Fourier (1772-1837)*. Frank
Cass & Co., 1969.

VII. - Proudhonism.

Proudhon et notre temps. Guy-Grand, Pirou, Puech, etc. Paris, Chiron,
1920, 255 p.

P. Armand: *P.-J. Proudhon et le Fouriérisme.* Paris, Rivière, 1929, 61 p.

M. Aucuy: *Les systèmes socialistes d'échange.* Paris, Alean, 1908, 366 p.

E. Berth: *Guerre des États ou guerre des classes.* Paris, Rivière, 1924, 437
p.

A. Berthod: *P.-J. Proudhon et la propriété.* Paris, Giard et Brière, 1910,
227 p.

Introduction à l'Idée générale de la Révolution au XIXème siècle.
Paris, 1924, Rivière, 462 p.

A. Berthod & G. Guy-Grand: *Proudhon et l'enseignement du peuple.*
Paris, Chiron, 1920, 28 p.

C. Bouglé: *La sociologie de Proudhon.* Paris, A. Colin, 1911, 333 p.

Proudhon. Paris, Alcan, 1930, 153 p.

N. Bourgeois: *Les théories du droit international chez Proudhon. Le
fédéralisme et la paix.* Paris, Rivière, 1927, 136 p.

H. Bourgin: *Proudhon.* Paris, Bibliothèque socialiste, 1901, 96 p.

P. Desjardins: *P.-J. Proudhon.* Paris, 1896, 2 vol., 279-297 p.

K. Diehl: *P.-J. Proudhon.* Iena, Fischer, 1888-1896, 3 vol., 126; 388; 239
p.

L. Dimier: *Les maîtres de la contre-révolution au XIXème siècle.* Paris, Nouvelle Librairie Nationale, 1907, 357 p.

J. Duprat: *Proudhon sociologue et moraliste.* Paris, Alcan, 1929, 311 p.

R. Labry: *Herzen et Proudhon.* Paris, Bossard, 1928, 244 p.

F. Pillon: *La morale indépendante et le principe de dignité.* Paris, Baillière, 1868.

G. Pirou: *Proudhonisme et syndicalisme révolutionnaire.* Paris, Rousseau, 1910, 422 p.

J.-L. Puech: *Le proudhonisme dans l'Association internationale des travailleurs.* Paris, Alcan, 1907, 268 p.

G. Séailles: *Proudhon moraliste.* Paris, Chiron, 1922, pamphlet 30 p.

G. Sorel: *Essai sur la philosophie de Proudhon.* (Dans Revue philosophique, 1892, tome 33, pp. 622 et seqq.; tome 34, pp. 41 et seqq.).

Resources in English.

P. Ansart: *Proudhon's Sociology.* Translated by S. Murdock, R. Berthier, & J. Cohn. AK Press, 2023.

T. B. Backer: *The Mutualists: The Heirs of Proudhon in the First International, 1865–1878.* Dissertation at the University of Cincinnati, 1978.

R. Berthier: *Proudhon and the Problem of Method.* 2012. Available at: monde-nouveau.net/spip.php?article407.

C. Bouglé: *The Sociology of Proudhon.* Translated by S. Murdock. little big eye publishing, forthcoming.

K. Carson: *Studies in Mutualist Political Economy.* Self-published, 2007.

Organization Theory: A Libertarian Perspective. BookSurge, 2008.

E. Castleton: *The Education of Pierre-Joseph Proudhon, 1836–39.* PhD Thesis at King's College, University of Cambridge, 2007.

The Origins of 'Collectivism': Pierre-Joseph Proudhon's Contested Legacy and the Debate about Property in the International Workingmen's Association and the League of Peace and Freedom. Pp. 169–195 in *Global Intellectual History,* 2(2), 2017.

Association, Mutualism, and Corporate Form in the Published and Unpublished Writings of Pierre-Joseph Proudhon. Pp. 143–172 in *History of Economic Ideas,* 15(1), 2017.

The Reception of German Thought in the Mind of Pierre-Joseph Proudhon. Pp. 87–141 in *Hegel and Schelling in Early Nineteenth-Century France, Volume 2.* Springer, 2023.

An Anarchist Take on Royalty: Pierre-Joseph Proudhon's Evolving Assessment of Post- Revolutionary Monarchy, 1839–64. Parts 1 & 2. *History of European Ideas,* 2024.

J. Cohn: *Anarchism and the Crisis of Representation: Hermeneutics, Aesthetics, Politics.* Susquehanna University Press, 2006.

Underground Passages: Anarchist Resistance Culture 1848–2011. AK Press, 2011.

D. D. Dillard: *Proudhon, Gesell, and Keynes: An Investigation of Some "Anti-Marxian-Socialist" Antecedents of Keynes' General Theory of Employment, Interest, and Money.* University of California, Berkley, 1940.

W. B. Greene: *Mutual Banking.* O. S. Cooke & Co., 1850.

The Radical Deficiency of the Existing Circulating Medium, and the Advantages of a Mutual Currency. B. H. Greene, 1857.

Socialistic, Communistic, Mutualistic, and Financial Fragments. Lee and Shephard Publishers, 1875.

D. Guerin: *Anarchism: From Theory to Practice.* Monthly Review Press, 1970.

C. M. Hall: *The Sociology of Pierre Joseph Proudhon, 1809–1865.* Philosophical library, 1971.

R. L. Hoffman: *Revolutionary Justice: The Social and Political Theory of P.-J Proudhon.* University of Illinois Press, 1972.

B. Horvat, M. Markovic, R. Super (eds.): *Self-Governing Socialism.* 2 volumes. International Arts and Sciences Press, Inc. 1975.

H. de Lubac: *The Un-Marxian Socialist: A Study of Proudhon.* Translated by R. E. Scantlebury. Sheed & Ward, 1948.

E. Lunn: *Prophet of Community: The Romantic Socialism of Gustav Landauer.* University of California Press, 1973.

I. McKay (ed): *Property is Theft! A Pierre-Joseph Proudhon Anthology.* AK Press, 2011.

M. Nettlau: *A Short History of Anarchism.* Translated by I. P. Isca. Freedom Press, 1996.

A. Noland: Pierre-Joseph Proudhon: Socialist as Social Scientist. Pp. 313–328 in *The American Journal of Economics and Sociology* 26(3), 1967.

Proudhon and Rousseau. Pp. 33–54 in *Journal of the History of Ideas* 28(1), 1967.

Proudhon's Sociology of War. Pp. 289–304 in *The American Journal of Economics and Sociology* 29(3), 1970.

History and Humanity: The Proudhonian Vision. Pp. 59–106 in W. Bosenbrook & H. White (eds.): *The Uses of History*. Wayne State University Press, 1968.

A. Prichard: *Justice, Order, and Anarchy: The International Political Theory of Pierre-Joseph Proudhon*. Routledge, 2013.

Anarchism: A Very Short Introduction. Oxford University Press, 2022.

A. Prichard, R. Kinna, S. Pinta, & D. Berry (eds.): *Libertarian Socialism: Politics in Black and Red*. Palgrave Macmillan, 2017.

A. Ritter: *The Political Thought of Pierre-Joseph Proudhon*. Princeton University Press, 1969.

H. Seymour: *The Fallacy of Marx's Theory of Surplus-Value*. Murdoch, 1897.

PJ Proudhon: A Biographical Sketch. International Publishing Company, 1887.

G. Sozen: *"The Straight Path That Leads to Sodom": Pierre-Joseph Proudhon's Sexual Politics and 19th Century French Feminist Responses*. Thesis at the University of Victoria, 2022.

M. Tyldesley: *The Political and Social Thought of Sidney and Beatrice Webb, 1884-1914: A Study in Democratic Socialism*. Dissertation at the University of Manchester, 1985.

Liberate and Federate: Three Proudhonian Socialists in an Age of Fascism, Stalinism and War. Irene Publishing, 2024.

K. S. Vincent: *Pierre-Joseph Proudhon and the Rise of French Republican Socialism.* Oxford University Press, 1984.

S. Wilbur: The New Proudhon Library. *The Libertarian Labyrinth. Available at: www.libertarian-labyrinth.org/proudhon-library/welcome-proudhon-library/.*

Pierre-Joseph Proudhon: Self-Government and the Citizen-State: Explorations in Proudhonian Sociology. *Corvus Editions,* Volume 2, 2013.

P. Winters: *Politics and Society in Marx and Proudhon.* Thesis at the University of Manchester, 1984.

J. B. Wood: *Proudhonism and the French Working Class, 1848-1914.* Thesis at the University of Richmond, 1970.

G. Woodcock: *Pierre-Joseph Proudhon.* MacMillan Company, 1956.

Anarchism: A History of Libertarian Ideas and Movements. World Publishing Company, 1962.

VIII. - Programs and Doctrines of Political Parties in General.

C. Benoist: *Les lois de la politique française.* Paris, Fayard 1928, 309 p.

G. Bourgin, J. Carrère, & A. Guérin: *Manuel des, partis politiques en France.* Paris, Rieder, 1928.

C. Brouilhet: *Le conflit des doctrines dans l'économie politique contemporaine.* Paris, Alcan, 1910, 297 p.

F. Corcos: *Catéchisme des partis politiques.* Paris, Editions Montaigne, 1928, 298 p.

L. Duguit: *Le droit individuel, le droit social et la transformation de l'État.* Paris, Alcan, 1922, 160 p.

E. Fels (Comte de): *La Révolution en marche.* 10th ed., Paris, A. Fayard, 1925, 251 p.

G. Guy-Grand: *La démocratie et l'après-guerre.* Paris, Carnier, n. d., 275 p.

Le conflit des idées dans la France d'aujourd'hui. Paris, Rivière, 1921, 268 p.

L'avenir de la démocratie. Paris, Rivière, 1928, 214 p.

D. Halévy: *Décadence de la liberté.* Paris, Grasset, 1931, 243 p.

D. Parodi: *Traditionalisme et démocratie.* Paris, Colin, 2nd ed., 1924, 111-324 p.

G. Pirou: *Doctrines sociales et science économique.* Paris, Recueil Sirey, 1929, 202 p.

Les doctrines économiques en France depuis 1870. Paris., A. Colin, 1930, 205 p.

A. François-Poncet: *Réflexions d'un républicain moderne.* Paris, Grasset, 1925, 135 p.

L. Romier: *Explication de notre temps.* Paris, Grasset, 1925, 286 p.

A. Siegfried: *Tableau politique de la France de l'Ouest sous la Troisième République.* Paris, A. Colin, 1913, 528 p.

Tableau des partis en France. Paris, Grasset, 1930, 240 p.

G. Weill: *Histoire du parti républicain en France, 1814–1870.* Paris, Alcan, 1900, 582 p.

L. Weiss (ed.): *L'Europe nouvelle.* 15th year, 1932.

Augélaribé, Berthod, Borel, Bouglé, Daladier, Demangeon, Dumas, Herriot, Jéze, Lévy-Bruhl, Painlevé, Rist, Seignobos, & Scelle: *La politique républicaine*. Paris, Alcan, 1924, 586 p.

L'année politique française et étrangère. Mémoires, Chroniques, Bibliographie critique. Paris, Gamber.

Resources in English.

J. H. Aldrich: *The Origin and Transformation of Political Parties in America*. University of Chicago Press, 1995.

R. Boer: *Socialism in Power: On the History and Theory of Socialist Governance*. Springer, 2023.

W. Brus: *Socialist Ownership and Political Systems*. Translated by R. A. Clarke. Routledge & Keagan Paul, 1975.

H. M. Drucker: *Doctrine and Ethos in the Labour Party*. G. Allen & Unwin, 1979.

L. Duigit: *The Law and the State: French and German Doctrines*. Harvard University Press, 1917.

Law in the Modern State. Translated by F. & H. Laski. B. W. Huebsch, 1919.

P. V. Dutton: *Origins of the French Welfare State: The Struggle for Social Reform in France, 1914–1947*. Cambridge University Press, 2002.

A. Fouillée, J. Charmont, L. Duguit, & R. Demogue: *Modern French Legal Philosophy*. Boston Book Company, 1916.

G. J. Gill: *The Collapse of a Single-Party System: The Disintegration of the Communist Party of the Soviet Union*. Cambridge University Press, 1994.

R. T. Griffiths (ed.): *Socialist Parties and the Question of Europe in the 1950s.* E.J. Brill, 1993.

S. E. Hanson: *Post-Imperial Democracies: Ideology and Party Formation in Third Republic France, Weimar Germany, and Post-Soviet Russia.* Cambridge University Press, 2010.

T. Judt: *Socialism in Provence 1871-1914: A Study in the Origins of the Modern French Left.* Cambridge University Press, 1979.

E. Kier: *Imagining War: French and British Military Doctrine Between the Wars.* Princeton University Press, 2017.

Y. Kokosalakis: *Building Socialism: The Communist Party and the Making of the Soviet System, 1921-1941.* Cambridge University Press, 2023.

A. Laitinen & A. B. Pessi (eds): *Solidarity: Theory and Practice.* Lexington Books, 2015.

L. March: *Radical Left Parties in Europe.* Routledge, 2012.

J. Marangos: *Consistency and Viability of Socialist Economic Systems.* Palgrave Macmillan, 2013.

A. Noland: *The Founding of the French Socialist Party: 1893-1905.* Harvard University Press, 1956.

M. Oakeshott: *The Social and Political Doctrines of Contemporary Europe.* Cambridge University Press, 1950.

S. Rosefielde & D. Q. Mills: *Populists and Progressives: The New Forces in American Politics.* World Scientific Publishing Co., 2020.

M. G. Ross & Y. Borgmann-Prebil (eds): *Promoting Solidarity in the European Union.* Oxford University Press, 2010.

D. J. Russell: *Citizen Politics: Public Opinion and Political Parties in Advanced Industrial Democracies.* Cq Press, 2013.

S. J. Scholz: *Political Solidarity.* Penn State Press, 2008.

K. Thelen: *Varieties of Liberalization and the New Politics of Social Solidarity.* Cambridge University Press, 2014.

IX. - Radicalism.

Alain: *Éléments d'une doctrine radicale.* Paris, Gallimard, 1925, 312 p.

L. Bourgeois: *Solidarité.* Paris, A. Colin, 1902, 253 p.

C. Bouglé: *Le solidarisme.* Paris, Giard, 1924, 2nd ed., 204 p.

F. Buisson: *La politique radicale.* Paris, Giard et Brière, 1908, 451 p.

M. Charny: *Les atouts du cléricalisme.* Paris, Éditions du Progrès civique, n. d, 307 p.

A. Charpentier: *Le parti radical et radical-socialiste à travers ses congrès (1901-1911).* Paris, Giard et Brière, 1913, 457 p.

É. Herriot: *Pourquoi je suis radical-socialiste.* Paris, Les Éditions de France, 1928, 181 p.

G. Maurice: *Le parti radical.* Paris. Rivière, 1929, 220 p.

G. Weill: *Histoire de l'idée laïque en France au XIXème siècle.* Paris, Alcan, 1925, 361 p.

Resources in English.

C. K. Ansell. *Schism and Solidarity in Social Movements: The Politics of Labor in the French Third Republic.* Cambridge University Press, 2001.

D. R. Berman: *Radicalism in the Mountain West, 1890–1920: Socialists, Populists, Miners, and Wobblies.* University Press of Colorado, 2007.

A. Bonnet: *Radicalism, Anti-Racism and Representation.* Routledge, 1993.

C. Calhoun: *The Roots of Radicalism: Tradition, the Public Sphere, and Early Nineteenth-Century Social Movements.* University of Chicago Press, 2012.

J. A. Chacón: *Radicals in the Barrio: Magonistas, Socialists, Wobblies, and Communists in the Mexican American Working Class.* Haymarket Books, 2018.

C. A. Endress: *The Republican-Radical and Radical-Socialist Party in the French Popular Front, 1934–1938.* Dissertation at Tulane University, 1968.

M. C. Finn: *After Chartism: Class and Nation in English Radical Politics 1848–1874.* Cambridge University Press, 1993.

L. K. Ford: *Origins of Southern Radicalism: The South Carolina Upcountry 1800–1860.* Oxford University Press, 1988.

M. Gane (ed.): *The Radical Sociology of Durkheim and Mauss.* Routledge, 1992.

J. Q. Graham: *The French Radical and Radical-Socialist Party, 1906–1914.* Dissertation at The Ohio State University, 1962.

J. R. Green: *Grass-Roots Socialism: Radical Movements in the Southwest, 1895–1943.* LSU Press, 1978.

C. Hill: *The World Turned Upside Down: Radical Ideas during the English Revolution.* Penguin, 1975.

I. L. Horowitz: *Radicalism and the Revolt Against Reason: The Social Theories of Georges Sorel.* Southern Illinois University Press, 1968.

J. Israel: *Radical Enlightenment.* Oxford University Press, 2001.

A Revolution of the Mind: Radical Enlightenment and the Intellectual Origins of Modern Democracy. Princeton University Press, 2010.

M. Jacob: *The Radical Enlightenment: Pantheists, Freemasons and Republics.* George Allen and Unwin, 1981.

N. Kauppi: *Radicalism in French Culture: A Sociology of French Theory in the 1960s.* Routledge, 2016.

C. Lasch: *The New Radicalism in America 1889–1963: The Intellectual as a Social Type.* Alfred A. Knopf, 1965.

S. Lash: *The Militant Worker: Class and Radicalism in France and America.* Fairleigh Dickinson University Press, 1984.

L. A. Loubère: *Radicalism in Mediterranean France: Its Rise and Decline, 1848–1914.* SUNY Press, 1974.

C. Merchant: *Radical Ecology: The Search for a Livable World.* Routledge, 2005.

P. McLaughlin: *Radicalism: A Philosophical Study.* Palgrave Macmillan, 2012.

P. Osborne & S. Sayers (eds): *Socialism, Feminism, and Philosophy: A Radical Philosophy Reader.* Routledge, 2013.

M. Razsa: *Bastards of Utopia: Living Radical Politics after Socialism.* Indiana University Press, 2015.

D. Schecter: *Radical Theories: Paths Beyond Marxism and Social Democracy.* Manchester University Press, 1994.

W. Stafford: *Socialism, Radicalism, and Nostalgia: Social Criticism in Britain, 1775-1830.* Cambridge University Press, 1987.

G. S. Wood: *The Radicalism of the American Revolution.* First Vintage Books, 1993.

D. Zweig. *Agrarian Radicalism in China, 1968-1981.* Harvard University Press, 1989.

X. - Socialism and Communism.

A. Aftalion: *Les fondements du socialisme: Étude critique.* Paris, Rivière, 1923, 306 p.

C. Andler: *La civilisation socialiste.* Paris, Rivière, 1912, 52 p.

E. Berth: *Dialogues socialistes.* Paris, Rivière, 1901, 319 p.

Les nouveaux aspects du socialisme. Paris, Rivière, 1908, 64 p.

L. Blum: *Les congrès ouvriers et socialistes français.* Paris, Bellais, 1901, 2 vol.

Les problèmes de la paix. Paris, Stock, 1931, 213 p.

N. Boukharine: *ABC du communisme.* Paris, Librairie de l'Humanité. 1925, 171 p.

M. Déat: *Perspectives socialistes.* Paris, Valois, 1930, 246 p.

J. Guesde: *Le socialisme au jour le jour.* Paris, Giard, 1899, 488 p.

État, politique et morale de classe. Paris, Giard et Brière, 1901, 466 p.

J. Jaurés: *L'action socialiste.* Paris, Bellais, 1899, 558 p.

L'*armée nouvelle*, Paris, Rouff, n.d., 685 p.

Études socialistes. Paris, Cahiers de la quinzaine, 1902, 274 p.

Œuvres (published by M. Bonnafous). Paris, Rieder, 1931, 3 volumes.

H. Lagardelle: *Le socialisme ouvrier.* Paris, Giard, 1902, 424 p.

La grève générale et le socialisme. Paris, Cornély, 1905, 423 p.

E. Lévy: *La vision socialiste du Droit.* Paris, Giard, 1926, 179 p.

B. Malon: *Le socialisme intégral, 1892-1894*, Paris, Alcan, 1894, 2 vol., 469 and 462 p.

A. Mencer: *L'État socialiste* (translated by E. Michaud). Paris, Bellais, 1904, 374 p.

A. Millerand: *Le socialisme réformiste français.* Paris, Cornély, 1903, 121 p.

M. Raléa: *Révolution et socialisme. Essai de bibliographie.* Paris, Presse Universitaire, 1923, 80 p.

L'idée de révolution dans les doctrines socialistes. Paris, Rivière, 1923, 398 p.

G. Renard: *Le régime socialiste.* Paris, Alcan, 1898, 186 p.

G. Sorel: *La décomposition du marxisme.* Paris, Rivière, 1908, 64 p.

E. Vandervelde: *Le socialisme contre l'État.* Paris, Berger Levrault, 1918, 174 p.

Jaurès. Paris, Alcan, 1929, 150 p.

Resources in English.

M. Adams: *Kropotkin, Read, and the Intellectual History of British Anarchism: Between Reason and Romanticism.* Palgrave Macmillan, 2015.

Z. Baker: *Means and Ends: The Revolutionary Practice of Anarchism in Europe and the United States.* AK Press, 2023.

M. Bakunin: *Statism and Anarchy.* Translated by M. Shatz. Cambridge University Press, 1990.

C. Bantman: *The French Anarchists in London, 1880–1914: Exile and Transnationalism in the First Globalisation.* Liverpool University Press, 2013.

Jean Grave and the Networks of French Anarchism, 1854–1939. Palgrave Macmillan, 2021.

D. E. Barclay & E. D. Weitz (eds): *Between Reform and Revolution: German Socialism and Communism from 1840 to 1990.* Berghahn Books, 2022.

D. Berry: *A History of the French Anarchist Movement, 1917 to 1945.* AK Press, 2009.

J. Bockman: *Markets in the Name of Socialism: The Left-Wing Origins of Neoliberalism.* Stanford University Press, 2011.

R. Boer (ed.): *Socialism with Chinese Characteristics: A Guide for Foreigners.* Springer, 2021.

D. Bowie: *The Radical and Socialist Tradition in British Planning: From Puritan colonies to Garden Cities.* Routledge, 2017.

M. Bracke: *Which Socialism, Whose Détente? West European Communism and the Czechoslovak Crisis, 1968.* Central European University Press, 2007.

D. Brandenberger & M. Zelenov (eds.): *Stalin's Master Narrative: A Critical Edition of the History of the Communist Party of the Soviet Union (Bolsheviks): Short Course.* Yale University Press, 2019.

J. Braunthal: *History of the International, Vol 1: 1864–1914.* Translated by H. Collins & K. Mitchell. Frederick A. Praeger, 1967.

   Vol 2: 1914–1943. Translated by J. Clark. Frederick A. Praeger, 1967.

   Vol 3: 1943–1968. Translated by P. Ford & K. Mitchell. Westview Press, 1980.

P. J. Bryson: *Socialism: Origins, Expansion, Decline, and the Attempted Revival in the United States.* Xlibris, 2015.

N. Bukharin: *The ABC of Communism.* Translated by P. Lavin. The Marxian Educational Society, 1921.

M. J. Buhle: *Women and American Socialism, 1870–1920.* University of Illinois Press, 1981.

B. Chavance: *The Transformation of Communist Systems: Economic Reform since the 1950s.* Westview Press, 1994.

P. E. Corcoran (ed.): *Before Marx: Socialism and Communism in France, 1830–48.* Springer, 1983.

J. S. Curtiss (ed.): *Essays in Russian and Soviet History: In Honor of Geroid Tanquary Robinson.* Columbia University Press, 1965.

J.-N Ducange: *Jules Guesde: The Birth of Socialism and Marxism in France.* Translated by D. Broder. Palgrave Macmillan, 2020.

J.-N. Ducange & A. Burlaud (eds): *Marx, a French Passion.* Translated by D. Broder. Brill, 2023.

B. Franks: *Rebel Alliances: The Means and Ends of Contemporary British Anarchisms.* AK Press and Dark Star, 2006.

R. Graham: *'We Do Not Fear Anarchy- We Invoke It': The First International and the Origins of the Anarchist Movement.* AK Press, 2015.

W. Graham: *Socialism: New and Old.* Kegan Paul, Trench, Trubner & Co. Ltd., 1890.

D. Hodges: *Sandino's Communism: Spiritual Politics for the Twenty-First Century.* UT Press, 1992.

The Bureaucratization of Socialism. University of Massachusetts Press, 1981.

J. Jaurès: *Studies in Socialism.* Translated by M. Minturn. GP Putnam, 1906.

Selected Writings of Jean Jaurés: on Socialism, Pacifism and Marxism. Palgrave Translated by D. Broder. Palgrave Macmillan, 2021.

L. A. Kirschenbaum: *International Communism and the Spanish Civil War.* Cambridge University Press, 2015.

R. Knowles: *Political Economy from Below: Economic Thought in Communitarian Anarchism, 1840-1914.* Routledge, 2004.

J. Kornai: *The Socialist System: The Political Economy of Socialism.* Princeton University Press, 1992.

P. Kropotkin: *Modern Science and Anarchy.* AK Press, 2018.

A. Lehning: *From Buonarroti to Bakunin: Studies in International Socialism*. Brill, 1970.

C. Levy & M. S. Adams (eds): *The Palgrave Handbook of Anarchism*. Palgrave Macmillan, 2018.

A. S. Lindemann: *A History of European Socialism*. Yale University Press, 1983.

C. Malabou: *Stop Thief!: Anarchism and Philosophy*. Translated by C. Shread. Polity Press, 2023.

M. Malia: *Soviet Tragedy: A History of Socialism in Russia, 1917–1991*. Free Press, 1994.

L. Martell: *Alternative Societies: For a Pluralist Socialism*. Bristol University Press, 2023.

P. Minxin: *From Reform to Revolution: The Demise of Communism in China and the Soviet Union*. Harvard University Press, 1994.

K. Morgan: *International Communism and the Cult of the Individual: Leaders, Tribunes, and Martyrs under Lenin and Stalin*. Palgrave Macmillan, 2017.

C. Pierson: *Socialism after Communism: The New Market Socialism*. Penn State Press, 1995.

S. Restivo: *Red, Black, and Objective: Science, Sociology, and Anarchism*. Routledge, 2016.

S. Rosefielde: *Socialist Economic Systems: 21st Century Pathways*. Routledge, 2023.

R. Samuel (ed): *People's History and Socialist Theory*. Routledge & Keagan Paul, 1981.

D. Sassoon: *One Hundred Years of Socialism: The West European Left in the Twentieth Century.* I B. Tauris, 2010.

G. W. Seidman: *Manufacturing Militance: Workers' Movements in Brazil and South Africa, 1970-1985.* University of California Press, 1994.

G. Sorel: *The Decomposition of Marxism.* Translation by I. L. Horowtiz. Routledge & Kegan Paul, 1961.

From Georges Sorel: Essays in Socialism and Philosophy. Routledge, 2018.

O. Spengler: *Prussianism and Socialism.* Translated by C. V. Hoffmeister. Legend Books Sp. Z O. O., 2023.

R. Stuart: *Marxism at Work: Ideology, Class and French Socialism during the Third Republic.* Cambridge University Press, 1992.

M. Tyldesley: *No Heavenly Delusion? A Comparative Study of Three Communal Movements.* Liverpool University Press, 2003.

M. van der Linden: *Western Marxism and the Soviet Union: A Survey of Critical Theories and Debates since 1917.* Translated by J. Bendien. Brill, 2007.

E. Vandervelde: *Socialism Versus the State.* Translated by C. H. Kerr. C. H. Kerr & Company Co-operative, 1919.

K. S. Vincent: *Between Marxism and Anarchism: Benoît Malon and French Reformist Socialism.* University of California Press, 1992.

XI.—Syndicalism and the Workers' Movement.

C. Albert: *L'état moderne.* (Bibliothèque syndicaliste). Paris, Valois, 1929, 189 p.

C. Andler: *L'humanisme travailliste.* Paris, Bibliothèque de la "Civilisation française," 1927, 144 p.

E. Berth: *Les méfaits des intellectuels.* Paris, Rivière, 1914, 335 p.

C. Bouglé: *Syndicalisme et démocratie.* Paris, Cornély, 1908, 225 p.

E. Cazalis: *Syndicalisme ouvrier et évolution sociale.* Paris, Rivière, 1925, 324 p.

F. Challaye: *Syndicalisme révolutionnaire et syndicalisme réformiste.* Paris, Alcan, 1909, 154 p.

P. Dominique: *La Révolution créatrice.* Paris, Valois, 1929, 215 p.

H. Dubreuil: *La République industrielle.* Paris, Bibliothèque d'éducation, n. d., 315 p.

A. Fourgeaud: *Du code individualiste au droit syndical.* Paris, Valois, 1929, 188 p.

R. Francq: *Le travail au pouvoir.* Paris, Éditions de la Sirène, 1920, 198 p.

R. Guy-Grand: *La philosophie syndicaliste.* Paris, Grasset, 1911, 235 p.

V. Griffuelhes: *L'action syndicaliste.* Paris, Rivière, 1908, 67 p.

G. Gurvitch: *Le temps présent et l'idée du droit social.* Paris, Vrin, 1931, 333 p.

L. Jouhaux: *Le syndicalisme français.* Paris, Rivière, 1913, 60 p.

Le syndicalisme et la C. G. T. Paris, Éditions de la Sirène, 1920, 243 p.

B. de Jouvenel: *L'économie dirigée.* Paris, Valois, 1929, 194 p.

H. de Jouvenel: *Pourquoi je suis syndicaliste.* Paris, Éditions de France, 1928, 97 p.

H. Lagardelle: *Sud-Ouest. Une région française.* Paris, Valois, 1929, 186 p.

P. Lasserre: *Georges Sorel, théoricien de l'impérialisme.* Paris, L'Artisan du Livre, 1928, 265 p.

M. Leroy: *Les transformations de la puissance publique. Les syndicats de fonctionnaires.* Paris, Giard et Brière, 1907, 293 p.

La coutume ouvrière. Paris, Giard, 909 p.

Syndicats et services publics. Paris, A. Colin, 1909, 324 p.

Les techniques nouvelles du syndicalisme. Paris, Garnier, 1921, 212 p.

Ligue des droits de l'homme: *Le Congrès national de 1931,* verbatim transcript *I. Le syndicalisme et l'état.* Paris, 1931, 458 p.

P. Loewel: *Inventaire 1931.* Paris, Valois. 1931, 251 p.

P. Louis: *Histoire du mouvement syndical en France.* Paris, Alcan, 1907, 282 p.

Le syndicalisme contre l'État. Paris, Alcan, 1910, 276 p.

Histoire de la classe ouvrière en France de la Révolution à nos jours. Paris, Rivière, 1927, 412 p.

J. Luchaire: *Une génération réaliste.* Paris, Valois, 1929, 202 p.

E. Martin Saint-Léon: *Les deux C. G. T. syndicalisme et communisme.* Paris, Plon-Nourrit, 1923, 132 p.

G. Moreau: *Le syndicalisme, les mouvements politiques et l'évolution économique.* Paris, Rivière, 1925.

F. Pelloutier: *La vie ouvrière en France.* Paris, Schleicher, 1900, 342 p.

Histoire des bourses du travail. Paris, Costes, 1921, 338 p.

G. Pirou: *Georges Sorel (1847-1922).* Paris, Rivière, 1927, 67 p.

G. Scelle: *Le droit ouvrier.* Paris, A. Colin, 1922, 210 p.

L. de Seilhac: *Les congrès ouvriers en France, de 1876 à 1897.* Paris, A. Colin, 1899, 364 p.

G. Sorel: *Réflexions sur la violence.* Paris, Rivière, 1921, 457 p.

Matériaux pour une théorie du prolétariat. Paris, Rivière, 1921, 456 p.

Introduction à l'économie moderne. Paris, Rivière, 2nd ed., 1922, 385 p.

G. Valois: *Un nouvel âge de l'humanité.* Paris, Valois, 1929, 187 p.

Resources in English.

S. Aronowitz: *The Death and Life of American Labor: Toward a New Workers' Movement.* Verso Books, 2015.

D. Azzellini: *An Alternative Labour History: Worker Control and Workplace Democracy.* Zed Books, 2015.

C. Bantman & B. Altena (eds.): *Reassessing the Transnational Turn: Scales of Analysis in Anarchist and Syndicalist Studies.* Routledge, 2015.

C. Bantman & D. Berry (eds): *New Perspectives on Anarchism, Labour and Syndicalism: The Individual, the National and the Transnational.* Cambridge Scholars Publishing, 2010.

D. Berry: *A History of the French Anarchist Movement, 1917–1945,* AK Press, 2009.

M. Bray: *The Anarchist Inquisition: Assassins, Activists, and Martyrs in Spain and France (1891–1909).* AK Press, 2002.

M. Brinton: *The Bolsheviks and Workers Control, 1917 to 1921.* Solidarity, 1970.

P. F. Brissenden: *The IWW: A Study of American Syndicalism.* Columbia University, 1920.

V. Burgmann: *Revolutionary Industrial Unionism: The Industrial Workers of the World in Australia.* Cambridge University Press, 1995.

M. Carter (ed.): *Challenging Social Inequality: The Landless Rural Workers Movement and Agrarian Reform in Brazil.* Duke University Press, 2015.

P. Cole, D. Struthers, & K. Zimmer (eds): *Wobblies of the World: A Global History of the IWW.* Pluto press, 2017.

R. Darlington: *Syndicalism and the Transition to Communism: An International Comparative Analysis.* Ashgate, 2008.

V. V. Damier: *Anarcho-Syndicalism in the 20th Century.* Black Cat Press, 2009.

M. Dubofsky: *We Shall be All: A History of the Industrial Workers of the World.* Quadrangle Books, 1969.

C. Ealham: *Anarchism and the City: Revolution and Counter-Revolution in Barcelona, 1898–1937.* AK Press, 2010.

Living Anarchism: José Peirats and the Spanish Anarcho-Syndicalist Movement. AK Press, 2015.

S. Early: *The Civil Wars in US Labor: Birth of a New Workers' Movement or Death Throes of the Old?* Haymarket Books, 2011.

D. Evans: *Revolution and the State: Anarchism in the Spanish Civil War, 1936-1939.* Routledge, 2018.

M. Ganz: *Why David Sometimes Wins: Leadership, Organization, and Strategy in the California Farm Worker Movement.* Oxford University Press, 2009.

H. Hester & N. Srnicek: *After Work: A History of the Home and the Fight for Free Time.* Verso, 2023.

S. Hirsch & L. van der Walt: *Anarchism and Syndicalism in the Colonial and Postcolonial World, 1870-1940.* Brill, 2010.

R. Humphrey: *Georges Sorel: Prophet Without Honor: A Study in Anti-Intellectualism.* Harvard University Press, 1951.

S. Jayaraman & I. Ness: *The New Urban Immigrant Workforce: Innovative Models for Labor Organizing.* Routledge, 2015.

I. Ness: *Southern Insurgency: The Coming of the Global Working Class.* Pluto Press, 2016.

Organizing Insurgency: Workers' Movements in the Global South. Pluto Press, 2021.

I. Ness & D. Azzelini: *Ours to Master and to Own: Workers' Control from the Commune to the Present.* Haymarket Books, 2011.

T. Ngwane, I. Ness, & L. Sinwell: *Urban Revolt: State Power and the Rise of People's Movements in the Global South.* Haymarket Books, 2017.

J. R. Jennings: *Syndicalism in France: A Study of Ideas.* Palgrave Macmillan, 1990.

S. Katayama: *The Labor Movement in Japan.* Charles H. Kerr & Company, 1918.

G. Kelsey: *Anarchosyndicalism, Libertarian Communism and the State: The CNT in Zaragoza and Aragon, 1930-1937.* Springer Science & Business Media, 1991.

M. van der Linden & W. Thorpe (eds): *Revolutionary Syndicalism: An International Perspective.* Scolar Press, 1990.

E. Pataud & E. Pouget: *How Shall We Bring About the Revolution: Syndicalism and the Co-operative Commonwealth.* Translated by C. & F. Charles. The New International Publishing Company, 1913.

V. Richards. *Lessons of the Spanish Revolution: 1936-1939.* PM Press, 2019.

F. Ridley: *Revolutionary Syndicalism in France: The Direct Action of its Time.* Cambridge University Press, 1970.

D. D. Roberts: *The Syndicalist Tradition and Italian Fascism.* The University of North Carolina Press, 1979.

W. Robles & H. Veltmeyer: *The Politics of Agrarian Reform in Brazil: The Landless Rural Workers Movement.* Palgrave Macmillan, 2015.

R. Rocker: *Anarcho-Syndicalism: Theory and Practice.* Secker & Warburg, 1938.

G. W. Seidman: *Manufacturing Militance: Workers' Movements in Brazil and South Africa, 1970-1985.* University of California Press, 1994.

B. J. Silver: *Forces of Labor: Workers' Movements and Globalization since 1870.* Cambridge University Press, 2003.

M. Smith & J. Mac: *Revolting Prostitutes: The Fight for Sex Workers' Rights.* Verso, 2018.

P. Snowden: *Socialism and Syndicalism.* Collins'-Clear Type Press, 1913.

P. N. Stearns: *Revolutionary Syndicalism and French Labor: A Cause Without Rebels.* Rutgers University Press, 1971.

G. Sorel: *Reflections on Violence.* Translated by T. E. Hulme. George Allen & Unwin Ltd., 1915.

> *From Georges Sorel: Essays in Socialism & Philosophy.* Transaction Publishers, 1987.

> *Syndicalism: Writings on Revolutionary Socialist Unions.* Red and Black Publishers, 2010.

A. Smith: *Anarchism, Revolution, and Reaction: Catalan Labor and the Crisis of the Spanish State, 1898–1923.* Berghahn Book, 2007.

W. Thorpe: *The Workers Themselves': Revolutionary Syndicalism and International Labour, 1913–1923.* Kluwers, 1989.

K. H. Tucker: *French Revolutionary Syndicalism and the Public Sphere.* Cambridge University Press, 1996.

> *Workers of the World, Enjoy!: Aesthetic Politics from Revolutionary Syndicalism to the Global Justice Movement.* Temple University Press, 2010.

Volin: *The Unknown Revolution, 1917–1921.* Translated by H. Cantine & F. Perlman. PM Press, 2019.

J. M. Yeoman: *Print Culture and the Formation of the Anarchist Movement in Spain, 1890–1915.* Routledge, 2019.

XII. - Current Organization of Industry in France.

Bernard Falgas: *Les syndicats patronaux de l'industrie métallurgique en France.* Paris, Éditions de la Vie Universitaire, 1922, 422 p.

Cahiers de la nouvelle journée: No. 4: *La cité moderne et les transformations du droit.* Paris, Blond et Gay, 1925, 229 p.

Confédération générale de la production française: Annuaire 1930. *Répertoire des Syndicats patronaux français.*

G. Davy: *Le problème de l'industrialisation de l'État.* Revue de Métaphysique et de Morale, 1924, pp. 600–641.

H. Dubreuil: *Standards.* Paris, Grasset, 1929, 425 p.

Nouveaux standards. Paris, Grasset, 1931, 336 p.

L. Guillet & J. Durand: *L'industrie française.* Paris, Masson, 1920, 283 p.

E. Lambert, Paul Pic & P. Garraud: *Les sources et l'interprétation de la législation du travail en France.* Revue internationale du travail, July 1926.

C. Lautaud & A. Poudenx: *La représentation professionnelle. Les conseils économiques en Europe et en France.* Paris, Rivière, 1927, 282 p.

A. le Hénaff: *Le pouvoir politique et les forces sociales.* Paris, Recueil Sirey, 1931, 159 p.

J. Moch: *Socialisme et rationalisation.* Brussels, L'Églantine, 1927, 141 p.

Le rail et la nation. Paris, Valois, 1931, 472 p.

Organisation Internationale du Travail. *L'organisation syndicale du patronat français.* Revue internationale du travail, July 1927, pp. 56–82.

P. Pic: *L'actionnariat ouvrier dans la législation française récente.* Revue internationale du travail, July 1923.

R. Picard: *Le progrès de la législation ouvrière en France pendant et depuis la guerre.* Revue internationale du travail, July-August 1921.

Les Assurances sociales. Paris. Éditions Godde, 1930, 418 p.

R. Pinot: *Les oeuvres sociales des industries métallurgiques.* Paris, A. Colin, 1924.

É. Villey: *L'organisation professionnelle des employeurs dans l'industrie française.* Paris, Alcan, 1923, 395 p.

D. Yovanovitch: *Les stimulants modernes du travail ouvrier.* Paris, Presses universitaires, 1923, 378 p.

Le rendement optimum du travail ouvrier. Paris, Payot, 1923, 490 p.

Resources in English.

W. C. Baum: *The French Economy and the State.* Princeton University Press, 1958.

L.-A. Brunet: *Forging Europe: Industrial Organization in France, 1940–1952.* Palgrave Macmillan, 2017.

J. Clarke: *France in the Age of Organization: Factory, Home and Nation from 1920s to Vichy.* Berghahn Books, 2011.

M. C. Cleary: *Peasants, Politicians and Producers: The Organisation of Agriculture in France Since 1918.* Cambridge University Press, 1989.

G. S. Cross: *Immigrant Workers in Industrial France: The Making of a New Laboring Class.* Temple University Press, 1983.

M. Crozier: *The Bureaucratic Phenomenon.* The University of Chicago Press, 1963.

The World of the Office Worker. Translated by D. Landau. The University of Chicago Press, 1971.

The Stalled Society. Translated by R. Swyer. The Viking Press, 1973.

Strategies for Change: The Future of French Society. Translated by W. R. Beer. MIT Press, 1982.

G. P. Dyas, P. Gareth, & H. T. Thanheiser: *The Emerging European Enterprise: Strategy and Structure in French and German Industry.* Springer, 1976.

A. Fontaine: *French Industry During the War.* Yale University Publishing, 1926.

J. Forbes, N. Hewlett, & F. Nectoux: *Contemporary France: Essays and Texts on Politics, Economics and Society.* Routledge, 2000.

G. Friedmann: *Industrial Society: The Emergence of the Human Problems of Automation.* The Free Press of Glencoe, 1955.

The Anatomy of Work: Labor, Leisure, and the Implications of Automation. Translated by W. Rawson. The Free Press of Glencoe, 1961.

R. Gildea: *France Since 1945.* Oxford University Press, 1996.

J. L. S. Girling: *France: Political and Social Change*. Psychology Press, 1998.

G. Gurvitch: Social Structure of Pre-War France. Pp. 535–554 in *American Journal of Sociology*, 48(5), 1943.

R. Hancké: *Large Firms and Institutional Change: Industrial Renewal and Economic Restructuring in France*. Oxford University Press, 2002.

G. Hecht: *The Radiance of France: Nuclear Power and National Identity after World War II*. MIT Press, 2009.

C. Howell: *Regulating Labor: The State and Industrial Relations Reform in Postwar France*. Princeton University Press, 2011.

T. C. Imlay & M. Horn: *The Politics of Industrial Collaboration during World War II: Ford France, Vichy and Nazi Germany*. Cambridge University Press, 2014.

B. Jacquillat: *Nationalization and Privatization in Contemporary France*. Hoover Institution Press, 1988.

A. Jenkins: *Employment Relations in France: Evolution and Innovation*. Springer, 2000.

M. Jones & D. Hornsby: *Language and Social Structure in Urban France*. Routledge, 2013.

R. F. Kuisel: *Capitalism and the State in Modern France: Renovation and Economic Management in the Twentieth Century*. CUP Archive, 1983.

J. D. Levy: *Contested Liberalization: Historical Legacies and Contemporary Conflict in France*. Cambridge University Press, 2023.

F. M. B. Lynch: *France and the International Economy: From Vichy to the Treaty of Rome.* Routledge, 1997.

D. MacRae: *Parliament, Parties, and Society in France, 1946-1958.* St. Martin's Press, 1967.

M. Maurice, F. Sellier, & J. J. Silbestre: *The Social Foundations of Industrial Power: A Comparison of France and Germany.* Translated by A. Goldhammer. MIT Press, 1986.

N. Parsons: *French Industrial Relations in the New World.* Routledge, 2007.

R. Price: *The Economic Modernization of France.* Routledge, 2022.

R. Salais & N. Whiteside: *Governance, Industry and Labour Markets in Britain and France: The Modernizing State.* Routledge, 1998.

V. Schwartz: *Modern France: A Very Short Introduction.* Oxford University Press, 2011.

T. B. Smith: *France in Crisis: Welfare, Inequality, and Globalization Since 1980.* Cambridge University Press, 2004.

C. Sowerwine: *France Since 1870: Culture, Politics, and Society.* Bloomsbury Publishing, 2018.

A. Steinhouse: *Workers' Participation in Post-Liberation France.* Lexington Books, 2001.

G. J. Stigler: *The Organization of Industry.* University of Chicago Press, 1983.

M. Sutton: *France and the Construction of Europe, 1944-2007.* Berghahn Books, 2007.

W. Teckenberg (ed): *Comparative Studies of Social Structure: Recent German Research on France, the United States, and the Federal Republic.* M. E. Sharpe, 1987.

K. S. Vincent & A. Klairmont-Lingo (eds): *The Human Tradition in Modern France.* Taylor & Francis Group, 2014.

R. Vinen: *France, 1934–1970.* St. Martin's Press, 1996.

S. M. Zdatny: *The Politics of Survival: Artisans in Twentieth-Century France.* Oxford University Press, 1990.

Index

Proteus, 200

Proudhon, Pierre-Joseph, 17–20, 22, 26, 28-36, 38, 41-43, 49, 50, 56, 70, 78, 130, 137, 175, 199-229, 234, 236, 237, 242, 245, 247, 249, 254-256, 263, 264, 269, 284-286, 316, 331-336

Proudhonism, 4, 5, 34, 44, 48, 50, 199, 211, 213, 216, 221, 226, 249, 250, 255, 281, 285, 298, 331, 336

Prussia, 155

Puech, Jules-Louis, 221, 317, 331, 332

Quesnay, François, 9, 10, 73, 76, 77, 79-84, 88, 90, 93, 141, 210, 306, 307

Queuille, Henri, 92

Rabelais, François, 172, 186

Radical, 3, 13, 26, 34, 62, 92, 98, 105, 113, 114, 119, 169, 173, 197, 215, 229, 243, 262, 340, 341

Reagan, Ronald, 273, 283

Redern, Sigismund Ehrenreich Johann von, 132

Reign of Terror, 15, 21, 55, 59, 62, 96, 98, 104, 109, 229

Religion, 1, 6, 15, 18, 21, 22, 24, 27, 28, 40, 51, 117, 131, 134, 135, 137, 138, 151-153, 176, 186, 205, 206, 257, 258

Renan, Ernest, 115

Renard, Georges, 197, 345

Renouvier, Charles, 60, 203

Revolution of 1830, 112, 117, 141, 315

Revolution of 1848, 20, 45, 112, 113, 117, 183, 311, 315

Revolutionary, 8, 12, 14, 18, 23, 28, 33, 49, 51, 52, 59, 75, 87, 96, 98, 100, 106, 107, 109, 112, 115, 119, 120, 122, 168, 182, 213, 215, 218, 222, 224, 227, 244, 247, 258, 289, 295

Revue d'économie politique, 162, 172, 250

Revue des études cooperatives, 198

Reybaud, Louis, 48, 174, 202, 317

Riazanov, David, 35

Ricardo, David, 83

Rights, 10, 12, 13, 15, 17, 20, 27, 28, 52, 54, 55, 60, 64-66, 71, 77, 84, 100-102, 105, 106, 114, 118, 121, 125, 127, 135, 141, 146, 179, 187, 201, 203, 209, 215, 221, 224, 225, 227, 231-233, 243, 244, 254, 261, 268, 271, 272, 276, 278-281, 285, 286, 289, 291, 292-295, 299

Rist, Charles, 162, 250, 305, 306, 316, 319, 338

Robespierre, Maximilien, 14, 15, 96, 99, 105, 119, 229, 313, 314

Rochdale Society, 194

Rodbertus, Johann Karl, 146

Rodrigues, Olinde, 134, 137, 325

Romier, Lucien, 85, 90, 188, 234, 337

Rothschild family, 25, 134

Rouanet, Gustave, 197

Rouen, Pierre-Isidore, 160

Rousseau, Jean-Jacques, 8, 11, 16, 51, 53, 59, 60, 62-64, 69,

73, 77, 95, 96, 107, 120, 140, 154, 209, 223, 230, 301, 303, 332, 335

Roux, Jacques, 98, 105

Sagnac, Philippe, 96, 102, 309

Saint-Domingue, 13

Sainte-Beuve, Charles, 138

Saint-Étienne, Jean-Paul Rabaut, 59, 98, 99

Saint-Just, Louis Antoine de, 96

Saint-Simon, Henri de, 17–33, 36, 38, 43, 48, 50, 54, 55, 78, 81, 100, 102, 126, 129–142, 144, 146, 149, 152, 154, 155, 157, 158, 163, 165, 167, 168, 178, 181, 187,195, 200, 201, 210, 215, 227–229, 263–266, 271, 298, 317, 321–326

Saint-Simonism, 2, 4–5, 17, 39, 44, 49, 129–130, 134–138, 142, 147, 149, 151–154, 158–159, 162, 166–168, 171, 175, 196, 201–202, 211, 249–250, 252, 255, 266–267, 271, 273–274, 321, 323, 324, 326

Sans-culottes, 125

Savigny, Friedrich Carl von, 69

Say, Jean-Baptise, 22

Schelling, Friedrich Wilhelm Joseph, 47, 333

Science of man, 22, 30

Scientific management, 266

Scientific Revolution, 5, 7, 21

Séailles, Gabriel, 67, 332

Second French Empire, 39, 112, 134, 155

Second International, 38, 124, 157

Seneca, 68

Sensualism, 58

Seven Years War, 12

Siegfried, André, 85, 90, 232, 233, 338

Sieyès, Emmanuel Joseph, 81, 98, 101, 111, 141, 179

Simiand, François, 2, 40, 217, 218

Simmel, Georg, 4

Simon, Jules, 114

Sismondi, Jean Charles Léonard de, 176–177, 316

Sisyphus, 181, 258

Slavery, 13, 57

Smith, Adam, 9, 201, 306

Social Democratic Party (SPD), 35, 37, 38

Social science, 1–5, 9, 11, 16–18, 22, 24, 26, 28–30, 32–33, 35, 39, 40, 42, 52, 55, 57, 65, 67, 78, 203, 206, 259, 260, 263, 271, 272, 299

Social structure, 22, 51, 67, 288, 298

Socialism, 2, 3, 5, 11, 17–21, 24, 29, 35–44, 49, 58, 60–65, 69, 71, 73, 79, 83, 93, 95, 98, 103, 108, 111, 115, 116, 119, 123, 126 127, 129, 130, 136, 143, 144, 146–148, 151–153, 167, 168, 178–183, 185, 187, 195, 197, 199, 202, 211, 212, 216, 218, 221, 224, 227, 231, 232, 238, 244, 250, 251, 253, 254, 263–265, 269, 271, 275, 285, 291, 301, 303, 305, 308, 314, 318–321, 323, 324, 328, 330, 334–336, 338, 339, 342, 343, 345–350, 356

Socialist School, 2

Sociology. See *Social science*.

Solidarity economy, 275, 277, 280

About the author, editor, and translator:

Célestin Bouglé (1870–1940) was a professor of the history of social economy and the director of École Normale Supérieure in Paris. He was the key public spokesperson of the Durkheimians in the early 20th century, yet he was critical of Durkheim on several issues. He authored dozens of books, only two of which, besides this one, have been translated into English: *Essays on the Caste System* and *The Evolution of Values*.

Cayce Jamil is an independent researcher based in North Carolina. He holds a PhD in Public Policy from UNC Charlotte. His research investigates neglected social theories and their relevance for today. He is a cofounder of little big eye publishing (littlebigeyepublishing.com) and can be reached via email at cgjamil@gmail.com.

Shaun Murdock translates texts on the themes of economy, society, and environment from French, Spanish, Italian, Portuguese, and Catalan into English. He led the recent English translation of *Proudhon's Sociology* by Pierre Ansart. He is the founder of Root & Branch Translation (rootandbranch.online).

www.ingramcontent.com/pod-product-compliance
Lightning Source LLC
Chambersburg PA
CBHW020821270326
41928CB00006B/388